A QUILTER'S CHRISTMAS COOKBOOK

A QUILTER'S CHRISTMAS COOKBOOK

Louise Stoltzfus
and
Dawn J. Ranck

Good Books
Intercourse, PA 17534

Cover design and illustrations by Cheryl Benner
Design by Dawn J. Ranck

A QUILTER'S CHRISTMAS COOKBOOK
Copyright ©1996 by Good Books, Intercourse, PA 17534
International Standard Book Number: 1-56148-209-9
Library of Congress Catalog Card Number: 96-36409

Library of Congress Cataloging-in-Publication Data

Stoltzfus, Louise, 1952-
    A quilter's Christmas cookbook / Louise Stoltzfus and Dawn
J. Ranck.
           p. cm.
    Includes index.
    ISBN 1-56148-209-9
    1. Christmas cookery. I. Ranck, Dawn J. II. Title.
TX739.2.C45S76   1996   96-36409
641.8'68--DC20   CIP

Table of Contents

Introduction

This marvelous collection of holiday recipes proves once again that many people who quilt are also fine cooks. Here are choice dishes from quilters throughout North America—from Inverness, Florida to Los Alamos, New Mexico, from Paoli, Indiana, to Pine Grove Mills, Pennsylvania, and from St. Mary's, Ontario, to Gridley, California.

We hope these recipes warm your heart, your hearth, and home. We hope you discover new dishes and rediscover old favorites. We hope you and your family find the fellowship and camaraderie which come from gathering around a table laden with good food.

A Quilter's Christmas Cookbook is the result of many hours of time given by many different people. Hundreds of you, the people of the quilting community, responded to our call for recipes, and then also agreed to help us test them.

To each of you, we offer our sincere thanks. Thank you for hand-copying your treasured holiday recipes and sending them to us. Thank you for graciously testing recipes at the height of summer when "Christmas" ingredients are often difficult to find and the temperature outside is considerably different than at the time of the holidays.

Thank you for telling us the name of the quilt you were working with at the time you submitted recipes. Those patterns, listed with your names, provide a kaleidoscope of original patterns, along with familiar and frequently used designs.

We also thank Phyllis Pellman Good and Esther Becker for their editorial and organizational assistance without which we could not have completed this project.

—*Louise Stoltzfus and Dawn J. Ranck*

Appetizers

❖

Potato & Caviar Hors d'oeuvre
Susan L. Schwarz
N. Bethesda, MD
Americana Hearts

Makes 24 servings

6 medium red potatoes
1/3 cup plain yogurt
1/4 cup sour cream
2 Tbsp. finely chopped
**   fresh chives**
2 Tbsp. finely chopped
**   fresh parsley**
1 Tbsp. red caviar

1. Do not peel potatoes. Cut into 24 1/4-inch slices. In a vegetable steamer, cover and steam potato slices for 12 minutes or until tender. Set aside to cool.
2. In a bowl combine yogurt and sour cream, stirring well. Spread this mixture to 1/2" thickness onto several layers of strong paper towels. Cover with additional paper towels and let stand for 10-15 minutes.
3. Carefully scrape yogurt mixture into a pastry bag fitted with a fluted tip. Set aside.
4. Combine the chives and parsley and press 1/2 tsp. herbs onto each potato slice. Pipe 1/2 tsp. yogurt mixture over herbs. Top with 1/8 tsp. caviar. Serve immediately.

❖

Glazed Brie
Nancy Jo Marsden
Glen Mills, PA
Tumbling Blocks Charm

Makes 10-12 servings

1/4 cup packed brown
**   sugar**
1/4 cup chopped walnuts,
**   pecans, almonds, or**
**   hazelnuts**
1 Tbsp. whiskey or
**   brandy**
14-oz. round Brie, 5" in
**   diameter**
lemon juice

apple or pear wedges
seedless grapes
crackers

1. Mix together sugar, nuts, and liquor. Cover. Chill up to one week.
2. Place Brie onto 9" pie plate.
3. Bake at 500° for 4-5 minutes until slightly softened. Sprinkle sugar mixture on top. Bake 2-3 minutes until sugar is melted and cheese is heated, but not melted.
4. Brush fruit wedges with lemon juice. Serve Brie with fruit wedges, grapes, and crackers.

❖

Ceviche
Dianna Milhizer
Springfield, VA
Bargello

Makes 30 servings

**2 lbs. fresh haddock or
 cod**
2 cups fresh lemon juice
**1/2 cup seeded, chopped
 jalapeno peppers**
**1 cup slivered Spanish
 onions**
1/2 cup chopped cilantro
**1 cup seeded, peeled,
 chopped tomatoes**
1 tsp. salt
lettuce leaves

1. Freeze fish. Cut frozen fish
into 2" squares. Place in glass
bowl, pour lemon juice over
fish, and marinate overnight.
(The fish "cooks" in the
lemon juice marinade.)
2. Drain lemon juice. Add
peppers, onions, cilantro,
tomatoes, and salt.
3. Arrange on platter over
lettuce leaves and serve
with melba toast or herbed
crackers.

❖

Holiday Shrimp Ceviche
Susan Stephani Smith
Monument, CO
May Baskets

Makes 12 servings

2 lbs. fresh shrimp
**1 red onion, very thinly
 sliced**
juice of 1 lemon
juice of 10 oranges
3/4 cup ketchup
1/2 tsp. olive oil
1/2-1 tsp. hot sauce
1/2 tsp. chopped parsley
salt and pepper to taste

1. Peel, devein, and steam
shrimp. Set aside to cool.
Refrigerate.
2. Pour boiling water over
onion in a strainer. Place
onion in a small bowl. Pour
lemon juice over onion to
marinate. Soak about 10
minutes. Set aside.
Refrigerate.
3. Combine orange juice,
ketchup, oil, hot sauce,
parsley, salt, and pepper.
Refrigerate.
4. About one hour before
serving, combine the
shrimp, onions, and orange
juice mixture and refrigerate
to marinate.
5. Serve in individual bowls,
garnished with sprig of
parsley. Popcorn or toasted
corn may be provided to
sprinkle over the ceviche.

*Note: This is a recipe from
Ecuador which we have incor-
porated into our holiday meal.*

❖

Hidden Treasures
Gail Bush
Landenberg, PA
Appliquéd Bunny

Makes 12 servings

**6-oz. can large pitted ripe
 olives, drained**
1 pint cherry tomatoes
**2 4-oz. jars whole
 mushrooms, drained**
**8-oz. can sliced water
 chestnuts, drained**
1 cup cauliflower florets
**1 lb. shrimp, cooked and
 peeled**
2 cups mayonnaise
4-oz. jar horseradish
1 tsp. lemon juice
2 tsp. dry mustard
1/4 tsp. salt

1. Mix together olives, tomatoes, mushrooms, water
chestnuts, cauliflower, and
shrimp and arrange on shallow serving dish or platter.
2. Mix together mayonnaise,
horseradish, lemon juice,
dry mustard, and salt. Pour
over shrimp mixture. Toss
to mix. Chill for several
hours.
3. Serve with crackers.

Christmas Cornucopias
Bonita Ensenberger
Albuquerque, NM
Snowflake

Makes 20 servings

3-oz. pkg. cream cheese, softened
1 medium ripe avocado, peeled and cubed
2 Tbsp. mayonnaise
7^1/$_2$-oz. can red salmon
^{1}/$_4$ cup green onion, minced
2 Tbsp. pimiento, drained and chopped
^{1}/$_4$ cup ripe olives, chopped
few drops Tabasco sauce
20 thin slices white bread
mayonnaise
parsley

1. Mix together cream cheese, avocado, and 2 Tbsp. mayonnaise. Beat until fluffy.
2. Drain, flake, and remove all bones from salmon.
3. Combine salmon, onion, pimiento, olives, and Tabasco sauce. Fold into cheese mixture. Chill covered for several hours.
4. Using a 3^1/$_2$" round cookie cutter, cut a circle from each slice of bread. Flatten each round with rolling pin.
5. Spread mayonnaise generously on both sides of each circle. Lap one side over the other to form cornucopia shape (more open at top end) and fasten with a toothpick. Repeat with remaining 19 bread circles. Place on ungreased baking sheet.
6. Bake at 350° for 12-15 minutes or until lightly browned. Cool.
6. Remove toothpicks. Fill each cornucopia with 1 generous tsp. filling. Garnish each with a bit of parsley and serve.

Stuffed Mushroom Appetizer
Jaclyn Ferrell
Carlisle, PA
Sisters' Choice

Makes 24-30 servings

3-oz. pkg. cream cheese, softened
^{1}/$_4$ cup grated mozzarella cheese
1^1/$_2$ tsp. butter, melted
^{1}/$_4$ cup chopped ham
2 Tbsp. bread crumbs
2 Tbsp. finely chopped onion
^{1}/$_2$ tsp. Worcestershire sauce
1 lb. fresh mushrooms

1. Combine all ingredients except mushrooms and mix well. Set aside.
2. Wash and drain mushrooms. Cut off stems.
3. Fill mushrooms with cheese mixture and arrange on lightly greased baking sheet.
4. Bake at 350° for 15 minutes.

I love to make quilts. The one I am doing now is a Flower Garden for my daughter and son-in-law, Treva and Mervin Headings, for their 25th wedding anniversary. I have made seven of these quilts, one for each of our seven children.

In my time I have made lots of quilts in many different patterns for many different people in many different places. These days, I'm only making quilts for our family. We have sixteen married grandchildren, and I have made each of them a quilt as a wedding gift.

—*Ida Schrock, Haven, KS*

Tortilla Hors d'oeuvre
Cora J. Peterson
Frederic, WI
Peachy Nine Patch

Makes many servings

5 10" flour tortillas
6-oz. can ripe olives, chopped
7 1/2-oz. can tuna or chicken
2 8-oz. pkgs. cream cheese
1 Tbsp. salad dressing
paprika

1. Mix all ingredients except tortillas and paprika. Spread mixture evenly onto tortillas. Roll each tortilla tightly.
2. Chill for 2 hours. Slice and garnish with paprika. Serve.

Tortilla Roll Ups
Lucille Reagan
Salem, OR

Makes many servings

10 large flour tortillas
1 pkg. Hidden Valley Ranch dressing mix
2 8-oz. pkgs. cream cheese, softened
4-oz. can chopped green chilies, drained
4-oz. can chopped black olives, drained
1 bunch green onions, chopped
1 stalk celery, chopped

2-3 slices bacon, crisp, crumbled
1/4 cup chopped red or green pepper

1. Mix together all ingredients except tortillas. Spread evenly on tortillas. Roll up, cover with plastic wrap, and refrigerate for at least 2 hours.
2. Immediately before serving, slice into wheels and microwave on high for 10-15 seconds.

Ham and Cheese Roll Ups
Mary Lou Kirtland
Berkeley Heights, NJ
Baby Bunting Basket

Makes many servings

1 lb. ham, thickly sliced
8-oz. pkg. cream cheese, softened
16 scallions
6 whole sweet pickles

1. Blot ham slices dry with a paper towel. Spread each slice of ham with cream cheese.
2. Trim and cut the scallions to same size as short side of ham. Cut sweet pickles into halves, lengthwise.
3. Place either 2 scallions or 1/2 sweet pickle on short side of ham. Roll up. Wrap in plastic wrap. Chill.
4. Slice each rolled up ham slice into 5 pieces.

Wonton Tassie
Gwendolyn P. Chapman
Gwinn, MI
Dresden Plate

Makes 30-36 servings

1 lb. cooked pork sausage, drained
1 1/2 cups grated sharp cheddar cheese
1 1/2 cups grated Monterey Jack cheese
1 cup prepared Hidden Valley Ranch dressing
1/2 cup sliced black olives
1/2 cup chopped red or green pepper
1 pkg. wonton wrappers
cooking oil

1. Mix together sausage, cheeses, dressing, black olives, and pepper. Set aside.
2. Lightly brush each side of wonton wrapper with oil and fit into mini muffin pan forming a cup.
3. Bake at 350° for 5 minutes or until lightly browned. Remove wonton cups and place on cookie sheet.
4. Fill each cup with filling 2/3 full. Return to oven for 7 minutes or until cheeses melt. May be served hot or cold.

Pickle Pinwheels
Lucille Amos
Greensboro, NC
Ohio Star

Makes many servings

8-oz. pkg. cream cheese, softened
1 tsp. garlic powder
2 pkgs. cooked corned beef or pastrami
1 large jar dill pickles

1. Mix together cream cheese and garlic powder.
2. Blot meat slices dry with a paper towel. Spread cream cheese mixture onto 3 slices of meat. Wrap each piece around a pickle to make 3 layers of meat and cheese for each pickle. Repeat, until all ingredients are used.
3. Chill for 1 hour. Slice into pinwheels and serve.

Pesto Cheese
Betty Hall
Fallbrook, CA
Point of No Return

Makes 12-16 servings

1/4 cup fine bread crumbs
2 Tbsp. grated Parmesan cheese
2 8-oz. pkgs. cream cheese, softened
1 cup ricotta cheese
1/2 cup Parmesan cheese
1/8 tsp. cayenne pepper
3 eggs
1/2 cup pesto*
sprigs parsley

1. Mix bread crumbs with 2 Tbsp. Parmesan cheese. Grease the bottom and sides of an 8" springform pan. Coat pan with crumb mixture.
2. Beat together cream cheese, ricotta cheese, 1/2 cup Parmesan cheese, and cayenne pepper until light and fluffy. Add eggs, one at a time, beating well.
3. Transfer 1/2 of cream cheese mixture to medium-sized bowl and stir in pesto. Pour into springform pan. Top with remaining 1/2 of cream cheese mixture.
4. Bake at 325° for 45 minutes or until center no longer shakes. Cool in refrigerator until cold. Garnish with parsley and serve with crackers.

*See page 325 for pesto recipe.

Pesto Sun Dried Tomato Paté
Susan L. Schwarz
N. Bethesda, MD
Americana Hearts

Makes 16 servings

1/2 cup sun dried tomato in oil, drained and coarsely chopped

Pesto:
1 cup basil leaves
1 cup grated Parmesan cheese
2-4 Tbsp. olive oil
2 cloves garlic
salt and pepper to taste

Garlic Cream Cheese:
3 4-oz. pkgs. cream cheese, softened
2 Tbsp. butter, softened
1 clove garlic
pinch white pepper

1. To prepare pesto combine basil leaves, Parmesan cheese, olive oil, 2 cloves garlic, salt, and pepper in food processor. Blend well.
2. To prepare garlic cream cheese combine cream cheese, butter, 1 clove garlic, and white pepper in food processor. Blend well.
3. Line a 3" x 7" loaf pan or fancy mold with plastic wrap. Let wrap overhang the edges. Layer ingredients in the following order: 1/2 of garlic cream cheese, pesto, 1/2 of garlic cream cheese, sun dried tomatoes. Cover with plastic wrap and refrigerate at least 4 hours or overnight. Unmold carefully onto serving plate.
4. Serve with assorted crackers or toasted baguette slices.

Vicliff's Wagon Wheels Spread

Myrtle Mansfield
Alfred, ME
Good Wishes from Quiltmaker #44

Makes 2¹/2 cups

16-oz. carton cottage
  cheese
¹/4 cup mayonnaise
dash Worcestershire
  sauce
¹/4 cup ketchup
dash salt
dash pepper
4-oz. pkg. cream cheese,
  softened
¹/2 small onion, chopped
¹/4 cup sweet pickles,
  chopped
¹/8 tsp. paprika
1 small clove garlic,
  minced

1. If cottage cheese is thin, drain slightly. Mix together all ingredients and blend well.
2. Chill for several hours. Serve with choice of crackers or bread.

Note: Many years ago this recipe was served at Chickland and Vicliff's restaurants in the area around Saugus, MA. Both restaurants are gone, but many of us Saugonians can still taste the wonderful food they served.

Zippy Cheese Spread

Mary Puskar
Forest Hill, MD

Makes 4 cups

10-oz. jar pineapple
  preserves
2 10-oz. jars apple jelly
5-oz. jar horseradish
1 small jar dry mustard
pepper to taste
8-oz. pkg. cream cheese

1. Mix all together all ingredients except cream cheese. Spread over a block of cream cheese.
2. Serve with crackers.

Note: This makes a lot of spread. Keep spread in a container in the refrigerator and use as needed. It keeps indefinitely.

Walnut Cheese Spread

Char Hagner
Montague, MI
Sunbonnet Sue

Makes 2 cups

8-oz. pkg. cream cheese,
  softened
¹/2 cup sour cream
¹/2 cup walnuts
2 Tbsp. chopped green
  pepper
2 Tbsp. chopped onion
3 ozs. chipped beef
2 Tbsp. milk

1. In glass bowl combine all ingredients and mix well. Microwave on high for 2 minutes. Stir and microwave 2 more minutes.
2. To serve spread on an assortment of crackers.

Red Onion Cheese Spread

Jan Carroll
Morton, IL
Wedding Autograph Quilt

Makes 1¹/2-2 cups

8 ozs. Colby or cheddar
  cheese, coarsely grated
1 red onion, finely
  chopped
¹/2-1 cup mayonnaise

1. Mix cheese, onion, and enough mayonnaise to spread easily.
2. Serve with crackers.

Note: This is so quick that I use it for unexpected company. A variety of cheeses such as pizza cheese or Swiss cheese also works well.

Boursin Cheese Spread

Suzanne S. Nobrega
Duxbury, MA
Madeline's Secret
Cindi Dafoe
Marquette, MI
Tami's Memory Quilt

Makes 3¹/2 cups

2 8-oz. pkgs. cream
  cheese, softened
¹/2 cup unsalted butter,
  softened
2 cloves garlic, minced
¹/4 tsp. pepper
¹/4 tsp. thyme
¹/4 tsp. chopped sweet
  basil
1 tsp. oregano
¹/4 tsp. dill weed
¹/2 tsp. salt
¹/8 tsp. chives
¹/8 tsp. parsley

1. Cream together all ingredients. Refrigerate a few hours before serving.
2. Serve with crackers, as stuffing for broiled mushroom caps, or topping for baked potatoes.

Note: Fresh herbs may be used instead of dry. Increase to 1 Tbsp. of each. This will keep in the refrigerator for at least two weeks.

Almond Cheese Ball Spread

Gwen Oberg
Albuquerque, NM
Fin and Fir

Makes many servings

10 slices bacon
6 green onions, chopped
8-ozs. medium sharp
  cheddar cheese, grated
2¹/2 ozs. sliced almonds
¹/2 cup mayonnaise
¹/2 tsp. black pepper

1. Fry, drain, and crumble bacon.
2. Mix together all ingredients and place in serving bowl. Chill at least several hours.
3. Serve with crackers or bagel chips.

Not Your Everyday Cheese Ball

Jean A. Schoettmer
Greensburg, IN
Road to California

Makes many servings

2 8-oz. pkgs. cream
  cheese, softened
1 cup sour cream
3 green onions, chopped
2¹/2-oz. jar smoked dried
  beef, chopped
12 ozs. cheddar cheese,
  shredded

1. Mix together all ingredients, reserving ¹/4 cup cheddar cheese for topping. Pour into an 8" square baking pan.
2. Bake at 350° for 15 minutes. Sprinkle cheddar cheese on top and serve with favorite crackers.

Special Cheese Ball

Susan Sneer
Mountain Lake, MN

1 lb. grated cheddar
  cheese
1 cup finely chopped
  pecans
1 cup mayonnaise
1 small onion, finely
  grated
¹/4 tsp. pepper

1. Combine all ingredients and mix well. Spoon into greased 5- or 6-cup mold. Refrigerate overnight or for several hours until firm.
2. Unmold and serve with a variety of crackers.

Mom's Cheese Ball

Dawn J. Ranck
Strasburg, PA
Patchwork
Susan Cook
Coshocton, OH

*Makes 2 small cheese balls
or 1 large cheese ball*

2 8-oz. pkgs. cream
 cheese, softened
8-oz. wedge sharp natural
 cheddar cheese,
 shredded
1 Tbsp. chopped
 pimiento
1 Tbsp. chopped green
 pepper
2 tsp. Worcestershire
 sauce
1 tsp. lemon juice
dash cayenne pepper
1 cup finely chopped
 pecans or finely
 chopped parsley

1. Combine cream cheese
and cheddar cheese. Mix
well. Stir in pimiento, green
pepper, Worcestershire
sauce, lemon juice, and
cayenne. Mix well. Chill.
2. Form into ball and roll in
chopped pecans or parsley.

Cheese Ball

Mrs. Clarence E. Mitchell
Frederick, MD
Appliqué

Makes 2 large cheese balls

3 8-oz. pkgs. cream
 cheese
4-oz. pkg. blue cheese
8 ozs. processed cheddar
 cheese spread
6 tsp. grated onion
1 tsp. Worcestershire
 sauce
1/8 tsp. Accent
parsley flakes or chopped
 nuts

1. Mix together all ingredients except parsley flakes or
nuts.
2. Form into 2 cheese balls.
3. Sprinkle with parsley
flakes or chopped nuts.

Holiday Cheese Ball

Ann Sunday McDowell
Newtown, PA
Jessica's Froggy Patchwork

Makes 1 medium cheese ball

3 4-oz. pkgs. cream
 cheese, softened
6 ozs. blue cheese,
 softened
6 ozs. processed cheddar
 cheese spread
2 Tbsp. Worcestershire
 sauce
1 cup ground pecans,
 divided in half
1/2 cup parsley, finely
 chopped

1. Combine all ingredients,
except 1/2 cup pecans and
1/4 cup parsley. Mix well.
2. Spoon onto sheet of plastic wrap. Shape into ball.
Wrap in plastic wrap and
chill overnight.
3. Immediately before serving, roll cheese ball in
remaining nuts and parsley.

One of my best ever quilting moments came on
Christmas Day 1994. For several years I had been
working away, painstakingly piecing a Hexagon quilt.
Whenever my mother-in-law would visit us, she
would always comment on its beauty and ask ques-
tions about what I planned to do with it. I would
just smile and keep on sewing and piecing.

When I gave it to her on Christmas Day, she first
sat there and cried. Then she looked at me and
asked, "Why would you do all this work for me?"
Telling the story brings tears to my own eyes and
reminds me that all the work was worth doing for
that one very special moment.

—*Char Hagner, Montague, MI*

Donna's Cheese Ball
Rhonda Yoder
Goshen, IN

Makes 1 large cheese ball

2 8-oz. pkgs. cream
  cheese, softened
2 2$^{1}/_{2}$-oz. pkgs. dried
  beef, chopped
2 tsp. dried onion
1 tsp. Accent
1 tsp. garlic powder
2 tsp. parsley flakes

1. Mix together all ingredients except parsley flakes.
2. Form into ball.
3. Roll in parsley flakes and serve with choice of crackers.

My Favorite Cheese Ball
Katherine Lombard
Deerfield, NH
Wear Warm Clothes

Makes 3 small cheese balls

8-oz. pkg. cream cheese,
  softened
4 cups shredded cheddar
  cheese
2 Tbsp. milk
$^{1}/_{8}$ tsp. pepper
3 Tbsp. Worcestershire
  sauce
4 ozs. crumbled blue
  cheese
$^{1}/_{4}$ tsp. garlic powder
$^{1}/_{2}$ cup finely chopped
  walnuts

1. Mix together cream cheese, cheddar cheese, milk, pepper, Worcestershire sauce, blue cheese, and garlic powder. Mix well.
2. Divide mixture into thirds. Roll each third into a ball. Roll balls in walnuts. Chill for at least 6 hours before serving.

Corned Beef Cheese Ball
Kay Miller
Mitchell, SD
Courthouse Steps

Makes 1 large cheese ball

2 8-oz. pkgs. cream
  cheese, softened
8 ozs. sharp cheddar
  cheese, shredded
6 green onions, chopped
2 2$^{1}/_{2}$-oz. pkgs. corned
  beef, chopped
1 tsp. Accent
1 Tbsp. Worcestershire
  sauce
1 cup chopped nuts

1. Mix together all ingredients. Chill for 2 hours.
2. Shape into ball and roll into chopped nuts. Chill for at least 6 hours before serving.

Smoked Turkey Cheese Ball
Gwen Oberg
Albuquerque, NM
Fin and Fir

Makes 1 medium cheese ball

1 cup finely ground
  smoked turkey
8-oz. pkg. cream cheese,
  softened
3 Tbsp. mayonnaise
$^{1}/_{2}$ tsp. cayenne pepper
$^{1}/_{2}$ cup chopped pecans
2 Tbsp. chopped parsley
  (optional)

1. Combine turkey, cream cheese, mayonnaise, and pepper. Mix well. Chill for several hours.
2. Shape into ball. Roll in pecans and parsley. Refrigerate until ready to serve.
3. Serve with crackers or as a filling for appetizer sandwiches.

Salmon Pecan Ball

Alyce C. Kauffman
Gridley, CA
Sailing Away
Betty Ziegler
Bay City, OR
Dresden Plate

Makes 1 large cheese ball

1-lb. can salmon
8-oz. pkg. cream cheese, softened
1 Tbsp. fresh lemon juice
1 Tbsp. grated onion
1 tsp. horseradish or
   1/2 tsp. dried dill
1/2 cup chopped pecans
1/3 cup chopped fresh parsley

1. Drain and flake salmon, being very sure to remove any bones.
2. Combine all ingredients except parsley and mix well. Chill for 2 hours.
3. Shape into a ball. Roll into parsley. Wrap in foil or plastic wrap and chill for at least 6 hours. Serve with crackers.

Pineapple Cheese Ball

Mildred Duley
Yates City, IL
Woven Heart

Makes 1 large cheese ball

2 8-oz. pkgs. cream cheese, softened
1 medium green pepper, chopped
1 small onion, chopped
8-oz. can crushed pineapple, well drained
1 tsp. seasoning salt
2 cups chopped nuts

1. Mix together cream cheese, green pepper, onion, pineapple, and salt. Mix well. Refrigerate for several hours or overnight.
2. Shape into a ball and roll in chopped nuts. Serve with favorite crackers.

Chipped Beef Log

Lois Stoltzfus
Honey Brook, PA
Colonial Star

Makes 1 large cheese log

8-oz. pkg. cream cheese, softened
3 tsp. horseradish
2 2 1/2-oz. pkgs. dried chipped beef
2 Tbsp. butter
1/2 cup chopped pecans

1. Mix together cream cheese and horseradish.
2. Chop dried beef into fine shreds and fry in butter until frizzled and curly.
3. Mix together dried beef and cream cheese mixture.
4. Form into a log and roll in pecans.
5. Wrap in plastic wrap and refrigerate for several hours or overnight.
6. Serve with assorted crackers.

Garlic Cheese Log

Mary Jane Wackford
Oxford, NY
Log Cabin

Makes 1 medium cheese log

3-oz. pkg. cream cheese, softened
2 cups shredded American cheese
1 large clove garlic, finely minced
1 cup chopped nuts
2 Tbsp. chili powder

1. Beat cheeses together with mixer until smooth. Add garlic and mix well. Carefully fold in chopped nuts. Refrigerate for 30 minutes.
2. Shape into a log. Roll log in chili powder. Wrap and refrigerate. Let stand at room temperature for 30 minutes before serving. Serve with crackers.

Spinach Bread Boat

Marjorie Patterson
North Point, PA
Radiant Broken Star
Maxine Cooper
Danville, IL
Maple Leaf

Makes 4 cups

1 cup sour cream
1 cup mayonnaise
4 scallions, chopped
8-oz. can water chestnuts, drained and chopped
1 pkg. Knorr vegetable soup mix
10-oz. pkg. frozen chopped spinach, well drained
1 loaf round rye bread

1. Mix together sour cream, mayonnaise, scallions, water chestnuts, vegetable soup mix, and spinach (squeeze out excess liquid from spinach). Refrigerate for 3-4 hours.
2. Cut top off round rye bread. Remove center of bread, leaving 3/4" around bottom part and sides of the bread. Cut the top and center of bread into cubes. Cover bread cubes and set aside.
3. Spoon spinach filling into center of rye bread. Use cubes for dipping.

Rye Bowl

Mary Seielstad
Schenectady, NY
Sampler

Makes 5 cups dip

2²/₃ cups mayonnaise
2²/₃ cups sour cream
4 tsp. Beaumonde seasoning
2 tsp. dill weed
4 Tbsp. minced onion
4 Tbsp. chopped fresh parsley
2 2¹/₂-oz. jars dried beef, finely chopped
1 large loaf round rye bread

1. Mix all ingredients except bread. Let stand 4 to 5 hours or overnight.
2. Hollow out the round bread loaf. Cut bread which was taken out of loaf into chunks or cubes.
3. Immediately before serving, fill rye bread shell with dip mixture and place bread cubes nearby for dipping. Serve.

Note: When you get down to "the bowl," cut it up and put it under the broiler for 2-3 minutes. Serve.

French Bread Dip

Loann Haegele
Woodland Hills, CA
Pink Tidings

Makes 3 cups

1 cup mayonnaise
1 cup Parmesan cheese
4 8-oz. pkgs. cream cheese, softened
1/2 tsp. garlic salt
1 bunch green onions, chopped
2 loaves french bread

1. Mix together mayonnaise, Parmesan cheese, cream cheese, garlic salt, and onions.
2. Cut one loaf of bread in half lengthwise. Hollow out, saving the two tops. Fill each half of bread with filling. Cover with tops. Wrap in foil.
3. Bake at 325° for 1¹/2 hours.
4. Cut second loaf of bread into small pieces and use for dipping.

Beef Bread Dip

Sue Graziadio
White Mills, PA
Double Irish Chain

Makes 2 cups

2¹/2-oz. pkg. chipped
  beef, shredded
8-oz. carton sour cream
1 cup mayonnaise
¹/4 tsp. garlic powder
1 small onion, chopped
1 small round loaf rye
  bread

1. Mix together beef, sour
cream, mayonnaise, garlic
powder, and onion.
2. Cut center out of bread.
Fill with chipped beef mixture. Cut center and top of
bread into cubes and serve
with dip.

Dill Bread Dip

Audrey Romonosky
Austin, TX
Pineapple

Makes 4 cups

1 pint mayonnaise
1 pint sour cream
1 Tbsp. dried minced
  onion
1 Tbsp. dried parsley
  flakes
1 Tbsp. Beaumonde
  seasoning
1 Tbsp. dill weed
1 large loaf wheat or
  pumpernickel bread

1. Mix together all ingredients except bread.
2. Carve out center of bread
to make a bowl for the dip.
Cut the removed bread into
pieces.
3. Pour dip into the bread
bowl and serve with bread
pieces.

Bagel Dip

Sharon Hillman
Waukesha, WI
Victorian Log Cabin

Makes 2¹/2 cups

1 cup sour cream
1 cup mayonnaise
2 Tbsp. Accent
2 Tbsp. dill weed
2 2¹/2-oz. pkgs. dried
  chipped beef, chopped
1 small onion, chopped
6 onion bagels

1. Mix together all ingredients except bagels. Chill for
2-3 hours.
2. Cut bagels into bite-sized
pieces. Serve with dip.

Crab and Cream
Cheese Dip

Marian Bentz
Arcadia, CA

Makes 6-10 servings

8-oz. pkg. cream cheese,
  softened
2 Tbsp. Worcestershire
  sauce
2 Tbsp. mayonnaise
1 Tbsp. fresh lemon juice
¹/2 onion, chopped
¹/2 cup cocktail sauce
¹/2 lb. crab
parsley

1. Mix together cream
cheese, Worcestershire
sauce, mayonnaise, lemon
juice, and onion. Spread
onto dinner plate.
2. Spread cocktail sauce
over cream cheese mixture.
Sprinkle crab on cocktail
sauce. Garnish with parsley.
Serve with crackers.

Philly Cream
Cheese Dip

Nanci C. Keatley
Salem, OR
Brian's Sea of Cabins

Makes 1 cup

8-oz. pkg. cream cheese
3 hard-boiled eggs
1 small clove garlic,
  crushed
¹/2 Tbsp. chopped green
  onion tops
salt and pepper to taste
5 Tbsp. mayonnaise
5 Tbsp. half-and-half

1. Mix together all ingredients. Chill overnight or at
least 8 hours.
2. Serve with crackers and
raw vegetables.

Crab and Mushroom Dip
Barbara Neuhauser
Parkesburg, PA

Makes 3 cups

1 cup sour cream
1 cup mayonnaise
2¹/2-oz. jar sliced
    mushrooms, drained
7¹/2-oz. can crabmeat,
    drained
1 cup coconut
¹/2 cup chopped red
    onion
1 Tbsp. parsley
¹/2 tsp. curry powder

1. Combine all ingredients
and mix well. Chill.
2. Serve with crackers.

Aldean's Shrimp Butter
LuAnne Taylor
Canton, PA
Dresden Plate

Makes 1¹/2 cups dip

8-oz. pkg. cream cheese,
    softened
1 cup butter, melted
1 small onion, grated
7¹/2-oz. can shrimp,
    drained
parsley

1. Blend all ingredients in
food processor or blender
until smooth. Chill.
2. Serve with crackers or
choice of raw vegetables.

Holiday Dip
Dorothy Dyer
Lee's Summit, MO
Butterflies in the Garden

Makes 5 cups

2 cups cottage cheese
1 cup sour cream
2 cups mayonnaise
1 pkg. Hidden Valley
    Ranch dressing mix

1. Mix together all ingredients. Chill overnight or at
least 8 hours.
2. Serve with vegetables or
chips.

Shrimp Dip
Ruth Day
Sturgis, SD

3-oz. pkg. cream cheese
12-oz. carton sour cream
2 Tbsp. lemon juice
1 pkg. Italian dressing
    mix
7¹/2-oz. can shrimp,
    drained

1. Mix together all ingredients. Chill several hours.
2. Serve with crackers.

To make Christmas more meaningful for our small children, we established a set of traditions, many with roots in our German heritage and background. On December 6th, St. Nicholas Day, the children were greeted with candies and fruits in their shoes (no charcoal lumps in our home!). Then during Advent, we prepared for and anticipated Christmas by following an old European tradition of having no parties or premature gift-giving. On Christmas Day the children celebrated with a beautiful white cake for the birthday of Jesus. They received religious or spiritually encouraging gifts—Bible storybooks, Christmas song books, or nativity play sets.

Then the twelve days of Christmas ensued. Each morning the children found one gift per child under the tree. Some gifts were small, such as new socks, others were substantial, such as a new bike. The best gifts were always given on the twelfth day. This way the children did not receive a mountain of gifts all at once, and they learned that Christmas was a season, not just a single day.

—*Karen Weber, Alexandria, SD*

Pineapple Dip

Kathie Weatherford
Stockton, CA
In Memory of Samantha

Makes 2 cups

2 8-oz. pkgs. cream
cheese, softened
20-oz. can crushed
pineapple, well drained
1/2 cup finely crushed
walnuts or pecans
2 Tbsp. finely chopped
onion
2 Tbsp. finely chopped
bell pepper
1/2-3/4 tsp. seasoning salt

1. Mix together all
ingredients. Refrigerate for
several hours.
2. Serve with choice of
crackers.

Hummus Dip

Sally A. Price
Reston, VA
Jewel Box

Makes 10-12 servings

2-3 cloves garlic, peeled
1/4 cup lemon juice
1/4 tsp. cumin
1/4 tsp. paprika
dash cayenne pepper
15-oz. can cooked
chickpeas or garbanzo
beans
1/4 cup tahini (toasted
sesame seed)
pita bread, cut into
wedges

pepper slices, carrot
sticks, celery, and
parsley

1. Process garlic, lemon
juice, and seasonings in
blender.
2. Drain chickpeas, reserving liquid.
3. Add beans and tahini and
process. Gradually add
small amounts of reserved
liquid until mixture reaches
a spreading consistency. Do
not over process.
4. Serve with pita bread.
Garnish with pepper slices,
carrot sticks, celery, and
parsley.

Artichoke Crab Dip

Suzie Humphries
Fort Smith, AR
Around the World

Makes 10 servings

1 chopped bell pepper
1 Tbsp. cooking oil
2 14-oz. cans artichoke
hearts, drained and
chopped
2 cups mayonnaise
1/2 cup chopped green
onions
1/2 cup chopped sweet
red pepper
1 cup Parmesan cheese
1 Tbsp. lemon juice
4 tsp. Worcestershire sauce
3 large jalapeno peppers,
seeded and minced
1 lb. imitation crab meat
1/3 cup sliced almonds,
toasted

1. Sauté bell pepper in oil
over medium heat, stirring
until soft. Let cool.
2. Mix together bell pepper,
artichokes, mayonnaise,
onions, red pepper,
Parmesan cheese, lemon
juice, Worcestershire sauce,
and jalapeno peppers. Mix
well. Stir in crab meat.
3. Pour mixture into greased
casserole dish. Sprinkle
almonds over top.
4. Bake at 375° for 30
minutes. Serve with crackers or bread.

Dried Beef Dip

Judy Sharer
Port Matilda, PA
Stained Glass Window

Makes many servings

8-oz. pkg. cream cheese,
softened
3 Tbsp. milk
4 ozs. sour cream
2 Tbsp. diced onion
2 Tbsp. diced green
pepper
1/2 tsp. pepper
21/2-oz. pkg. dried beef,
shredded
1/4 cup chopped walnuts

1. Mix together cream
cheese and milk. Stir in sour
cream, onion, green pepper,
and pepper. Mix well. Add
dried beef and mix.
2. Transfer mixture to a
greased casserole dish. Top
with walnuts.
3. Cover and bake at 300°
for 20 minutes. Uncover

and bake for another 10 minutes.
4. Serve with bread sticks, crackers, or a variety of cubed breads.

Hot Macadamia Dip
Faye Blair
Mt. Pleasant, SC
Ribbon Star

Makes 12-15 servings

3 4-oz. pkgs. cream cheese, softened
2 Tbsp. milk
2 1/2-oz. jar dried chipped beef, shredded
1/3 cup onion, finely chopped
1 clove garlic, minced
1/2 tsp. pepper
1/8 tsp. ground ginger
3/4 cup sour cream
1/2 cup coarsely chopped macadamia nuts
1 Tbsp. butter or margarine

1. Combine cream cheese and milk, blending until smooth. Stir in chipped beef. Add onion, garlic, pepper, and ginger. Fold in sour cream. Pour into shallow baking dish.
2. In small skillet sauté nuts in butter until glazed. Sprinkle over beef mixture.
3. Bake at 350° for 20-25 minutes.
4. Serve hot with crackers.

Hot Beef Dip
Esther Lantz
Leola, PA
Broken Star

Makes 12 servings

2 lbs. ground beef
1 cup chopped onion
16-oz. can tomato sauce
1/2 cup ketchup
3/4 tsp. oregano
1/2 tsp. sugar
1/2 tsp. salt
2 8-oz. pkgs. cream cheese, softened
1 cup grated sharp cheddar cheese

1. Sauté ground beef and onion. Drain well. Stir in tomato sauce, ketchup, oregano, sugar, and salt. Cover and simmer for 10 minutes.
2. Remove from heat. Stir in cream cheese and cheddar cheese. Stir until cheese is melted. Serve hot with corn chips.

Favorite Chip Dip
Mary Ann England
Rosamond, CA
Dresden Hearts

Makes many servings

2 lbs. Velveeta cheese
10-oz. can tomatoes with green chilies
10 3/4-oz. can cream of mushroom soup
15-oz. can chili

1. Put all ingredients in crockpot. Heat on medium for 1-2 hours, stirring as cheese melts.
2. Serve with chips.

Hot Cheddar Bean Dip
Janice Way
Warrington, PA
Appliqué

Makes many servings

1/2 cup mayonnaise
16-oz. can pinto beans, drained and mashed
1 cup shredded cheddar cheese
4-oz. can chopped green chilies, drained
1/4 tsp. hot pepper sauce
tortilla chips

1. Mix together all ingredients except chips. Stir to mix well. Spoon into small casserole dish.
2. Bake at 350° for 30 minutes. Serve with chips.

Chili Conqueso
Colleen Konetzni
Rio Rancho, NM
Double Wedding Ring

Makes 12 servings

1/2 cup butter
1 onion, chopped
1 bell pepper, chopped
2 1/2 lbs. Velveeta cheese, cubed
1 lb. longhorn cheese, grated
4-oz. can chopped green chilies
1/8 tsp. garlic powder
milk as needed
5 tomatoes, chopped
corn chips or raw vegetables

1. Sauté onion and pepper in butter until soft.
2. Combine onion, pepper, cheeses, green chilies, and garlic powder in crockpot.
3. Cook on low 2-3 hours, stirring occasionally until melted together. Add milk to thin, as necessary. Stir in tomatoes. Serve with corn chips and raw vegetables.

Pizza Pan Dip
Nancy Wagner Graves
Manhattan, KS
Memories of an English Garden

Makes many servings

8-oz. pkg. cream cheese, softened
12-oz. bottle chili sauce
6-oz. can ripe black olives, chopped
1 medium green pepper, chopped
1 medium onion, chopped
2 cups shredded cheddar cheese
2 cups shredded mozzeralla cheese
corn chips

1. On a large pizza pan, layer all ingredients except corn chips in the order given.
2. Serve with corn chips.

Guacamole Dip
Donna Lantgen
Rapid City, SD
Interlock

Makes 1 1/2 cups

8-oz. carton sour cream
1/2 pkg. dry onion soup mix
1 avocado, mashed
1 medium tomato, diced
1/4 cup chopped green pepper
tortilla chips

1. Mix together all ingredients except chips.
2. Serve with tortilla chips.

Vegetable Pizza
Ruth Day
Sturgis, SD
Sampler

Makes 12 servings

1 pkg. crescent rolls
8-oz. pkg. cream cheese, softened
1/2 pkg. Hidden Valley Ranch dressing mix
1/2 tsp. garlic powder
1/2 tsp. dill weed
assortment of fresh vegetables, sliced

1. Roll out crescent rolls on medium-sized, ungreased, rectangular pizza pan and bake according to directions on package. Cool.
2. Mix cream cheese with ranch dressing, garlic powder, and dill weed. Spread over cooled crust.
3. Top with fresh vegetables of choice: cauliflower, black olives, broccoli, green peppers, carrots, green onion, cherry tomatoes.
4. Cut into squares and serve.

Honey-Baked Chicken Wings
Margaret A. Papuga
Prospect Heights, IL
Callie Lu's Sunflower

Makes 16 wings

16 chicken wings
1 cup honey
1/2 cup ketchup
1/2 cup soy sauce
2 tsp. cooking oil
2 large cloves garlic, crushed and minced
1/4 tsp. pepper

1. Cut off tips of wings. Cut each wing in half at joint. Arrange in a single layer in a shallow 3-quart baking dish.
2. Stir together honey, ketchup, soy sauce, oil, garlic, and pepper. Pour over chicken pieces, turning to coat.
3. Bake at 350° for 1 1/4-1 1/2 hours or until browned, basting occasionally.
4. To serve transfer to a chafing dish or hot tray. Serve with small plates and napkins.

Chicken Wings
Maryann Markano
Wilmington, DE

Makes 12-15 servings

4-5 lbs. chicken wings
1/2 cup sugar
3/4 cup soy sauce
2 tsp. ginger
1 clove garlic, minced
1/4 tsp. pepper
2 tsp. paprika
1/2 tsp. chili powder

1. Rinse chicken wings. Pat dry. Place in large greased roasting pan. Sprinkle with sugar. Let sit for 30 minutes.
2. Combine all remaining ingredients. Pour over chicken and refrigerate for 1 hour.
3. Drain off most but not all of liquid and reserve.
4. Bake at 350° for 1 hour. Reduce oven temperature to 275° and bake another 1 hour. Baste and turn chicken while baking. (Meat will be very tender.)

Maply Sausage Appetizer
Kathi Rogge
Alexandria, IN
Jewel Box

Makes 14-16 servings

20-oz. can pineapple chunks
4 tsp. cornstarch
1/2 tsp. salt
3/4 cup maple syrup
1/3 cup water
1/4 cup vinegar
1 lb. small sausages
1 large green pepper
1 cup maraschino cherries, drained

1. Drain pineapple and reserve juice.
2. In saucepan blend reserved juice, cornstarch, salt, maple syrup, water, and vinegar. Heat just to boiling, stirring constantly.
3. Brown sausages and drain all excess fat. Cut green pepper into 1" pieces.
4. Add pineapple, sausages, peppers, and cherries to maple syrup mixture. Cook for 5 minutes or until sausages are heated through. Serve in chafing dish with toothpicks.

Appetizer Sausage Balls
Donna A. Lessmann
Commack, NY
May Flowers

Makes 3 dozen

1 1/2 cups sifted flour
2 tsp. curry powder
1 tsp. paprika
1/4 tsp. salt
8 ozs. cheddar cheese, shredded
1/2 cup butter or margarine
1 lb. sausage meat

1. Mix flour, curry powder, paprika, salt, and cheese. Cut in butter with pastry blender until mixture resembles coarse crumbs. Shape into a ball, cover, and refrigerate.
2. Shape teaspoons of sausage meat into small balls. Fry over medium heat until well browned. Drain on paper towels.
3. Divide cheese dough into as many pieces as you have sausage balls. Shape dough around balls. Wrap and freeze until ready to use.
4. Preheat oven to 400°. Place frozen balls on cookie sheet. Bake 12 to 15 minutes until golden brown. Serve with toothpicks.

Hot Dips for Sausages
Mary Lou Maher
Williamsfield, IL
Tumbling Star

Dip One:
4-oz. jar brown horseradish mustard
6-oz. jar currant jelly

Dip Two:
1 cup ketchup
1 cup grape jelly

Dip Three:
1 cup raspberry brandy
1 cup brown sugar
1 cup ketchup

1. To prepare each dip combine ingredients and mix thoroughly.
2. Choose dip of choice and combine it with small sausages or meatballs in a crockpot. Heat on medium for 3-4 hours or until sausages are cooked. Serve hot with toothpicks.

Hot Crab Meat Dip
Mary Seielstad
Schenectady, NY
Offset Star

Makes many servings

2 8-oz. pkgs. cream cheese, softened
7 1/2-oz. can king crab meat, drained
1 small onion, finely chopped
1/8 tsp. salt
2 Tbsp. finely chopped green pepper

1. Mix together all ingredients.
2. Pour into a small, greased casserole dish.
3. Bake at 300° for 30 minutes or until bubbly.
4. Serve with crackers.

Hot Crab Spread
Mary K. Mitchell
Battle Creek, MI
Miniature Wild Goose Chase
Maricarol Magill
Freehold, NJ
Round Robin

Makes 10-20 servings

8-oz. pkg. cream cheese, softened
7 1/2-oz. can crab meat, drained
2 Tbsp. chopped onion
1 Tbsp. milk
1/2 tsp. cream-style horseradish

1/4 tsp. salt
1/8 tsp. pepper
1/3 cup sliced almonds
1-2 Tbsp. butter

1. Mix together cream cheese, crab meat, onion, milk, horseradish, salt, and pepper. Spread mixture into greased, shallow chafing dish.
2. Sauté almonds in butter. Spread over crab mixture.
3. Bake at 375° for 15 minutes until hot and bubbly. Serve with assorted crackers.

Mom's Hot Crab Meat Appetizer
Susan Stephani Smith
Monument, CO
May Baskets

Makes 6-10 servings

7 1/2-oz. can crab meat
8-oz. pkg. cream cheese, softened
1 tsp. grated onion
dash Worcestershire sauce
salt and pepper to taste
dash Tabasco sauce
1 tsp. lemon juice
1/3 cup slivered almonds

1. Mix together crab meat, cream cheese, onion, Worcestershire sauce, salt, pepper, Tabasco sauce, and lemon juice. Pour into oven-proof serving dish. Top with slivered almonds.
2. Bake at 350° for 25 minutes. Serve with crackers.

Shrimp Mold
Margaret A. Papuga
Prospect Heights, IL
Callie Lu's Sunflower

Makes 10-12 servings

1 pkg. unflavored gelatin
1/4 cup hot water
10 3/4-oz. can tomato soup
8-oz. pkg. cream cheese, softened
1 cup mayonnaise
3/4 cup chopped celery
3/4 cup chopped onion
2 4 1/2-oz. cans tiny shrimp, drained

1. Dissolve gelatin in hot water. Pour into saucepan. Stir in tomato soup and cream cheese. Cook slowly until cream cheese has melted, stirring frequently. Beat with a mixer and cool.
2. Stir in mayonnaise, celery, onion, and drained shrimp. Mix well.
3. Pour mixture into a well greased mold. Refrigerate overnight or at least 8 hours. Unmold and serve with crackers.

Variation:
Substitute cream of mushroom soup for the tomato soup. Use 3/4 lb. fresh cocktail shrimp, peeled, deveined, and steamed.

Jean Johnson
Dallas, OR
Ducky Weather

Crab Mold
Rayann Rohrer
Allentown, PA
The Twist

Makes 10-12 servings

1/2 of 10 3/4-oz. can cream of mushroom soup
1 pkg. unflavored gelatin
1/8 cup hot water
8-oz. pkg. cream cheese, softened
1/2 cup mayonnaise
1 small onion, grated
1/2 cup finely chopped celery
12 ozs. crab meat*

* *It is best not to use imitation crab meat for this recipe.*

1. Heat soup over medium heat.
2. Dissolve gelatin in hot water and add to mushroom soup.
3. Over low heat add cream cheese, mayonnaise, onion, celery, and crab meat. Blend well.
4. Pour into well greased mold. Refrigerate overnight or at least 8 hours until set. Serve with crackers.

Stuffed Celery Sticks
Linda Gruhlkey Pond
Los Alamos, NM
Fields of Purple

Makes 24-30 servings

8-oz. pkg. cream cheese
3 ozs. Velveeta cheese
1 bunch green onions,
sliced
1/8 tsp. garlic salt
8-10 stalks celery
paprika

1. Microwave cheeses until soft enough to blend. Stir in onions and garlic salt.
2. Spread evenly over celery stalks. Garnish with paprika. Cut each stalk into 3 pieces and serve.

Pickled Eggs
Barbara Hummel
Punxsutawney, PA
April Showers

Makes 12 eggs

1 dozen eggs
2 16-oz. cans sliced beets
1 1/2 cups sugar
3/4 cup vinegar
2 3" cinnamon sticks

1. Boil eggs. Cool. Peel and place in deep container such as a 2-quart glass canning jar.
2. Drain beets. Pour liquid into saucepan. Pour sliced beets over eggs.

3. Add sugar, vinegar, and cinnamon sticks to reserved beet liquid. Heat to boiling, stirring constantly. Remove from heat and pour over beets and eggs. Cool. Cover. Refrigerate for at least 8 hours.
4. To serve remove eggs and beets with slotted spoon.

Fall Apple Dip
Carol Peszynski
Carpentersville, IL
Voices of the Past

Makes 2 cups

8-oz. pkg. cream cheese,
softened
3/4 cup brown sugar
1 tsp. vanilla
1 cup chopped peanuts
golden delicious apples
orange juice

1. Combine cream cheese, brown sugar, vanilla, and peanuts and mix well. Spoon dip into small serving bowl.
2. Cut cores out of apples. Slice into wedges and dip into orange juice.
3. Arrange apple wedges around dip on a platter and serve.

Cheese Blintzes
Joyce Parker
North Plainfield, NJ
Round Robin Friendship Quilt

Makes 56-70 pieces

14 slices thin white bread
8-oz. pkg. cream cheese,
softened
1 egg yolk
1 tsp. cinnamon
1 Tbsp. sugar
1/2 cup butter or
margarine, melted
sour cream

1. Cut crusts off bread and flatten with a rolling pin.
2. Mix together cream cheese and egg yolk. Spread on bread and roll each piece into a log.
3. Mix together cinnamon and sugar.
4. Roll logs in butter, then in cinnamon-sugar mixture. Freeze.
5. To serve cut each log into 4-5 bite-sized pieces. Place on ungreased cookie sheet.
6. Bake at 350° for 10-15 minutes. Serve hot with sour cream available as a dip.

Salads

Easy Caesar Salad
Jeanne Allen
Los Alamos, NM
Best Friends

Makes 4-6 servings

2 Tbsp. olive oil
1/2 tsp. salt
1 large clove garlic
2 tomatoes, peeled, cut in eighths
2 heads romaine lettuce, cut in 1" strips
1/4 cup chopped green onions
1/2 cup freshly grated Romano cheese
1 lb. bacon, cooked crisp and chopped fine
1/3 cup olive oil
juice of 2 medium-sized lemons
1/2 tsp. pepper
1/2 tsp. oregano
1 lightly soft-boiled egg
1 cup croutons

1. Pour 2 Tbsp. oil into a large wooden bowl. Sprinkle with salt and rub with a clove of garlic. Remove garlic and place the tomatoes in bowl. Add romaine, onions, cheese, and bacon.
2. Mix together 1/3 cup oil, lemon juice, pepper, and oregano in a medium-sized bowl. Add egg and whip vigorously.
3. Pour dressing over salad when ready to serve. Add croutons. Toss and serve.

Eggless Caesar Salad
Joyce Cox
Port Angeles, WA
Amish Star

Makes 6-8 servings

1 large head romaine lettuce
1 cup olive oil
juice of 1 lemon
4 large garlic cloves, minced
1/3 cup balsamic vinegar
1/4 tsp. salt
1/4 tsp. fresh ground pepper
2/3 cup Romano cheese, shredded

1. Wash, dry, and break lettuce into bite-sized pieces. Chill.
2. Mix together oil, lemon juice, garlic, vinegar, salt, and pepper. Shake well and chill.
3. Place lettuce in bowl. Toss with dressing, mixing well. Sprinkle cheese over top. Serve immediately.

Korean Salad
Cindi Dafoe
Marquette, MI
Tami's Memory Quilt

Makes 6-8 servings

1 1/4 lbs. fresh spinach
1/2 lb. fresh bean sprouts
8 slices bacon, cooked
  and crumbled
3 hard-boiled eggs,
  chopped

Dressing:
3/4 cup salad oil
1/3 cup sugar
1/3 cup ketchup
2 tsp. Worcestershire
  sauce
1 medium onion, sliced
  in rings
3 Tbsp. red wine vinegar

1. Toss together spinach,
bean sprouts, bacon, and
eggs and set aside.
2. Mix dressing ingredients
together. Dressing can be
heated and served warm, or
served cold.
3. Pour dressing over salad
and toss well. Serve immediately.

Sherril's Tossed Salad
Sherril Bieberly
Salina, KS
My Watercolor Heart

Makes 6-8 servings

1 large head lettuce
1/4 lb. mushrooms, sliced
1 cup cauliflower pieces
1 green pepper, sliced
1/2 cup sliced onions
4 ozs. stuffed olives, cut
  in half
4 ozs. blue cheese,
  crumbled
1/4 cup olive oil
1/2 tsp. garlic salt
1/2 tsp. salt
1/4 tsp. pepper
1/4 cup tarragon vinegar

1. Combine lettuce, mush-
rooms, cauliflower, green
pepper, onions, and olives.
Refrigerate.
2. Before serving, sprinkle
blue cheese and olive oil
over lettuce mixture. Cover
and gently shake until all
salad pieces glisten. Add
garlic salt, salt, and pepper.
Sprinkle tarragon vinegar on
top. Toss and serve.

Seven Layer Salad
Lucille Brubacker
Barnett, MO
Double Wedding Ring

Makes 6-8 servings

4 cups shredded lettuce
1 cup chopped celery
4 eggs, hard-boiled and
  sliced
1 cup frozen peas
1 cup shredded carrots
8 slices bacon, fried and
  crumbled
2 cups salad dressing
2 tsp. sugar
4 ozs. cheese, grated

1. Arrange lettuce, celery,
eggs, peas, carrots, and
bacon in layers in 9" x 13"
pan.
2. Mix together salad dressing and sugar. Spread on top
of vegetables.
3. Sprinkle top with cheese.
4. Refrigerate for up to one
day before tossing and serving.

Mandarin Orange Salad
Dorothy Reise
Severna Park, MD
Honeybee

Makes 6-8 servings

1/4 cup sliced almonds
1 Tbsp. plus 1 tsp. sugar
1/4 head iceberg or
  butternut lettuce
1/4 head romaine lettuce

1 cup chopped celery
2 green onions with tops,
   thinly sliced
1/2 tsp. salt
1/8 tsp. pepper
2 Tbsp. sugar
2 Tbsp. vinegar
1/4 cup salad oil
1/8 tsp. red pepper sauce
1 Tbsp. chopped parsley
11-oz. can mandarin
   oranges, drained

1. Cook almonds and sugar over low heat, stirring constantly until sugar is melted and almonds are coated. Cool and break apart.
2. Tear lettuce into bite-sized pieces. Place greens in plastic bag. Add celery and onions.
3. Place salt, pepper, sugar, vinegar, oil, red pepper sauce, and parsley in jar. Cover tightly and shake.
4. Five minutes before serving, pour dressing into bag. Add drained mandarin oranges. Fasten bag. Shake until greens are coated. Add almonds and shake.
5. Pour into salad bowl. Serve immediately.

Spinach Salad
Carmen Kleager
Scottsbluff, NE
Carrie Nation

Makes 4-6 servings

1 Tbsp. onion juice
   (scraped from onion)
1/2 cup vinegar
1 tsp. dry mustard
1/4 cup sugar
3/4 cup oil
1 tsp. salt
1 1/2 tsp. poppy seeds
1 1/2 cups large curd
   cottage cheese
1/2 lb. bacon, fried and
   crumbled
1 lb. fresh spinach, torn
   into pieces
1/2 head lettuce, torn into
   pieces

1. Mix together onion juice, vinegar, mustard, sugar, oil, salt, poppy seeds, 3/4 cup cottage cheese, and 1/4 lb. bacon.
2. Toss together spinach, lettuce, remaining 1/4 lb. bacon, and remaining 3/4 cup cottage cheese.

3. Pour dressing over spinach mixture and toss well. Serve immediately.

Cottage-Tomato Salad
Marion Snead
Montgomery, AL
Half Log Cabin

Makes 6 servings

4-6 cups fresh green
   beans
2 cups cottage cheese
1/3 cup mayonnaise
1/2 cup shredded carrots
1/4 cup salted, chopped
   peanuts
2 Tbsp. chopped green
   onion
4 medium tomatoes,
   sliced
lettuce leaves

1. Cook beans in boiling water for 15 minutes or until crisp tender. Drain and plunge into cold water. Drain.
2. Combine green beans, cottage cheese, mayonnaise, carrots, peanuts, and onion.
3. Line serving platter with lettuce leaves and sliced tomatoes. Cover with green bean mixture.

The first Christmas after we were married, my husband and I discovered we did not agree on how to decorate our Christmas tree. He preferred a plain tree with a only few lights. I liked a tree filled and overflowing with ornaments (often homemade) and covered with lights. So we made a compromise.
   On the even years we would decorate the tree my way and on the odd years his way. While our friends thought this a bit strange, they have spent the past thirty-six years watching our tree. If it is sparsely decorated, they know it's an odd year!
   —*Joyce Parker, North Plainfield, NJ*

Tomatoes and Cucumbers with Fresh Mint Dressing

Jean Hannemann
Marquette, MI

Makes 10-12 servings

1/2 cup tarragon vinegar
2/3 cup salad oil
1/4 cup sugar
1/2 tsp. salt
1/8 tsp. pepper
1/2 cup chopped fresh
   mint leaves
2-3 cucumbers
6 ripe tomatoes, sliced
1/2 head romaine lettuce
mint sprigs

1. Combine vinegar, oil, sugar, salt, pepper, and 1/4 cup chopped mint in a jar with a tight-fitting lid. Shake vigorously to mix well.
2. Wash and score cucumbers. (To score, run tines of fork down length of cucumbers to make a pattern.) Slice cucumbers 1/8 inch thick.
3. Place cucumber and tomato slices in a 9" x 13" glass baking dish, grouping tomatoes in one end and cucumbers in the other.
4. Shake dressing well, and drizzle evenly over all. Refrigerate covered for at least 1 hour, spooning dressing over vegetables occasionally.
5. To serve line a large, shallow platter with romaine lettuce. Arrange tomato slices around edge and cucumber slices in center. Spoon dressing over all. Sprinkle with remaining mint and garnish with mint sprigs.

Cucumbers in Sour Cream

Charmaine Caesar
Lancaster, PA
Bits and Pieces Wallhanging

Makes 2-4 servings

1/2 tsp. salt
2 cucumbers, peeled and
   sliced thin
1 small onion, sliced very
   thin
1 tsp. minced fresh dill
2/3 cup sour cream
1 tsp. vinegar

1. Salt cucumbers and drain on paper towel for 45 minutes.
2. Mix together all ingredients and serve.

Minted Wild Rice Salad

Flo Neiman
Islamorada, FL
1930's Material in a Mini Quilt

Makes 6-8 servings

1 cup raw wild rice
5 1/2 cups chicken broth
   or water
1 cup pecans, chopped
1 cup yellow raisins
grated rind of 1 orange
1/4 cup chopped fresh mint
4 scallions, sliced thin
1/4 cup oil
1/3 cup orange juice
1 tsp. salt
1/4 tsp. pepper

1. Rinse rice. Mix together rice and broth and simmer uncovered for 40-50 minutes. (Rice should not be too soft.) Drain.
2. Gently toss remaining ingredients with rice.
3. Let stand for 2 hours before serving. Serve at room temperature.

Fresh Mushroom Salad

Cindy Dorzab
Fort Smith, AR
The Geese Have Finally Flown!

Makes 8 servings

1 lb. fresh mushrooms,
   washed and sliced
1/2 lb. Swiss cheese,
   grated
2-3 chopped green onions
1/4 cup fresh parsley,
   chopped
1/2 cup oil
1/4 cup red wine vinegar
3 tsp. mixed dried herbs
   (basil, thyme,
   rosemary, etc.)

1. In a large serving dish, layer mushrooms, cheese, green onions, and parsley. Chill.

2. Combine oil, vinegar, and herbs. Toss with other ingredients and serve.

Broccoli Salad
Carlene Horne
Bedford, NH
Mariners Compass

Makes 6-8 servings

2 heads broccoli florets, cut in bite-sized pieces
1 cup cubed Monterey Jack cheese
1/2 cup pepperoni chunks or slices
1 large red onion, sliced
1/2 cup vinegar
1/2 cup sugar
1/2-3/4 cup mayonnaise

1. Combine broccoli, cheese, pepperoni, and onion.
2. Mix together vinegar, sugar, and mayonnaise. Pour over broccoli mixture. Refrigerate for 2 hours before serving.

Broccoli Slaw
Jean A. Schoettmer
Greensburg, IN
Road to California

Makes 8 servings

1 lb. broccoli, cut up in small pieces
3/4 cup oil
1/2 cup sugar
1/3 cup plus 2 Tbsp. vinegar

2 pkgs. chicken-flavored Ramen noodles
1 medium red onion, chopped
1 cup diced celery
3 ozs. toasted almond slivers
3 ozs. sunflower seeds

1. Mix together oil, sugar, vinegar, and broken Ramen noodles. Pour over broccoli. Add onion and chopped celery and stir.
2. Cover and put in refrigerator for 12 hours. Before serving add almonds and sunflower seeds.

Cabbage Salad
Margaret F. Moehl
Pinckney, MI
Christmas Treasures

Makes 6-8 servings

1/2 head cabbage, shredded
2-3 green onions, chopped
2-oz. pkg. slivered almonds
1/2 cup oil
3 Tbsp. vinegar
2 tsp. sugar
1 tsp. salt
1/2 tsp. pepper
1/2 pkg. Ramen flavoring that comes with noodles
1 pkg. chicken-flavored Ramen noodles

1. Mix cabbage and onions together.
2. Toast almonds on baking sheet at 300°.

3. Mix together oil, vinegar, sugar, salt, pepper, and Ramen flavoring.
4. When ready to serve, mix noodles into vegetables and gently fold in dressing. Top with slivered almonds.

Coleslaw Souffle Salad
Mrs. Gordon Dorothy
Madelia, MN

Makes 6-8 servings

3-oz. pkg. lemon gelatin
1 cup boiling water
1/2 cup mayonnaise
1/2 cup cold water
2 Tbsp. vinegar
1/4 tsp. salt
1 1/2 cups finely shredded cabbage
1/2 cup diced celery
1 Tbsp. grated onion
2 Tbsp. chopped pimiento

1. Dissolve gelatin in boiling water. Stir in mayonnaise, cold water, vinegar, and salt. Chill until partially set. Then beat until fluffy.
2. Stir in cabbage, celery, onion, and pimiento. Pour into a 1-quart mold and chill until set.

Cabbage Crock Salad

Lorene P. Meyer
Wayland, IA
Sampler

Makes 3-4 quarts

4 Tbsp. salt
4 individual quarts of
  water
1 medium head of
  cabbage, shredded
3 medium onions,
  shredded
2 peppers (green, red,
  yellow), shredded
2 carrots, shredded
2 cups vinegar
2 cups sugar
2 tsp. celery seed
2 tsp. mustard seed

1. Dissolve 1 Tbsp. salt in each quart of water. Mix together shredded cabbage, onions, peppers, and carrots. Divide vegetables equally among the 4 quarts of salt water. Allow to set for several hours.
2. Drain each quart of water, and squeeze out the excess water by hand. Mix all the vegetables together in a large mixing bowl.
3. In a saucepan stir together vinegar, sugar, celery seed, and mustard seed. Heat to boiling. Stir until sugar is dissolved. Cool.
4. Mix together vegetables and vinegar mixture. Put in container with tight-fitting lid so the container can be turned over at intervals in order to fully season all the vegetables. The salad will keep in the refrigerator for several months.

Sauerkraut Salad

Janie Canupp
Millersville, MD
Double Wedding Ring

Makes 12-15 servings

1 large green pepper,
  chopped
1 large red pepper,
  chopped
1 large onion, chopped
1 cup celery, diced
4-oz. jar pimientos
1 quart sauerkraut,
  drained and cut up
2 cups sugar
1/4 cup water
1/2 cup vinegar
1 tsp. celery seed

1. Mix together peppers, onion, celery, pimientos, and sauerkraut.
2. Mix together sugar, water, vinegar, and celery seed. Pour over sauerkraut mixture.
3. Place in refrigerator for 24 hours.

Crazy Quilt Bean Salad

Pauline J. Morrison
St. Marys, Ontario
Cinderella

Makes 12-16 servings

15-oz. can cut green
  beans, drained
15-oz. can cut wax beans,
  drained
15-oz. can red kidney
  beans, drained
15-oz. can lima beans,
  drained
1 cup diced celery
1/2 cup red onions, rings
  or chunks
1/4 cup diced green, red,
  or yellow pepper
1/2 tsp. salt

Dressing:
1/4 cup white vinegar
1/2 cup oil
1/4 tsp. pepper
1 tsp. dry mustard
1 tsp. thyme
1/2 tsp. garlic powder

1. Mix together beans, celery, onions, and green pepper. Sprinkle with salt and mix well.
2. Mix together vinegar, oil, pepper, mustard, thyme, and garlic powder. Pour over vegetables and mix well.
3. Cover and refrigerate for one day before serving. Stir occasionally to make sure bean mixture is well marinated.

Calico Salad

Mary Davis
Akron, MI
Road to Oklahoma

Makes 10-12 servings

2 15-oz. cans mixed
  vegetables
1 small onion, chopped
1/2 cup chopped celery
1 small green pepper,
  chopped
15-oz. can kidney beans,
  drained
1 tsp. dill weed
1/3 cup sugar
1/2 cup white vinegar
1 Tbsp. prepared mustard

1. Combine vegetables,
onion, celery, pepper, and
kidney beans.
2. Mix together dill weed,
sugar, white vinegar, and
mustard. Pour over vegetables and mix well.
3. Refrigerate for 1 hour,
stirring occasionally.

Christmas Pea Salad

Flo Neiman
Islamorada, FL
1930's Material in a Mini Quilt

Makes 6-8 servings

2 cups baby peas, cooked
  and drained
1 1/2 cups corn, cooked
  and drained
1 cup green onions and
  tops, chopped

1 green pepper, chopped
4-oz. jar pimientos,
  drained and cut up
1 cup chopped celery
1 large carrot, grated
1/2 cup white vinegar
1/4 cup oil
1/2 cup sugar
1/2 tsp. salt
1/4 tsp. pepper
1 tsp. celery salt

1. Combine peas, corn,
onions, green pepper, pimientos, celery, and carrot.
2. Mix together vinegar, oil,
sugar, salt, pepper, and celery
salt. Pour over vegetables.

*Note: This lasts for weeks in
the refrigerator.*

Christmas Vegetable Salad

Dorothy B. Williams
Keezletown, VA
Tumbler Charm

Makes 8 servings

2 cups corn, cooked and
  drained
2 cups small green peas,
  cooked and drained
2 cups French-style green
  beans, cooked and
  drained
1 red pepper, chopped
1 bunch green onions,
  sliced
2 stalks celery, chopped
2 Tbsp. sugar
1 cup vinegar
1/2 cup vegetable oil
dash of black pepper
1/4 tsp. garlic powder

1. Mix together corn, peas,
beans, red pepper, onions,
and celery.
2. In saucepan mix together
sugar, vinegar, oil, and seasonings and bring to a boil.
Cool.
3. Pour over vegetables and
chill for 8 hours.

Marinated Carrots

Carolyn D. Burkett
Punxsutawney, PA
Tulip Quilt by Eleanor Burns

Makes 12 servings

3 1-lb. cans whole baby
  carrots
1 small green pepper,
  coarsely chopped
1 small red pepper,
  coarsely chopped
10 3/4-oz. can tomato soup
1/2 cup olive oil
1 cup sugar
3/4 cup apple cider
  vinegar
1 tsp. dry mustard
1 med. onion, sliced

1. Mix together carrots and
peppers. Set aside.
2. Warm soup. Blend with
olive oil, sugar, vinegar, and
dry mustard. Mix together
with carrot mixture.
3. Cook onions until tender.
Stir into carrot mixture.
4. Serve as a vegetable or
relish.

Macaroni Salad
Dorothy Dyer
Lee's Summit, MO
Falling Leaves

Makes 8-10 servings

16-oz. pkg. shell macaroni,
   cooked and drained
2-3 carrots, shredded
1 onion, chopped
1 red or green pepper,
   chopped
1 cup salad dressing
1/2 cup vinegar
3/4 cup sugar
5-oz. can evaporated milk

1. Mix together all ingredients.
2. Let stand for at least 8 hours before serving.

Sunshine Salad
Mary Davis
Akron, MI
Road to Oklahoma

Makes 6 servings

2 cups grated carrots
1 cup drained, crushed
   pineapple
1/2 cup golden raisins
1/4 cup pineapple juice
1 Tbsp. sugar
2 Tbsp. low-fat salad
   dressing

1. Combine carrots, pineapple, and raisins.
2. Mix together pineapple juice, sugar, and salad dressing. Mix into carrot mixture.

Potato Salad
Anita Coker
Bellville, TX
12 Days of Christmas

Makes 8-10 servings

8 large red potatoes
2 Tbsp. oil
3-4 green onions,
   chopped
1/2 cup chopped dill
   pickles
4-oz. jar pimientos
1 cup mayonnaise
1/2 tsp. salt
1/4 tsp. pepper

1. Boil potatoes until soft. Peel and dice while warm.
2. Drizzle oil over potatoes. Add onions, pickles, pimientos, and mayonnaise and mix well. Stir in salt and pepper.

Gelatin Pineapple Cranberry Salad
Susan Tjon
Austin, TX
Mary Brubacker
Barnett, MO
Cheryl Bartel
Hillsboro, KS

Makes 10-12 servings

2 cups water
3/4 cup sugar
3 cups cranberries,
   chopped or ground
6-oz. pkg. orange,
   strawberry, cherry, or
   raspberry gelatin

8-oz. can crushed
   pineapple
1/2 cup chopped walnuts
3 apples, chopped
   (optional)
2 oranges, chopped
   (optional)
salad greens
sour cream
pineapple chunks

1. In saucepan heat water and sugar to boiling. Boil 1 minute.
2. Add cranberries. Heat to boiling; boil 5 minutes.
3. Stir in gelatin until dissolved. Stir in pineapple, walnuts, apples, or oranges.
4. Pour into 6-cup mold. Refrigerate until firm, at least 6 hours.
5. Unmold onto salad greens. Garnish with sour cream and pineapple chunks.

Gingered Cranberry Mold
Nicole Koloski
East Sandwich, MA
Piecemakers 1995
Calendar Quilt

Makes 10-14 servings

4 cups cranberries
2 cups sugar
juice from 3 oranges
2 pkgs. unflavored gelatin
1/2 cup cold water
1/2 cup boiling water
1/2 cup pineapple juice
1 tsp. ginger
1 cup chopped walnuts
4-6 ozs. crushed pineapple,
   drained (reserve juice)

1. Coarsely grind cranberries in food processor.
2. Combine sugar and orange juice and add to cranberries. Allow mixture to set for 3-4 hours.
3. Sprinkle gelatin in cold water and allow to soften. Stir in boiling water, pineapple juice, and ginger. Place in refrigerator and allow to set until thickened, but not completely set.
4. Stir in walnuts, cranberries, and pineapple.
5. Pour into greased 8-cup mold. Refrigerate until set.

Orange Cranberry Salad
Judi Robb
Manhattan, KS
Seven Sisters

Makes 8 servings

4 cups fresh cranberries, chopped
1 cup sugar
1 pkg. unflavored gelatin
1/2 cup orange juice
1 cup chopped celery
1 cup chopped apple
1 cup chopped pecans or walnuts

1. Mix together cranberries and sugar. Let stand 15 minutes, stirring occasionally.
2. In saucepan sprinkle gelatin over orange juice to soften. Heat, stirring until gelatin is dissolved.
3. Add gelatin mixture, celery, apple, and nuts to cran-

berries. Mix well. Turn into 1-quart mold.
4. Refrigerate until firm, from 6-8 hours.

Cranberry Salad
Lynn Crowe
Anderson, IN
Ann Driscoll
Albuquerque, NM
Lena Mae Janes
Lane KS

Makes 6-8 servings

6-oz. pkg. strawberry, raspberry, or cherry gelatin
1 cup sugar
1 cup boiling water
1 cup cold water
1 cup chopped celery
1 cup chopped apples
1 cup chopped cranberries
1 cup chopped pecans or English walnuts
15 large marshmallows, cut into pieces

1. Dissolve gelatin and sugar in boiling water. Stir in cold water.
2. Stir in celery, apples, cranberries, nuts, and marshmallows. Refrigerate several hours until set.

Merry Cranberry Salad
Myrna Schroder
Savannah, MO
Block of the Month Sampler
Rita I. Friesen
Paoli, IN
Rosebud

Makes 12 servings

1 cup water
2 cups sugar
12-oz. pkg. fresh cranberries
2 cups miniature marshmallows
2 apples, diced
3 bananas, sliced
3 cups orange sections
1-2 cups seedless grapes, halved
1/2 cup chopped pecans
1/2 cup diced celery

1. Boil water and sugar until mixture becomes thick and syrupy. Add cranberries. Cook until cranberries burst. Remove from heat and let stand covered for 10 minutes.
2. Remove cover and cook for another 5 minutes. Chill.
3. When cool, add marshmallows, apples, bananas, oranges, grapes, pecans, and celery. Chill. Serve cold.

My mother always prepared this cranberry salad for our family Thanksgiving and Christmas dinners. She always served it in a thick cut-glass antique bowl that belonged to my grandmother.
—Myrna Schroder

Gelatin Cranberry Salad

Charlotte Shaffer
Ephrata, PA
Millie Hohimer
Independence, MO
Ruth Ann Penner
Hillsboro, KS
Cyndie Marrara
Port Matilda, PA
F. Elaine Asper
Stroudsburg, PA
Lori Berezovsky
Salina, KS

Makes 10-12 servings

2 cups boiling water
6-oz. pkg. cherry, raspberry, or strawberry gelatin
16-oz. can whole cranberries
3 apples, cubed
1/2 cup walnuts, coarsely chopped
1/2 cup diced celery (optional)
1 orange, chopped (optional)

1. Stir gelatin into water until dissolved. Stir in cranberries.
2. Mix in apples, walnuts, celery, and orange, if desired.
3. Pour into 6-cup mold. Chill until firm.

Cranberry Cherry Salad

Jean A. Schoettmer
Greensburg, IN
Rachel's Quilt

Makes 8 servings

2 cups juice, drained from cherries, with water added
6-oz. pkg. cherry gelatin
20-oz. can Bing cherries, drained (save juice)
16-oz. can whole cranberry sauce
3/4 cup chopped celery
1/2 cup diced apples
1/2 cup chopped nuts

1. Heat juice and water mixture to boiling. Remove from heat and stir in gelatin until completely dissolved. Chill until slightly thickened.
2. Stir in remaining ingredients. Chill until firm.

Cranberry Pineapple Relish

Jeanne Sanson
Chatham, IL
Sunbonnet Sue

Makes 8 servings

12-oz. pkg. fresh cranberries
1 orange
2 celery ribs
1 cup diced pineapple
1 cup broken walnut pieces
1 scant cup sugar

1. Grind cranberries and orange in food processor. Grind in celery.
2. Grind in pineapple and walnut pieces.
3. Stir in sugar. Refrigerate for at least 24 hours.

This dish can be prepared in advance and frozen. Thaw overnight in the refrigerator before using.

Baked Cranberry Relish

Alyce C. Kauffman
Gridley, CA
Sailing Away

Makes 8-10 servings

1 orange
1 lb. fresh cranberries
2 cups sugar
1/4 tsp. salt
1 cup coarsely chopped nuts

1. Peel orange. Cut segments into 1" pieces. Grate half the peel.
2. Wash cranberries. Place in a 2-quart casserole. Add sugar, salt, orange pieces, and orange peel. Mix well. Cover tightly.
3. Bake at 325° for 75 minutes.
4. Remove from oven and cool slightly. Stir in nuts. Allow to chill in refrigerator overnight

Christmas Cranberry Sauce
Lynn Loveland
East Hampton, CT
House Quilt

Makes 6 servings

12-oz. pkg. cranberries, chopped or ground
3/4 tsp. lime zest
1/4 cup lime juice
3/4 cup water
1 1/2 cups sugar
3/4 tsp. orange zest
1/4 cup orange juice

1. In saucepan combine all ingredients and bring to a boil. Simmer on low for 10 minutes.
2. Cool and serve.

Cranberry Strawberry Salad
Eldeen Carter
Charleston, SC
A Charleston Basket

Makes 12 servings

6-oz. pkg. strawberry gelatin
2 cups boiling water
10-oz. pkg. frozen sliced strawberries, partially thawed
15 1/4-oz. can crushed pineapple, undrained
16-oz. can whole berry cranberry sauce
1 cup chopped celery
1/2 cup chopped pecans

1. Dissolve gelatin in water. Cool.
2. Add strawberries, pineapple, cranberry sauce, celery, and pecans.
3. Pour into a 12" x 8" pan or mold. Cover and chill until firm.

Spicy Cranberry Sauce
Marlene Fonken
Upland, CA
Crazy Patch

Makes 2 cups

6" stick cinnamon
1/4 tsp. cloves
1/4 tsp. nutmeg
4 cups cranberries
1/2 tsp. grated orange peel
1 cup orange juice
2 scant cups sugar

1. Cook together cinnamon, cloves, nutmeg, cranberries, and orange juice until cranberries start to pop.
2. Stir in sugar and cook until mixture starts to thicken. Chill and serve.

Creamy Cranberry Salad
Suzanne S. Nobrega
Duxbury, MA
Irma Harder
Mountain Lake, MN
Elizabeth L. Richards
Rapid City, SC

Makes 8-10 servings

1 cup coarsely chopped cranberries
1 cup coarsely chopped apples
1 cup canned, crushed pineapple, drained
2 cups miniature marshmallows
1 cup fresh cream

1. Mix together cranberries, apples, and pineapple. Add marshmallows and mix well. Place in refrigerator for several hours or overnight.
2. Whip the cream and fold into fruit mixture just before serving.

Cranberry Relish

Naomi Stoltzfus
Leola, PA
Lois J. Cassidy
Willow Street, PA
Joyce Valley
Pelican Rapids, MN
Anna Tompkins
Greenfield, OH
Mary-Lou Miller
Rochester, NY
Mary Jane Musser
Manheim, PA
Leona Cook
Falmouth, MA

Makes 8 servings

4 cups cranberries,
  ground
2 oranges, ground
3 apples, chopped fine
2 cups sugar

1. Mix together all ingredients.
2. Let stand in refrigerator for 12 to 24 hours before servings.

Cranberry Grape Salad

Sheila Plock
Boalsburg, PA
Jeanne Allen
Los Alamos, NM
Debbie Divine
Salina, KS

Makes 6-8 servings

2 cups fresh cranberries,
  ground
3/4 cup sugar
1 cup seedless red or
  green grapes, halved
1/4 cup broken walnuts
2 cups miniature
  marshmallows
1/2 cup whipping cream

1. Mix together cranberries and sugar. Cover and chill overnight.
2. Drain, pressing lightly to remove excess juice. Stir in grapes, nuts, and marshmallows.
3. Whip cream and fold into fruit mixture.

Fluffy Cranberry Salad

Sharon Shadburn
Ft. Leavenworth, KS
Northern Stars

Makes 6-8 servings

8-oz. pkg. cream cheese
2 Tbsp. sugar
16-oz. can whole berry
  cranberry sauce
15-oz. can drained,
  crushed pineapple
8-oz. pkg. whipped
  topping
Additional ingredients:
  chopped pecans, sliced
  bananas, chopped
  apples, miniature
  marshmallows

1. Beat together cream cheese and sugar. Stir in cranberry sauce.
2. Add crushed pineapple, whipped topping, and any additional ingredients. Mix well.
3. Chill before serving.

My uncle has been seriously ill with diabetes. To brighten his days, I decided to make a Best Friends quilt and sent it out to be machine quilted. When it was returned, I threw it across a sofa and my family admired it. Without seeing the design as a whole, I suddenly felt there was something wrong with the quilt. I laid it out and discovered I had reversed four of the blocks, light was where dark should be. I had been very proud of the quilt and when I saw the flaw, I couldn't put the binding on. After about three months, my husband reminded me that it was a quilt made out of love and it should be finished. I swallowed my pride and finished it, sending it to my uncle who keeps it on his bed for all to see.
—*Jeanne Allen, Los Alamos, NM*

Cranberry Christmas

Carolyn W. Carmichael
Berkeley Heights, NJ
Lover's Knot

Makes 8 servings

16 oz. carton whipped
  topping
16-oz. can whole
  cranberry sauce
15-oz. can crushed
  pineapple, drained
3 bananas, sliced
1 cup chopped nuts

1. Mix together all ingredients.
2. Pour into ring mold and freeze.
3. Unmold and serve.

Christmas Gelatin Salad

Stacy Petersheim
Mechanicsburg, PA

Makes 12 servings

20-oz. can crushed
  pineapple
1/4 cup sugar
1 Tbsp. lemon juice
2 3-oz. pkgs. strawberry
  gelatin
4 Tbsp. cold water
8-oz. pkg. cream cheese
12-oz. can evaporated
  milk
3 Tbsp. sugar
1 tsp. vanilla
8 oz. carton whipped
  topping

1/4 cup chopped nuts
  (optional)
1/4 cup coconut, dyed red
  and green (optional)

1. In saucepan mix together pineapple, sugar, lemon juice, gelatin, and water. Bring to a boil. Cool.
2. Beat together cream cheese, evaporated milk, sugar, and vanilla. Mix with cooked mixture. Fold in whipped topping.
3. Pour into jello mold or 9" x 13" pan and chill.
4. Sprinkle top with nuts and/or coconut.

Christmas Salad

Lorene Diener
Arthur, IL
Lydia Jane Zimmerman
Versailles, MO
Mrs. Jean Weller
State College, PA

Makes 12 servings

2 3-oz. pkgs. strawberry
  gelatin
2 cups boiling water
1 1/2 cups cold water
20-oz. can crushed
  pineapple, drained
  (reserve juice)
1/2 cup chopped pecans
1 pkg. unflavored gelatin
1/4 cup cold water
8-oz. pkg. cream cheese,
  softened
1/3 cup raisins (optional)
1/3 cup salted nuts,
  chopped (optional)
1 cup whipped topping
2 3-oz. pkgs. lime gelatin

2 cups boiling water
1 1/2 cups cold water

1. Dissolve strawberry gelatin in 2 cups boiling water. Add 1 1/2 cups cold water. Let cool to jelly stage.
2. Add half of drained pineapple and pecans to strawberry gelatin. Pour into 9" x 13" pan or jello mold. Chill until set.
3. Mix together unflavored gelatin and 1/4 cup cold water.
4. In saucepan bring reserved pineapple juice to boil. Stir in unflavored gelatin mixture. Mix in cream cheese. Stir in raisins and nuts. Allow to partially set. Fold in whipped topping. Pour on top of first layer and let set until firm.
5. Dissolve lime gelatin in 2 cups boiling water. Add 1 1/2 cups cold water. Let cool to jelly stage. Add remaining half of pineapple. Pour on top of second layer. Chill until firm.
6. Cut into squares and serve on lettuce leaves.

Fizzy Lime Salad
Amanda A. Schlabach
Millersburg, OH
Star Spin

Makes 16-20 servings

6-oz. pkg. lime gelatin
1 cup boiling water
8-oz. pkg. cream cheese,
  softened
1/2 tsp. vanilla
15-oz. can mandarin
  oranges, drained
8-oz. can crushed
  pineapple, drained
1 cup lemon-lime soda
1/2 cup chopped pecans
8 oz. carton frozen
  whipped topping

1. Dissolve gelatin in hot water.
2. In a mixing bowl beat cream cheese until fluffy. Stir in gelatin mixture and beat until smooth.
3. Stir in vanilla, oranges, pineapple, soda, and pecans.
4. Chill until mixture mounds slightly when dropped from a spoon. Fold in 3/4 of the whipped topping. Pour into a 9" x 13" pan and refrigerate 3-4 hours.
5. To serve cut into squares and top with remaining whipped topping.

Lime Jello Salad
Debra Botelho Zeida
Mashpee, MA
Sunbonnet Sue
F. Elaine Asper
Stroudsburg, PA
Split Rail

Makes 12-16 servings

2 3-oz. pkgs. lime or
  lemon gelatin
2 cups boiling water
8 oz. pkg. cream cheese,
  softened, or
  1 pint cottage cheese
1 cup evaporated milk
20-oz. can crushed
  pineapple
1 cup mayonnaise
1/2 cup chopped
  maraschino cherries
1 cup chopped pecans

1. Dissolve gelatin in boiling water. Let chill until thickened.
2. Beat together cream cheese and milk until smooth.
3. Stir in gelatin, pineapple, mayonnaise, cherries, and pecans.
4. Pour into mold and chill until set. Unmold onto lettuce leaves.

Lemon Pineapple Salad
Elaine Patton
West Middletown, PA
Puss in the Corner

Makes 9 servings

20-oz. can crushed
  pineapple, drained
  (reserve juice)
1/2 cup sugar
2 Tbsp. flour
2 Tbsp. butter
1 egg, beaten
3-oz. pkg. lemon gelatin
3 bananas
1 cup whipped topping

1. In saucepan mix together pineapple juice, sugar, flour, butter, and egg. Cook until thickened. Cool.
2. Make gelatin as directed on package. Stir in pineapple and bananas. Refrigerate until almost set.
3. Stir cooked mixture into gelatin mixture. Fold in whipped topping. Pour into 9" x 13" pan or mold. Chill until firm.

Variation: Substitute any flavor of gelatin for the lemon gelatin, and substitute any variety of fruits for the pineapple and bananas, providing you have fruit juice for the dressing.

Lime Pear Salad

Jeanne Allen
Los Alamos, NM
Clams in the Cabin

Makes 6-8 servings

3-oz. pkg. lime gelatin
8-oz. pkg. cream cheese
29-oz. can pears, diced
   and drained (reserve
   juice)
8-oz. can crushed
   pineapple (reserve
   juice)
8-oz. carton whipped
   topping
1/2 cup chopped nuts

1. In saucepan mix together
1 1/3 cups pear juice, and
pineapple juice. Bring to
boiling point. Pour into
blender.
2. Add gelatin and cream
cheese and blend until
smooth. Transfer to larger
bowl.
3. Stir in pears and pineapple. Fold in whipped top-
ping and nuts. Pour into
mold or bowl and refrigerate until firm.

Cherry Salad Supreme

Jaclyn Ferrell
Carlisle, PA
Sisters Choice

Makes 16 servings

3-oz. pkg. raspberry
   gelatin
1 cup boiling water
21-oz. can cherry pie
   filling
3-oz. pkg. lemon gelatin
1 cup boiling water
1 cup crushed pineapple,
   drained
1 cup miniature
   marshmallows
3-oz. pkg. cream cheese
1/3 cup mayonnaise
1/2 cup whipped topping
2 Tbsp. chopped nuts

1. Dissolve raspberry gelatin
in 1 cup boiling water. Stir
in pie filling. Turn into a 9"
square pan. Chill.
2. Dissolve lemon gelatin in
1 cup boiling water. Stir in
crushed pineapple and
miniature marshmallows.
3. Beat together cream
cheese and mayonnaise.
Gradually add to lemon
mixture. Fold in whipped
topping.
4. Spread on cherry layer.
Top with nuts. Chill until
firm.

Make-Ahead Salad

Betty B. Dennison
Grove City, PA
Sampler

Makes 10 servings

2 egg yolks
2 Tbsp. flour
1 cup milk
juice of 2 lemons
1 pint whipping cream
1 lb. marshmallows, cut
   up
20-oz. can sliced
   pineapple, drained
16-oz. can white cherries,
   drained

1. In saucepan mix together
egg yolks and flour. Stir in
milk. Slowly add lemon
juice. Stir constantly until
mixture boils and thickens.
Cool.
2. Whip the cream and fold
into custard mixture. Stir in
marshmallows, pineapple,
and cherries.
3. Refrigerate for 24 hours.

White Salad
Ruth Bruffey
Nipomo, CA
Duck in a Flower Garden

Makes 10 servings

1 egg, beaten
1/2 cup sugar
1 heaping Tbsp. flour
1 cup pineapple juice
   (from can of pineapple)
20-oz. can pineapple
   chunks, drained
   (reserve juice)
1/2 pint whipping cream
2-3 bananas
1 cup sliced, seedless red
   grapes
1 cup mini-marshmallows
1/2 cup broken nuts
1/2 cup maraschino
   cherries, cut up
8-10 whole maraschino
   cherries

1. In saucepan mix together
egg, sugar, and flour.
Gradually whisk in pineapple juice. Bring to boil, stirring constantly until thickened. Chill for several
hours.
2. Whip cream to soft
peaks. Fold into well chilled
custard. Fold in pineapple,
bananas, grapes, marshmallows, nuts, and cut-up cherries.
3. Decorate with whole
maraschino cherries and
additional nuts.

Aunt Lil's Frozen Salad
Laurie Rott
Fargo, ND
Rose and Tulip Appliqué

Makes 8 servings

2 3-oz. pkgs. cream
   cheese
2 Tbsp. mayonnaise
60 small marshmallows
8-oz. can crushed
   pineapple
2 Tbsp. pineapple juice
6-oz. jar maraschino
   cherries, cut fine
2 Tbsp. cherry juice
1/8 tsp. salt
1/2 pint whipping cream

1. Combine all ingredients
except cream.
2. Beat cream until stiff and
fold into the mixture.
3. Pour into 9" x 13" pan.
Freeze for at least 3 hours.
Cut into squares and serve
on lettuce.

Orange Salad
Nadine Martinitz
Salina, KS
Midnight Sky

Makes 12 servings

2 3-oz. pkgs. orange
   gelatin
1 cup boiling water
juice from canned
   oranges and pineapple,
   plus enough water to
   equal 2 cups liquid

6-oz. can frozen orange
   juice concentrate
2 11-oz. cans mandarin
   oranges
8-oz. can crushed
   pineapple
8-oz. carton frozen
   whipped topping
1 cup milk
1 pkg. instant lemon
   pudding

1. Dissolve gelatin in boiling
water. Add pineapple juice,
orange juice, and water and
stir well.
2. Add frozen orange juice
concentrate, mandarin
oranges, and crushed
pineapple.
3. Pour into 9" x 13" dish.
Chill until set.
4. Mix together whipped topping mix, milk, and pudding.
Spread over chilled gelatin.
Cut into squares and serve.

Orange Buttermilk Salad
Audrey L. Kneer
Williamsfield, IL
Sunbonnet Sue

Makes 10-12 servings

20-oz. can crushed
   pineapple with juice
6-oz. pkg. orange gelatin
2 cups buttermilk
8 oz. carton whipped
   topping
1/4-1/2 cup chopped nuts

1. In saucepan bring pineapple and juice to boiling. Mix
in gelatin and stir until dis-

solved. Cool to room temperature.

2. Stir in buttermilk. Fold in whipped topping and nuts.

3. Pour into serving dish. Chill for at least 4 hours.

Pistachio Salad

Sue Graziadio
White Mills, PA
Shirley A. Carlson
Green Bay, WI
JoAnn Pelletier
Longmeadow, MA

Makes 8-10 servings

1 pkg. instant pistachio pudding
8-oz. carton whipped topping
16-oz. can crushed pineapple, drained
3/4 cup small marshmallows
1/4-1/2 cup chopped nuts

1. Mix together dry pudding and whipped topping.

2. Stir in pineapple.

3. Add marshmallows. Refrigerate at least 4 hours before serving.

Party Salad

Lydia Jane Zimmerman
Versailles, MO
Boston Commons
Martha Darr
Dexter, MI
Noah's Ark

Makes 12 servings

1 pint boiling water
3-oz. pkg. lime gelatin
3-oz. pkg. lemon gelatin
20-oz. can crushed pineapple
1 tsp. fresh or reconstituted lemon juice
1 cup cottage cheese
1 cup mayonnaise
1 tsp. horseradish
1 cup pecan pieces

1. Dissolve gelatins in water. Let stand until mixture reaches room temperature. Add undrained pineapple and lemon juice.

2. In separate bowl mix together cottage cheese, mayonnaise, horseradish, and pecans. Stir into gelatin mixture.

3. Pour into 9" x 13" pan. Chill. Serve on lettuce.

Frozen Fruit Salad

Pat Garrow
Lodi, CA
Seven Sisters

Makes 8-10 servings

8-oz. can crushed pineapple, well drained (reserve syrup)
2 eggs, slightly beaten
1/2 cup sugar
1/8 tsp. salt
3 Tbsp. lemon juice
2 cups finely chopped, unpeeled red apples
1/2 cup finely chopped celery or seedless grapes, halved
1 cup whipping cream

1. Add water to pineapple syrup to make 1/2 cup. In saucepan combine syrup, eggs, sugar, salt, and lemon juice. Cook over low heat, stirring constantly until thickened. Chill.

2. Stir in pineapple, apples, and celery.

3. Whip cream and fold into fruit mixture.

4. Pour into 11/2-quart baking dish. Cover with plastic wrap and freeze until firm.

5. To serve slice and place on beds of greens on individual salad plates.

Blueberry Gelatin Salad

Nancy Vance
Carterville, IL
Scrap Quilt
Carla Woodworth
Lyndonville, NY

Makes 15 servings

3-oz. pkg. lemon gelatin
3-oz. pkg. raspbery
  gelatin
2 cups boiling water
1 cup cold water
21-oz. can blueberry pie
  filling
whipped topping

1. Mix together gelatin and boiling water until gelatin is dissolved. Stir in cold water and pie filling. Cool.
2. Serve with whipped topping.

Variation: Substitute 1 can undrained crushed pineapple in place of the 2 cups boiling water and 1 cup cold water.

Strawberry Banana Salad

Janice Muller
Derwood, MD
Anna L. Kauffman
Arthur, IL
Doris Travis
Sedona, AZ

Makes 10-12 servings

6-oz. pkg. strawberry
  gelatin

l cup boiling water
2 10¹/₂ oz. pkgs. frozen
  strawberries, thawed
3 bananas, mashed
8-oz. can crushed
  pineapple, drained
16-oz. carton sour cream
  or cottage cheese

1. Dissolve gelatin in hot water. Stir in strawberries, bananas, and pineapple.
2. Pour half of mixture into 9" x 13" pan and chill. Cover with sour cream. Pour remaining gelatin mixture over sour cream.
3. Refrigerate until set. Serve chilled.

Champagne Salad

Audrey L. Kneer
Williamsfield, IL
Sunbonnet Sue

Makes 12 servings

8-oz. pkg. cream cheese,
  softened
1/2 cup white sugar
10-oz. pkg. frozen
  strawberries, thawed
20-oz. can crushed
  pineapple, drained
2 bananas, diced
1 cup chopped pecans
8-oz. carton whipped
  topping

1. Mix together cream cheese, white sugar, strawberries, pineapple, bananas, and pecans.
2. Fold in whipped topping. Pour into a 9" square pan. Freeze overnight.

3. Remove from freezer 30 minutes before serving.

Waldorf Salad Ring

Katie Zimmerman
Leola, PA

Makes 8 servings

2 3-oz. pkgs. lemon
  gelatin
1¹/₂ cups boiling water
1¹/₂ cups cold water
1/4 cup cooked raisins
1 cup chopped red apples
1/4 cup chopped celery
1/2 cup shredded cheddar
  cheese
1/4 cup grated carrots
1/3 cup chopped nuts

1. Dissolve gelatin in boiling water. Add cold water. Chill until partially set.
2. Mix in raisins, apples, celery, cheese, carrots, and nuts.
3. Pour into 4¹/₂-cup mold. Chill.

Variation: Substitute seedless grapes in place of carrots.

Apple Raisin Salad

Lucille Metzler
Conestoga, PA
Country Love

Makes 6 servings

6 apples
1 cup raisins
1/4 cup mayonnaise
1/4 cup peanut butter

1. Peel, core, and dice apples. Mix with raisins.
2. Combine peanut butter and mayonnaise. Pour over apples and raisins and mix well.

Raspberry Applesauce Salad

Blanche M. Cahill
Willow Grove, PA
Tumbling Packages

Makes 4-6 servings

2 cups applesauce
2 3-oz. pkgs. raspberry gelatin
2 10-oz. pkgs. frozen raspberries, thawed

1. Heat applesauce to boiling. Add gelatin. Mix well.
2. Stir in raspberries.
3. Pour into mold and chill. Best to make at least a day ahead.

Note: Can be made with strawberry gelatin and strawberries.

Crunchy Apple Salad

Karen M. Rusten
Waseca, MN
Angela's Kitty Quilt

Makes 10-12 servings

20-oz. can crushed pineapple
2/3 cup sugar
3-oz. pkg. lemon gelatin
8-oz. pkg. cream cheese, softened
1 cup chopped, unpeeled apples
1/2-1 cup chopped walnuts
1 cup chopped celery
1 cup whipped topping

1. In saucepan mix together pineapple with its juice and sugar. Boil for 3 minutes.
2. Add lemon gelatin and stir until dissolved. Mix in cream cheese and stir until mixture is well blended. Cool.
2. Fold in apples, walnuts, celery, and whipped topping. Pour into 9" square pan. Chill until firm.
3. Cut into squares and serve on lettuce leaves.

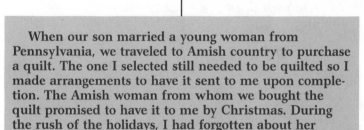

When our son married a young woman from Pennsylvania, we traveled to Amish country to purchase a quilt. The one I selected still needed to be quilted so I made arrangements to have it sent to me upon completion. The Amish woman from whom we bought the quilt promised to have it to me by Christmas. During the rush of the holidays, I had forgotten about her promise.

On Christmas Eve day, I received a call from a person who had moved into a house where we had once lived with the message that a package addressed to me had been delivered to my old home. As it turned out, I had given the quilter a box number and UPS had found an old street address where they dropped the package.

Snow was falling as we drove home from our candlelight Christmas Eve church service when I remembered the call about the package. At that moment I knew it was my quilt from Pennsylvania. And, indeed, there on that warmly lighted porch at our former home was the package with my Amish quilt.

—*Becky J. Harder, Monument, CO*

Apple, Cheese, and Nut Salad

Marion Snead
Montgomery, AL
Half Log Cabin

Makes 4-6 servings

3 large red apples, unpeeled and chopped
2 Tbsp. lemon juice
1 cup seedless green grapes
1/2 cup chopped celery
1/2 cup chopped almonds
1/2 cup cheese (cheddar, Swiss, or American)
1/3 cup mayonnaise

1. Sprinkle apples with lemon juice.
2. Mix in grapes, celery, almonds, cheese, and mayonnaise.
3. Chill and serve on lettuce leaves.

Apple Salad

Eldeen Carter
Charleston, SC
A Charleston Basket

Makes 12-15 servings

6 apples, cubed
2 cups seedless grapes, halved
1 cup chopped celery
1 cup chopped pecans
1 cup cubed cheddar cheese
15-oz. can pineapple chunks, drained (reserve juice)
3/4 cup sugar
1/4 tsp. salt
2 Tbsp. flour
3 eggs, beaten
3 Tbsp. vinegar
1 cup reserved pineapple juice
8-oz. carton whipped topping

1. Combine apples, grapes, celery, pecans, cheese, and pineapple.
2. In saucepan mix together sugar, salt, and flour. Add eggs, vinegar, and pineapple juice. Cook until thickened. Chill. Fold in whipped topping.
3. Pour creamed mixture over fruit and mix well. Chill.

Cut Glass Gelatin

Ruth Ann Hoover
New Holland, PA
Spinning Star

Makes 8 servings

3-oz. pkg. orange gelatin
3-oz. pkg. lime gelatin
3-oz. pkg. cherry gelatin
4 1/2 cups boiling water
1 cup pineapple juice
1/4 cup sugar
3-oz. pkg. lemon gelatin
2 pkgs. whipped topping mix

1. In three separate bowls, dissolve each gelatin except lemon in 1 1/2 cups boiling water. Pour each flavor into its own shallow pan. Chill until firm. Cut each gelatin into 1/2-inch squares.
2. In saucepan combine pineapple juice and sugar and bring to a boil. Add lemon gelatin and stir until dissolved. Chill until syrupy.
3. Prepare whipped topping as directed on package. Blend into pineapple mixture.
4. Fold gelatin cubes into pineapple mixture. Refrigerate.

Nut Salad
Elaine Anderson
Mitchell, SD
Sampler

Makes 8 servings

1 pkg. unflavored gelatin
1/3 cup cold water
2 eggs, beaten
3/4 cup sugar
2 cups milk
2 cups whipping cream
1 1/2 tsp. vanilla
1 cup crushed walnuts

1. Soak gelatin in water.
2. In saucepan mix together eggs, sugar, and milk. Bring to a boil and boil for 5 minutes.
3. Mix together softened gelatin and cooked mixture. Cool.
4. Whip cream until stiff. Fold into cooled mixture. Gently stir in vanilla and nuts. Chill for 12-18 hours.

Ribbon Gelatin Salad
Joyce Parker
North Plainfield, NJ
Friendship Quilt
Char Hagner
Montague, MI
Sunbonnet Sue

Makes 12-15 servings

2 3-oz. pkgs. red gelatin
3 cups boiling water
2 3-oz. pkgs. green gelatin
3 cups boiling water
2 cups milk
1 cup sugar
2 tsp. vanilla
1 cup sour cream
2 pkgs. unflavored gelatin
1/2 cup boiling water

1. Dissolve red gelatin in 3 cups boiling water. Set aside to cool.
2. Dissolve green gelatin in 3 cups boiling water. Set aside to cool.
3. In saucepan heat milk. Add sugar, vanilla, and sour cream. Mix well.
4. Dissolve unflavored gelatin in 1/2 cup boiling water. Add to milk mixture.
5. Pour 1 cup white milk mixture into 9" x 13" pan. Chill until set (about 30 minutes). Then pour half of red gelatin over white mixture. Chill until firm.
6. Add another white layer and chill. Then add half the green gelatin. Chill.
7 Add another white layer and chill. Repeat the process again with the red and green gelatins. Chill

until final layer is firm.
6. Cut into squares and serve.

Seafood Salad
Joyce B. Suiter
Garysburg, NC
Pieced Tulip

Makes 8 servings

1 cup finely chopped green pepper
1/2 cup finely chopped onion
2 cups finely chopped celery
2 7 1/2-oz. cans crab meat, drained and flaked
2 4 1/2-oz. cans shrimp, drained and rinsed
5-oz. can lobster, drained and flaked
7-oz. can tuna, drained and flaked
1 1/4 cups mayonnaise
1 tsp. Worcestershire sauce
1/8 tsp. pepper
dash Tabasco
1 tsp. garlic salt
crushed potato chips

1. Mix together pepper, onion, celery, crab meat, shrimp, lobster, and tuna.
2. Combine mayonnaise, Worcestershire sauce, pepper, Tabasco, and garlic salt. Pour over seafood. Mix well. Pour into greased casserole dish.
3. Sprinkle with crushed potato chips.
4. To eat hot, bake at 350° for 30 minutes. To eat cold, chill well.

Soups

Black Bean Chili
Cindy Ewert
Salem, OR

Makes 6 servings

1 cup chopped yellow
 onion
3/4 cup finely chopped
 celery
4 garlic cloves, finely
 minced
3 Tbsp. olive oil
2 15-oz. cans black beans,
 not drained
2 16-oz. cans diced
 tomatoes
4-oz. can diced chilies
10 3/4-oz. can beef broth
 concentrate
1/2 tsp. cumin powder
shredded cheddar or jack
 cheese
sour cream
chopped green onions
diced avocado
diced tomato
tortilla chips
Parmesan cheese

1. In heavy saucepan sauté
onion, celery, and garlic in
olive oil over medium heat
until onions begin to soften,
about 3 minutes.
2. Stir in beans, tomatoes,
chilies, broth, and cumin
powder. Simmer gently,
uncovered, for 20 minutes.
3. Serve with suggested
accompaniments.

White Chili
Sherril Bieberly
Salina, KS
My Watercolor Heart

Makes 4 servings

1 Tbsp. olive oil
1 lb. boneless chicken
 breast, cut into cubes
1/4 cup chopped onion
1 cup chicken broth
4-oz. can chopped green
 chilies
1 tsp. garlic powder
1 tsp. ground cumin
1/2 tsp. oregano
1/2 tsp. cilantro leaves
1/4 tsp. ground red pepper
16-oz. can white kidney
 beans, undrained
shredded Monterey Jack
 cheese
chopped onion
cilantro

1. In saucepan sauté
chicken in oil for 4-5 minutes, stirring often. Remove
chicken. Keep warm.
2. Sauté onion in saucepan
for 2 minutes. Stir in broth,
green chilies, and spices.
Simmer for 30 minutes.
3. Stir in chicken and beans.
Simmer 10 minutes.
Garnish with cheese and
chopped onion or cilantro.

Yellow-Eye Bean Soup
Ann Mather
Lansing, MI
Miniature Churn Dash

Makes 6 servings

2 cups dry yellow-eye
   beans (5 cups cooked
   and drained)
1 ham shank
2 carrots, diced
2 onions, thinly sliced
2 potatoes, sliced
1/2 tsp. black pepper

1. Soak beans for at least 8
hours in water in refrigerator. (Quick-soak in 6 cups
water, heat to boiling, and
cook beans for 2 minutes.
Then cover pot and let
beans stand for 2 hours.)
2. Drain and rinse. Combine
soaked beans with 6 cups
water and all remaining
ingredients. Cook until
beans are tender (approx.
1 1/2 hours), adding more hot
water if necessary.
3. Serve bean soup whole or
mashed, or rub mixture
through a sieve and season.
Add hot water if soup is too
thick.

Christmas Chili
Nancy Wagner Graves
Manhattan, KS
Diane Potenta
Oxford, NJ
Marian V. Bentz
Arcadia, CA

Makes 8-10 servings

4 lbs. ground beef
1 cup chopped onion
2 garlic cloves, minced
2 cups chopped green or
   red peppers
1 Tbsp. oil
2 28-oz. cans chopped
   tomatoes
2 15-oz. cans tomato
   sauce
4 Tbsp. chili powder
2 tsp. Worcestershire
   sauce
2 tsp. salt
1/2 tsp. cayenne red
   pepper
1/2 tsp. oregano
1/2 tsp. cinnamon
1/4 tsp. paprika
1 cup water, or more, to
   reach desired
   consistency
2 15-oz. cans kidney
   beans

1. Brown meat, onion, garlic
cloves, and chopped pep-
pers in oil until meat is
brown. Drain fat.
2. Stir in tomatoes, tomato
sauce, chili powder,
Worcestershire sauce, salt,
pepper, oregano, cinnamon,
paprika, and water. Simmer 2
hours.
3. Stir in kidney beans
before serving.

4. Serve with cheddar
cheese and sour cream.

Variation: Add 7-oz. can
*chili salsa and 1 small
jalapeno chili pepper, seeded
and chopped to Step 2.*

Green Chili Stew
Barbara Striegel
Rio Rancho, NM
Boots & Bow Ties

Makes 4-5 servings

3/4 lb. pork pieces
1 large onion, diced
2 cloves minced garlic
1 Tbsp. olive oil
16-oz. can stewed
   tomatoes
2 cups diced potatoes
4-oz. can chopped green
   chilies
2 cups chicken broth

1. In saucepan brown pork,
onions, and garlic in olive
oil.
2. Add tomatoes, potatoes,
green chilies and broth.
Simmer on low until pota-
toes are done, about 30 minutes.

Microwave Chili
Janie Canupp
Millersville, MD
Double Wedding Ring

Makes 4 servings

1 lb. ground beef
1 medium onion, diced
2 tsp. chili powder
1 1/2 tsp. salt
1 tsp. dry mustard
1 clove garlic, minced
15-oz. can pork and
   beans
16-oz. can tomatoes
2 Tbsp. brown sugar
1 Tbsp. vinegar

1. Brown ground beef by microwaving on high for 10 minutes. Drain.
2. Mix in remaining ingredients and microwave on high for 15 to 20 minutes.

Hearty Bean Soup
Jean Johnson
Dallas, OR
Ducky Weather

Makes 8-10 servings

1 cup chopped potatoes
2 cups chopped carrots
1 cup chopped onion
1 cup chopped celery
3 cups water
10 1/2-oz. can beef broth
8-oz. can tomato sauce
15-oz. can kidney beans
16-oz. can ready-cut
   tomatoes
3 cloves garlic, minced

2 tsp. basil
1 tsp. salt
1 tsp. sugar

1. In saucepan mix together potatoes, carrots, onion, celery, water, and beef broth. Boil until vegetables are almost cooked.
2. Stir in tomato sauce, kidney beans, tomatoes, garlic, basil, salt, and sugar. Simmer until vegetables are cooked.

Tiffany's Bean Pot Soup
Jeanne Allen
Los Alamos, NM
Scrap-a-holic

Makes 16 servings

2 cups dry pinto beans
1 lb. ham, cubed
1 quart water
2 16-oz. cans tomato juice
4 cups chicken stock or
   bouillon
1 medium onion,
   chopped
3 medium cloves garlic,
   minced
3 Tbsp. chopped parsley
1/4 cup chopped green
   pepper
4 Tbsp. brown sugar
1 Tbsp. chili powder
1 tsp. salt
1 tsp. crushed bay leaves
1 tsp. oregano
1/2 tsp. ground cumin
1/2 tsp. crushed rosemary
   leaves
1/2 tsp. celery seed
1/2 tsp. ground thyme

1/2 tsp. ground marjoram
1/2 tsp. sweet basil
1/4 tsp. curry powder
1 cup sherry

1. Thoroughly wash beans; then soak them for 8 hours. Drain.
2. Stir in remaining ingredients, except sherry. Bring to boil.
3. Reduce heat and simmer covered until beans are tender, about 1 hour.
4. Stir in sherry. Heat to serving temperature.

Beef and Bean Soup
Alyce C. Kauffman
Gridley, CA
Sailing Away

Makes 5-6 servings

1 cup dry lima beans
2 1/2 cups boiling water
1 lb. stewing beef
1 Tbsp. oil
1 garlic clove, minced
1 onion, chopped
16-oz. can tomato sauce
1 1/2 tsp. salt
1/4 tsp. basil
1/4 tsp. caraway seed
1/2 bay leaf
1/2 tsp. thyme
2 carrots, sliced
1/2 cup chopped celery

1. Rinse beans. Mix together beans and water and boil for 2 minutes. Cover and let stand for 1 hour. Drain, reserving 1 cup of water.
2. Cut beef into 1 1/2-inch

cubes and brown in oil. Add onion and garlic. Brown lightly. Stir in tomato sauce.
3. Add beans and reserved water to beef. Stir in salt, basil, caraway seed, bay leaf, and thyme. Cover and simmer for 1¹/2 hours.
4. Add sliced carrots and celery and cook about 30 minutes longer. Remove bay leaf and serve.

Mom's Hamburger Stew
Lisa Schafer
Hampton, VA

Makes 4-6 servings

1 small onion, chopped
2-4 celery stalks, chopped
1 Tbsp. butter
1¹/2 lbs. ground beef
2 10³/4-oz. cans tomato soup
2 soup cans water
15-oz. can red kidney beans
2-4 potatoes, cut into bite-sized pieces

1. In large saucepan sauté celery and onion in butter.
2. Add ground beef and brown.
3. Stir in tomato soup, water, and kidney beans with juice. Add potatoes.
4. Simmer until potatoes are soft.

Minestrone Soup
Nanci Keatley
Salem, OR
Brian's Sea of Cabins
Joyce Kaut
Rochester, NY

Makes 6-8 servings

1 Tbsp. oil
1 lb. Italian sausage, sliced thin
1 cup diced onion
1 clove garlic, minced
2 cups finely shredded carrots
1 tsp. basil
2 small zucchini, cubed
16-oz. can tomatoes, undrained
2 10³/4-oz. cans beef stock
2 cups finely chopped cabbage
1 tsp. salt
1/4 tsp. pepper
16-oz. can Great Northern beans, undrained

2 Tbsp. fresh chopped parsley
grated Parmesan cheese

1. Brown sausage, onion, and garlic in oil. Stir in carrots and basil. Cook for 5 minutes.
2. Add zucchini, tomatoes, beef stock, cabbage, salt, and pepper. Bring soup to boil. Reduce heat and simmer covered for 30 minutes.
3. Add beans and cook another 20 minutes.
4. Sprinkle parsley and Parmesan cheese over soup in serving bowls.

I was born and raised in the Arizona desert where we rarely have white Christmases. When I was about five, it finally happened. And in the way that only mothers seem to have, Mom must have known my brother and I would need warm hands that year. She had knitted blue mittens for me and red ones for Bob. We were giddy with excitement and could almost not wait to put on our mittens and head for the front yard. Much to our delight, we found what appeared to be reindeer and sleigh tracks in the fresh snow. How Mom got the tracks from the roof to the ground, we did not know! We busied ourselves with the job of building our first-ever snowman. When completed, Frosty needed a doll quilt to keep his shoulders warm because it was a cold Christmas that year in Arizona.

—*Mary Evangeline Dillon, Tucson, AZ*

Quick Minestrone Soup

Alyce C. Kauffman
Gridley, CA
Sailing Away

Makes 3-4 servings

1 cup shredded cabbage
1/2 cup sliced celery
1/3 cup sliced carrots
1/4 cup small noodles
1 medium tomato, cut in wedges
1 medium onion, cut in wedges
1 Tbsp. parsley
1/2 tsp. salt
1 bay leaf
1 2/3 cups water
1 1/3 cups condensed beef broth

1. Combine all ingredients. Bring to a boil.
2. Reduce heat. Simmer covered for 30-35 minutes.
3. Remove bay leaf. Serve hot.

Chicken Soup

Doris Roberts
Fairbank, IA
Trip Around the World

Makes 12-14 servings

1 quart chicken broth
2 1/2 cups chopped potatoes
1 cup chopped celery
1/2 cup chopped onions
10-oz. pkg. frozen mixed vegetables (cauliflower, broccoli, and carrots)
10 3/4-oz. can cream of mushroom soup
10 3/4-oz. can cream of chicken soup
2 soup cans water
2 7-oz. cans mushrooms, drained
2 cups chicken, cooked and cubed
1 lb. cubed Velveeta cheese

1. In saucepan mix together broth, potatoes, celery, and onions. Simmer for 10 minutes.
2. Add mixed vegetables, soups, water, mushrooms, chicken, and cheese. Continue to simmer until frozen vegetables are tender.

Turkey Soup

Linda Gruhlkey Pond
Los Alamos, NM
Fields of Purple

Makes 8 servings

1 cup cubed red potatoes
1 cup chopped onion
1 clove garlic, minced
1 cup cubed zucchini
2 quarts water
5 chicken bouillon cubes
1 tsp. salt
1/4 tsp. pepper
1 cup chopped celery
1 cup sliced carrots
1/2 cup butter
2 cups cubed, cooked turkey
12 ozs. Velveeta cheese, cubed
2 cups cooked spaghetti or macaroni

1. In saucepan mix together potatoes, onion, garlic, zucchini, and bouillon cubes in water. Bring to boil and simmer for 25 minutes. Add salt and pepper.
2. Sauté celery and carrots in butter until just tender. Add to potato mixture.
3. Stir in turkey and Velveeta. Heat, stirring until cheese melts. Do not boil.
4. Add cooked spaghetti and serve.

Turkey Leek Potato Soup
Doris L. Orthmann
Wantage, NJ
Log Cabin

Makes 6 servings

6 medium well trimmed, coarsely chopped leeks
1 cup chopped onion
2 Tbsp. margarine
5 large potatoes, peeled and diced
3 cups chicken broth
2 cups water
1 tsp. salt
1/4 tsp. pepper
1/4 tsp. nutmeg
1/2-1 cup cooked chicken or turkey, shredded or ground
1 1/2 cups evaporated skim milk

1. In Dutch oven melt margarine. Add leeks and onions. Cover and cook slowly for 5 minutes, or until soft and wilted.
2. Add potatoes, broth, water, salt, pepper, and nutmeg. Cover and cook for 45 minutes until potatoes are very soft. Purée soup in blender or food processor until smooth.
3. Stir in turkey or chicken. Add evaporated milk. Heat, but do not boil before serving.

Leek and Potato Soup
Jeanne Allen
Los Alamos, NM
Clams in the Cabin

Makes 8 servings

1/2 bunch leeks
1 lb. potatoes, cubed
1/4 cup butter
1/2 cup flour
1 quart milk, heated
2 quarts chicken stock, heated
1 tsp. salt
1/4 tsp. pepper
2 Tbsp. minced parsley

1. Remove outside leaves of leeks and cut into 1/2-inch pieces. Parboil in 1 cup water. Do not drain.
2. Parboil potatoes.
3. Melt butter in saucepan. Stir in flour. Gradually add milk, stock, and water in which leeks were cooked. Simmer for 10 minutes.
4. Stir in salt, pepper, leeks, and potatoes. Purée briefly in blender.
5. Garnish with parsley.

Swiss Potato Soup
Nan Mitchell
Peru, NY
Kansas Album Quilt

Makes 6 servings

3 cups water
2 10 3/4-oz. cans condensed chicken broth
10 3/4-oz. can condensed beef broth
2 onions, diced
4 large potatoes, cubed
2 cups sliced celery
8 large mushrooms, sliced
1/3 cup butter
1/3 cup flour
1 tsp. salt
1/4 tsp. pepper
1 cup shredded Swiss cheese
parsley

1. Combine water, chicken broth, and beef broth. Stir in onions, potatoes, celery, and mushrooms and simmer for 30 minutes.
2. Melt butter in saucepan. Add flour, stirring constantly until golden brown. Add to soup and stir until thickened. Mix in salt and pepper.
3. Ladle into bowls and top with shredded cheese and parsley.

Potato and Ham Chowder

Eleanor Larson
Glen Lyon, PA
Friendship Quilt

Makes 3-4 servings

1 cup diced white
  potatoes
1¹/2 cups water
¹/2 cup chopped onion
1¹/2 Tbsp. butter
1¹/2 Tbsp. flour
1¹/2 cups milk
³/4 cup diced ham
³/4 cup grated sharp
  cheese
salt and pepper to taste

1. Cook potatoes until soft
in 1¹/2 cups water.
2. Sauté onion in butter.
3. Combine potatoes, cooking water, and onion. Beat
flour into milk until smooth
and stir into vegetables.
Cook, stirring constantly,
until thickened.
4. Add ham, cheese, salt,
and pepper, stirring until
cheese melts. Serve.

Baked Potato Soup

Gail Bush
Landenberg, PA
Appliquéd Bunny

Makes 6 servings

4 large potatoes, baked
²/3 cup margarine
²/3 cup flour
6 cups milk
³/4 tsp. salt
¹/2 tsp. pepper
4 green onions, chopped,
  or a handful of fresh
  chives
12 slices bacon, cooked
  and crumbled
1¹/4 cups shredded
  cheddar cheese
1 cup sour cream or plain
yogurt

1. Cool potatoes. Scoop
baked potatoes out of skins
in bite-sized chunks.
2. In large saucepan melt
margarine. Add flour and
milk and cook until white
sauce has thickened.
3. Stir in potatoes, salt,
pepper, 2 tsp. green onions,
¹/2 cup crumbled bacon, and
1 cup cheese. Stir until mixture is heated and cheese
has melted. Stir in sour
cream and heat.
4. Serve in individual bowls
with a garnish of remaining
green onions, bacon, and
cheese.

Potato Soup

Carole M. Mackie
Williamsfield, IL
Sunbonnet Sue

Makes 4 servings

1/4-1/2 cup butter
4 Tbsp. flour
3 cups chicken broth
2 cups milk
1 tsp. salt
1/4 tsp. pepper
1 onion, finely chopped
1 carrot, grated
2-3 stalks celery, diced
1/4-1/2 cup minced parsley
1 Tbsp. oil
4-5 cups diced, cooked
  potatoes

1. Melt butter over low
heat. Stir in flour until well
blended. Stir in 1 cup
chicken broth. As mixture
begins to thicken, add
remaining chicken broth
and milk. Cook to desired
consistency. Stir in salt and
pepper.
2. In skillet sauté onion, carrot, celery, and parsley in
oil. When cooked, add to
soup. Add diced potatoes.
Refrigerate 24 hours before
using.
3. Reheat and serve.

Kohlrabi Soup
Roseann Wilson
Albuquerque, NM
Patchwork

Makes 6 servings

2 lbs. kohlrabi (5 or 6
 medium bulbs)
2 large leeks, trimmed of
 all but 2 inches of
 green
1/4 cup unsalted butter
2 medium carrots, thinly
 sliced
6 cups chicken broth
1 cup fresh shelled peas
2 cups fresh spinach
 leaves
salt
freshly ground pepper

1. Peel kohlrabi and cut into
1/2-inch cubes. Set aside.
2. Cut leeks lengthwise and
then crosswise into thin
slices. Rinse under warm
water. Drain.
3. Melt butter over low heat
in large casserole. Add leeks
and carrots. Cook 2 to 3
minutes without browning.
4. Add kohlrabi and chicken
broth. Heat to a boil. Reduce
the heat and simmer, partly
covered, for 30 minutes.
5. Add the peas and cook
until tender.
6. Add the spinach and cook
until just wilted.
7. Add salt and pepper to
taste.
8. Serve hot or chilled.

Mama's Green Soup
Joyce Swinney
Mooresville, IN
Flower Garden

Makes 8-10 servings

8 Tbsp. butter, melted
1 1/2 cups chopped green
 onion
1 quart chicken broth
4 Tbsp. or 4 cubes
 chicken bouillon
2 tsp. salt
3 large potatoes, finely
 diced
3 large carrots, finely diced
3 cups finely cut
 cauliflower
3 cups finely cut broccoli
1/2 cup rice, uncooked
3 cups fresh asparagus,
 cut into 1/2" slices
3 cups chopped, fresh
 spinach
1 quart milk
1/2 tsp. pepper
2 cups shredded cheddar
 cheese

1. In 6-8 quart soup pot,
sauté onion in butter. Stir in
chicken broth and bouillon.
Add salt, potatoes, carrots,
cauliflower, broccoli, and
rice. Cook gently for 15
minutes.
2. Add asparagus and
spinach. Cook for 5 minutes.
3. Add milk and pepper,
and stir throughly. Add
water if soup is too thick.
Simmer until vegetables are
tender, 20-30 minutes.
4. Sprinkle with cheese just
before serving.

Broccoli Chowder
Jeanne Allen
Los Alamos, NM
Clams in the Cabin

Makes 4-6 servings

2 lbs. coarsely chopped
 fresh broccoli
6 cups chicken broth
3 cups milk
l cup chopped, cooked
 ham
2 tsp. salt
1/4 tsp. pepper
1 cup light cream
1/2 lb. grated Swiss cheese
1/4 cup butter

1. Cook broccoli in chicken
broth until just tender
(about 7 minutes). Remove
broccoli from broth.
2. Add milk, ham, salt, and
pepper. Bring to a boil over
medium heat, stirring occasionally.
3. Stir in remaining ingredients and chopped broccoli.
Heat until cheese is melted.

Broccoli Spinach Soup
Elaine Headley
Salina, KS
Strippy Grandmother's Fan

Makes 6-8 servings

5 cups chicken broth
1/2 lb. fettuccine, broken in half
3 cups finely chopped broccoli
1 1/4 cups water
10-oz. pkg. frozen chopped spinach, thawed
1 small onion, finely chopped
1/4 tsp. salt
1/2 tsp. pepper
1/2 to 3/4 lb. Velveeta cheese

1. Cook together chicken broth, fettuccine, broccoli, and water until fettuccine is soft.
2. Stir in spinach, onion, salt, and pepper. Simmer for 3 minutes, stirring occasionally.
3. Just before serving, add cheese. Stir until melted and smooth.

Broccoli Soup
Claire Amick
Pine Grove Mills, PA
Autumn Stars

Makes 4 servings

4 cups chopped fresh broccoli
1 small onion, quartered
2 cups chicken or vegetable broth
1 garlic clove, minced
1 tsp. fresh lemon juice
1/4 tsp. pepper

1. In large saucepan combine broccoli, onion, broth, and garlic. Cook until broccoli is tender, about 10-15 minutes. Transfer by batches to blender and purée until smooth.
2. Return to saucepan. Add lemon juice and pepper. Cook until heated through.

Broccoli Noodle Soup
Lynn Clark
Emmitsburg, MD
Graduation Quillos

Makes 4 quarts

2 Tbsp. margarine
3/4 cup chopped onion
6 cups water
6 chicken bouillon cubes
8 ozs. fine egg noodles
1 tsp. salt
2 10-oz. pkgs. chopped frozen broccoli
1/8 tsp. garlic powder
6 cups milk
1 lb. grated cheese (your choice)
pepper to taste

1. Sauté onion in margarine for 3 minutes. Add water and bouillon. Heat to boiling, stirring until cubes dissolve.
2. Gradually stir in noodles and salt. Cook uncovered for 3 minutes, stirring occasionally.
3. Stir in broccoli and garlic powder. Cook 4 minutes.
4. Add milk, cheese, and pepper. Continue cooking until cheese melts, stirring constantly.

I will always remember a special Christmas dinner that we had with friends. It came at the end of a very sad year when we had both lost our fathers. Other tragic happenings kept us from having the so-called Christmas spirit. We were in no mood for cookies, turkey, or feasting.

I told our friends to come over anyway on Christmas Day, and we decided to make a picnic meal, complete with cheeseburger roll (see page 110), tossed salad, watermelon, and strawberries. The light cuisine helped to lighten our hearts and spirits.
—*Sue Hamilton, Minooka, IL*

Cream of Crab Broccoli Soup

Rachel Thomas Pellman
Lancaster, PA
Little Angel Miniature Quilt

Makes 4-6 servings

8-oz. pkg. frozen Alaska
   King Crab, thawed
10-oz. pkg. frozen
   chopped broccoli,
   cooked
1/2 cup chopped onion
3 Tbsp. butter
2 Tbsp. flour
2 cups milk
2 cups half-and-half
2 chicken bouillon cubes
1/2 tsp. salt
1/8 tsp. pepper
1/8 tsp. cayenne pepper
1/8 tsp. thyme
1 Tbsp. Worcestershire
   sauce
4-6 Tbsp. sherry

1. Drain and slice crab. Set aside.
2. Sauté onion in butter. Stir in flour. Add milk and half-and-half and cook until thickened and smooth, stirring constantly.
3. Dissolve bouillon in hot soup.
4. Add salt, peppers, thyme, Worcestershire sauce, crab, and broccoli. Heat through.
5. Pour 1 Tbsp. sherry in each serving bowl. Ladle soup into bowl and serve immediately.

Simple Mushroom Soup

Joan Kowalsky
Shelton, WA
Trip Around the World

Makes 6-8 servings

1 medium onion, diced
1 clove garlic, minced
1 Tbsp. butter
1 Tbsp. olive oil
5 cups sliced mushrooms
2 10³/4-oz. cans chicken
   or vegetable broth
1³/4 cups water
1/4 cup dry sherry
   (optional)
1/4 cup tomato paste
1/4 tsp. pepper (optional)
1/4 cup grated Parmesan
   cheese
2 Tbsp. snipped parsley

1. Sauté onion and garlic in butter and oil until soft. Stir in mushrooms. Sauté for 2 minutes.
2. Add broth, water, sherry, tomato paste, and pepper. Simmer for 30 minutes.
3. Ladle soup into serving bowls, and sprinkle cheese and parsley over each.

Creamy Mushroom Broccoli Soup

Barbara Dunham
Knowlesville, NY
Irish Chain

Makes 8-10 servings

12 ozs. fresh mushrooms
5 Tbsp. margarine
1 medium onion,
   chopped
1/4 cup flour
1/2 tsp. salt
1/4 tsp. white pepper
10-oz. pkg. frozen
   broccoli, chopped
1¹/2 cups milk
10³/4-oz. can chicken
   broth
1 cup half-and-half

1. Chop half the mushrooms. Slice remaining half.
2. In saucepan melt 2 Tbsp. margarine. Add sliced mushrooms and cook until tender. Set aside.
3. In same saucepan melt 3 Tbsp. margarine. Add chopped mushrooms and onion and cook until tender. Stir in flour, salt, and pepper until smooth.
4. Add chopped broccoli. Cook for one minute, stirring constantly.
5. Gradually add milk and chicken broth. Bring to a boil, stirring constantly until thickened. Add chopped mushrooms.
6. Remove from heat and add half-and-half. Heat, but do not boil.

Exotic Mushroom Soup

Eleanor Fabiszak
Columbia, MD
Paddington Bear Baby Quilt

Makes 4-5 servings

6-8 large dry Polish or
  cepes mushrooms
1 cup boiling water
1/2 lb. fresh mushrooms,
  sliced
1/2 cup chopped celery
1/4 cup sliced onion
1/8 cup shredded parsley
2-3 Tbsp. butter
2 cups chicken stock
2 Tbsp. butter
2-3 Tbsp. flour
1 cup milk
1 small onion
4 whole cloves
1/2 small bay leaf
1 tsp. salt
1/4 tsp. pepper

1. Soak Polish mushrooms
in 1 cup boiling water for
30 minutes.
2. In saucepan sauté fresh
mushrooms, celery, onions,
and parsley in 2-3 Tbsp.
butter. Stir in chicken stock.
Simmer covered for 20 minutes.
3. Blend sautéed vegetables
and stock in blender or food
processor. Set aside.
4. Drain Polish mushrooms.
Strain liquid through coffee
filter. Add liquid to puréed
vegetables. Wash mush-
rooms in cold water and
chop. Add to vegetables.
5. In saucepan melt 2 Tbsp.
butter over low heat. Stir in

flour. Slowly add milk and
mix well. Add onion studded
with cloves and bay leaf.
Cook and stir sauce until
thickened and smooth.
6. Add cream sauce to soup
and heat just until soup
reaches a boil. Stir in seasonings, remove onion, and
serve.

Cream of Carrot Soup

Jean Johnson
Dallas, OR
Ducky Weather

Makes 4 servings

1 large onion, sliced
1 tsp. oil
2 cups chicken broth
1/2 cup sliced carrots
1 large potato, cubed
1/2 tsp. thyme
1-2 cups evaporated skim
  milk, according to taste

1. In saucepan sauté onion
in oil until soft, about 5
minutes.
2. Stir in chicken broth, carrots, potato, and thyme.
Simmer until tender, about
25 minutes.
3. Purée a small amount at
a time in a blender. Stir in
evaporated milk.
4. Reheat and serve.

Wild Rice Soup

Sharon Leali
Jackson, OH
Maple Leaf

Makes 6-8 servings

1 lb. bacon, chopped in
  small pieces
1/2 cup chopped onion
1/2 cup chopped celery
2 cups chicken broth
2 10³/4-oz. cans cream of
  mushroom soup
2 cups cooked wild rice

1. Brown bacon until crisp.
Set aside. Drain off all but
1/4 cup drippings. Add onion
and celery. Sauté lightly.
2. Add chicken broth and
simmer until vegetables are
tender.
3. Stir in soup and wild rice.
Heat, but do not boil. Add
water if soup is too thick.

Tomato Rice Soup

Mary Lou Rowe
Batavia, IL
Garden Twist

Makes 12 servings

1 large onion, diced
1 Tbsp. oil
28-oz. can diced tomatoes
1 quart V-8 juice
6 cups chicken broth
1 cup converted rice,
  uncooked
1/8 tsp. pepper
1-2 Tbsp. fresh basil
1 cup buttermilk

1/4 bunch fresh parsley
10-oz. pkg. frozen
    spinach, thawed

1. Sauté onion in oil until tender. Stir in tomatoes, V-8 juice, chicken broth, rice, and pepper. Simmer for 45-60 minutes.
2. Stir in basil and buttermilk. Heat, but do not boil. Add parsley.
3. Remove as much moisture as possible from spinach. Add to soup just before serving. Heat throughly.

Chicken and Wild Rice Soup

Gwendolyn P. Chapman
Gwinn, MI
Dresden Plate

Makes 6 servings

1/2 cup uncooked wild
    rice
1 1/2 cups water
2 green onions, thinly
    sliced
8 ozs. mushrooms, sliced
1 lb. chicken breast filets,
    cut up
1 clove garlic, minced
3 Tbsp. butter
1/4 cup flour
1 quart chicken broth
1 cup whipping cream or
    half-and-half
2 Tbsp. dry sherry
white pepper to taste

1. Rinse wild rice 3 times. Combine rice and water in saucepan. Mix well. Bring to boil, reduce heat and simmer covered for 35-45 minutes or until rice is tender.
2. Sauté onions, mushrooms, chicken, and garlic in butter for 5-7 minutes or until vegetables are tender.
3. Stir in flour. Cook for 2 minutes, stirring constantly.
4. Add broth and mix well. Bring to boil. Cook until thickened, stirring constantly.
5. Stir in wild rice, cream, and sherry. Cook until heated through, stirring frequently. Season with white pepper.

French Onion Soup

Tracey B. Stenger
Gretna, LA
*Original Whole Cloth
Baby Quilt*

Makes 4 servings

4 medium onions, sliced
3 Tbsp. butter
1 Tbsp. flour
2 10 3/4-oz. cans beef
    consommé, heated
1 tsp. salt
1/4 tsp. pepper
toasted croutons
Gruyère cheese, grated

1. Sauté onions in butter until golden brown. Add flour and cook for 5 minutes, stirring so that flour does not burn. Stir in beef consommé. Season with salt and pepper.
2. Place soup in oven-proof serving bowls. Top with toasted croutons and cheese.
3. Place under oven broiler until cheese melts.

Canadian Cheese Soup

Cindy Dorzab
Fort Smith, AR
*The Geese
Have Finally Flown*

Makes 8 servings

1/2 cup margarine
1/4 cup minced onion
1 cup thinly sliced carrots
1 1/2 cup finely chopped
    celery
4 cups chicken broth
1 tsp. seasoned salt
1/2 cup flour
3 cups milk
Tabasco
pepper
5 cups shredded cheese,
    American or cheddar
1 tsp. parsley

1. In saucepan sauté onion in margarine until clear. Add carrots and celery and sauté for 2-3 minutes.
2. Stir in chicken broth and seasoned salt and cook for 10-15 minutes, or until vegetables are soft.
3. Mix together flour and 1 cup milk. Stir in remaining milk and add to vegetable mixture. Cook slowly until thickened.
4. Add Tabasco and pepper to taste. Add shredded cheese and parsley. Serve.

George's Fish Chowder

Jennie Walsh
Port Hawkesbury,
Nova Scotia
Casey's Stars

Makes 6 servings

3 slices bacon
1/3 cup diced onion
1 1/2 cups sliced potatoes
1/2 tsp. salt
1/8 tsp. pepper
1/2 cup water
1 lb. fish fillets
7-oz. can clams, drained
7-oz. can oysters, drained
7-oz. can shrimp, drained
3 cups milk
2 Tbsp. butter
7-oz. can lobster paste
  (optional)

1. Fry bacon until crisp.
Remove bacon and add
onion to drippings. Cook
onions until tender.
2. Stir in potatoes, salt, pepper, and water. Cover and
cook 10 minutes, or until
potatoes are tender.
3. Add fish, clams, oysters,
and shrimp. Cook 15 min-
utes, adding more water if
necessary.
4. Add milk, butter, and lobster paste. Heat but do not
boil.

Savory Seafood Chowder

Donna M. Mulkey
Oregon City, OR
Bow Tie

Makes 6-8 servings

6-oz. pkg. frozen crab,
  sliced
4 1/2-oz. can shrimp
7-oz. can minced clams
4 strips bacon, diced
1 clove garlic, minced
2 cups diced potatoes
1 cup white wine
2 tsp. salt
1/4 tsp. pepper
1/2 tsp. thyme
16-oz. can cream-style
  corn
3 cups milk
2 cups half-and-half
1/2 cup chopped green
  onions
2 Tbsp. minced parsley

1. Drain crab, shrimp, and
clams, reserving liquid.
2. In large kettle sauté
bacon and garlic until bacon
is crisp. Stir in potatoes,
wine and reserved liquid
from seafoods. Stir in salt,
pepper, and thyme. Cover
and simmer 15-20 minutes,
or until potatoes are tender.
3. Add seafood, corn, milk,
half-and-half, green onions,
and parsley. Heat slowly.
Simmer but do not boil.

New England Clam Chowder

Gertrude Hedrick
Willow Grove, PA
Patchwork in Double-Time

Makes 10-12 servings

4 medium potatoes,
  peeled and cubed
2 medium onions,
  chopped
1/2 cup butter or
  margarine
3/4 cup flour
2 quarts milk
3 6 1/2-oz. cans chopped
  clams, undrained
2-3 tsp. salt
1/8 tsp. ground sage
1/8 tsp. ground thyme
1/2 tsp. celery salt
1/2 tsp. pepper
2 strips bacon, cooked
  and crumbled
dash of Worcestershire
  sauce

1. In saucepan cook potatoes
until tender.
2. In Dutch oven sauté
onions in butter until tender. Add flour. Mix until
smooth. Stir in milk. Cook
over medium heat, stirring
constantly until thickened
and bubbly.
3. Add potatoes to Dutch
oven. Stir in clams, salt,
sage, thyme, celery salt,
pepper, bacon, and
Worcestershire sauce. Heat
but do not boil.

Sue's Clam Chowder
Shirley Odell
Manteca, CA
Dresden Plate

Makes 8-10 servings

20-oz. bag frozen hash
browns, thawed
5 10-oz. cans clams,
undrained
1/4 lb. bacon, cooked and
crumbled
1/2 bunch celery, sliced
thin
1 large onion, chopped
1 Tbsp. thyme
2 Tbsp. Worcestershire
sauce
1/2 cup flour
1 cup milk, or more

1. Mix together all ingredients
except flour and milk. Heat,
but do not boil.
2. Make paste from flour and
milk and stir into simmering
mixture.
3. Cook on low heat, stirring
constantly until thickened.
Add more milk if desired to
increase creaminess.

Clam Chowder
Sherril Beiberly
Salina, KS
My Watercolor Heart

Makes 2-3 servings

1 slice bacon, chopped
2 Tbsp. minced onion
10³/₄-oz. cream of potato
soup
7-oz. can minced clams
1 cup light cream or half-
and-half
chopped parsley

1. In saucepan cook bacon
until crisp. Add onion and
sauté until softened. Add
soup and clams.
2. Gradually add cream,
stirring until mixture is
smooth. Heat to serving
temperature. Garnish with
chopped parsley.

When we lived in Virginia, I started a neighborhood cookie exchange during the holiday season. Anyone who wanted to participate baked six dozen of their favorite Christmas cookies and brought them to a get together in my home on an afternoon during the first week in December. Each person contributed five dozen cookies to boxes which were then divided among us, plus four or five extra packages which were delivered to new people in the neighborhood or to people who had been sick or hospitalized.

The remaining dozen cookies from each person were arranged on a table and enjoyed with coffee, hot cocoa, tea, fruit salad, and fellowship. When school closed for the day, all our children were invited to come and help themselves to what was left of the cookies on the table. The first year there were twelve women and within a few years the group had grown to nearly fifty. I think many of the kids coerced their mothers into participating so they could join in for the "clean-up" party.

Everyone got into the Christmas spirit, went home with a nice assortment of Christmas cookies, and felt good because we had given to other people. Twelve years after moving out of the neighborhood, I still receive letters from neighbors reminiscing about our cookie exchanges.

—*Jean Hannemann, Marquette, MI*

Breads, Rolls, and Muffins

Oatmeal Bread
Lorene P. Meyer
Wayland, IA
Sampler

Makes 2 loaves

2 cups boiling water
1 cup oatmeal, rolled or
   quick
2 Tbsp. shortening
1/2 cup molasses
2 tsp. salt
1 pkg. dry yeast
1/2 cup warm water
5-6 cups flour

1. Pour hot water over oatmeal. Stir in shortening, molasses, and salt. Cool.
2. Dissolve yeast in warm water. Add to oatmeal mixture. Add flour, mixing well.
3. Turn onto floured board and knead well. Put in greased bowl. Let rise until double in size. Punch down and let rise again.
4. Divide into 2 greased full-sized loaf pans. Let rise until double in size.
5. Bake at 350° for 30-40 minutes.

Mama's Swedish Rye Bread
Joyce R. Swinney
Mooresville, IN
Double Wedding Ring

Makes 4 loaves

2 pkgs. dry yeast
1/2 cup warm water
1 quart warm water
1 Tbsp. lard
1 cup sugar
1/2 cup oatmeal
1/2 cup molasses
1 tsp. salt
3 Tbsp. anise seed
1 Tbsp. orange rind
3 1/2 cups rye flour
5 cups sifted bread flour

1. Dissolve yeast in 1/2 cup warm water.
2. Pour 1 quart warm water into large bowl, and stir in dissolved yeast, lard, sugar, oatmeal, molasses, salt, anise seed, and orange rind. Mix well.
3. Stir in rye flour. Let stand until bubbly. Add bread flour. Knead until smooth and elastic. Put dough into greased bowl. Turn to coat top. Cover lightly and let rise until double in size.
4. Shape into 4 loaves. Place in greased, full-sized bread pans. Cover with waxed paper and let rise until double in size.
5. Bake at 350° for 45 minutes. Remove bread from pans and butter tops while still warm.

Pilgrim Bread
Jeanne Allen
Los Alamos, NM
Baltimore Beauty

Makes 2 loaves

1/2 cup yellow cornmeal
1/3 cup brown sugar
1 Tbsp. salt
2 cups boiling water
1/2 cup vegetable oil or
   melted butter
2 pkgs. dry yeast
1/2 cup lukewarm water
3/4 cup stirred whole
   wheat flour
1/2 cup stirred rye flour
41/4-41/2 cups sifted all-
   purpose flour

1. Thoroughly combine cornmeal, brown sugar, salt, boiling water, and oil. Let cool to lukewarm, about 30 minutes.
2. Soften yeast in lukewarm water. Stir into cornmeal mixture.
3. Add whole wheat and rye flours. Mix well. Stir in enough all-purpose flour to make a moderately stiff dough.
4. Turn out on lightly floured surface and knead till smooth and elastic, 6-8 minutes. Place in greased bowl, turning once to grease surface. Cover and let rise in warm place until double in size, 50-60 minutes. Punch down.
5. Turn out on lightly floured surface and divide in half. Cover and let rest 10 minutes.
6. Shape into 2 loaves and place in greased, full-sized loaf pans. Let rise again till almost double, about 30 minutes.
7. Bake at 375° for 45 minutes. Top loosely with foil after first 25 minutes if bread browns rapidly.
8. Remove from pans to cool.

Oatmeal Cinnamon Bread
Mary Martins
Fairbank, IA
Mystery Quilt Wall Hanging

Makes 3 loaves

2 pkgs. dry yeast
1/2 cup warm water
11/2 cups scalded milk
2/3 cup melted shortening
1/2 cup sugar
2 tsp. salt
51/2-6 cups sifted flour
2 eggs, beaten
2 cups uncooked
   oatmeal, quick or
   regular
31/2 cups sugar
4-6 tsp. cinnamon
2 Tbsp. melted butter

1. Dissolve yeast in warm water.
2. In large bowl pour scalded milk over mixture of shortening, sugar, and salt, stirring lightly.
3. Cool to lukewarm and stir in 1 cup flour and eggs. Add dissolved yeast and oatmeal. Stir in enough more flour to make soft dough.
4. Turn out on floured board and knead about 10 minutes, or until satiny. Shape into a ball and place in greased bowl, turning to grease dough. Cover and let rise in warm place until doubled, about 1 hour.
5. Punch down and let rest 10 minutes. Divide into 3 parts. Roll out each part to form a rectangle 8" x 24."
6. Mix together 31/2 cups sugar and 4-6 tsp. cinnamon. Brush 1/3 of mixture over each rectangle.
7. Roll each up, starting at short end. Place each in well greased, full-sized loaf pan. Let rise until doubled, about 45 minutes.
6. Bake at 375° for 45 minutes. Remove from pans and brush with melted butter.

I live in the small farming and fishing village of Half Moon Bay, California. Our main crops are flowers, Christmas trees, and pumpkins. Every year in October, we have a huge pumpkin festival and our small town of approximately 12,000 swells to hundreds of thousands. Pumpkins decorate houses and shops throughout the holidays, and I have cookbooks full of pumpkin recipes which I bake and prepare as the season progresses.
—*Marina Salume, Half Moon Bay, CA*

Oatmeal Bread with Cinnamon and Raisins

Cindy Ewert
Salem, OR

Makes 2 loaves

1¹/2 cups oatmeal
1¹/2 cups boiling water
3 Tbsp. butter or
    margarine
3 Tbsp. honey
1 Tbsp. brown sugar
2 tsp. salt
¹/2 cup raisins
1 pkg. dry yeast
2 eggs, room temperature
4-5 cups flour
3 Tbsp. butter, melted
1 cup sugar
2 Tbsp. cinnamon

1. In large bowl pour boiling water over oatmeal. Stir to blend. Add butter, honey, brown sugar, salt, and raisins. Cool to 130°.
2. Stir in yeast. Add eggs and 2 cups flour. Stir vigorously for 2-3 minutes. Work in additional flour, ¹/2 cup at a time.
3. Pour onto floured surface. Knead for 8 minutes, adding flour as needed. Place dough in greased bowl. Cover with plastic wrap and allow to rise in warm place until double in size, about 1 hour.
4. Divide dough into 2 pieces. Shape each piece into a 8" x 12" rectangle. Butter the dough and sprinkle with sugar and cinnamon. Roll up each rectangle

of dough from the narrow end like a jelly roll. Press seams securely together. Place each on a greased cookie sheet, seam side down. Cover with waxed paper and allow to rise for 45 minutes.
5. Bake at 375° for 40 minutes. Brush with melted butter and turn out onto a metal rack to cool.

Mama's Herb Bread Treat

Joyce R. Swinney
Mooresville, IN
Dresden Heart

Makes 2 loaves

2 cups milk
1 pkg. dry yeast
4 Tbsp. sugar
4 Tbsp. shortening
2 tsp. salt
2 eggs
1 tsp. nutmeg
4 tsp. rubbed sage
4 tsp. caraway seed
6 cups sifted flour

1. Scald milk and cool to room temperature. Stir in yeast and sugar. Let set until bubbly.
2. Stir in shortening and salt. Mix well.
3. Beat eggs. Add nutmeg, sage, and caraway. Stir into yeast mixture. Add 4 cups flour and beat for 2 minutes.
4. Pour dough onto board spread with 2 cups flour. Knead well for 5 minutes.

Place dough in greased bowl. Turn to coat top. Let rise until double, about 2 hours.
5. Shape into 2 loaves. Place in greased bread pans. Let rise until double, about 1 hour.
6. Bake at 425° for 15 minutes; then reduce heat to 350° and bake for 25-35 minutes. Remove from pan and cool on racks.

Cardamom Bread

Marion Matson
Bloomington, MN
Winding Ways

Makes 3 loaves

2 pkgs. dry yeast
1 tsp. sugar
¹/3 cup warm water
¹/2 cup sugar
1 tsp. salt
¹/2 cup oil
1 cup warm milk
3 beaten eggs (reserve 1
    Tbsp. and mix with 1
    Tbsp. water; save for
    egg wash to brush over
    braid)
3 heaping tsp. freshly
    ground cardamom
5¹/2-6 cups flour
decorative or pearl sugar

1. Dissolve yeast and 1 tsp. sugar in water.
2. Mix together ¹/2 cup sugar, salt, oil, milk, eggs, cardamom, and 2 cups flour. Stir in yeast mixture. Let stand for 15 minutes.
3. Stir in 3¹/2-4 cups flour.

Turn out on a floured surface and knead 5-10 minutes.
4. Place in a greased bowl, turning once to grease top. Let rise 30 minutes.
5. Divide into three parts. Divide each part into 3 18"-long pieces and braid 3 strands together. Place each braid on a greased cookie sheet. Let rise for 30 minutes.
6. Brush with egg wash. Sprinkle generously with decorative or pearl sugar.
7. Bake at 350° for 20 minutes.

Dinner Rolls
Janet Groff
Stevens, PA
Dorothy Shank
Sterling, IL
Bethel T. Moore
Fairfax, VA

Makes 3-4 dozen rolls

2 eggs
3/4 cup sugar
1/2 cup shortening
1 tsp. salt
1 cup warm water
2 pkgs. dry yeast
1 cup milk
7 cups flour

1. Cream together eggs, sugar, shortening, and salt.
2. Dissolve yeast in warm water. Add to creamed mixture. Stir in milk and flour. Mix well. Let rise in warm place for 2 hours.
3. Punch down. Shape into golf ball-sized balls and place 1" apart in greased

pans. Let rise until pan is full.
4. Bake at 350° for 20-25 minutes. Butter tops while still warm.

Elizabeth's Dinner Rolls
Elizabeth J. Yoder
Millersburg, OH
Country Love

Makes 2 dozen rolls

1 pkg. dry yeast
1/4 cup warm water
1/2 cup shortening
1/2 cup sugar
3 eggs, well beaten
2 tsp. salt
1 cup lukewarm milk
5 cups flour

1. Dissolve yeast in lukewarm water.
2. Cream together sugar and shortening.
3. Beat eggs into creamed mixture.
4. Mix in salt, milk, and yeast mixture.
5. Stir in about half the flour and mix well. Add remaining flour. Turn onto floured board and knead several minutes.
6. Let rise until double. Punch down and divide into 24 smooth balls.
7. Place in 2 round pans or 1 9" x 13" pan. Cover. Let rise until almost double.
8. Bake at 350° for 15-20 minutes or until light brown on top.

Note: 1 cup whole wheat flour may be substituted for 1 cup regular flour to make wheat dinner rolls.

Oatmeal Dinner Rolls
Nettie J. Miller
Millersburg, OH

Makes 15 dinner rolls

1 Tbsp. yeast
1 cup warm water
1/4 cup sugar
1 1/2 tsp. salt
1/2 cup rolled oats
1 egg, beaten
3 Tbsp. oil
3 cups bread flour

1. Dissolve yeast in warm water. Add sugar, salt, rolled oats, egg, oil, and 2 1/4 cups flour. Turn onto floured surface and knead in remaining flour. Knead for a few more minutes.
2. Let rise in warm place for 1 to 1 1/2 hours.
3. Shape dough into balls and place in greased pans. Let rise about 1 hour.
4. Bake at 350° for 20-25 minutes. Butter tops while still warm.

Honeybee Rolls

Charlotte Bull
Cassville, MD
Pieced Sunburst with
Appliquéd Florals

Makes 4 dozen rolls

4 cups skim milk
3/4 cup margarine
1/2 cup sugar
1/2 cup honey
1/4 cup lukewarm water
2 pkgs. dry yeast
1/8 tsp. nutmeg
10-12 cups flour

1. Scald milk in saucepan. Stir in margarine, sugar, and honey. Stir until dissolved. Cool to lukewarm.
2. Dissolve yeast in lukewarm water. Add to milk mixture. Add nutmeg and 6 cups flour. Stir well.
3. Add 4-6 cups of flour, 1 cup at a time, until dough is no longer sticky. Turn onto floured surface and knead well.
4. Place in greased bowl. Cover and let rise in warm place until double, about 1 hour. Punch down.
5. Divide into half or thirds for easier handling. Form into rolls and place into greased pans. Cover. Let rise until double.
4. Bake at 350° for 20 minutes.

Note: From this basic dough you can make raisin bread, sweet rolls, fruited wreaths, or many other variations.

Variation 1: Add 2 eggs to milk mixture for richer dough to make sweet rolls.

Variation 2: Substitute 3 cups of whole wheat flour for 3 of white flour.

Golden Potato Rolls

Barbara Tenney
Delta, PA
Glenna K. Smith
Punxsutawney, PA
North Star Tree Skirt

Makes 3 dozen rolls

1 pkg. dry yeast
1/2 cup warm water
1 cup milk
3/4 cup shortening or
** margarine**
1 1/4 cups mashed
** potatoes**
1/2 cup sugar
2 tsp. salt
8-8 1/2 cups flour
2 eggs, beaten

1. Dissolve yeast in water and set aside.
2. In saucepan combine milk, shortening, and mashed potatoes. Heat on low until shortening is melted. Remove from heat.
3. In large bowl combine sugar, salt, 2 cups flour, and yeast mixture. Stir in mashed potato mixture. Add eggs and mix well. Cover loosely and allow to stand for 2 hours. The mixture will eventually look like a sponge.
4. Stir in enough remaining flour to make a soft dough. Turn onto a floured surface and knead until smooth and elastic, about 6 minutes. Place in greased bowl. Turn to grease top. Cover and let rise in warm place until double in size, about 1 hour.
5. Punch down and divide into thirds. On floured surface, roll each into a 12" circle. Cut each circle into 12 pie-shaped wedges. Roll up from wide end like a crescent roll. Lay point side down, with rolls 2" apart, on baking sheet. Cover and let rise for 30 minutes.
6. Bake at 400° for 15 minutes until golden brown.

Potato Refrigerator Rolls

Elsie Russett
Fairbank, IA
Starry Path

Makes 4 dozen rolls

1 1/2 cups warm water
1 pkg. dry yeast
2/3 cup sugar
1 1/2 tsp. salt
2/3 cup soft shortening
2 eggs
1 cup lukewarm mashed
** potatoes**
7-7 1/2 cups flour

1. Mix yeast into warm water. Stir to dissolve and allow to bubble.
2. Stir in sugar, salt, and shortening. Add eggs and mashed potatoes. Mix well.
3. Stir in flour until easy to

handle. Turn out onto floured board and knead until smooth.

4. Place in greased bowl. Turn dough to grease top. Cover with damp cloth. Place in refrigerator for 2 hours.

5. Shape into desired rolls or cut with biscuit cutter into buns. Grease top and bottom of rolls and place on cookie sheet. Let rise until double, about 1 hour.

6. Bake at 400° for 12-15 minutes.

Variation: Instead of shaping into rolls or buns, divide dough into 3 pieces. Roll each piece into a cord 18" long. Braid 3 cords together. Place on pan and let rise until double in size. Bake at 400° for 15-20 minutes.

Mix together 1 egg white, 2 cups powdered sugar, 3 Tbsp. melted butter, and enough water to make liquid glaze. Drizzle glaze over braid and decorate with pecan halves and red and green cherries.

Refrigerator Dinner Rolls
Judi Robb
Manhattan, KS
Seven Sisters

Makes 1 dozen

1 egg
1/2 cup sugar
1 cup butter
1 cup hot water
1 cup cold water
1 pkg. yeast

1 1/2 tsp. salt
1/2 tsp mace (optional)
6 to 7 cups flour, sifted

1. Beat egg until thick and lemon colored. Add sugar and beat.

2. Melt butter in hot water and add to egg and sugar mixture. Stir in cold water.

3. When mixture is luke-warm, add yeast, salt, and mace.

4. Mix in flour. Beat well. Refrigerate and use as needed.

5. Roll out on floured surface. Cut with round cookie cutter and fold circle in half. Put on greased cookie sheet. Let rise for 1 hour. Bake at 425° for 12 to 15 minutes.

Refrigerator Rolls
Elaine Headley
Salina, KS
Here's to Bears!
Barbara R. Zitzmann
Metairie, LA
Illusion

Makes 5 dozen rolls

1/2 cup warm water
2 pkgs. dry yeast
1 cup lard
3/4 cup sugar
1 1/2 cups boiling water
1 tsp. salt
2 eggs
6 cups unsifted flour

1. Dissolve yeast in warm water and let set for 5 minutes.

2. Cut lard in thin slices in large mixer bowl. Add sugar. Pour boiling water over the sugar and lard. Mix at low speed to soften lard.

3. Cool to about 150°. Add salt and eggs and beat well. Cool to 105-115°. Stir in yeast. Sift flour and add one cup at a time, mixing well after each addition.

4. The dough can be refrigerated at this point for up to one week. Store it in a covered container. The dough may need to be punched down occasionally. When you are ready to use it, remove it from the refrigerator and let it stand for 10 minutes before shaping it into rolls.

5. If you are ready to use the dough immediately, place it in a greased bowl. Cover and let rise in warm place until double in size, 1 1/2-2 hours.

6. Divide dough into 5 parts. Flour board and roll out 1 part into a circle. Using a pizza cutter, cut the circle into 12 equal wedges. Roll up each wedge, starting with wide end. Place on lightly greased cookie sheet. Repeat with remaining dough. Let rise 30-45 minutes.

7. Bake at 375° for 12-15 minutes.

Wheat Crescent Rolls

Martha Bender
New Paris, IN
Boston Commons

Makes 2¹/2 dozen rolls

2 Tbsp. yeast
1 cup warm water
¹/2 cup sugar
¹/2 cup shortening
1 tsp. salt
1 cup boiling water
2 eggs, beaten
2 cups wheat flour
5 cups flour

1. Dissolve yeast in warm water. Set aside.
2. Melt sugar, shortening, and salt in boiling water. Cool to lukewarm and add to yeast mixture.
3. Add eggs and stir.
4. Add flours. Turn onto floured board and knead well.
5. Place in greased bowl. Let rise until double in size.
6. Punch down. Split dough into two pieces.
7. Roll out one piece on floured surface into a 14-15 inch round.
8. Cut into 16 pie-shaped pieces. Roll up, beginning at rounded edge. Place on greased cookie sheet. Repeat with second piece of dough.
9. Bake at 350° for 20 minutes.

Note: I have made these rolls for many church dinners and everyone seems to really like

them. *I make them regularly for family dinners during the holidays and for other family get-togethers. Our grandchildren, when they were quite young, preferred to eat the rolls rather than other food!*

Whole Wheat Rolls

Marian Brubacker
Barnett, MO
Country Bride

Makes 2 dozen rolls

2 pkgs. dry yeast
2 cups lukewarm water
¹/2 cup sugar
3 tsp. salt
3 cups whole wheat flour
¹/2 cup margarine, melted
3 eggs, beaten
3¹/2 cups white flour

1. Dissolve yeast in water. Stir in sugar, salt, and 2 cups whole wheat flour. Beat until smooth.
2. Add margarine and eggs, beating well. Add remaining whole wheat flour and enough white flour to form dough.

3. Knead and place in a greased bowl. Turn dough to grease top. Cover and set in warm place until double in size.
4. Shape into rolls and place in well greased pans. Cover and let rise until light, about 30-45 minutes.
5. Bake at 350° for 25 minutes.

Mushroom Cheese Bread

Lynne Fritz
Bel Air, MD
Mom's Star

Makes 2 loaves

4 Tbsp. butter
2 lbs. fresh mushrooms, sliced
1 large clove garlic, minced
1¹/2 tsp. garlic powder
1 Tbsp. fresh parsley
¹/2 tsp. salt
4 Tbsp. butter
2 Tbsp. fresh chives
¹/2 lb. fresh mushrooms, sliced
2 Tbsp. flour
1 cup heavy cream
¹/2 tsp. salt

My grandmother was a very giving person. Some of my fondest memories of her are linked to her Christmas care packages. These usually included things like fudge, shortbread, Christmas pudding, and cookies. She would take them around to the old folks in her small town of Lacome, Alberta. She did this until she was eighty-five years old and many of the "old folks" were younger than she.
—*Jean Turner, Williams Lake, BC*

2 dashes Tabasco sauce
1 Tbsp. fresh parsley
2 tsp. lemon juice
2 Tbsp. Parmesan cheese
1 cup flour
1 1/2 tsp. wheat germ
1/2 cup Parmesan cheese
1/2 cup white cornmeal
1 Tbsp. sugar
1/2 tsp. salt
1 pkg. rapid-rising dry
   yeast
1 1/2 cups hot water (120-
   130°)
2 tsp. butter
12-ozs. mozzarella cheese,
   grated
1 egg, slightly beaten
1 Tbsp butter, melted
2-3 Tbsp. sesame seeds
1 Tbsp. poppy seeds

1. In saucepan saute 2 lbs. mushrooms and garlic in butter until all moisture is gone. Add 1 tsp. garlic powder, 1 Tbsp. parsley, and 1/2 tsp. salt. Set aside.
2. Melt 4 Tbsp. butter. Add chives and cook 1 minute. Add 1/2 lb. mushrooms. Cook until moisture is gone. Sprinkle with 2 Tbsp. flour and pour heavy cream on top. Cook until thickened.
3. Add 1/2 tsp. salt, Tabasco sauce, 1 Tbsp. fresh parsley, lemon juice, and 2 Tbsp. Parmesan cheese. Set aside.
4. Combine 1 cup flour, wheat germ, 1/2 cup Parmesan cheese, cornmeal, 1 Tbsp. sugar, 1/2 tsp. salt, and rapid-rising yeast. Stir in hot water and 2 tsp. butter. Mix well. Stir in remaining flour (1 1/2 cups) to form soft dough.
5. Cover in bowl and let rise for 15 minutes. Punch dough down.
6. Press 1/3 of dough in bottom of greased 10" springform pan. Press a small amount up the sides. Layer in half the sautéed mushrooms and then half the mozzarella cheese, followed by the remaining mushrooms and the remaining mozzarella cheese. Pour mushroom cream sauce over top, keeping all in the center of dough.
7. When layering is finished, press filling toward edges of pan, leaving 1/2" rim of dough at sides.
8. Split remaining dough in half. Form a thin log to fit around rim of pan, pushing down into dough around the sides.
9. Roll out last third of dough into a circle the size of pan. Carefully place on top and push into dough around the edges to totally enclose the filling.
10. Cover dough loosely with a cloth and let rise until double in size, approx. 30-40 minutes.
11. Brush top dough with beaten egg mixed with 1 Tbsp. butter. Sprinkle with sesame seeds and poppy seeds.
12. Bake at 400° for 30 minutes, or until dough pulls away from the sides of the pan and is golden brown.
13. Cool 5-10 minutes. Remove sides of pan. Cut into wedges to serve.

Butterhorn Crescent Rolls
Judy Steiner Buller
Beatrice, NE
Shifting Mountains
Elizabeth Miller
Walnut Creek, OH
Rose Trellis

Makes 2-2 1/2 dozen rolls

1 pkg. dry yeast
1 Tbsp. sugar
2 Tbsp. warm water
1/2 cup margarine
1 cup milk
1/2 cup sugar
1 tsp. salt
3 eggs, well beaten
4 1/2 cups flour

1. Dissolve yeast and 1 Tbsp. sugar in large bowl in warm water.
2. In saucepan melt margarine. Add milk to cool it. Stir in sugar, salt, and eggs. Mix well. Add to yeast mixture. Stir in 4 cups flour. Dough will be sticky.
3. Place piece of plastic wrap over bowl and let rise for at least 8 hours, either in refrigerator or on counter top.
4. Divide dough into 4 pieces. Roll each piece into a circle on well floured board. Cut each circle into 8 wedges. Starting with wide edge, roll to center to make crescent shape. Pinch ends to hold shape. Place on greased cookie sheets, allowing room for rolls to rise. Let rise for 1-2 hours, until light.
5. Bake at 375° for 10-12 minutes.

Grandma's Onion Bread
Lydia Lapp
Kinzers, PA
Double Wedding Ring

Makes 2 loaves

5¹/2-6 cups flour
2 pkgs. dry yeast
2¹/4 cups water
1 pkg. dry onion soup mix
2 Tbsp. sugar
2 Tbsp. shortening
1 tsp. salt
1 Tbsp. liquid smoke (optional)
1 Tbsp. cornmeal
1 beaten egg white
1 Tbsp. water

1. Combine 2¹/2 cups flour with yeast.
2. In saucepan combine 2¹/4 cups water and soup mix. Simmer covered for 10 minutes. Stir in sugar, shortening, salt, and liquid smoke. Add to dry mixture.
3. Beat at low speed with mixer for half a minute, scraping bowl. Beat 3 minutes at high speed. Stir in remaining flour to make a moderately stiff dough.
3. Knead on floured surface until smooth, 8-10 minutes. Shape into ball. Place in greased bowl. Turn once. Cover and let rise in warm place until double, about 1 hour.
4. Punch down. Divide in half. Cover. Let rest 10 minutes.
5. Shape into 2 long loaves, tapering ends. Place on greased baking sheet sprinkled with cornmeal. Gash tops diagonally, 1/4 inch deep. Cover.
6. Let rise until double, about 30 minutes.
7. Bake at 375° for 20 minutes. Brush with mixture of egg white and 1 Tbsp. water. Bake 10-15 minutes longer. Remove from baking sheet. Cool.

Popovers
Margaret F. Moehl
Pinckney, MI
Christmas Treasures
Mary-Lou Miller
Rochester, NY
Cross-stitch

Makes 5-9 popovers

1 cup flour
1/2 tsp. salt
1 cup milk
2 eggs, beaten
1 Tbsp. melted butter

1. Beat together flour, salt, milk, eggs, and butter until mixture reaches the consistency of heavy cream.
2. Pour into greased muffin tins or popover tins.
3. Bake at 425° for 35-45 minutes. Remove immediately from pans and serve.

Cloud Biscuits
Martha Darr
Dexter, MI
Dorothy Farmwald
Sullivan, IL
Anniversary Quilt

Makes 12-15 servings

2 cups flour
2 Tbsp. sugar
3 tsp. baking powder
1/2 tsp. cream of tartar
1/2 tsp. salt
1/2 cup shortening
1 egg
2/3 cup milk

1. Sift together dry ingredients. Cut in shortening.
2. Combine egg and milk. Stir into dry mixture until dough follows fork.
3. Turn out on floured board. Knead gently, about 20 strokes.
4. Pat or roll to 1/2-inch thick. Cut with round cutter and place on ungreased baking sheet.
5. Bake at 450° for 10-14 minutes.

Tortillas de Harina
Lisa Schafer
Hampton, VA

Makes 6-10 tortillas

1/2 pkg. dry yeast or 1/2 tsp. baking powder
1/2 cup warm water
2 cups flour
1/2 tsp. salt
1/4 cup shortening
1/4 cup sugar

1. Dissolve yeast in warm water. Mix in remaining ingredients. Let stand at room temperature for 30 minutes.
2. Pinch off pieces of dough and flatten into tortillas. Brown in skillet in a little oil.
3. Use with any of various tortilla dishes.

Scottish Tea Scones
Lynn Clark
Emmitsburg, MD
Dad's Cozy Comforter

Makes approximately 16 scones

2 cups flour
1/2 cup sugar
2 tsp. cream of tartar
1 tsp. baking soda
3/4 tsp. salt
1/2 cup shortening
1/2 cup raisins or currants
2 eggs, slightly beaten
1/4 cup milk

1. Sift together flour, sugar, cream of tartar, baking soda, and salt. Blend in shortening until mixture resembles fine bread crumbs.
2. Gently stir in remaining ingredients. Mix with fork.
3. Divide into two parts. Turn each part out on a floured board. Do not handle. Flatten with a rolling pin into circles about 1/2" thick. Cut each circle into 8 wedges and place on greased cookie sheets.
3. Bake at 400° for 15 minutes, or until golden brown.
4. Serve warm, lightly buttered. Cover with towel to keep warm.

Sugarloaf Scones
Beverly Simmons
Boulder, CO
Spirit of the Carousel

Makes 8-10 scones

2 cups flour
1/4 cup sugar
2 tsp. baking powder
1/2 tsp. salt
3 Tbsp. oil
1/2 cup raisins or dried cranberries
3 Tbsp. chopped crystallized ginger
3/4 cup milk
1 Tbsp. milk
1 tsp. sugar
lemon or orange zest
1/8 tsp. cinnamon

1. Combine flour, sugar, baking powder, and salt. Using a fork, stir in oil until mixture forms pea-sized lumps.
2. Add raisins and ginger. Add 3/4 cup milk, stirring to form soft dough.
3. Turn out onto lightly floured surface and gently pat and turn into 8-10" round, approximately 1/2" thick.
4. Cut into 8-10 wedges and place on cookie sheet. Brush with 1 Tbsp. milk and sprinkle with sugar, zest, and cinnamon.
5. Bake at 400° for 10-12 minutes.

Variation: Instead of raisins and ginger, add chocolate chips and nuts.

Bailey's Irish Cream Scones

Mary Ann Wasick
West Allis, WI
Baltimore Album

Makes 24-26 scones

3¹/2 cups biscuit mix
2 Tbsp. sugar
2 tsp. margarine, melted
1 egg, beaten
¹/2 cup vanilla yogurt
¹/2 cup Bailey's Irish Cream
2-3 Tbsp. sugar

1. Mix together biscuit mix and 2 Tbsp. sugar. Cut margarine into dry mixture with a fork.
2. Beat together egg, yogurt, and Bailey's Irish Cream until smooth.
3. Add to dry mixture. Mix well.
4. Knead dough about 10 times on floured surface. Cut dough in half. Flatten each half on an ungreased, non-stick jelly roll pan. Sprinkle dough with 2-3 Tbsp. sugar.

5. Cut each dough square into 12-13 smaller squares.
4. Bake at 425° for 12-14 minutes.

Lemon Blueberry Muffins

Jan Moore
Wellsville, KS
Grandmother's Flower Garden

Makes 12 muffins

2 cups flour
¹/4 cup sugar
1¹/2 tsp. baking powder
¹/2 tsp. baking soda
²/3 cup plain nonfat yogurt
1 egg
2 Tbsp. vegetable oil
1 tsp. finely shredded lemon peel
1 cup fresh or frozen blueberries

1. In large mixing bowl, stir together dry ingredients. Make a well in the center of dry mixture.

2. In medium bowl combine yogurt, egg, oil, and lemon peel. Mix well and add to well in dry mixture. Stir only until moistened (batter will be lumpy).
3. Add blueberries. Fill greased muffin cups ²/3 full.
4. Bake at 400° for 20-25 minutes or until toothpick in center comes out clean.
5. Cool for 5 minutes. Serve warm.

Blueberry Muffins

Betty J. Smith
Punxsutawney, PA
Country Bride

Makes 2 dozen muffins

¹/2 cup shortening
1 cup sugar
1 egg
2 cups flour
4 tsp. baking powder
1 cup blueberries

1. Cream together shortening and sugar. Beat in egg.
2. Stir flour and baking powder together. Gently stir into creamed mixture, being careful not to overmix.
2. Fold in blueberries.
3. Fill greased muffin tins ²/3 full.
4. Bake at 350° for 30 minutes.

It was a Christmas in the early 1930s, the middle of the Great Depression. I was nine years old, and we had no money to spend on storebought gifts. Without my mother's knowledge, I went to each of our farm neighbors and asked if they would please save scraps of material from their sewing and let me have them.

By Christmas I had a large box of colorful prints for a quilt, and my mother always said it was the best gift she ever received. I now own the Dresden Plate she made with those scraps and remember the prints from my own dresses and those of my friends.
—*Leila Orr Gormley, Van Nuys, CA*

Cherry Buttermilk Muffins

Tanya Potenta
Bridgewater, NJ
Biscuit Crib Quilt

Makes 12 muffins

1/2 cup dried cherries
3 Tbsp. orange juice
1 cup flour
3/4 cup cornmeal
1/2 tsp. baking powder
1 tsp. baking soda
1/4 tsp. salt
1 egg, beaten
1/4 cup sugar
1 cup buttermilk
6 Tbsp. butter, melted

1. Combine cherries and orange juice in bowl and microwave for 3 minutes. Cool to lukewarm.
2. In medium-sized bowl, mix together flour, cornmeal, baking powder, baking soda, and salt.
3. In large bowl cream together egg and sugar. Stir in buttermilk and butter. Gently stir in dry ingredients. Fold in cherries, being careful not to overmix.
4. Pour into greased muffin tins. Bake at 375° for 15 minutes, or until golden brown.

Christmas Muffins

Carla Woodworth
Lyndonville, NY

Makes 12 muffins

2 cups flour
2/3 cup sugar
1 Tbsp. baking powder
1/2 tsp. baking soda
1 tsp. ground cinnamon
1/2 tsp. salt
1/2 cup fresh or frozen cranberries, coarsely chopped
1/2 cup dried cranberries
3/4 cup plain yogurt
1/2 cup unsalted butter, melted
1/2 cup milk
1 egg
1/2 cup chopped unsalted pistachios

1. Combine flour, sugar, baking powder, baking soda, cinnamon, and salt. Stir fresh and dried cranberries into the dry ingredients.
2. Whisk together yogurt, butter, milk, and egg until smooth. Add to dry ingredients. Fold just until evenly moistened. Do not overmix.
3. Divide batter evenly among the muffin cups. Sprinkle pistachios evenly on top.
4. Bake at 400° for 18-20 minutes, or until tops are golden and toothpick inserted in center comes out clean.
5. Cool before removing from muffin tins.

Orange-Glazed Raisin Muffins

Roseann Wilson
Albuquerque, NM
Patchwork

Makes 12 muffins

1 2/3 cups flour
1/2 cup wheat germ
1/3 cup sugar
1 Tbsp. baking powder
1/2 tsp. salt
3/4 cup raisins
1 cup milk
1/4 cup oil
1 egg, slightly beaten
2 Tbsp. grated orange peel
1/2 cup powdered sugar
1 Tbsp. orange juice

1. Combine flour, wheat germ, sugar, baking powder, salt, and raisins. Mix well.
2. Combine milk, oil, egg, and orange peel. Stir into dry mixture, just until ingredients are moistened.
3. Fill greased or paper-lined muffin cups 2/3 full.
4. Bake at 400° for 18-20 minutes. Cool on wire rack.
5. Combine powdered sugar and orange juice. Drizzle over slightly cooled muffins.

Pumpkin Raisin Muffins

Marina Salume
Half Moon Bay, CA

Makes 12 muffins

2 cups flour
4 tsp. baking powder
1/2 tsp. salt
1 tsp. cinnamon
1/2 cup raisins
1 egg
4 Tbsp. sugar
1/2 cup cooked mashed
   pumpkin
1/2 cup milk
4 Tbsp. butter, melted

1. Sift together flour, baking powder, salt, and cinnamon. Stir in raisins.
2. Beat egg. Add sugar, pumpkin, milk, and butter. Stir into dry ingredients, just until blended.
3. Fill greased muffin pans 2/3 full.
4. Bake at 400° for 20-25 minutes.

Chocolate Chip Banana Muffins

Susan J. Miller
Millersburg, OH
Patchwork

Makes 12 large muffins

1 Tbsp. instant coffee
   granules
1 Tbsp. hot water
3 bananas, mashed
1 cup butter, softened
1 1/4 cups sugar
1 egg
2 1/2 cups flour
1 tsp. baking powder
1/2 tsp. baking soda
1/2 tsp. salt
1 cup chocolate chips

1. Dissolve coffee in hot water. Stir in bananas.
2. Cream together butter, sugar, and egg until fluffy. Add to banana mixture.
3. Sift together flour, baking powder, baking soda, and salt. Stir gently into creamed mixture. Fold in chocolate chips.
4. Pour into greased muffin tins.
5. Bake at 350° for 18-20 minutes.

Gingerbread Muffins

Nicole Koloski
East Sandwich, MA
*Piecemakers 1995
Calendar Quilt*

Makes 12 muffins

1/2 cup butter, softened
2 Tbsp. packed brown
   sugar
1 cup sour cream
1/2 cup light molasses
2 eggs
2 cups flour
1 Tbsp. baking powder
1/2 tsp. baking soda
3 cups bran flakes
1/2 cup raisins

1. Beat butter until smooth. Add brown sugar and beat until fluffy. Add sour cream and molasses and beat until blended. Beat in eggs.
2. Sift together flour, baking powder, and baking soda.
3. Gently fold dry ingredinets into creamed mixture, being careful not to overmix. Carefully fold in bran flakes and raisins.
4. Evenly divide mix into greased muffin tins.
5. Bake at 350° for 20-25 minutes. Cool in pan for 5 minutes before removing.

Swedish Christmas Muffins
Sharon Peterson
Hemet, CA
Christmas Wallhanging

Makes 18 muffins

2 cups flour
1/2 cup wheat germ
1 tsp. ground cardamom
1 tsp. salt
1/2 cup sugar
4 tsp. baking powder
1 tsp. baking soda
1/2 cup chopped almonds
1/2 cup raisins
1 cup glazed fruit
2 eggs
1 cup buttermilk
1/2 cup butter, melted

1. Combine flour, wheat germ, cardamom, salt, sugar, baking powder, baking soda, chopped almonds, raisins, and glazed fruit.
2. Whisk together eggs, buttermilk, and butter. Add to dry ingredients. Stir well.
3. Spoon into greased muffin tins.
4. Bake at 375° for 20 minutes.

Icebox Cinnamon Muffins
Rosaria Strachan
Old Greenwich, CT
Friendship Quilt

Makes 20 muffins

2 cups flour
2 Tbsp. cinnamon
pinch of salt
4 tsp. baking powder
1 cup sugar
1 cup milk
1/2 cup butter, melted
2 eggs, beaten
1/2 cup chopped nuts

1. Sift flour twice, then sift with cinnamon, salt, and baking powder.
2. Add remaining ingredients and mix well.
3. Store in refrigerator or put in greased muffin pans and bake at 350° for 20-25 minutes.

This batter may be stored in the refrigerator for a few days. The batter can be taken directly from the refrigerator and baked immediately.

Refrigerator Bran Muffins
Karen M. Rusten
Waseca, MN
Angela's Kitty Quilt
Patti Boston
Newark, OH
Cathedral Window

Makes about 60 muffins

2 cups 100% bran or bran flakes cereal
2 cups boiling water
1-3 cups sugar, according to your preference
1 cup shortening
4 eggs, beaten, or 6 egg whites
1 quart buttermilk
5 cups flour or 2 1/2 cups flour and 2 1/2 cups wheat flour
5 tsp. baking soda
1 tsp. salt (optional)
4 cups all-bran cereal

1. Pour hot water over 100% bran. Set aside.
2. Cream together sugar and shortening. Add eggs and buttermilk. Mix well.
3. Stir in flour, baking soda, salt, all-bran, and 100% bran and water. Stir until mixed.
4. Place in large jars in refrigerator.
5. Bake, as needed, in greased muffin tins at 400° for 15-20 minutes.

Long Horn Sweet Rolls
Faye Meyers
San Jose, CA
Grandmother's Fan

Makes 2 dozen rolls

1 1/2 cups milk
1 cake yeast or 2 pkgs. dry yeast
1/2 cup shortening, melted
1/2 cup sugar
1 tsp. salt
3 eggs
4 cups flour

1. Scald milk and cool to lukewarm. Dissolve yeast in milk.
2. Stir in shortening, sugar, salt, eggs, and as much flour as possible.
3. Knead in the rest of the flour on a floured board until the dough is no longer sticky.
4. Divide dough into 3 balls. Roll out each like a pie crust, about 1/2 inch thick.
5. Cut each circle into 8 pie wedges. Start at the big end of each wedge and roll up.
6. Let rise until double in size.
7. Bake at 400° for 10-15 minutes.

Cinnamon Knots
Jean Johnson
Dallas, OR
Ducky Weather

Makes 16 knots

2 pkgs. dry yeast
2 cups milk, scalded and cooled
2 eggs, beaten slightly
2 Tbsp. sugar
1 1/2 tsp. salt
6 cups flour, or more
4 Tbsp. oil
1 cup margarine, melted
2 cups sugar
3 Tbsp. cinnamon

1. Dissolve yeast in 1/4 cup milk. Stir in remaining milk, eggs, sugar, and salt. Add half of flour, then the oil, then the remaining flour. Stir well.
2. Grease top of dough. Cover with plastic and let rise until double in bulk, about 1 1/2 hours. Dough will look sticky.
3. Pour margarine into flat dish. In bowl, mix together sugar and cinnamon.
4. Punch dough down. Take about 1/3 cup dough in hand. Roll into rope about 8" long. Dip in margarine, then in sugar/cinnamon mixture and tie into a knot. Place in jelly roll pan. Repeat with all remaining dough. Let rise until double in bulk.
5. Bake at 400° for 15-20 minutes.

Cinnamon Rolls
Lorene P. Meyer
Wayland, IA
Sampler

Makes 4 dozen rolls

1 pkg. dry yeast
1/2 cup warm water
2 cups sugar
2 tsp. salt
2 tsp. vanilla
1/2 cup shortening, lard, or margarine
3 cups milk, scalded
3 eggs, beaten
9-10 cups flour
1/4 cup butter, melted
2 cups brown sugar
4 tsp. cinnamon
2 cups nuts

Frosting:
6 Tbsp. margarine, softened
2 Tbsp. flour
1/4 cup milk
2 tsp. vanilla or maple flavoring
4 cups powdered sugar

1. Dissolve yeast in warm water. Set aside.
2. Mix together sugar, salt, vanilla, and shortening. Add milk. Mix until shortening is melted. Cool to lukewarm. Add eggs.
3. Stir in 4 cups flour and mix well. Let rest 20 minutes. Add more flour and knead as soon as dough can be handled. Knead at least 10 minutes. Place in greased bowl. Turn over to grease top. Let rise until double.
4. Punch down and let rise

again until double.
5. Divide dough and roll out. Spread with melted butter. Sprinkle with brown sugar, cinnamon, and nuts. Roll up jelly-roll fashion. Slice 1-inch thick. Place in greased pans. Let rise until double.
6. Bake at 425° for 12 minutes, or until lightly browned. Frost while warm.
7. Mix together all frosting ingredients. Beat well. Spread frosting over individual rolls.

Sweet Rolls
Barbara Dunham
Knowlesville, NY
Irish Chain

Makes 3 dozen rolls

2 pkgs. dry yeast
2 cups lukewarm water
4 Tbsp. shortening
3 heaping Tbsp. sugar
1 tsp. salt
6 cups flour
3 Tbsp. margarine, softened
1 Tbsp. cinnamon
1 cup brown sugar

1. Dissolve yeast in water. Mix well. Stir in shortening, sugar, and salt. Gradually stir in flour.
2. Turn onto floured surface and knead well. Place in greased bowl. Cover and allow to rise in warm place till double in size.
2. Divide dough in half. Roll out each half into 6" x 18"

rectangle. Spread top with margarine. Sprinkle with brown sugar and cinnamon.
3. Roll jelly-roll fashion and cut into 1½-inch rolls. Place in 9" x 13" pan. Cover and let rise until double in size.
4. Bake at 400° for 20-25 minutes. Frost while still warm with a light glaze.

Easy Cinnamon Buns
Trella Kauffman
East Petersburg, PA
Railroad Crossing

Makes 30 servings

4 pkgs. dry yeast
1 cup warm water
1 cup margarine
1 cup sugar
4 tsp. salt
3½ cups hot water
10-12 cups flour
⅓ cup butter, melted
2 cups brown sugar
1½ tsp. cinnamon
1 cup nuts, chopped

Topping 1:
(optional—mix together and place in bottom of pan before adding dough, step 6, below)
1 cup heavy cream
1 cup brown sugar
1 cup chopped nuts

Topping 2:
(optional—mix together and frost buns after they have cooled)
4 cups powdered sugar
1 tsp. vanilla
⅓ cup hot water

1. Dissolve yeast in warm water. Set aside.
2. Dissolve margarine, sugar, and salt in hot water. Cool to lukewarm and add to yeast mixture.
3. Beat in enough flour to make a thick, but still sticky, dough (not stiff enough for kneading).
4. Place in greased bowl. Grease top and let rise until double in size. Sprinkle flour on counter and roll dough into 8" x 42", ½" thick, rectangle.
5. Spread with melted butter, brown sugar, cinnamon, and nuts.
6. Roll up and cut into 1-inch slices. Place into greased pans and let rise until double in size.
7. Bake at 350° for 15-20 minutes, or until lightly browned.

Apple Cinnamon Rolls

Ev-Ann Johnson
Marquette, MI
Dresden Plate Heart

Makes 4 dozen rolls

3-3³/4 cups flour
1/2 tsp. salt
1/4 cup sugar
1 pkg. dry yeast
1/4 cup margarine
1 cup applesauce
1 egg

Filling:
1/4 cup butter or margarine
3/4 cup cinnamon-
    flavored, or chunky
    applesauce
1/4 cup brown sugar
1/4 cup chopped nuts
1¹/2 tsp. cinnamon

1. In large bowl combine 1 cup flour, salt, sugar, and yeast.
2. In saucepan melt margarine. Stir in applesauce. Add to yeast mixture. Stir in egg. Blend to moisten. Stir in 1³/4-2 cups flour.
3. On floured surface knead in 1/4-3/4 cup more flour.
4. Let rise until double in size. Divide dough in half. Roll each half into 12" x 15" rectangle.
5. Mix together all filling ingredients and spread half on each rectangle. Roll up jelly-roll fashion. Cut in 1" slices and place in 2 greased 9" x 13" pans. Refrigerate for at least 8 hours.
6. Let stand for 30 minutes

before baking. Bake at 375° for 25-30 minutes.

Sticky Rolls

Carole Whaling
New Tripoli, PA
Drunkard's Path
Gloria R. Yoder
Dundee, OH

Makes 24 rolls

1/2 cup milk
1/2 cup sugar
1 tsp. salt
2/3 cup shortening
1/2 cup warm water
2 pkgs. dry yeast
4 eggs, slightly beaten
4¹/2 cups flour
1¹/2 cups brown sugar
1 cup light corn syrup
1/2 cup margarine
3 Tbsp. margarine,
    softened
1 Tbsp. cinnamon
1/4 cup sugar
1/4-1/2 cup raisins
    (optional)

1. In saucepan combine milk, sugar, salt, and shortening. Heat until shortening is melted. Cool to lukewarm.
2. In large bowl sprinkle yeast over warm water. Stir to dissolve. Add milk mixture, eggs, and 2 cups flour. Beat until smooth.
3. Add enough remaining flour to make soft dough. Turn onto floured surface and knead well. Let rise 1-1¹/2 hours until double in size.

4. While dough is rising, cook together brown sugar, syrup, and 1/2 cup margarine in saucepan. Boil for 3 minutes, stirring constantly. Divide between 2 9" x 9" pans.
5. Punch down dough. Knead a few times. Let stand for 5 minutes. Divide into 2 pieces. Roll each into a rectangle. Spread with 3 Tbsp. margarine. Sprinkle with 1/4 cup sugar, cinnamon, and raisins.
6. Roll up jelly-roll fashion and cut into 12 slices. Place in prepared 9" x 9" pans. Let rise 1 hour.
7. Bake at 350° for 25 minutes.

Raspberry Sweet Rolls

Rebecca Meyerkorth
Wamego, KS
Challenge Quilt

Makes 24 rolls

3¹/2-4 cups flour, or more
1/2 cup sugar
1 tsp. salt
2 pkgs. active dry yeast
1 cup milk
1/2 cup margarine or
    butter
2 eggs
1/4 cup melted margarine
1/2 cup red raspberry
    preserves
1 cup powdered sugar
2-3 Tbsp. milk

1. Combine 1¹/2 cups flour, sugar, salt, and yeast.

2. In saucepan heat milk and 1/2 cup margarine until very warm. Add to flour mixture. Stir in eggs. Blend until moistened.

3. Stir in an additional 1 3/4-2 cups flour until dough pulls away from sides of bowl.

4. On floured surface knead in 1/4-1/2 cup flour until dough is smooth and elastic, about 3-5 minutes. Place dough in greased bowl and cover with plastic. Let rise in warm place until double in size, 45-60 minutes.

5. Punch down dough. Turn onto lightly floured surface. Divide into 24 pieces. Roll each piece into 15" rope. On greased cookie sheets, loosely coil each rope into a small circle, sealing ends underneath. Cover. Let rise in warm place until double, 15-20 minutes.

6. Brush rolls carefully with melted margarine. Make deep thumbprint in center of each roll. Fill with 1 tsp. preserves.

7. Bake at 350° for 10-20 minutes. Remove from pan and brush again with melted margarine. Cool.

8. Combine powdered sugar and milk. Drizzle over rolls.

Quick Danish Sweet Rolls

Dorothea K. Ladd
Ballston Lake, NY
Amish Easter Baskets

Makes 30 rolls

1 cup milk
4 cups flour
1/4 cup sugar
1 tsp. salt
1 tsp. lemon peel
1 cup butter or margarine,
   room temperature
1 pkg. dry yeast
1/4 cup warm water
2 eggs, beaten

Filling:
1 1/2 cups chopped, peeled
   apples
3/4 cup chopped walnuts
1/3 cup sugar
1 1/2 tsp. cinnamon

1. In saucepan scald milk. Cool to lukewarm.

2. In large bowl combine flour, sugar, salt, and lemon peel. Cut in butter.

3. Dissolve yeast in warm water. Add yeast mixture, milk, and eggs to flour mixture. Combine lightly. Cover tightly with plastic wrap and refrigerate from 2 hours to 2 days.

4. Make filling by combining apples, walnuts, sugar, and cinnamon.

5. On a well floured surface, roll half of dough into a 15" x 18" rectangle. Spread half of the filling over the dough. Fold down 1/3 of the dough and fold up 1/3 of the dough, overlapping in order to create 3 layers of dough. Rectangle should now measure 6" x 15."

6. Cut into 2" strips and twist. Bring ends of each strip together to form a circle and pinch. Place each circle on a greased cookie sheet. Repeat with second half of dough.

7. Bake at 400° for 15 minutes. When cool, drizzle light frosting on top.

My mother-in-law was a wonderful cook. She always brought these rolls to every family gathering. She made them fresh the morning of the event, regardless of what the weather was. She usually had to double the recipe as the family of five children grew and grew with newer generations.

Don't be scared by the use of yeast in this recipe. It really is an easy one. I have made them without the nuts because my daughter doesn't care for nuts. I have also made them with just butter spread on the rectangle of dough. They are more like a plain dinner roll that way. You may also change the nuts from pecans to your favorite!
—*Marilyn Bloom Wallace, Alfred, ME*

Auntie Anna's Houska (Slavic Bread)
Barb Jensen
Troy, MI
Trip to Tucson

Makes 1 braid or 2 loaves

1 pkg. dry yeast
1 pint milk, warmed
1/2 cup sugar
6 cups flour
1 tsp. salt
1-2 eggs
1/2 cup butter or
   margarine, softened
1/2 tsp. cinnamon,
   nutmeg, or mace

Filling:
1/4 cup brown sugar
2 Tbsp. cinnamon

1. Dissolve yeast in 1/2 cup warmed milk. Stir in 2 tsp. sugar. Let stand.
2. Sift together flour and salt.
3. Beat eggs. Add remaining sugar and milk, butter, cinnamon, flour, and salt, and yeast mixture. Dough should be soft and springy.
4. Knead on floured surface until very smooth. Cover with cloth and let rise in a warm place until double in size.
5. To make a braid, lay dough on a floured surface and cut it into 3 sections. Roll each into a long cord. Lay sections across one another and braid them from the center toward the ends. Put in breadpan.
5. Bake at 350° for 45-60 minutes. Bread is done when you tap the outside and it sounds hollow.
6. To make two loaves, divide dough in half. Roll out each piece 1/4" thick into a 12" x 18" rectangle.
7. To prepare filling combine brown sugar and cinnamon.
8. Spread each half of dough with half of cinnamon sugar. Roll up from short end and pinch ends to keep filling from leaking out. Bake as directed in Step 5.

Note: This recipe is very old. My great-aunt used to make this Slavic bread for us when we were little. She had no written recipe, so she simply told us how to make it.

Grammie Wallace's Pecan Rolls
Marilyn Bloom Wallace
Alfred, ME
Sailboats

Makes 16 rolls

Dough:
1/2 cup milk, scalded
3 Tbsp. butter
3 Tbsp. sugar
1 1/2 tsp. salt
1/2 cup warm water
1 pkg. yeast
1 egg, well beaten
3 1/4 to 3 1/2 cups flour

Topping:
1/2 cup brown sugar
3 Tbsp. maple syrup
1 Tbsp. butter, melted
1/4 cup chopped pecans

Filling:
1/4 cup brown sugar
1 tsp. cinnamon
1/4 cup chopped pecans

1. In large bowl combine scalded milk with butter, sugar, and salt. Stir until melted. Cool to lukewarm.
2. Dissolve yeast in warm water. Add to milk mixture.
3. Add egg and flour. Mix until mixture is no longer sticky. Cover and let rise for 15 to 30 minutes.
4. Meanwhile, in saucepan combine brown sugar, maple syrup, butter, and pecans. Bring to a boil and cook for 3 minutes.
5. Roll dough into an 8" x 20" rectangle on a floured board.
6. Mix together filling ingredients. Sprinkle over dough. Roll lengthwise. Cut into 16 pieces with a sharp knife.
7. Grease 16 muffin tins well. Put about 1 tsp. of topping mixture into the bottom of each muffin tin. Add rolls, cut side into the mixture. Cover and let rise for 15-30 minutes.
8. Bake at 350° for 18 to 20 minutes or until light brown.
9. Immediately invert muffins onto tin foil. Scrape any remaining buttery mixture out of muffin cups and add to the rolls.
10. These are wonderful served hot or cold.

Nut Rolls
Patricia M. Olinger
Lyndonville, NY

Makes 3-4 dozen rolls

1 pkg. dry yeast
2 Tbsp. sugar
1/2-3/4 cup warm water
2 cups butter
6 egg yolks
2 whole eggs
5 cups flour
1/2 cup powdered sugar

Filling:
2 cups sugar
1/2-3/4 cup water
1 tsp. vanilla
2 cups chopped nuts
powdered sugar

1. Dissolve yeast and sugar in warm water. Mix in butter, egg yolks, eggs, and flour. Chill dough.
2. Roll into walnut-sized balls and chill again.
3. Roll each ball in powdered sugar, in order to keep them from sticking. Then flatten each into a 2-inch circle.
4. Mix together filling ingredients. Put a spoonful of filling in the center of each circle and roll up.
4. Place on greased cookie sheets and bake at 350° for 10 minutes, or until lightly browned. Cool, then sprinkle with powdered sugar.

Potica (Nut Roll)
Peggy Smith
Hamlin, KY
Basket of Blooms

Makes 2 rolls (about 20 servings)

Dough:
1/2 cup butter or
     margarine
1/4 cup sour cream
1/2 cup evaporated milk
2 egg yolks
1 pkg. dry yeast
1 Tbsp. sugar
1/4 tsp. salt
2 1/2 to 2 3/4 cups flour
powdered sugar

Filling:
1 cup ground nuts
     (pecans or walnuts)
1/4 cup sugar
1 Tbsp. honey
2 egg whites, beaten until
     frothy

1. Melt butter. Cool. Add sour cream, milk, egg yolks, and yeast to butter in medium-sized bowl.
2. Add sugar, salt, and flour. Mix well.
3. Divide into two balls. Wrap each in plastic and refrigerate overnight in plastic bags.
4. Mix all filling ingredients together. Chill until ready to use.
5. On the next day, allow the dough to warm up a bit, then roll out each ball very thin into powdered sugar. Spread each rectangle of dough with half the filling.
6. Roll each up jelly-roll style. Place each seam-side

down on greased cookie sheet. Let rise until double, about 1 hour.
7. Bake at 375° for 30 minutes. Remove from pan. Cool.
8. To serve slice into serving size pieces. Dust with powdered sugar.

Each year we make 8 Potica around Thanksgiving and freeze them individually. When we send Christmas gifts to my brother's family in California, we use the Potica as fillers in the box. When the package arrives in California, they enjoy a little touch of home. One year we were running late on making the Potica and my brother said, "Don't send the package without the Potica, even if it arrives in January."

Holiday Bread
Nicole Koloski
East Sandwich, MA
Piecemakers 1995
Calendar Quilt

Makes 4 loaves

2 pkgs. dry yeast
2 cups lukewarm water
1/2 cup sugar
2 tsp. salt
2/3 cup instant nonfat dry
  milk
2 eggs
1/2 cup soft shortening
1/4 tsp. yellow food
  coloring
1 1/4 cups raisins
1/2 cup slivered toasted
  almonds
7 2/3 cups flour

Frosting:
3 cups powdered sugar
3 Tbsp. water
1 tsp. lemon juice
1 tsp. lemon rind

1. Dissolve yeast in 1/2 cup water. Add sugar, salt, dry milk, eggs, shortening, remaining 1 1/2 cups water, food coloring, raisins, and almonds. Mix well.
2. Stir in 3 1/2 cups flour. Mix well. Continue adding flour until dough begins to cling together.
3. Turn out onto a well floured surface and knead until a smooth elastic dough is formed. Place dough in a well greased bowl. Turn to grease top. Cover tightly with plastic wrap and place in warm place to rise until double in bulk, about 45 minutes.
4. Punch down dough and divide into four equal pieces. Form dough into balls and place in 4 well greased coffee cans. Place cans on cookie sheet and let rise until doubled.
5. Bake in cans at 375° for 40 minutes, or until well browned. Gently loosen from cans and cool on wire racks.
6. Combine powdered sugar, water, lemon juice, and lemon rind in bowl. Pour over bread while still warm.

Christmas Morning Bread
Shirley Hedman
Schenectady, NY
Stars for Many Mornings

Makes 1 braid

4 1/2-5 cups flour
2 pkgs. dry yeast
1/2 cup nonfat dry milk
1/4 tsp. cinnamon
1/4 tsp. nutmeg
1 cup water
1/2 cup sugar
1/2 cup margarine
1/2 tsp. salt
3 eggs, beaten (reserve 2
  Tbsp. for glaze)
sliced almonds
sugar

1. Mix together 2 cups flour, yeast, dry milk, cinnamon, and nutmeg.
2. Heat water, sugar, margarine, and salt to 120°. Add to flour mixture.
3. Add eggs and beat at low speed until blended, then at high speed for 3 minutes.
4. Stir in enough remaining flour to make moderately soft dough that pulls away from sides of bowl. Cover bowl and refrigerate 2 to 48 hours.
5. Divide dough into thirds. Shape into 3 22-inch strands. Braid 3 strands together.
6. Make a circle with braid. Seal ends together and put an oven-proof glass in center of circle (so dough won't fill in from rising). Let rise until nearly double, about 1 hour.
5. Brush with reserved beaten egg and sprinkle with sugar and almonds.
6. Bake at 350° for 25-30 minutes until golden brown.

Jule Kage (Scandinavian Christmas Bread)

Adelle Horst Ward
Scotia, NY
Johnny's Airplane

Makes 3 loaves

2 Tbsp. yeast
2 cups warm water
2 Tbsp. sugar
1 tsp. salt
1/2 cup flour
1 cup lukewarm water
1/4 cup dry milk
1/2 cup sugar
2 tsp. salt
2 eggs
1/2 cup shortening
2 cups flour
2 tsp. cardamom
1 cup raisins
1/2 cup candied cherries
1/2 cup mixed candied
    fruit
1/2 cup sliced almonds
3 1/2 cups flour

1. Combine yeast and 2 cups warm water. Let stand 5 minutes.
2. Add 2 Tbsp. sugar, 1 tsp. salt, and 1/2 cup flour. Beat and let rise 12-15 minutes.
3. Stir in 1 cup lukewarm water, dry milk, 1/2 cup sugar, 2 tsp. salt, eggs, shortening, and 2 cups flour. Beat for 2 minutes.
4. Add cardamom, raisins, cherries, fruit, and almonds. Mix well.
5. Knead in remaining 3 1/2 cups flour. Let rest for 10 minutes.
6. Divide into 3 balls and let

rest 10 minutes longer.
7. Shape into round loaves and place in greased pie pans. Let rise for 40-45 minutes.
8. Bake at 375° for 30-35 minutes. Cool. Frost and decorate wtih cherries and sliced almonds.

Christmas Bread

Mary Ann Calhoun
Johns Island, SC
Michael's Quilt

Makes 2 full-sized loaves

2 pkgs. dry yeast
1/2 cup lukewarm water
1 cup milk, scalded
1/2 cup sugar
1/4 cup shortening
1 1/2 tsp. salt
5-5 1/4 cups flour, sifted
2 eggs, beaten
1/2 tsp. vanilla
1/4 tsp. nutmeg
1/2 cup chopped mixed
    fruits and peels
1 cup seedless raisins

Frosting:
2 cups powdered sugar
2 Tbsp. milk,
    approximately
1 tsp. vanilla
red and green candied
    cherries

1. Dissolve yeast in water.
2. Combine scalded milk, sugar, shortening, and salt. Cool to lukewarm. Stir in about 1 1/2 cups flour. Beat vigorously.
3. Add eggs, beat well. Stir

in yeast, vanilla, and nutmeg. Stir in chopped fruits, raisins, and enough remaining flour to make a soft dough.
4. Turn dough onto well-floured surface. Knead until smooth and elastic, about 6-8 minutes. Place dough in a lightly greased bowl, turning once to grease the surface. Cover dough and let rise until double in size, about 2 hours.
5. Punch down. Divide dough in half. Cover dough and let rest 10 minutes. Form dough into round shapes and place on greased baking sheet or place in greased bread pans. Cover and let rise until double, about 2 hours.
6. Bake at 350° for 30 minutes. Cool and frost.
7. To prepare frosting add milk to sugar until desired consistency is reached. Add vanilla. Mix well. Drizzle on top of each loaf. Decorate wtih candied cherries.

Mama's Holiday Yeast Bread

Joyce R. Swinney
Mooresville, IN
Double Wedding Ring

Makes 1 large loaf

1/4 cup warm water
1 Tbsp. sugar
1 pkg. dry yeast
1 cup buttermilk or sour milk
2 tsp. salt
1/3 cup sugar
1/4 cup butter, melted
2 eggs, beaten
4 cups flour
1/2 cup white raisins (optional)
1 Tbsp. grated orange rind
1 1/2 tsp. cinnamon
3/4 cup finely chopped nuts
1/3 cup packed brown sugar
3 Tbsp. orange juice concentrate
2 tsp. grated lemon rind
1/3 cup honey

1. Mix together warm water, 1 Tbsp. sugar, and yeast. Stir until yeast is dissolved. Let set until bubbly.
2. Heat buttermilk. Stir in salt, sugar, and butter until sugar is dissolved. Stir into yeast mixture. Add eggs. Mix well.
3. Stir in flour. Turn out onto floured surface and knead until elastic. Place dough in greased bowl. Turn to grease top. Let stand in warm place until double in size, about 2 hours.

4. Punch down. Place dough on floured surface and roll into 18" x 18" square.
5. Mix together raisins, orange rind, cinnamon, nuts, brown sugar, orange juice concentrate, lemon rind, and honey. Spread half of mixture over dough.
6. Roll up like jelly roll. Cut into 1" slices. Layer into 9"-10" greased tube pan. Let rise until double in size.
7. Bake at 350° for 1 hour.
8. Slide knife around edges to loosen. Turn out on cake rack to cool. Pour remaining raisin honey mixture over top of cake. Cool completely before cutting.

Stollen

Mary Evangeline Dillon
Tucson, AZ
Bunnies and Bows

Makes 2 loaves

2 cups warm water
2 cups milk
3 pkgs. dry yeast
2 eggs
1 tsp. salt
1 cup sugar
1 cup shortening
1 tsp. nutmeg
8 cups flour
1 cup chopped, blanched almonds
1 cup chopped citron
1/2 cup chopped candied cherries
1 cup raisins
2 Tbsp. grated lemon rind
1/4 cup soft butter

Frosting:
1 cup sifted powdered sugar
1-2 Tbsp. warm water
1/2 tsp. vanilla
1/2 tsp. lemon extract
1 tsp. grated lemon rind
candied red and green cherries

1. Mix together water and milk. Stir in yeast. Let set until yeast dissolves. Stir in eggs, salt, sugar, shortening, and nutmeg. Stir well.
2. Add 4 cups flour and stir well. Stir in remaining 4 cups and knead well. If dough is still soft, add a little more flour. Turn onto lightly floured board and knead until dough is smooth, elastic, and doesn't stick to board.
3. Place in greased bowl, turning once. Cover with damp cloth and let rise until double in size, about 1 1/2-2 hours.
4. When double, punch down. Turn in bowl. Let rise again until amost double, 30-45 minutes.
5. Turn onto lightly floured board. Flatten. Sprinkle with almonds, citron, cherries, raisins, and lemon rind. Knead into dough.
6. Divide dough in half. Pat each half into an oval about 8" x 12." Spread with soft butter. Fold in half the long way, and shape into crescent. Press folded edge firmly so it won't open.
7. Repeat for second half of dough. Place loaves on lightly greased heavy baking sheets. Brush tops with

melted butter. Let rise until double in size, about 35-45 minutes.

8. Bake at 375° for 20-25 minutes. Frost while warm and decorate with red and green cherries, cut and positioned to create holly clusters.

9. For frosting mix together all ingredients and drizzle over slightly warm stollen.

Christmas Poinsettia Bread

Linda V. Caldwell
Lockeford, CA
Log Cabin

Makes 10 servings

1/2 cup warm water
1 tsp. sugar
2 pkgs. dry yeast
3/4 cup warm milk
1/2 cup butter, softened
1/2 cup sugar
1 tsp. salt
1 tsp. ground cardamom
2 eggs, beaten
5-51/2 cups flour
2 Tbsp. melted butter
2 tsp. honey
candied cherries

1. Dissolve yeast and 1 tsp. sugar in water.

2. Combine milk and yeast mixture. Stir in butter, 1/2 cup sugar, salt, cardamom, eggs, and enough flour to make dough easy to handle.

3. Turn dough out on a lightly floured surface. Knead until smooth, about

10 minutes. Place in buttered bowl. Turn buttered side up. Cover and let rise until double, about 11/2 hours.

4. Punch down and divide into 2 parts. Roll each into a 12"-14" circle. Cut each circle into eight pie-shaped wedges.

5. Mix together melted butter and honey. Brush onto each wedge. Place wedges pinwheel fashion on lightly greased cookie sheet.

6. Brush tops with remaining honey mixture and garnish each with 3 candied cherries. Let rise until double.

7. Bake at 375° for 10-12 minutes until golden.

Christmas Braid

Judi Robb
Manhattan, KS
Mary Helen Wade
Sterling, IL
Reba M. Sharp
Manheim, PA

Makes 3 braids

5 to 51/2 cups flour
1 pkg. active dry yeast
2 cups milk
1/2 cup sugar
6 Tbsp. butter
1 tsp. salt
1 egg
1 cup raisins
1 cup finely chopped
    mixed candied fruits
    and peels
1 egg yolk

1. In large mixing bowl combine 3 cups of flour and the yeast.

2. In saucepan heat together milk, sugar, butter, and salt until warm (115° to 120°), stirring constantly. Add to dry mixture.

3. Add egg. Beat at low speed for 1/2 minute, scraping sides of bowl constantly.

4. Beat for 3 minutes at high speed. Stir in raisins, candied fruits and peels, and enough of the remaining flour to make a moderately stiff dough.

5. Turn out on floured surface. Knead until smooth and elastic (8 to 10 minutes). Place in greased bowl, turning once. Cover. Let rise in warm place until double (11/2 hours).

6. Divide dough into 3 portions. Then divide each portion into thirds. Roll each piece into a 15" rope.

7. Place 3 ropes on a greased baking sheet. Braid. Repeat with remaining ropes, forming 3 braids in all.

8. Cover and let rise in warm place until double (about 30-40 minutes). Combine egg yolk and 1 Tbsp. water. Brush about half of mixture over braids.

9. Bake at 350° for 10 minutes. Brush with remaining egg yolk mixture. Bake 10 minutes more. Cover with foil. Continue baking for 5 more minutes. Cool.

Eggnog Bread
Nicole Koloski
East Sandwich, MA
*Piecemakers 1995
Calendar Quilt*

Makes 1 loaf

3¹/2-4¹/2 cups flour, sifted
2 pkgs. dry yeast
¹/2 tsp. nutmeg or 1 tsp.
  freshly grated nutmeg
1 cup eggnog
¹/4 cup water
¹/4 cup butter
¹/4 cup sugar
1 tsp. salt
1 egg
1 cup chopped candied
  fruit
¹/2 cup raisins
¹/2 cup chopped pecans
1 Tbsp. cornmeal
1¹/2 cups powdered sugar
2-3 Tbsp. eggnog

1. Combine 1¹/2 cups flour,
yeast, and nutmeg in large
mixer bowl.
2. In saucepan heat eggnog,
water, butter, sugar, and
salt, stirring constantly until
warm. (Butter does not have
to be fully melted.) Add to
flour mixture.
3. Add egg and beat at
medium speed for 30 sec-
onds. Scrape sides of bowl.
Beat on high for 3 minutes.
Stir in dried fruit, raisins,
and nuts.
4. Add enough flour until
dough clings together and
forms smooth elastic dough.
Shape into ball and place in
greased bowl, turning dough
to grease the top. Cover with

plastic wrap and allow to rise
in warm spot for 1 to 1¹/2
hours, or until double in size.
5. Punch down. Place on
lightly floured surface and
let stand for 10 minutes.
Divide dough into 3 equal
pieces. Roll each piece into
an 18" rope.
6. Loosely braid ropes
together. Seal ends by pressing together and tucking
under. Cover and let rise
until double, 45-60 minutes.
Place on sheet which has
been lightly dusted with
cornmeal.
7. Bake at 350° for 10 minutes. Place tin foil loosely
over bread and bake an additional 15-20 minutes. To test
for doneness, tap bread. It
will sound hollow when done.
8. Combine powdered sugar
and 2-3 Tbsp. eggnog to make
glaze. Drizzle over loaf.

Almond Braid
Dottie Geraci
Burtonsville, MD
The Homestead

Makes 10 servings

Dough:
1 pkg. dry yeast
¹/2 cup warm water
¹/2 cup butter or
  margarine
¹/4 cup sugar
1¹/2 tsp. grated lemon
  rind
¹/2 tsp. salt
1 egg
2¹/2 cups sifted flour
1 tsp. vegetable oil

Filling:
¹/2 cup powdered sugar
¹/2 cup butter or
  margarine, softened
¹/2 tsp. grated lemon rind
  or vanilla
¹/2 cup ground almonds

Topping:
1 Tbsp. butter or
  margarine, melted
1 cup sifted powdered
  sugar
2 Tbsp. boiling water
¹/2 tsp. vanilla

1. Dissolve yeast in warm
water. Set aside.
2. In large bowl cream
together butter, sugar,
lemon rind, and salt until
light and fluffy. Beat in egg.
Alternately stir in flour and
dissolved yeast. Beat with a
spoon for 5 minutes.
3. Brush top of dough with
vegetable oil. Cover with
towel. Let rise in a warm
place until doubled, about
2 hours.
4. Meanwhile, to prepare
filling mix together ¹/2 cup
powdered sugar, butter,
lemon rind, and almonds.
Set aside.
5. Punch down dough. Roll
dough into a 9" x 12" rectangle on a greased, lightly
floured cookie sheet. Spread
filling down center third of
dough.
6. Along each side of filling,
cut crosswise slits into
dough, 1" apart, from edge
to filling. Fold strips at an
angle across filling, alternating from side to side, making sure end of preceding
strip is covered.

7. Let braid rise until doubled, about 30 minutes. Brush top with melted butter.

8. Bake at 350° for 30 minutes, or until golden. Cool on cake rack.

9. To make glaze mix together powdered sugar, boiling water, and vanilla. When braid has cooled, drizzle with sugar glaze.

Cheery Cherry Bread
Kay Miller
Mitchell, SD
Courthouse Steps

Makes 1 loaf

6-oz. jar red maraschino cherries
2 1/2 cups flour
1 cup sugar
4 tsp. baking powder
1/2 tsp. salt
2 eggs
2/3 cup milk
1/3 cup melted butter or margarine
8-oz. jar green cherries, drained and cut up
1/2 cup chopped pecans or walnuts
1 Tbsp. grated orange peel

1. Drain red cherries, reserving liquid. Add enough water to cherry juice to make 1/3 cup. Cut up cherries.
2. In large bowl combine flour, sugar, baking powder, and salt.

3. In small bowl lightly beat eggs. Stir in milk, butter, and cherry liquid.
4. Stir into dry ingredients, just until well combined.
5. Fold in red and green cherries, nuts, and orange peel. Pour into greased 9" x 5" pan.
6. Bake at 350° for 1 hour.

Cherry Pecan Bread
Sheila Plock
Boalsburg, PA
Christmas Sampler

Makes 1 loaf

3/4 cup sugar
1/2 cup butter or margarine
2 eggs
2 cups flour
1 tsp. baking soda
1/2 tsp. salt
1 cup buttermilk
1 cup chopped pecans
11-oz. jar maraschino cherries, drained and chopped (reserve juice for glaze)
1 tsp. vanilla

Glaze:
2 1/2 Tbsp. butter or margarine
1 cup powdered sugar
3/4 tsp. vanilla
2-3 Tbsp. reserved cherry juice, heated

1. Cream together sugar, butter, and eggs until light and fluffy.
2. Sift together flour, baking soda, and salt. Add alternately with buttermilk to creamed mixture.
3. Stir in pecans, cherries, and vanilla. Pour batter into a well greased, full-sized loaf pan.
4. Bake at 350° for 55-60 minutes, or until tester comes out clean. Remove from pan and cool. Glaze if desired.
5. For glaze melt butter. Blend in sugar and vanilla. Stir in juice, 1 tablespoon at a time, until glaze is of proper consistency.

In 1945 I was a very young teacher back in West Virginia when I decided to use up a supply of pretty wool scraps. Some were good parts from wool clothing which I had washed and pressed. I made a Crazy quilt by sewing the pieces onto squares of old sheets. I embroidered over some seams and did a few other designs. My mother-in-law offered to put in a batting and lining, and she tied it with wool yarn. Thus was created my first warm, cozy quilt. Through the years, it was well used and I still own it.

—*Cova Rexroad, Kingsville, MD*

Cranberry Anadama Bread
M. Jeanne Osborne
Wells, ME
Teddy Bear Love

Makes 2 loaves

1 orange peel, grated
1/4 cup sugar
1 1/2 cups fresh
    cranberries, washed
    and coarsely chopped
2 pkgs. dry yeast
1/2 cup warm water
1/2 tsp. sugar
1 Tbsp. flour
2/3 cup yellow cornmeal
2 1/2 cups boiling water
1/4 cup margarine
1/2 cup dark molasses
2 1/2 tsp. salt
7-8 cups flour

1. Mix together grated orange peel and 1/4 cup sugar. Add cranberries and process in food processor for 30 seconds.
2. Dissolve yeast in warm water. Stir in 1/2 tsp. sugar and 1 Tbsp. flour. Let stand until bubbly.
3. Stir cornmeal slowly into boiling water and cook until thickened. Stir in margarine, molasses, and salt. Cool to lukewarm.
4. Stir in yeast mixture, berries, and orange peel. Knead in flour to form smooth elastic dough. Allow to rise until double, about 50 minutes.
5. Turn out on lightly floured board and knead again. Divide dough in half and place each in greased, full-sized loaf pan. Let rise to the top of pan, 45 minutes to 1 hour.
6. Bake at 350° for 45 minutes. Remove from pans and cool on racks.

Cranberry Nut Bread
Eleanor Botelho
Falmouth, MA
Ann L. Boyer
Baltimore, MD
Leona Cook
Falmouth, MA
Ethel C. Fopeano
Clarence, NY
Carol Homewood
Stevensville, MD
Elizabeth L. Richards
Rapid City, SD
Margaret Sherman
Pompano Beach. FL
Berenice M. Wagner
Dodge City, KS

Makes 1 loaf

2 cups sifted flour
1 cup sugar
1 1/2 tsp. baking powder
1 tsp. salt
1/2 tsp. baking soda
1/4 cup butter or
    margarine, room
    temperature
1 egg, beaten
1 Tbsp. grated orange peel
3/4 cup orange juice
1 1/2 cups fresh or frozen
    cranberries, chopped
1/2 cup chopped nuts

1. Sift together flour, sugar, baking powder, salt, and baking soda. Cut in butter until mixture is crumbly.
2. Stir in egg, orange peel, and orange juice. Stir just until mixture is evenly moist. Fold in cranberries and nuts.
3. Spoon into a greased 9" x 5" x 3" loaf pan.
4. Bake at 350° for 70 minutes, or until a toothpick inserted in center comes out clean. Remove from pan and cool on wire rack.

Cranberry Nut Bread with Filling
Lois Niebauer
Pedricktown, NJ
Original Paper-cut Appliqué

Makes 1 loaf

1/3 cup butter or
    margarine, softened
1 cup sugar
2 eggs
3 cups flour
2 tsp. baking powder
1/2 tsp. baking soda
1/4 tsp. salt
1 cup orange juice
1 1/2 cups coarsely
    chopped cranberries
1/2 cup chopped nuts
2 tsp. grated orange peel
    (optional)

Filling:
8-oz. pkg. cream cheese
8-oz. can crushed
    pineapple, drained

1. Beat butter and sugar together until light and fluffy.
2. Add eggs one at a time, mixing well.

3. Mix together dry ingredients. Add dry ingredients alternately with juice to butter and sugar mixture, mixing well after each addition.
4. Stir in cranberries, nuts, and orange peel. Pour into a greased, full-sized loaf pan.
5. Bake at 350° for 70 minutes or until done. Cool thoroughly.
6. Slice the entire loaf into thin slices. Mix together the cream cheese and pineapple and spread between two slices of the bread, using the whole loaf. Cut each sandwich into 2 pieces and arrange on a festive plate.

Date and Nut Loaf
Katie Stoltzfus
Leola, PA
Log Cabin

Makes 2 full-sized loaves

1 1/2 cups boiling water
2 cups finely chopped dates
2 Tbsp. lard or shortening
2 cups sugar
2 eggs
3 cups flour
2 tsp. baking soda
1/2 cup hot water
2 tsp. vanilla
1-2 cups chopped nuts

1. Pour boiling water over dates. Set aside.
2. Cream lard. Add sugar and mix well. Add eggs.
3. Gradually stir in date

mixture and flour.
4. Mix together baking soda and hot water. Add to batter. Stir in vanilla. Mix well. Fold in chopped nuts.
5. Pour into greased 9" x 5" loaf pans.
6. Bake at 350° for 25-30 minutes. After bread has baked for about 20 minutes, check to see if it is browning excessively. If so, cover top with a sheet of aluminum foil and continue to bake until tester inserted in center of loaf comes out clean.

Date Nut Bread
Audrey L Kneer
Williamsfield, IL
Sunbonnet Sue

Makes 1 loaf

1 cup chopped dates
1 cup boiling water
1 Tbsp. butter
1 tsp. baking soda
3/4 cup sugar
1 egg
2 cups flour
1/2 tsp. salt
1 tsp. baking powder
1 cup chopped nuts

1. Mix dates, boiling water, butter, and baking soda together in a large bowl. Cool.
2. Beat sugar and egg together. Stir into date mixture.
3. Sift together flour, salt, and baking powder. Add to wet mixture. Stir in nuts.

4. Pour into greased and floured loaf pan.
5. Bake at 350° for 45 minutes.

Kona Inn Banana Bread
Mary A. Moya
West Hills, CA
Alphabet for Stephanie

Makes 2 full-sized loaves

1 cup vegetable shortening
2 cups sugar
2 cups mashed ripe bananas (about 6 bananas)
4 eggs, slightly beaten
1 cup chopped walnuts
2 cups flour
1 tsp. salt
2 tsp. baking soda

1. Cream together shortening, sugar, mashed bananas, eggs, and walnuts.
2. Mix together flour, salt, and baking soda. Add to creamed mixture. Mix well.
3. Pour batter into 2 greased and floured 9" x 5" loaf pans.
4. Bake at 350° for 55-65 minutes, until toothpick inserted in center comes out clean. Let bread cool in pan for about 5 minutes. Turn loaves onto rack to cool completely.

Best Banana Bread
Gail Skiff
Clifton Park, NY
Swirling Peony

Makes 2 loaves

1 1/2 cups sugar
1/2 cup shortening
2 eggs
1 tsp. vanilla
3 cups flour
2 tsp. baking soda
1/2 tsp. salt
2/3 cup sour milk
3 very ripe bananas
1/2 cup chopped walnuts
 (optional)

1. Cream together sugar and shortening. Add eggs and vanilla and mix well.
2. Sift together flour, baking soda, and salt. Add dry mixture alternately with sour milk and bananas to creamed mixture, beating until well mixed.
3. Add nuts if desired, reserving 2 tablespoons to sprinkle on top of loaves for garnish. Pour into 2 lightly greased, full-sized loaf pans.
4. Bake at 325° for 1 hour, or until toothpick inserted in center comes out clean.
5. Cool in pans for 15 minutes. Turn out onto foil and wrap immediatley.

Banana Surprise Bread
Jean Harris Robinson
Cinnaminson, NJ
My Secret Garden

Makes 1 full-sized loaf

1/2 cup shortening or
 margarine, room
 temperature
1 cup sugar
2 eggs
1 1/2 cups mashed
 bananas (3-5 bananas)
3/4 cup grated carrots
2/3 cup snipped dried
 apricots or prunes
1 tsp. vanilla
2 cups sifted flour
1 tsp. salt
1/2 tsp. baking soda
2/3 cup chopped pecans
1 tsp. lemon juice

1. Cream together shortening and sugar. Add eggs and mix well.
2. Mix in bananas, carrots, dried fruit, and vanilla.
3. Sift together flour, salt, and baking soda and mix well into creamed mixture.
4. Stir in pecans and lemon juice. Pour into greased full-sized loaf pan.
5. Bake at 325° for 75 minutes.

Apricot Banana Bread
Carole M. Mackie
Williamsfield, IL
Sunbonnet Sue

Makes 1 loaf

1/3 cup margarine,
 softened
2/3 cup sugar
2 eggs
1 cup mashed bananas
 (2-3 bananas)
1/4 cup buttermilk
1 1/4 cups flour
1 tsp. baking powder
1/2 tsp. baking soda
1/2 tsp. salt
1 cup bran cereal (not
 flakes)
3/4 cup chopped dried
 apricots
1/2 cup chopped walnuts

1. Cream together margarine and sugar. Stir in eggs and mix well.
2. Combine bananas and buttermilk.
3. Combine flour, baking powder, baking soda, and salt. Alternately add banana mixture and flour mixture to creamed mixture.
4. Stir in cereal, apricots, and walnuts. Pour into greased, full-sized loaf pan.
5. Bake at 350° for 55-60 minutes. Cool 10 minutes before removing from pan.

John's Zucchini Bread

Mary Ann Potenta
Bridgewater, NJ
Double Irish Chain

*Makes 1 tube pan or
2 full-sized loaves*

3 eggs
1 cup sugar
3/4 cup oil
1 tsp. grated lemon peel
1/2 tsp. orange extract
1/4 tsp. vanilla
2 cups grated zucchini,
   packed tightly
2 1/2 cups flour
2 tsp. baking powder
3/4 tsp. salt
1 tsp. baking soda
1/2 tsp. ginger
1/2 cup chopped walnuts
   or pecans

1. Beat eggs and sugar together until pale yellow. Add oil. Mix well.
2. Stir in lemon peel, orange extract, vanilla, and zucchini.
3. Mix together flour, baking powder, salt, baking soda, and ginger. Stir into zucchini mixture. Fold in nuts.
4. Pour into greased and floured tube pan or 2 greased and floured full-sized loaf pans.
5. Bake at 350° for 60 minutes, or until tester comes out clean.

Zucchini Bread

Debbie Divine
Salina, KS
Friendship Sampler Quilt

Makes 2 full-sized loaves

3 eggs, beaten
1 cup oil
2 cups sugar
2 cups grated zucchini
2 tsp. vanilla
3 cups flour
1 tsp. baking soda
1/2 tsp. baking powder
1 tsp. salt
1 tsp. cinnamon
1/2 cup chopped nuts

1. Mix together ingredients in order given. Pour into 2 greased full-sized loaf pans.
2. Bake at 325° for 1 hour, or until tester inserted in center comes out clean.

Orange-Almond Poppy Seed Bread

Jeanne Allen
Los Alamos, NM
Baltimore Beauty

Makes 2 full-sized loaves

3 1/2 cups flour
1 1/2 tsp. salt
1 1/2 tsp. baking powder
2 1/4 cups sugar
1 3/4 cups milk
1 1/3 cups oil
1 1/2 Tbsp. poppy seeds
3 eggs
1 1/2 tsp. almond extract
1 1/2 tsp. vanilla extract

Glaze:
3/4 cup sugar
1/4 cup orange juice
1/2 tsp. vanilla
1/2 tsp. almond extract
2 tsp. melted butter

1. Mix together all bread ingredients with an electric mixer for two minutes.
2. Pour into 2 greased and floured full-sized loaf pans.
3. Bake at 350° for 60 minutes. Remove from pans.
4. Mix together glaze ingredients and pour over loaves of slightly warm bread.

Orange Poppy Seed Bread with Blueberries

Jean Moore
Pendleton, IN
Miniature Anvil

Makes 1 full-sized loaf

3/4 cup milk
1/4 cup oil
1 egg, beaten
1 Tbsp. finely shredded
  orange peel
1 Tbsp. orange juice
1 3/4 cups flour
1/2 cup sugar
1 1/2 tsp. baking powder
1 Tbsp. poppy seeds
1/4 tsp. salt
3/4 cup fresh or frozen
  blueberries
1/2-3/4 cup chopped nuts
  (optional)

1. Cream together milk, oil, egg, orange peel, and orange juice.
2. Combine flour, sugar, baking powder, poppy seeds, and salt. Add to creamed mixture. Stir until just moist. Fold in blueberries and nuts.
3. Pour into greased, full-sized loaf pan.
4. Bake at 350° for 45-50 minutes, or until toothpick inserted near center comes out clean. Cool in pan for 10 minutes. Remove from pan and cool on wire rack.

Lemon Poppy Seed Bread

Geraldine A. Ebersole
Hershey, PA
Old Maids Puzzle

Makes 4 small loaves

2 2/3 cups flour
1 1/2 tsp. baking powder
1 tsp. salt
1/4 cup poppy seeds
1 cup unsalted butter,
  softened
1 1/4 cups sugar
1 Tbsp. plus 1 tsp.
  freshly grated lemon
  peel
1 1/2 tsp. vanilla
3 large eggs
1/3 cup milk

Syrup:
1/2 cup fresh lemon juice
1/2 cup sugar

1. Sift together flour, baking powder, and salt. Stir in poppy seeds.
2. In separate bowl cream together butter and sugar. Beat in lemon peel and vanilla. Beat in eggs, one at a time. Add milk and mix well.
3. Add flour mixture and stir until combined.
4. Divide the batter among 4 buttered and floured small loaf pans. Bake the breads in the middle of a 350° oven for 40 to 45 minutes, or until toothpick comes out clean.
5. While bread is baking, combine lemon juice and sugar in a small saucepan. Bring mixture to a boil, stir-

ring until the sugar is dissolved. Keep the syrup warm until bread is baked.
6. While bread is still hot, poke holes in top of bread with a skewer. Brush bread with half of the syrup. Let the bread cool in the pans for 5 minutes.
7. Invert the bread. Poke all sides with skewer, and brush with remaining syrup. Cool.
8. Wrap breads in plastic wrap and foil and let stand overnight.

Glaze Variation:
3/4 cup sugar
1/4 cup orange juice
1/2 tsp. vanilla
1/2 tsp. almond extract
1/2 tsp. butter-flavored
  extract

After baked breads have cooled for 5 minutes, brush tops with glaze.
Leigh Booth
Kintnersville, PA
Sampler

Pumpkin Bread
Mary Seielstad
Schenectady, NY
Janie Steele
Moore, OK
Sunbonnet Sue

Makes 3 loaves

4 eggs
3 cups sugar
1 cup oil
2/3 cup water
2 cups pumpkin
31/2 cups flour
2 tsp. baking soda
11/2 tsp. salt
1 tsp. nutmeg
1 tsp. cinnamon
1 tsp. allspice
1 cup raisins (optional)
1 cup walnuts

1. Mix together eggs, sugar, oil, water, and pumpkin.
2. Add remaining ingredients and mix well.
3. Pour into 3 greased loaf pans.
4. Bake at 350° for 1 hour.

Note: Baked loaves freeze well.

Pumpkin Nut Bread
Janice Muller
Derwood, MD
Canadian Geese
Pat Segal
Woodbury, NY
Mariners Compass in Space

Makes 2 full-sized loaves

2 cups pumpkin
1 cup oil
4 eggs
31/2 cups flour
3 cups sugar
1/2 tsp. baking soda
11/2 tsp. salt
11/2 tsp. allspice
11/2 tsp. nutmeg
2 tsp. cinnamon
1/2 cup chopped nuts

1. Combine pumpkin, oil, and eggs.
2. Sift together dry ingredients. Blend into pumpkin mixture. Mix well. Fold in nuts.
3. Pour into 2 greased full-sized loaf pans.
4. Bake at 300° for 60 minutes, or until tester comes out clean.

Pumpkin Raisin Bread
Sue Graziadio
White Mills, PA
Double Irish Chain

Makes 2 full-sized loaves

3 eggs
2 cups cooked pumpkin
11/2 cups sugar
11/2 cups firmly packed brown sugar
1 cup water
1/2 cup oil
31/3 cups flour
1/2 cup dry milk
1/2 cup wheat germ
2 tsp. baking soda
1/2 tsp. baking powder
1 tsp. cinnamon
1/2 tsp. nutmeg
1/2 tsp. salt
1 cup raisins

1. Beat eggs at medium speed. Stir in pumpkin, sugars, water, and oil. Beat until well blended.
2. Combine flour, dry milk, wheat germ, baking soda, baking powder, cinnamon, nutmeg, and salt. Beat into pumpkin mixture until well blended. Stir in raisins.
3. Pour into 2 greased and floured full-sized loaf pans.
3. Bake at 325° for 50-60 minutes. Remove from pans and cool on wire racks.

My great-aunt Meddie was born in the late 1800s and raised on a farm in Mississippi. As a young married woman, she wanted to make a special dish for her husband for their first Christmas together. She had heard people raving about smothered chicken and decided to try it. Aunt Meddie took a pillowcase to the chicken house and used it to smother and kill a chicken. She cleaned it and fried the chicken as usual. After serving it, she remarked that the chicken did not taste any differently than regular fried chicken.
—*Cathie Favret, Tillamook, OR*

Holiday Orange Pumpkin Loaf
Ann Sunday McDowell
Newtown, PA
Jessica's Froggy Patchwork

Makes 3 full-sized loaves

2 cups cooked pumpkin
1 cup orange juice
1 cup margarine,
  softened
3 cups sugar
4 eggs, beaten
1 tsp. salt
2 tsp. baking soda
1 tsp. nutmeg
1 tsp. cinnamon
4 cups flour
1 cup chopped nuts
1 cup golden raisins

1. Beat together first five ingredients. Stir together dry ingredients, except nuts and raisins.
2. Add dry ingredients to creamed ones and blend well. Stir in nuts and raisins.
3. Grease and lightly flour 3 full-sized loaf pans. Fill them half full.
4. Bake at 350° for 1 hour, or until toothpick comes out clean.

I make at least 12 Holiday Orange Pumpkin Loaves each holiday season. When my children were young, I gave the breads to their elementary school teachers, ballet and riding and music teachers, our neighbors and co-workers. These breads are also great as hostess gifts. I make them ahead and freeze them so they're ready for a ribbon and gift tag when an occasion arises.

Pumpkin Biscuits
Lois Niebauer
Pedricktown, NJ
Original Paper-cut Appliqué

Makes 20 biscuits

2 cups flour
3 Tbsp. sugar
4 tsp. baking powder
1/2 tsp. salt
1/2 tsp. cinnamon
1/2 cup butter or
  margarine, softened
1/2 cup light cream
2/3 cup pumpkin

1. Sift together dry ingredients.
2. Cut in butter until consistency of coarse crumbs.
3. Combine cream and pumpkin and stir into the crumb mixture. Stir only until moistened.
4. Turn onto floured surface and knead gently a few times.
5. Roll to 1/2" thick and cut with a 2" round cutter.
6. Place 1 inch apart on a greased cookie sheet.
7. Bake at 425° for 12 minutes.

Christmas Bread in a Jar
Joan Brown
Warriors Mark, PA
Group Quilt with 4th Graders

Makes 8 pint jars

2/3 cup shortening
2 2/3 cups sugar
4 eggs
2 cups pumpkin
2/3 cup water
3 1/3 cups flour
1/2 tsp. baking powder
2 tsp. baking soda
1 1/2 tsp. salt
1 tsp. cinnamon
1 tsp. ground cloves

1. Cream together shortening and sugar. Beat in eggs, pumpkin, and water.
2. Mix together flour, baking powder, baking soda, salt, cinnamon, and ground cloves. Stir into pumpkin mixture. Mix well.
3. Pour into 8 greased widemouth pint jars, filling them half full.
4. Bake at 325° for 45-55 minutes.
5. When done, remove one jar at a time from the oven. If bread has risen over edge, cut off excess to the top of the jar rim and wipe edges of jar clean. Scald lids of jars in boiling water and have them ready to attach to jars by the time the bread is cooked. Tightly screw on lids. Set aside to cool. Lids should pop when they are sealed. Breads can be stored on shelf for months.

Variations: Instead of 2 cups pumpkin add:
a) 2 cups mashed bananas
b) 1 3/4 cups mashed bananas and 1/4 cup orange marmalade
c) 2 cups shredded zucchini
d) 2 cups shredded apple
e) 1 cup shredded carrot and 1 cup shredded apple
f) 1 3/4 cup mashed banana and 1/4 cup crushed pineapple
g) 1 3/4 cup applesauce and 1/4 cup crushed pineapple
h) 1 can cranberries
i) 1 lb. ground cranberries

Rhubarb Bread
Patricia Snow
Lane, KS

Makes 2 loaves

1 cup brown sugar
1/2 cup white sugar
2/3 cup oil
1 egg
1 tsp. salt
1 cup sour milk or buttermilk
1 tsp. baking soda
1 tsp. vanilla
2 1/2 cups flour
1 1/2 cups diced rhubarb
1/2 cup chopped nuts

Topping:
1/2 cup sugar
1 tsp. cinnamon
1 Tbsp. margarine or butter, melted

1. Mix together all bread ingredients in order given. Pour dough into 2 greased and floured full-sized loaf pans.

2. Mix together topping ingredients. Sprinkle over bread.
3. Bake at 325° for 60 minutes.

Carrot Bread Mini-Loaves
Laura Barrus Bishop
Boerne, TX
Log Cabin

Makes 6 mini-loaves

1 1/2 cups flour
1 cup sugar
1 tsp. baking soda
1 1/2 tsp. cinnamon
1/4 tsp. salt
2 eggs, well beaten
3/4 cup oil
1 tsp. vanilla
1 1/2 cups grated carrots

1. Sift together flour, sugar, baking soda, cinnamon, and salt.
2. Stir in eggs, oil, vanilla, and carrots. Pour into 6 greased mini-loaf pans.
3. Bake at 350° for 35 minutes.

Green Tomato Bread
Jo Haberkamp
Fairbank, IA
Card Tricks

Makes 2 full-sized loaves

3 eggs
1 cup oil
2 cups sugar
2 cups ground green tomatoes, drained
2 tsp. vanilla
3 cups flour
1 tsp. baking soda
1 tsp. salt
1/2 tsp. baking powder
1/4 tsp. nutmeg
1/4 tsp. cloves
2 1/2 tsp. cinnamon

1. Mix together eggs, oil, sugar, green tomatoes, and vanilla.
2. Mix together flour, baking soda, salt, baking powder, nutmeg, cloves, and cinnamon. Add to green tomato mixture. Mix well.
3. Pour into 2 greased 9" x 5" loaf pans.
4. Bake at 350° for 60 minutes.

I make this bread in the fall, at the end of the growing season and freeze it to give as Christmas gifts for friends.

Raisin Loaf
Lois J. Cassidy
Willow Street, PA
Star Light

Makes 4 small loaves

1 1/2 cups raisins
2 cups boiling water
2 tsp. baking soda
1/2 cup shortening
2 cups sugar
3 eggs
4 cups flour
1/2 tsp. salt
1 tsp. vanilla
1/2 cup chopped walnuts

1. Combine raisins, boiling water, and baking soda. Set aside for 1 hour.
2. Cream together shortening and sugar. Add eggs and beat well.
3. Add flour and salt alternately with raisin mixture to creamed mixture.
4. Add vanilla and nuts and stir well.
5. Pour into four small greased bread pans (3 1/2 x 7 1/4).
6. Bake at 350° for 40-45 minutes.

Note: When cool, wrap the loaves separately and refrigerate or freeze them. Use as needed for drop-in guests or last-minute gifts.

Cinnamon Loaf
Janice Yoskovich
Carmichaels, PA
Rising Sun

Makes 2 full-sized loaves

2 cups sugar
1 cup oil
4 eggs
3 cups flour
2 tsp. baking powder
1/2 tsp. salt
1 cup milk
2 Tbsp. sugar
2 Tbsp. cinnamon

1. Cream together sugar and oil. Stir in eggs one at a time. Beat well after each addition.
2. Mix together dry ingredients. Add alternately with milk to creamed mixture.
3. Pour 1/4 of batter into each of 2 greased 9" x 5" loaf pans.
4. Mix together sugar and cinnamon. Pour 1/4 of sugar/cinnamon mixture onto batter in loaf pans. Swirl with a spoon or table knife.
5. Divide remaining batter between pans. Top with remaining sugar/cinnamon mixture.
6. Bake at 350° for 45 minutes.

Raised Potato Doughnuts
Elva Engel
Gap, PA
Snowman Sampler Panel

Makes 100 doughnuts

1 quart mashed potatoes
1 pint warm water
1/2 cup sugar
2 pkgs. yeast
1 1/2 Tbsp. salt
3 eggs, beaten
1 1/2 cups sugar
2 cups butter
5 lbs. flour
2 1/2 cups whole wheat flour

1. Mix together mashed potatoes and water. Stir in sugar, yeast, and salt. Cover and let set in warm place for 4 hours.
2. Stir in eggs, sugar, and butter. Mix well. Mix in flours. Turn onto floured surface and knead well.
3. Roll out on floured board until 1/2" thick. Cut with doughnut cutter. Let rise for 10 minutes.
4. Fry in deep fat until lightly brown. Cool.

Note: This recipe makes a large quantity. Extra doughnuts freeze well.

Doughnuts
JoAnn Pelletier
Longmeadow, MA
Interlocking Log Cabin

Makes 20 small doughnuts

1^1/3 cups flour, sifted
2 tsp. baking powder
1/3 tsp. salt
1/3 cup sugar
1 egg, slightly beaten
1/2 cup milk
1 Tbsp. oil
1 tsp. vanilla

1. Sift together flour, baking powder, salt, and sugar.
2. Mix together egg, milk, oil, and vanilla. Stir into dry ingredients, just until moistened.
3. Drop by spoonfuls into hot fat (365°) and fry 2-3 minutes. Turn after first minute.
4. Drain on paper towels.
5. Roll in mixture of cinnamon and sugar.

Kruschinky
Bea Gagliano
Lakewood, NJ

Makes 2-3 dozen

3/4 cup sugar
1/2 cup margarine
3 eggs
1 tsp. vanilla
4^1/2 cups flour
1 tsp. baking powder
1 tsp. salt
1 Tbsp. whiskey
1 cup milk
2 cups sugar
2-3 tsp. cinnamon

1. Cream together 3/4 cup sugar, margarine, eggs, and vanilla. Mix well.
2. Mix together flour, baking powder, and salt.
3. Mix together whiskey and milk. Add alternately with flour mixture to creamed mixture.
4. Roll out 1/3 of dough on a floured board. Cut into 2" x 3" strips. Slit centers and then pull one end of strip through slit from behind to front.
5. Fry in hot oil until light brown. Drain on paper towels.
6. Divide remaining dough in half and repeat procedure with each half.
5. Mix together 2 cups sugar and cinnamon. Sprinkle hot kruschinky with cinnamon-sugar mixture.

Soft Pretzels
Janie Steele
Moore, OK
Winter Geese

Makes 25-30 pretzels

1/8 cup hot water
1 pkg. dry yeast
1^1/3 cups warm water
1/3 cup brown sugar
5 cups flour
coarse kosher salt
baking soda

1. Mix yeast and water. Stir in warm water, brown sugar, and flour.
2. Knead on lightly floured board until smooth and elastic.
3. Grease cookie sheets and sprinkle with kosher salt.
4. Pinch off golf-ball sized pieces of dough and roll each into a long thin cigar shape. Shape into pretzels.
5. Fill skillet with water and add 1 Tbsp. baking soda per cup of water. Bring to a boil. Lower pretzel into water for 30 seconds. Then place the pretzel onto cookie sheet.
6. Bake at 400° for 8 minutes, or until golden brown.
7. Serve with mustard or melted cheese.

Twisted Cinnamon Treats
Debbie Chisholm
Fallston, MD
Whole Cloth Quilt

Makes 2-3 dozen

Filling:
2/3 cup chopped nuts
1/3 cup brown sugar
1/3 cup powdered sugar
1 1/4 tsp. cinnamon
1/4 cup butter, melted

Dough:
2 8-oz. cans crescent rolls

Glaze:
1 cup powdered sugar
2 Tbsp. milk

1. In a small bowl combine filling ingredients.
2. Shape one can of crescent dough into a 13" x 7" rectangle. (Pinch dough together where it's perforated.)
3. Sprinkle with filling mixture.
4. Shape second can of dough into a 13" x 7" rectangle. Place over the first layer and filling mixture.
5. Pinch the edges of the dough to seal the layers.
6. Cut into 1/2" wide sticks. Carefully pick up each stick and twist it several times as you place it on an ungreased cookie sheet.
7. Bake 15-20 minutes at 375°.
8. Mix together powdered sugar and milk and pour over baked sticks.

Note: Twisted Cinnamon Treats can be shaped into candy canes or wreaths.

Christmas Morning Rolls
Carma Popp
Mitchell, SD
Pheasant Comforter
Marsha Sabus
Fallbrook, CA
Diamond in the Rough

Makes 12 servings

1/2 cup chopped nuts or pecan halves
1 bag of 24 frozen dinner rolls
3 3/4-oz. pkg. butterscotch pudding mix
1/2 cup butter
3/4 cup brown sugar
3/4 tsp. cinnamon

1. Generously grease 10" fluted bundt pan. Sprinkle nuts in bottom of pan. Arrange frozen rolls on top of nuts. Sprinkle dry pudding mix over rolls.
2. In saucepan mix together butter, sugar, and cinnamon. Cook over low heat until sugar is dissolved and mixture bubbles. Pour over rolls.
3. Cover tightly with foil and let stand for at least 8 hours.
4. Bake at 350° for 30 minutes. Let stand 5 minutes, then invert carefully onto serving dish.

Cheese Bread
Cyndie Marrara
Port Matilda, PA
Sampler

Makes 12-15 slices

4 ozs. mozzarella cheese, shredded
4 ozs. cheddar cheese, shredded
8 ozs. Monterey Jack cheese, shredded
1 cup mayonnaise
1 Tbsp. garlic powder
1 loaf French bread

1. Mix together cheeses, mayonnaise, and garlic powder.
2. Cut French bread loaf in half length-wise. Spread cheese mixture on both pieces of bread.
3. Bake at 350° for 20 minutes.

Main Dishes

Christmas Eve Cornish Game Hens

Grace Ketcham
Wilmington, DE
Baby's Heart Quilt

Makes 4 servings

4 Cornish game hens
2 cups brown sugar
2 cups orange juice
4 Tbsp. margarine or
  butter
1/2 tsp. allspice
2 tsp. dry mustard

1. Coat medium roasting pan with non-stick cooking spray. Place hens in roasting pan.
2. In saucepan mix together brown sugar, orange juice, margarine, allspice, and mustard. Heat to boiling. Pour sauce over hens.
3. Bake at 375° for 1¼ hours, basting occasionally.
4. Serve with wild rice and a vegetable medley.

Cherry-Roasted Goose

Nicole Koloski
East Sandwich, MA
*Piecemakers 1995
Calender Quilt*

Makes 8-10 servings

8-10-lb. domestic goose
2 Tbsp. lemon juice
3/4 cup apple-cherry juice
9" cinnamon stick
1/3 cup sugar
6 whole cloves
1 Tbsp. cornstarch
1 Tbsp. cold water
16-oz. jar pitted cherries,
  drained
2 Tbsp. kirsch

1. Rinse goose and pat dry. Season with salt. Prepare goose for roasting by tucking the drumsticks below the skin, across the tail. Skewer the neck to the back. Twist wing tips under the back. Prick skin. Place bird in roasting pan, breast side up. Brush with lemon juice.
2. Insert meat thermometer in thigh part of goose. Roast uncovered at 350° for 2³/4-3¹/4 hours. (Meat thermometer should read 180-185°.)
3. During roasting process, remove fat. When done, remove from heat, cover, and let stand for 15 minutes.
4. While goose is roasting, mix together apple-cherry juice, cinnamon stick, sugar, and cloves in a saucepan. Bring to boil. Reduce heat, cover, and simmer 15 minutes. Strain through fine sieve, saving juice.
5. Combine cornstarch and cold water. Mix well. Add to juice mixture. Return to heat and cook until bubbly. Continue cooking for 2 minutes, stirring constantly.
6. Stir in cherries and kirsch and heat through.
7. Place goose on serving plate and spread sauce over goose. Serve.

Roast Duck with Red Cabbage

Charmaine Caesar
Lancaster, PA
Bits and Pieces

Makes 4 servings

Duck:
1 medium to large duck
salt
2 medium onions, peeled
  and quartered
2 apples, pared and
  quartered
3 strips bacon
1 cup water

Cabbage:
1 medium head red
  cabbage
1/4 lb. bacon, sliced
1 medium onion, minced
1/2 cup red wine
1/4 cup lemon juice

1. Rinse the duck, then pat it dry. Rub inside cavity with salt.
2. Place onions and apples into cavity of duck.
3. Place duck, breast side up, on a rack in a roasting pan.
4. Place bacon strips on top to keep the duck breast moist. Add water.
5. Bake at 325° for 20 minutes per pound (for example, bake 4-lb. duck for 80 minutes), basting frequently in juices.
7. When done, remove onions and apple from cavity and discard.
8. During last 15 minutes of roasting time, prepare cabbage. Brown bacon, draining excess fat. Add cabbage, onion, wine, and lemon juice to bacon. Cover and simmer for 15 minutes.
9. Mound cabbage onto a heated platter. Carve duck into serving pieces and arrange around and over cabbage. Serve immediately.

Mustard-Roasted Leg of Lamb

Nicole Koloski
East Sandwich, MA
*Piecemakers 1995
Calendar Quilt*

Makes 8 servings

8-lb. leg of lamb
1/2 cup olive oil
salt and pepper to taste
2 1/2 cups Dijon mustard
1/2 loaf of bread
1/4 cup fresh chopped or
  dried parsley

1. Debone lamb, 3 main pieces and some small pieces should remain. (Or have the butcher do this for you.)
2. Lightly coat all pieces with olive oil. Sprinkle with salt and pepper. Take smaller pieces and tightly tuck them into larger pieces. Roll the pieces tightly.
3. Make bread crumbs by slicing bread into cubes and running through food processor until coarse, fairly large crumbs appear. Combine with parsley to flavor.
4. Brush a thick layer of mustard over each piece of lamb. Coat heavily in fresh bread crumbs.
5. Place lamb on roasting rack in shallow pan. Roast at 450° for 10 minutes. Reduce heat to 350° and continue roasting until meat ther-

Every Wednesday from 8 a.m. to 4 p.m., I meet with a group of friends to quilt. We call ourselves the quilting bee and are a diverse group which includes women with high school educations as well as those with Ph.Ds. Our average age is around seventy, and each week we sit around two or three frames and quilt. We solve all the problems in the world, we laugh, and occasionally, we also shed a tear or two.

Those whose quilts are in the frames are responsible for the lunch that week. Not only can we quilt, but most of us are also quite good cooks. The food is always adequate and often marvelous.

The Christmas meal is especially celebrative. One of the women is a chef by profession, and she prepares the meat. Each of us contributes a dish to pass, bringing our favorite and most delicious recipe. While there are only thirty of us, we often have enough food to serve twice that many people.

—*Mary Lou Rowe, Batavia, IL*

mometer reaches 140°, about one hour. Do not overcook.
5. Remove lamb from oven and let rest for 15 minutes before slicing.

Teriyaki Lamb Chops
Joan Lemmler
Albuquerque, NM
Marissa

Makes 2 servings

1/3 **cup soy sauce**
2 **Tbsp. fresh lemon juice**
1 **Tbsp. brown sugar**
1/4 **tsp. ground ginger**
2 **lamb chops, 1**1/4**" thick**

1. Combine soy sauce, lemon juice, brown sugar, and ginger. Marinate chops in mixture for 6-8 hours, turning frequently.
2. Broil chops for 3-5 minutes on each side, basting frequently with marinade. Serve.

Mama's Christmas Ham
Joyce R. Swinney
Mooresville, IN
Dresden Heart

Makes 24-30 servings

12-15-lb. **smoked, sugar cured ham**
2 **20-oz. cans sweetened chunk pineapple**
2 **cups brown sugar**

2 **Tbsp. cinnamon**
1 1/4-oz. **box whole cloves**
4 **cups grape wine**

1. Trim the skin or rind from the ham. Keep rind. Trim all excess fat. Score ham surface 1/2" deep and 1" apart, creating diamond shapes over entire surface of ham.
2. Mix together brown sugar and cinnamon. Rub generously over entire surface. Place 1 whole clove in each diamond space and push in deeply.
3. Drain pineapple, reserving liquid. Using plain white toothpicks or toothpicks that have been soaked in water, secure pineapple chunks to ham surface. Place in roasting pan.
5. Push meat thermometer into thickest part of ham, be sure not to touch bone. Bake until ham setting is reached.
6. At the beginning of baking time, baste ham with 1 cup wine and pineapple juice. Repeat this step about every 20 minutes. After using 4 cups wine, ladle liquid from baking pan when basting. Each time after basting, take ham rind and lay it over ham to keep ham from drying out.
7. When done, place ham on a wire rack which has been placed on top of roasting pan, allowing excess liquid to drain from ham. Serve.

Raspberry-Glazed Ham
Elizabeth Miller
Walnut Creek, OH
Rose Trellis

Makes 16-20 servings

8-10-lb. **boneless, fully cooked ham**
1/4 **cup apple juice or dry white wine**
2 **Tbsp. lemon juice**
2 **tsp. cornstarch**
1/3 **cup seedless raspberry jam**
1 **Tbsp. butter**
watercress, parsley, or other greens

1. Score ham into diamond shapes. Place on a rack in shallow roasting pan.
2. Bake at 325° for about 2 hours or until meat thermometer registers 140°.
3. In saucepan blend apple juice or wine with lemon juice and cornstarch. Add about 1/2 of jam. Cook and stir until thickened and bubbly.
4. Stir in remaining jam and butter. Heat and stir until butter is melted. Brush ham with glaze. Bake ham 10 minutes longer. Spoon any additional glaze over ham. (You may want to double the glaze recipe and thin extra glaze slightly with water to pass around with ham.)
5. Garnish ham with choice of greens and serve.

Honey-Baked Ham

Nicole Koloski
East Sandwich, MA
*Piecemakers 1995
Calendar Quilt*

Makes 12-15 servings

10-lb. whole cooked ham
1¼ cups brown sugar
½ cup dry sherry
¼ cup plus 2 Tbsp. honey
6 Tbsp. Dijon mustard
½ tsp. fresh ground pepper
¾ cup pineapple chunks
¾ cup fresh cranberries

1. Place ham on rack in shallow roasting pan. Roast at 325° for 1¾ hours. Remove ham from oven and turn oven temperature to 425°.
2. Collect all juice from the pan, skim, and set aside. Trim fat from ham and score ham in a diagonal pattern, forming diamond shapes about ¾" wide.
3. Mix together brown sugar, sherry, honey, mustard, and pepper. Coat ham with honey mixture, return oven temperature to 325°, and put ham back into oven. Bake 15 minutes.
4. Glaze ham again with honey mixture. Using toothpicks (which have been dipped in water to prevent burning), decorate ham with cranberries and pineapple chunks, spreading pieces evenly. Bake another 15 minutes.

5. Remove from oven and glaze a final time. Bake another 15 minutes or until meat thermometer shows 135-140°. Remove from oven and let stand for 20 minutes before carving.
6. Skim fat from ham juices and heat through. Serve with ham.

Ham Balls with Cherry Sauce

Evelyn L. Ward
Greeley, CO
Watercolor

Makes 12 servings

Ham Balls:
2 lbs. ground ham
1 lb. ground pork
½ lb. ground beef
2 eggs
1 Tbsp. grated onion
¼ tsp. pepper
1 cup cracker crumbs
10¾-oz. can cream of tomato soup

Cherry Sauce:
21-oz. can cherry pie filling
½ cup brown sugar
¼ cup pineapple juice
¼ cup vinegar
½ tsp. dry mustard

1. Mix together meats, eggs, onion, pepper, cracker crumbs, and tomato soup. Form into balls the size of large walnuts. Place balls in large glass baking dish.
2. To prepare sauce mix together pie filling, brown

sugar, pineapple juice, vinegar, and dry mustard. Pour over ham balls and marinate for at least 1 hour.
3. Bake at 300° for 1½ hours.
4. Transfer to crockpot to keep warm for serving.

Ham Meatballs

Elsie Russett
Fairbank, IA

Makes 24 meatballs

Meatballs:
1 lb. ground smoked ham
1½ lbs. ground pork
2 eggs, slightly beaten
1 cup milk
2 cups cracker crumbs

Sauce:
1 cup brown sugar
1 Tbsp. dry mustard
½ cup vinegar
½ cup water

1. Mix together ham, pork, eggs, milk, and cracker crumbs. Form into 24 balls. Place in greased shallow pan.
2. Mix together brown sugar and mustard. Add vinegar and water. Pour over meatballs.
3. Bake at 350° for 1½ hours, basting often.

Note: For Christmas parties make smaller meatballs, about the size of a large walnut. Bake for 1 hour only and serve with toothpicks.

Crown Roast of Pork

Barbara G. Winiarski
South Dennis, MA
*Sunbonnet Sue
Through the Years*

Makes 6-8 servings

5-lb. crown roast of pork
1 tsp. salt
1/2 tsp. pepper
6 bacon slices, cut into
  1/2" pieces
1/2 cup chopped onion
1/2 cup chopped celery
3 cups fresh white bread
  crumbs
1 tsp. salt
1/4 tsp. pepper
1/4 tsp. dried thyme
  leaves
1/2 tsp. poultry seasoning
1 1/2 cups chopped, pared
  apples
1/4 cup butter or
  margarine, melted
crab apples
parsley sprigs

1. Pat pork roast with damp paper towels. Place in shallow roasting pan. Sprinkle with salt and pepper. Insert a meat thermometer into thick part of meat, without touching bone. Protect each rib bone with foil during roasting time and fill center of roast with crushed foil to keep crown shape during roasting.
2. Roast uncovered at 325° for 2 1/2 hours.
3. To prepare stuffing cook bacon in skillet until crisp. Drain off fat, reserving 2 Tbsp. Set bacon aside.
4. Sauté onion and celery in bacon fat, stirring until tender, about 5 minutes. Remove from heat.
5. Stir in bread crumbs, salt, pepper, thyme leaves, poultry seasoning, apples, and butter. Toss lightly to combine.
6. Remove foil from center of roast. Fill center with stuffing. Cover stuffing loosely with foil.
7. Continue roasting until thermometer reaches 185°. Remove foil from each of rib bones.
8. Place roast on serving platter. Garnish with crab apples and parsley sprigs.

The first year we were married, we spent the Christmas holidays with my husband's family. I wanted to share my favorite fresh ham recipe from Puerto Rico, my birthplace. As I prepared the seasoning, I noticed that my mother-in-law seemed apprehensive about the large quantity of fresh garlic I was using. Very soon the whole house was permeated with the overpowering smell of garlic. It was winter and their house was tightly insulated to keep out the cold. As the ham was roasting, it became necessary to open windows despite the cold outside. Since Puerto Rico has a tropical climate where we keep our windows open year round, I had not considered the lack of ventilation.

As we sat down to eat, my husband kept reassuring his mother that despite the smell, it was quite safe to try out the ham. She was pleasantly surprised that it tasted good, but for days afterward she continued to air out the house by opening windows and placing scented candles in various strategic places. Thirty-three years later, we still tell the story whenever we sit down for our Christmas fresh ham in memory of our dear Mom Harkins, who braved the cultural shock and made me feel welcome in spite of the garlic fiasco.

—*Michelle Harkins, Punxsutawney, PA*

Crown Roast of Pork with Sausage Stuffing

Nicole Koloski
East Sandwich, MA
*Piecemakers 1995
Calendar Quilt*

Makes 8-10 servings

6-8-lb. crown roast of
  pork
1¹/2 tsp. rosemary
salt and pepper to taste
8-oz. pkg. cornbread
  stuffing mix
¹/2 cup minced celery
2 Tbsp. green onion,
  chopped
2 Tbsp. butter
1 lb. sausage
1 apple, chopped
¹/2 cup raisins
¹/2 cup pecans, chopped
1 cup applesauce
crab apples, parsley, or
  watercress

1. Place roast in roasting
pan. Rub rosemary, salt, and
pepper over roast.
2. Prepare cornbread stuffing mix according to package directions.
3. Sauté celery and onion in
butter and add to stuffing
mixture.
4. Brown sausage and drain
all excess fat. Stir into stuffing. Add apple, raisins, and
pecans and mix well.
5. Stuff roast to top of the
crown. Spread applesauce
over the top. Wrap bone
ends tightly in aluminum
foil.
6. Roast uncovered at 325°

for 3 hours. Remove from
oven and let stand for 10
minutes.
7. Garnish with parsley,
watercress, or crab apples
and serve.

Roast Pork with Mustard Herb Crust

Nicole Koloski
East Sandwich, MA
*Piecemakers 1995
Calendar Quilt*

Makes 24-28 servings

14-lb. whole pork leg
¹/4 tsp. pepper
1 tsp. garlic salt
¹/2 cup prepared mustard
3 tsp. Worcestershire
  sauce
1 tsp. ground ginger
¹/2 cup butter, melted
6 slices bread, crumbled
¹/2 cup chopped fresh
  parsley

1. Remove skin and excess
fat from pork. Leave thin
layer of fat. Place on rack in
large roasting pan, fat side
up. Rub with pepper and
garlic salt.
2. Roast at 325° for 3¹/2
hours or until meat ther-
mometer reads 170-180°.
Remove from oven.
3. While pork is roasting,
mix together mustard,
Worcestershire sauce, and
ginger. Remove 2 Tbsp. fat
from pork pan drippings
and add to mustard mixture.

Mix well.
4. In separate bowl combine
butter, bread crumbs, and
parsley.
5. Using a pastry brush,
spread mustard mixture
over pork leg evenly. Gently
pat bread crumbs onto pork
leg and return to oven. Bake
an additional 15 minutes
until bread crumbs are
lightly toasted. Remove
from pan and let rest 15
minutes. Carve and serve.

*Note: This stuffing mixture
may also be used as a stuffing
for individual pork chops.*

Barbecue Roast of Pork

Patti Boston
Newark, OH
Cathedral Window

Makes 4-6 servings

3-5-lb. pork roast
10³/4-oz. can tomato soup
¹/3 cup chopped onion
¹/3 cup chopped celery
1 clove garlic, minced
2 Tbsp. brown sugar
2 Tbsp. Worcestershire
  sauce
2 Tbsp. lemon juice
2 tsp. prepared mustard
4 drops Tabasco sauce

1. Place roast in shallow
pan. Roast at 325° for 45
minutes per pound (3-lb.
pork roast needs 2¹/4 hours).
One hour before meat is
done, remove from oven
and pour off juices.

2. Combine all remaining ingredients and pour over meat. Return to oven and continue roasting, basting frequently with sauce.

Baked Pork Tenderloin with Mustard Sauce
Bobbie Jean Weidner Muscarella
State College, PA
State College Centennial Quilt

Makes 10-12 servings

Roast Pork:
1/2 cup soy sauce
1/2 cup bourbon
4 Tbsp. brown sugar
3 1-lb. pork tenderloins

Mustard Sauce:
1 Tbsp. dry mustard
4 Tbsp. Dijon mustard
2 Tbsp. sugar
1/2 tsp. salt
2 Tbsp. vinegar
4 egg yolks, beaten
1 cup cream

1. Mix together soy sauce, bourbon, and brown sugar.
2. Place pork tenderloins in shallow dish and pour marinade over them. Marinate meat for 2-3 hours at room temperature, turning occasionally.
3. Place meat in roasting pan and roast at 325° for 1 1/4 hours or until meat is tender and its juices run clear when pierced with a fork. Carve pork into thin,

diagonal slices and serve with mustard sauce.
4. To prepare sauce combine dry mustard, Dijon mustard, sugar, salt, vinegar, and egg yolks in top of double boiler. Cook over simmering water, stirring constantly until thickened. Cool slightly. Stir in cream. Serve the sauce just heated or at room temperature.

Note: This sauce may be prepared ahead of time and kept in the refrigerator for up to 3 days. It is also delicious on ham.

Grilled Pork
Ann Mather
Lansing, MI
Miniature Churn Dash

Makes 6-8 servings

1/4 cup soy sauce
2 Tbsp. dry red wine
1 Tbsp. brown sugar
1 Tbsp. honey
1 green onion, chopped
1 clove garlic, crushed
1/2 tsp. cinnamon
2-lb. pork tenderloin

1. Combine all ingredients, except pork, in large bowl.
2. Place pork in bowl. Cover and let stand in refrigerator from 1 hour to overnight, turning occasionally.
3. Drain marinade and grill pork, basting occasionally with marinade.

Pork Chop Casserole
Jean Hannemann
Marquette, MI
Love Is My Gift

Makes 6 servings

6 strips bacon
8 ozs. sauerkraut, drained
6 pork chops
3 onions, sliced into rings
4 large potatoes, peeled and sliced
20-oz. can stewed tomatoes, undrained
1/2 tsp. salt
1/4 tsp. pepper
caraway seeds

1. Line bottom of 5-quart casserole dish with bacon. Layer sauerkraut, pork chops, onion rings, and potatoes over bacon. Pour stewed tomatoes over entire casserole. Sprinkle with salt, pepper, and caraway seeds.
2. Bake at 350° for 2 hours.

Posole
Jeanne Allen
Los Alamos, NM
Clams in the Cabin

Makes 8-10 servings

1 lb. pork, trimmed of fat
1 onion, chopped
1 clove garlic, finely diced
1 tsp. oregano
2 4-oz. cans green chilies
12-16-oz. pkg. frozen
   hominy
2 cups water
salt and pepper to taste

1. Mix together all ingredients in a crockpot. Cook for 6-8 hours on medium heat, stirring once after about 3-4 hours.
2. Slice pork and serve.

Sausage Casserole
Anne Fiedler
Barrington, IL
Alaskan Sampler

Makes 4 servings

6 mild or hot Italian link
   sausages
1 pint whipping cream
1 cup diced zucchini
1/2 cup chopped onion
2 cloves garlic, diced
1 cup grated fontina
   cheese
2-3 cups cooked pasta

1. Boil sausage until done. Crumble while still warm, removing casings.

2. Heat cream just to boiling point.
3. Mix together sausage, whipping cream, zucchini, onion, garlic, 3/4 cup cheese, and pasta.
4. Pour into greased casserole dish. Top with remaining cheese.
5. Bake at 350° for 20 minutes.

Note: Flavor is enhanced if prepared a day ahead and refrigerated. I like to prepare this dish when I have guests arriving from out of town.

Sausage Cornbread Stuffing
Joyce Shackelford
Green Bay, WI
Double Irish Chain
Laura M. Rohwedder
Pittsburgh, PA
Garden Path

Makes 10-12 servings

3/4 lb. bulk pork sausage
3/4 cup chopped onion
1/2 cup chopped celery
1/2 cup chopped green
   pepper
1/2 cup margarine or butter
2 eggs, beaten
1/8 tsp. pepper
1 tsp. poultry seasoning
5 cups dry bread cubes
5 cups crumbled
   cornbread
3/4 cup toasted pecans,
   chopped
1 1/2 cups chicken broth

1. Cook sausage until browned. Drain excess fat, reserving 2 Tbsp. drippings.
2. In same pan cook onion, celery, and green pepper in margarine or butter until tender.
3. Mix together eggs, pepper, and poultry seasoning. Add bread cubes and cornbread. Toss to coat.
4. Stir in sausage, reserved drippings, vegetables, and pecans. Add enough broth to moisten (3/4 to 1 cup).
5. Place in a casserole dish. Drizzle with remaining broth.
6. Bake covered at 325° for 40 minutes.

Note: This stuffing is wonderful for stuffing a 9-10-lb. turkey.

Sweet and Sour Brisket
Alyce C. Kauffman
Gridley, CA
Sailing Away

Makes 6-8 servings

16-oz. can stewed
  tomatoes, cut-up
8-oz. can sauerkraut
1 cup applesauce
2 Tbsp. brown sugar
2¹/2-3¹/2-lb. beef brisket
2 Tbsp. cold water
2 Tbsp. cornstarch
parsley sprigs

1. In a 10-inch skillet, combine undrained tomatoes, undrained sauerkraut, applesauce, and brown sugar. Bring to a boil. Reduce heat.
2. Add brisket, spooning some of sauce over meat. Cover and simmer 2¹/2-3 hours or until meat is tender, spooning sauce over meat occasionally.
3. Transfer meat to serving dish and keep warm. Skim off excess fat from juices. Combine cold water and cornstarch. Stir into tomato juices. Cook and stir until thickened and bubbly. Cook and stir 2 minutes longer.
4. Spoon some of sauce over brisket. Serve the remaining sauce as a gravy. Garnish sliced meat with parsley sprigs.

Sauerbraten
Irene Klaeger
Inverness, FL

Makes 10-12 servings

Sauerbraten:
5-6-lb. rump roast
2 cups wine vinegar
2 cups water
¹/4 cup brown sugar
1 Tbsp. salt
1 bay leaf
¹/2 tsp. pepper
3 medium onions,
  chopped
2 large carrots, pared and
  diced
1¹/2 cups diced celery
2 Tbsp. vegetable
  shortening

Gravy:
4 Tbsp. butter
4 Tbsp. flour
4 cups broth

1. Place roast in large bowl. Mix together vinegar, water, brown sugar, salt, bay leaf, pepper, onions, carrots, and celery and pour over meat. Cover. Marinate in refrigerator for 2-3 days, turning roast several times.
2. Remove meat from marinade and pat dry. Brown meat in shortening in large Dutch oven. Add vegetable marinade. Bring to a boil and cover. Simmer for 3 hours, or until meat is tender.
3. Remove meat from broth and keep warm.
4. To prepare gravy strain broth from roast into 4-cup

measure and let stand a minute until fat rises. Skim off fat and add enough water to make 4 cups. Melt butter in Dutch oven and add flour, stirring constantly until flour is lightly browned. Stir in broth over low heat, stirring constantly until gravy is smooth and thickened.
5. Serve roast and gravy with mashed potatoes.

French Dip
Barbara Walker
Sturgis, SD
Grapevine

Makes 6 servings

3-lb. rump roast
¹/2 cup soy sauce
1 beef bouillon cube
1 bay leaf
1 tsp. thyme
3-4 peppercorns
1 tsp. garlic powder
water

1. Place meat in crockpot. Add remaining ingredients, including enough water to cover roast.
2. Cook on low for 10 hours.

Saki Flank Steak
Dorothy Reise
Severna Park, MD
Honey Bee

Makes 3-4 servings

1/4 cup soy sauce
1/4 cup saki or sherry
1/4 cup cooking oil
2 tsp. powdered ginger
1 clove garlic, crushed
1 tsp. sugar
1 1/2 lbs. flank steak, not
   scored

1. Combine soy sauce, saki, oil, ginger, garlic, and sugar for marinade.
2. Marinate steak for 24-48 hours in refrigerator. Drain well.
3. Grill over hot charcoal for 4-5 minutes. Slice very thinly on the diagonal.
4. Serve hot as an entree or cold as an hors d'oeuvre.

Classic Beef Stroganoff
Tracy Supcoe
Barclay, MD
Patience Corner

Makes 4 servings

1 lb. beef tenderloin or
   sirloin steak
2 Tbsp. margarine or
   butter
1/2 lb. mushrooms, washed,
   trimmed, and sliced
1 medium onion,
   chopped
10 3/4-oz. can beef broth
2 Tbsp. ketchup
1 small clove garlic,
   minced
1 tsp. salt
3 Tbsp. flour
1 cup sour cream
4 cups uncooked noodles

1. Cut meat across the grain into 1/2" strips, about 1 1/2" long. (Ask butcher to do this for you.)
2. Melt butter or margarine in large skillet. Add mushrooms and onion. Cook and stir until onion is tender. Remove from skillet.
3. In same skillet cook meat until light brown. Reserve 1/3 cup beef broth. Stir remaining broth, ketchup, garlic, and salt into meat.

Cover and simmer for 15 minutes.
4. Stir flour into 1/3 cup beef broth and add to meat mixture. Add mushrooms and onion and heat to boiling, stirring constantly. Boil and stir 1 minute. Reduce heat.
5. Stir in sour cream and heat just to boiling point.
6. Meanwhile, prepare noodles according to package directions.
7. Remove beef mixture from heat and serve over noodles.

Meatball Stroganoff
Shan D. Lear
Middleton, MA
Let's Twist Again

Makes 6 servings

Meatballs:
1 1/2 lbs. ground beef
1/2 cup dry bread crumbs
1 tsp. salt
1/2 cup milk
3/4 cup chopped onion
1/8 tsp. garlic powder
1/4 tsp. pepper
3 Tbsp. cooking oil

Sauce:
1 cup sour cream
1/4 cup flour
10 3/4-oz. can beef
   consommé
3 Tbsp. tomato paste
1 tsp. Worcestershire
   sauce
1/4 tsp. salt
1/4 cup sherry (optional)

Christmas is a time for being with family, and anytime family is together is a special memory. The love of family and friends, along with the sights, sounds, and smells of the holiday season all add up to warm my heart and leave memories to last a lifetime.
—*Mary Rogers, Waseca, MN*

1. Mix together ground beef, bread crumbs, salt, milk, onion, garlic powder, and pepper. Mix well and shape into 1" balls.
2. Brown meatballs in cooking oil. Drain well and set aside.
3. Blend together sour cream and flour. Add beef consommé, tomato paste, Worcestershire sauce, and salt. Pour over meatballs and cook for 10-15 minutes. If adding wine, stir into sauce and cook until heated through.
4. Serve over cooked noodles or hot rice.

No-Peek Stew
Nancy Rexrode Clark
Ellicott City, MD
Sampler

Makes 4-6 servings

1 1/2 lbs. beef cubes
10 3/4-oz. can golden
  mushroom soup
1 cup red wine
1 pkg. dry onion soup mix

1. In casserole dish mix together all ingredients. Cover.
2. Bake at 300° for 3 hours without lifting cover.

Note: This is an easy and delicious dish to prepare during the busy holiday season.

Mom's Best Meatloaf
Ruth Ann Hoover
New Holland, PA
Spinning Star

Makes 6-8 servings

1 1/2 lbs. ground beef
1 cup milk
1 egg, slightly beaten
3/4 cup soft bread crumbs
1 medium onion,
  chopped
1 Tbsp. chopped green
  pepper
3 Tbsp. ketchup
1 1/2 tsp. salt
1 tsp. sugar

1. Combine ground beef, milk, egg, bread crumbs, onion, green pepper, 1 Tbsp. ketchup, salt, and sugar. Mix well.
2. Press into an ungreased 4" x 8" loaf pan.
3. Bake at 350° for 1 hour.
4. Remove from oven and drizzle remaining 2 Tbsp. ketchup over top of loaf. Return to oven and bake another 15 minutes.

Sweet and Sour Meatballs
Bea Gagliano
Lakewood, NJ
Appliqué Heart Dream Quilt

Makes 4-6 servings

Meatballs:
1 1/2 lbs. ground beef
2 Tbsp. cooked rice
1 egg
1/2 tsp. salt
1/4 tsp. pepper
1/2 tsp. paprika

Sauce:
1 onion
1 Tbsp. cooking oil
8-oz. can tomato sauce
1/2 cup brown sugar
2-3 Tbsp. lemon juice
1/3 cup raisins
3 gingersnaps, crushed
1 cup whole cranberry
  sauce

1. Mix together ground beef, rice, egg, salt, pepper, and paprika. Mix well and form into small balls.
2. To prepare sauce brown onion in cooking oil. Drain and mix in tomato sauce, brown sugar, lemon juice, raisins, gingersnaps, and cranberry sauce.
3. Put sauce and meatballs in a crockpot and cook on medium to low for 4-5 hours.

Chafing-Dish Meatballs

Donna A. Lessmann
Commack, NY
May Flowers

Makes 4 dozen meatballs

Meatballs:
1 1/2 lbs. ground beef
1/2 cup dry bread crumbs
1 tsp. salt
1/4 tsp. pepper
1 egg
1/2 cup milk

Sauce:
1/2 cup ketchup
1/2 cup molasses
1/2 cup vinegar
20-oz. can pineapple
   chunks
1 cup green olives

1. Mix together ground beef, bread crumbs, salt, pepper, egg, and milk. Shape into 1/2" meatballs and place on greased cookie sheet.
2. Brown at 350° for 15-20 minutes.
3. In large skillet mix together ketchup, molasses, and vinegar. Blend well. Add meatballs and cook uncovered over low heat for about 20 minutes or until sauce thickens and coats meatballs.
4. Immediately before serving, stir in pineapple chunks and olives.

Note: I serve these at parties using a chafing dish.

Cranberry Meatballs

Anna Petersheim
Paradise, PA
Noah's Ark Crib
Char Hagner
Montague, MI
Sunbonnet Sue

Makes 12 servings

Meatballs:
2 lbs. ground beef or
   pork
2 eggs, beaten
1 cup cornflake crumbs
1/3 cup ketchup
2 Tbsp. soy sauce
1 Tbsp. dried parsley
   flakes
2 Tbsp. dehydrated onion
1/2 tsp. salt
1/4 tsp. pepper

Sauce:
16-oz. can jellied
   cranberry sauce
1 cup ketchup or chili
   sauce
3 Tbsp. brown sugar
1 Tbsp. lemon juice

1. Mix together ground meat, eggs, cornflake crumbs, ketchup, soy sauce, parsley flakes, onion, salt, and pepper. Shape into 72 1" meatballs.
2. Place in large baking pan.
3. Bake at 350° for 20-25 minutes. Remove from oven and drain on paper towel.
4. Mix together cranberry sauce, ketchup or chili sauce, brown sugar, and lemon juice. Cook in large skillet or Dutch oven, stir-

ring frequently, until cranberry sauce is melted.
5. Add meatballs to sauce and heat thoroughly.

Cheeseburger Roll

Sue Hamilton
Minooka, IL
Garden Twist

Makes 6 servings

Dough:
1 cup warm water
1 Tbsp. cooking oil
1 tsp. salt
1 tsp. sugar
1 pkg. yeast
3 cups flour

Filling:
1 lb. ground beef
1/2 cup diced onions
1/4 cup ketchup
1/4 cup prepared mustard
1/4 cup dill pickles, diced
4 slices bacon
1 cup shredded cheddar
   cheese
sesame seeds

1. To prepare dough mix together water, oil, salt, sugar, and yeast. Mix until yeast is dissolved. Stir in flour. Work into a smooth ball. Leave in bowl and cover to rise.
2. Fry ground beef and onions together. Remove from heat and drain all excess fat. Mix in ketchup, mustard, pickles, bacon, and cheese and stir well. Set aside.
3. On a floured surface, roll

dough out into a 12" x 18" rectangle. Spread filling over dough. Roll up like a jelly roll.

4. Place seam side down on a greased jelly roll pan. Brush with water and cover with sesame seeds.

5. Bake at 350° for 30-35 minutes. Serve.

Scalloped Oysters
Karen Harer
Fort Hood, TX
Emma B. Ebersole
Lancaster, PA
Christine Weaver
Reinholds, PA

Makes 4-5 servings

4 cups coarsely crushed saltines
1 pint fresh or canned oysters
2 cups milk
1/4 tsp. pepper
1/4 tsp. salt
1/3 cup margarine

1. Line bottom of 1 1/2-quart casserole dish with 2 cups cracker crumbs. Place half of oysters on top of crackers. Layer remaining cracker crumbs over oysters.

2. Mix together milk, pepper, and salt. Pour over oysters and crackers. Dot with margarine. Let stand until milk is absorbed.

3. Bake at 375° for 30 minutes.

Note: Oyster juice can be substituted for part of the milk.

Crab Imperial
Jacquelyn Kreitzer
Mechanicsburg, PA
Starlit Flower Garden

Makes 6 servings

1 lb. crab meat
2 Tbsp. butter
2 Tbsp. flour
3/4 cup milk
1 egg, slightly beaten
1 hard-boiled egg, finely chopped
1 Tbsp. mayonnaise
6 drops Worcestershire sauce
1/2 tsp. dry mustard
1/2 tsp. parsley flakes
1/4 tsp. seafood seasoning
1 tsp. salt
1/4 tsp. pepper
6 baking shells
1/2 cup bread crumbs
1/4 cup melted butter
pimiento for garnish

1. Remove cartilage from crab meat and place in large bowl.

2. In saucepan melt butter over low heat. Stir in flour to make paste. Add milk and cook slowly until thickened, stirring constantly. Reserve 6 Tbsp. white sauce.

3. Stir remaining white sauce into crabmeat. Add egg, hard-boiled egg, mayonnaise, Worcestershire sauce, mustard, parsley, seafood seasoning, salt, and pepper. Mix gently but thoroughly.

4. Put crab meat mixture into 6 baking shells. Top

each with bread crumbs, melted butter, and reserved sauce. Garnish with pimiento.

5. Bake at 350° for 15-20 minutes until browned.

Shrimp Creole
Ann Mould
Mt. Pleasant, SC
Teacups

Makes 6 servings

3 cups shrimp
2 Tbsp. bacon drippings
2 medium onions, chopped
1 green pepper, chopped
1 1/2 cups chopped celery
1 quart canned tomatoes
3 Tbsp. tomato paste
1 tsp. sugar
salt and pepper to taste

1. Boil shrimp in shells briefly, just until pink. Remove shells and set aside.

2. Sauté onions, green pepper, and celery in bacon drippings. Stir in tomatoes and 1/2 of tomato liquid, tomato paste, and sugar. Simmer slowly for 30-45 minutes until thickened. Stir in salt and pepper.

3. 15 minutes before serving, add shrimp and serve over white rice.

Rich Man's Casserole
Jeanne Sanson
Chatham, IL
Log Cabin Blues

Makes 6 servings

2 7¹/2-oz. cans fancy crab meat
2 7¹/2-oz. cans medium or large shrimp
15-oz. jar artichoke hearts, drained
¹/2 lb. fresh mushrooms, halved
10-12 pitted ripe olives
2¹/2 Tbsp. butter or margarine
3 Tbsp. flour
¹/2 tsp. salt
1¹/2 cups half-and-half
3 Tbsp. dry sherry

3 Tbsp. cereal crumbs
2 Tbsp. grated Parmesan cheese
paprika

1. Drain crab meat and shrimp. Remove any shells. Cut artichokes in half and place in greased glass pan. Cover with crab, shrimp, mushrooms, and olives.
2. In saucepan melt butter. Blend in flour and salt. Gradually add half-and-half and cook until thickened, stirring constantly. Stir in sherry. Pour sauce over meat mixture.
3. Combine cereal crumbs and Parmesan cheese. Sprinkle over sauce. Top with sprinkle of paprika.
4. Bake at 450° for 30 minutes.

This is the story of the year we had spam sandwiches and cookies for our Christmas dinner. In the early years of my marriage, I bought groceries by the day as did everyone else in town. You put on a clean apron, walked up to the store, and bought your meat and whatever else you needed for the day. Each day you charged your purchases, and on Friday you paid up.

This particular Christmas we were invited to my folks for the day. But we woke up on Christmas morning to a blizzard and were not able to get out to their home, which was about two miles out of town. Needless to say, I was not prepared to cook a typical Christmas meal.

One of the men my husband worked with got stuck on his way to work and ended up stranded at our home. He shared our humble meal. And for many years after that, my husband's co-workers always asked what we were having for Christmas dinner.

—Mary Davis, Akron, MI

Catfish Court Bouillon
Carol Lyle
Jacksonville, FL
Grandmother's Fan

Makes 6 servings

Homemade Roux:
6 Tbsp. cooking oil
6 Tbsp. flour

Catfish Court Bouillon:
6 3-oz. catfish fillets
2 medium onions, chopped
¹/2 cup margarine
4-oz. can tomato paste
8-oz. can tomatoes
roux
6 cups water
2 10³/4-oz. cans cream of mushroom soup
1 tsp. salt
¹/4 tsp. red pepper
¹/4 tsp. pepper
¹/2 tsp. garlic powder
¹/4 cup green onions, chopped
2 Tbsp. parsley, chopped

1. To make roux (a thickening used in creole cooking), heat oil and flour together in an iron skillet. Cook very slowly, stirring until mixture turns a soft brown color.
2. In large skillet or Dutch oven, sauté onions in margarine. Stir in tomato paste, tomatoes, roux, and water. Simmer for 30 minutes, then add mushroom soup, seasonings, green onions, and parsley. Simmer another 15 minutes.
3. Add catfish fillets and

simmer another 10 minutes.
4. Serve over hot, cooked
rice.

Escargot Monaco
Mary Ann Mazur
Dublin, OH
ABC Quilt

Makes 6 servings

1/2 cup margarine,
softened
4 cloves garlic, minced
1 tsp. creole seasoning
24 large fresh mushroom
crowns
2 4³/4-oz. cans large snails
(24 snails)
4 Tbsp. white wine
1/2 cup Parmesan cheese,
grated
4 Tbsp. parsley, snipped

1. Combine margarine, garlic, and creole seasoning.
Spread 1/2 of mixture on the
bottom of 6 individual glass
casserole dishes or 2 glass
pie plates.
2. Coat mushroom crowns
with remaining garlic mixture and place 4 mushrooms
in each casserole dish or 12
mushrooms in each pie
plate.
3. Drain and rinse snails.
Fill each mushroom with 1
snail. Sprinkle with wine,
Parmesan cheese, and parsley. Cover with plastic wrap
and refrigerate until ready
to cook and serve.
4. Prepare in microwave. For
6 individual casserole dishes,
microwave 3 casseroles at a

time on high for 2 minutes.
For 2 pie plates, microwave
one plate at a time on high
for 2 minutes.
5. Serve immediately with
French bread.

Seafood Thermidor
Kathi Stingle
Lederach, PA
Star Gems

Makes 10 servings

1 lb. haddock
1 lb. shrimp
1 lb. scallops
2 10³/4-oz. cans cream of
mushroom
2 10³/4-oz. cans cream of
shrimp
1/2 cup half-and-half
1/3 cup dry sherry
2 Tbsp. brandy
1 lb. imitation seafood
flakes
2 Tbsp. dried chopped
parsley
grated Parmesan cheese

1. Put haddock in 9" x 13"
baking dish. Wrap shrimp
and scallops separately and
loosely in foil and bake at
same time as haddock. Bake
both at 350° for 15 minutes
or until fish flakes.
2. Mix together cream of
mushroom, cream of
shrimp, and half-and-half.
Heat until hot and smooth.
Stir in sherry and brandy.
3. Stir in haddock, shrimp,
scallops, seafood flakes, and
parsley.

4. Pour into 3-quart baking
dish. Sprinkle with
Parmesan cheese.
5. Bake at 350° for 30-40
minutes.

Seafood Bake
Muriel B. Haley
Dexter, ME
Trip Around the World

Makes 10 servings

1 lb. haddock, cut into
cubes
1 lb. scallops
1 lb. shrimp
1/2 cup butter
1/2 cup flour
3 cups milk
3/4 tsp. salt
1/2 cup cooking sherry
2 Tbsp. Ritz cracker
crumbs

1. Layer seafood in a
9" x 13" pan.
2. In saucepan melt butter
over medium heat. Stir in
flour. Gradually add milk.
Cook until white sauce
thickens. Remove from heat
and stir in salt and sherry.
Pour over fish. Top with
cracker crumbs.
3. Bake at 300° for 45 minutes. Serve over rice.

Tuna Foldovers
Alyce C. Kauffman
Gridley, CA
Sailing Away

Makes 6-8 servings

7$\frac{1}{2}$-oz. can tuna
1 hard-boiled egg,
  chopped
2 Tbsp. finely chopped
  onion
10$\frac{3}{4}$-oz. cream of
  mushroom soup
$\frac{1}{4}$ tsp. pepper
1 9" unbaked pie shell

1. Combine tuna, egg,
onion, 4 Tbsp. mushroom
soup, and pepper.
2. Cut pie shell into as
many 4" squares as possible.
3. Spoon portion of mixture
into center of squares. Fold
on diagonal to make a triangle and fasten with a toothpick. Place on lightly
greased cookie sheet.
4. Bake at 450° for 12 minutes.
5. Heat remaining mush-
room soup and serve with
baked tuna foldovers.

Tuna Noodle a la Vicki
Mary Lou Blount
Medina, NY
Churn Dash

Makes 6 servings

12-oz. pkg. egg noodles
4 Tbsp. margarine
4 Tbsp. flour
2 cups milk
7$\frac{1}{2}$-oz. can tuna, drained
2 cups shredded cheddar
  cheese

1. Prepare noodles according to package directions.
Drain and set aside.
2. In saucepan melt mar-
garine. Slowly stir in flour
until smooth and creamy.
Slowly stir in milk. Stir over
medium heat until white
sauce has thickened.
3. Stir in tuna, cheese, and
cooked egg noodles.
4. Cover and bake at 350°
for 30 minutes.

Roast Turkey with Sausage-Apple Stuffing
Carol Ambrose
Napa, CA
Kittens in the Attic

Makes 10 servings

10-12-lb. turkey
4 cups diced white or
  wheat bread
$\frac{1}{4}$ cup chopped parsley
$\frac{1}{2}$ cup chopped celery
1 tsp. tarragon or basil
$\frac{3}{4}$ tsp. salt
$\frac{1}{2}$ tsp. paprika
$\frac{1}{8}$ tsp. nutmeg
milk to moisten very
  lightly
3 eggs
1 cup crumbled, cooked
  sausage
1 cup grated, peeled
  apple
1 Tbsp. chopped onion
  (optional)

1. Mix together all ingredients and stuff turkey. Do
not stuff turkey tightly
because stuffing will expand
some while cooking. Place
any extra stuffing in lightly
greased covered casserole
dish.
2. Bake at 325°. For a
turkey under 12 lbs., allow
30-45 minutes per pound.
For a turkey 12 lbs. or more,
allow 20-30 minutes per
pound.
3. Bake extra stuffing at
325° for $\frac{1}{2}$ hour.

Main Dishes

Roast Turkey with Sausage Stuffing
Abbie Christie
Berkeley Heights, NJ
Double Wedding Ring

Makes 12-15 servings

15-lb. turkey
1 lb. sausage
2 medium onions, chopped
6 stalks celery, chopped
1/2-1 lb. mushrooms, sliced
1 Tbsp. salt
1 Tbsp. thyme
1 Tbsp. parsley flakes
1/2 tsp. pepper
1 Tbsp. cooking oil
1 loaf of bread, crumbled
2 eggs, slightly beaten
1-1 1/2 cups milk

1. Fry sausage, onions, celery, mushrooms, salt, thyme, parsley, and pepper in cooking oil over low heat. Do not drain.
2. Mix together bread, eggs, and 1 cup milk. Add sausage mixture including fat. Mix well. Add more milk if needed for moisture.
3. Stuff bird just before roasting. Place any extra stuffing in a covered, greased casserole dish.
4. Bake at 325° for 20-30 minutes per pound. Bake extra stuffing at 325° for 1/2 hour.

Note: This is my grand-mother's recipe and always brings back warm memories of love whenever I make it.

Turkey Fondue Bake
Katie Esh
Ronks, PA

Makes 8 servings

2 Tbsp. butter, melted
1 cup milk
1 cup turkey broth
1 Tbsp. chopped celery
1 3/4 cups bread cubes
1 tsp. salt
1/8 tsp. pepper
1 tsp. thyme
1 tsp. parsley flakes
1 tsp. onion salt
2 Tbsp. lemon juice
2 cups turkey, cut into small pieces
6 eggs yolks, beaten slightly
6 egg whites, beaten until stiff

1. Melt butter in saucepan. Add milk and turkey broth and heat through.
2. Blend celery, bread cubes, salt, pepper, thyme, parsley flakes, onion salt, lemon juice, turkey, and egg yolks into liquid mixture and mix well. Cook slowly until thickened, stirring frequently.
3. Remove from heat. Beat egg white until stiff. Fold into mixture.
4. Pour into lightly greased baking dish and bake at 350° for 1 1/4 hours.

Hot Turkey Hustle Up
Anne Townsend
Albuquerque, NM
Stripe Stars

Makes 8 servings

Turkey:
4 cups chopped, cooked turkey
2 cups chopped celery
2 Tbsp. lemon juice
4 hard-boiled eggs, sliced
1/2 cup slivered, blanched almonds
2-oz. jar chopped pimiento (optional)
1/2 cup mayonnaise
10 3/4-oz. can cream of mushroom soup
1 tsp. salt
1 Tbsp. onion flakes

Topping:
1/2 cup flour
1/2 tsp. salt
1/2 cup sesame seeds
1/2 cup grated American cheese
1/4 cup butter, melted

1. Mix together all turkey ingredients in the order given. Spread into 8" x 12" baking dish.
2. To prepare topping combine all ingredients. Spread over mixture in baking dish.
3. Bake at 325° for 30 to 35 minutes.

Note: This is an excellent way to use up your holiday bird.

113

Turkey or Chicken Meatballs
Dolly Jansen
DePere, WI
Victorian Hearts

Makes 6-8 servings

Meatballs:
1 medium onion,
   chopped
1 stalk celery, chopped
1 Tbsp. cooking oil
1 egg, beaten
2 Tbsp. milk
2 slices white bread,
   cubed
3 Tbsp. Parmesan cheese
1 Tbsp. dry parsley
1 tsp. salt and pepper
1 lb. ground turkey or
   chicken

Sauce:
10³/₄-oz. can cream of
   chicken or mushroom
   soup
1/3 cup milk
1/2 cup sour cream or
   cream cheese
2 4-oz. cans mushrooms
   (optional)
1/8 tsp. nutmeg

1. Sauté onion and celery in cooking oil. Drain.
2. Mix together onions, celery, egg, milk, bread, Parmesan cheese, parsley, salt, pepper, and meat. Shape into 1¹/₂" balls. Place balls on greased jelly roll pan.
3. Bake at 425° for 20 minutes.
4. To prepare sauce combine all ingredients in a saucepan. Heat, bringing just to boiling point.
5. Pour sauce over meatballs and serve.

Leftover Turkey Barbecue
Anona M. Teel
Bangor, PA
Irish Chain

Makes 10 servings

2 Tbsp. cooking oil
5 tsp. vinegar
2/3 cup turkey broth
1 cup ketchup
1/3 cup brown sugar
1/3 cup chopped onion
3/4 cup chopped celery

1 tsp. Worcestershire
   sauce
1/2 tsp. dry mustard
1/2 tsp. salt
5¹/₂ cups chopped turkey

1. Mix together all ingredients except turkey. Simmer for 15 minutes.
2. Add turkey and heat well. Serve on hamburger rolls.

Turkey Pot Pie
Barb Lucas
Fishers, IN

Makes 1 10" pie

1 cup chopped onion
1 cup chopped celery
1 cup chopped carrots
1/2 cup frozen green peas
1/3 cup butter, melted
1/2 cup flour
2 cups chicken broth
1 cup half-and-half
1/2 tsp. salt
1/4 tsp. pepper
4 cups diced, cooked
   turkey
2 10" unbaked pie shells

1. Sauté onion, celery, carrots, and peas in butter for 10 minutes. Add flour and cook one minute, stirring constantly.
2. Mix together chicken broth and half-and-half. Gradually stir into vegetable mixture. Cook over medium heat, stirring constantly until thick and bubbly.
3. Season with salt and pepper. Add turkey and stir. Pour into unbaked pie shell.

For Christmas 1995 my favorite aunt gave me a quilt top that had been in her trunk for fifty years. It was a primitive red and brown Log Cabin made by her grandmother—my great-grandmother—around 1900 in Monroe, South Dakota. I wish I knew the history behind every remnant, the dresses and shirts that appear in this wonderful treasure. My friends at the Methodist church in Yorba Linda, California, quilted the top, and I now have a priceless family heirloom.

—*Sharon Peterson, Hemet, CA*

4. Cover with pie shell, seal edges, and prick top with fork.
5. Bake at 400° for 40 minutes or until crust is golden brown.

Turkey Supreme
Beverly Roberts Kessler
Marietta, SC
Christmas Angel

Makes 12 servings

2 pkgs. long grain wild rice
1/2 cup butter
1/2 cup flour
1 tsp. salt
1/4 tsp. pepper
1 1/2 cups chicken broth
2/3 cups milk
3 cups diced, cooked turkey
1/2 cup chopped green pepper
1 cup sliced mushrooms
1/4 cup chopped pimiento
1/3 cup slivered almonds (optional)

1. Cook rice according to directions on box.
2. In a saucepan melt butter. Blend in flour, salt, and pepper. Cook over low heat until bubbly, stirring frequently. Remove from heat. Stir in broth and milk. Bring to a boil for 1 minute, stirring constantly.
3. Add all remaining ingredients, including rice. Pour into greased 9" x 13" casserole dish.
4. Bake at 350° for 40-45 minutes.

Orange-Flavored Chicken
Kaye Merrill
Olive Branch, MS
Bow Tie

Makes 4-6 servings

5-lb. whole chicken
1 orange
1 onion
salt and pepper to taste
1 tsp. thyme
1 tsp. rosemary
1/2 cup cooking wine
3 Tbsp. margarine, melted
3 Tbsp. Dijon mustard
3 Tbsp. honey
1 Tbsp. apricot marmalade
3 Tbsp. orange juice

1. Wash chicken and pat dry.
2. Cut orange into quarters and squeeze over chicken. Place orange quarters inside cavity of chicken. Quarter onion and place inside cavity of chicken.
3. Sprinkle outside of chicken with salt, pepper, thyme, and rosemary. Put in roasting pan. Pour cooking wine into bottom of pan.
4. Bake at 400° for 35-40 minutes.
5. Prepare glaze while chicken is roasting. In saucepan combine margarine, mustard, honey, and marmalade. Heat and add orange juice.
6. Spoon glaze over chicken. Reduce oven temperature to 350° and bake for 1-1 1/2 hours or until done. Carve and serve.

Roast Chicken Deluxe
Jeanne Allen
Los Alamos, NM
Clams in the Cabin

Makes 4 servings

1 medium onion, peeled
7 whole cloves
4-lb. stewing chicken
1 oz. brandy
salt to taste
1 lemon, peeled
1 orange, peeled
2 Tbsp. butter

1. Stud onion with cloves. Wash and dry chicken. Rinse chicken cavity with brandy. Salt cavity. Place lemon, orange, and onion in cavity. Truss with skewers.
2. Rub outside of chicken with butter. Wrap in aluminum foil and place in baking dish.
3. Bake at 450° for 1 1/2-1 3/4 hours. Unwrap foil. Bake several minutes longer to brown chicken. Carve and serve.

Deviled Barbecue Chicken

Audrey Lorence Couvillon
Dallas, TX
Friendship Quilt

Makes 4-6 servings

4-6 chicken breasts
1/4 cup flour
6 Tbsp. olive oil
1 onion, chopped
1 cup beef consommé
1 1/2 tsp. dry mustard
2 tsp. Worcestershire
sauce
1/2-3/4 cup ketchup
paprika to taste

1. Pat flour on chicken
breasts. Slowly brown in
olive oil in large skillet.
Remove chicken to plate.
2. Brown onion in same
pan. Return chicken to skillet and add all remaining
ingredients. Simmer covered
until chicken is done, turning chicken occasionally.
3. Sprinkle lightly with
paprika before serving.

Rolled Chicken Breast and Yellow Rice

Shirley Hedman
Schenectady, NY
Stars for Many Mornings

Makes 6 servings

Chicken:
6 half-breasts of chicken,
deboned and flattened
6 thin slices boiled ham
6 slices Swiss cheese
1 cup skim milk
1 cup dry bread crumbs
butter-flavored spray or
melted margarine
salt and pepper to taste

Rice:
2 cups uncooked rice
4 cups chicken broth
1 tsp. salt
1 tsp. curry powder
1/4 tsp. turmeric

1. Ask butcher to debone
and flatten chicken breasts.
2. Wrap cheese rectangle in
each slice of ham. Place on
flattened chicken breast and
roll up.
3. Hold seam in place while
you dip roll in skim milk
and then in bread crumbs.
4. Arrange seam side down
on lightly greased shallow
baking pan.
5. Spray chicken rolls with
butter-flavored spray or
drizzle lightly with melted
margarine. Season to taste.
6. Bake uncovered at 350°
for 45-60 minutes.
7. Mix together rice and
chicken broth. Add salt,

curry powder, and turmeric.
Pour into baking dish, cover,
and bake along with
chicken. Serve chicken on a
bed of rice.

Company Chicken

Nan Mitchell
Peru, NY
Celeste D. Coffelt
Pasadena, MD
Carolyn W. Carmichael
Berkeley Heights, NJ

Makes 8 servings

4 whole chicken breasts,
boned, skinned, and
split
8 slices Swiss cheese
10 3/4-oz. can cream of
mushroom soup
1/2 cup white wine
(optional)
1/3 cup herb-seasoned
stuffing mix, crushed
1/3 cup butter, melted

1. Place chicken into
greased 9" x 13" baking pan.
Put one slice cheese on each
half chicken breast.
2. Mix together mushroom
soup and wine. Pour soup
mixture over chicken.
3. Sprinkle stuffing mix over
chicken and drizzle with
butter.
4. Bake at 350° for 45-50
minutes.

Cranberry Chicken

Lucille Reagan
Salem, OR
Gertrude Hedrick
Willow Grove, PA
Elsie Widdel
Denver, IA
Dorothy Reise
Severna Park, MD

Makes 6-8 servings

6-8 chicken breasts, boned
16-oz. can whole cranberries
1 pkg. dry onion soup mix
8-oz. jar Russian salad dressing

1. Arrange chicken in a greased 9" x 13" baking pan.
2. Mix together cranberries, onion soup mix, and salad dressing. Pour over chicken.
3. Bake at 350° for 1 hour or until done.
4. Serve with cooked rice.

Chicken Acapulco

Pat Collins
Granada Hills, CA
Bow Tie

Makes 6 servings

6 chicken breasts, boned, skinned
3 Tbsp. margarine
3 Tbsp. flour
2 10³/4-oz. cans cream of chicken soup
16-oz. carton sour cream
4-oz. can green chilies
1/2 tsp. onion salt
1/4 tsp. pepper
2 cups shredded Swiss cheese

1. Place chicken in greased 9" x 13" baking pan.
2. Melt margarine in skillet. Add flour and cook until golden brown. Stir in soup, sour cream, chilies, salt, and pepper. Simmer for 10 minutes, stirring frequently. Pour sauce over chicken in pan.
3. Bake at 400° for 20 minutes. Cover dish with aluminum foil and reduce oven temperature to 350°. Bake for 1 hour.
4. Uncover and sprinkle cheese over chicken. Bake uncovered for 15 more minutes.

Baked Chicken Breasts

Anna Oberholtzer
Lititz, PA
Improved Nine Patch

Makes 12 servings

2 cups sour cream
4 tsp. Worcestershire sauce
1/4 cup lemon juice
1¹/2 tsp. garlic salt
1 tsp. salt
1 tsp. paprika
6 chicken breasts, deboned and skinned
1/2 cup bread crumbs
2 Tbsp. butter, melted

1. Mix together sour cream, Worcestershire sauce, lemon juice, salt, garlic salt, and paprika.
2. Cut each chicken breast in half. Dip each piece in cream mixture, covering both sides of chicken well. Lay chicken in shallow baking pan. Cover and refrigerate for at least 8 hours.
3. Sprinkle bread crumbs over chicken and pour butter over bread crumbs.
4. Bake at 350° for 45 minutes. Pour a little more butter on top and bake for another 15 minutes.

Chicken Dijon

Nancy Rexrode Clark
Ellicott City, MD
Sampler

Makes 4 servings

4-6 boneless, skinless chicken breasts
3 Tbsp. Dijon mustard
3 Tbsp. lemon juice
1/4 cup butter or margarine
1 tsp. fresh or dried tarragon

1. Layer chicken in shallow greased baking pan.
2. Mix together mustard, lemon juice, butter, and tarragon. Spread over chicken.
3. Bake at 350° for 45 minutes.

Country Chicken
Andrea O'Neil
Fairfield, CT
Irish Chain

Makes 6-8 servings

4 medium potatoes,
  peeled and cubed
1 lb. Italian sausage, cut
  into 1" pieces
1 Tbsp. salad oil
2¹/₂-3 lbs. chicken pieces
4 medium green peppers,
  diced
1 large onion, quartered
  and separated
¹/₂ cup water
¹/₂ tsp. salt
¹/₂ tsp. oregano
¹/₂ tsp. basil
2 10-oz. pkgs. frozen
  whole green beans

1. Combine potatoes,
sausage, and salad oil in
medium roasting pan.
2. Bake at 425° for 15 minutes.
3. Add chicken, peppers,
onion, water, salt, oregano,
and basil. Stir to cover
chicken pieces with seasonings. Bake for 40 minutes.
4. Separate frozen beans
under warm running water.
Drain on paper towels.
Sprinkle beans onto chicken
mixture and bake 15-20
minutes longer, stirring
occasionally.

Lemon Chicken
Dana Braden
Seattle, WA
May Baskets for Mother

Makes 2-3 servings

3-4-lb. chicken, cut in
  pieces
juice of 3 lemons
2¹/₂ Tbsp. chopped
  rosemary
¹/₄ cup cooking oil
salt and pepper to taste

1. Arrange chicken in
greased 9" x 13" baking pan.
Pour juice from 2 lemons
over chicken. Cover and
weight down in refrigerator
for at least 8 hours.
2. Pour remaining lemon
juice over chicken. Add
rosemary, oil, salt, and pepper. Cover with aluminum
foil.
3. Bake at 350° for 35-40
minutes. Remove foil and
brown by baking another
10-15 minutes.

Elva's Christmas Chicken Dinner
Elva Engel
Gap, PA
Snowman Sampler Panel

Makes 12 servings

12 chicken legs and
  thighs
¹/₄ cup cooking oil
1 loaf bread, cubed
1 onion, diced
4 eggs, beaten
¹/₂ tsp. salt
1 cup chopped celery
1 tsp. curry powder
1 cup water

1. Brown chicken in oil.
2. Line bottom of roasting
pan with chicken.
3. Mix together bread,
onion, eggs, salt, celery,
curry powder, and water.
Spoon over chicken in roasting pan.
4. Bake at 325° for 2 hours.

Christmas 1988 came on the heels of my husband
having been out of work for a very long time. We
were just making it, and I knew that the last thing
we could buy was a Christmas tree. This also happened to be our first Christmas in Oregon where
there are tree lots on every corner. I noticed one lot
that kept lowering its prices every couple of days.
Unfortunately, our budget still did not allow it. So I
finally resigned myself to not having a tree.

Several days before Christmas, I was talking to my
mother. When she realized how pained I was about
not having a tree, she immediately handed me
enough money to buy one of the most beautiful trees
still remaining on the lot.

—*Nanci C. Keatley, Salem, OR*

Scalloped Chicken and Stuffing

Doris H. Perkins
Mashpee, MA
Lone Star

Makes 12-15 servings

1 pkg. herb-seasoned stuffing mix
1/2 cup chopped green pepper
1 cup chopped celery
2 chicken bouillon cubes
1 1/2 cups margarine
1/2 cup flour
4 cups chicken broth
2 chicken bouillon cubes
6 eggs, slightly beaten
3-4 cups diced, cooked chicken
3/4 tsp. salt
10 3/4-oz. can cream of mushroom soup
1/4 cup milk
1/2 pint sour cream
1/4 cup chopped pimientos

1. Prepare stuffing mix according to package directions. Stir in green pepper, celery, and 2 bouillon cubes. Spread into well greased 9" x 13" baking pan.
2. In top of double boiler, melt margarine. Blend in flour. Add chicken broth. Cook and stir until thickened. Add 2 bouillon cubes to sauce and heat through.
3. Stir small amount of heated sauce into eggs. Stir egg mixture into sauce and heat through, stirring frequently.
4. Spoon cooked chicken over stuffing in baking pan and sprinkle with salt. Pour cream sauce over chicken.
5. Bake at 325° for 45 minutes or until knife inserted in center comes out clean. Let stand for 5-10 minutes, then cut into squares.
6. Meanwhile, prepare a sauce by combining mushroom soup and milk in double boiler. Heat through, then stir in sour cream and pimientos. Heat through and serve with scalloped chicken.

Chicken and Filling

Gladys M. High
Ephrata, PA
Log Cabin
Lizzie Weaver
Ephrata, PA
Medallion

Makes 8-10 servings

1/4 tsp. saffron
1/3 cup boiling water
1 Tbsp. butter
1 Tbsp. shortening
1-lb. loaf homemade white bread, cubed
3 eggs
1 tsp. salt
1/8 tsp. pepper
1/2 tsp. onion salt
1 cup milk
1 cup chicken broth
1/2 tsp. parsley flakes
2 cups diced, cooked chicken
1 Tbsp. butter

1. Add saffron to boiling water and set aside.
2. In saucepan melt 1 Tbsp. butter and shortening. Add 3 cups bread cubes and brown lightly. Brown remaining cubes in oven at 325° for 15 minutes.
3. Beat together eggs, salt, pepper, onion salt, milk, broth, saffron water, and parsley flakes and mix thoroughly. Pour over bread cubes.
4. Stir in browned cubes and chopped chicken and mix lightly with fork, adding more milk and broth if needed to moisten. Pour mixture into greased baking dish. Dot with 1 Tbsp. butter.
5. Bake covered at 325° for 30-45 minutes or until golden brown.

Note: This is a moist and delicious dish to serve with turkey. No one could make it exactly like my mother-in-law, Anna High, but this is close.

Chicken Risotto

Chris Poeller Kaczynski
Schenectady, NY
Wyoming Valley Star

Makes 4-6 servings

6 Tbsp. butter
1 lb. boneless chicken
  breast, cut into strips
1 clove garlic, minced
1 1/2 cups uncooked rice
1/4 lb. mushrooms, sliced
3 green onions, chopped
2 1/2 cups chicken broth
1 tsp. basil
1 cup shredded cheddar
  cheese

1. Melt 2 Tbsp. butter. Add chicken strips and cook until browned. Remove chicken.
2. Stir in remaining butter, garlic, and rice. Cook until lightly browned.
3. Add mushrooms and green onions. Continue cooking until mushrooms are tender.
4. Stir in chicken broth and basil. Bring to a boil. Cover and simmer for 15 minutes.
5. Stir in chicken and continue simmering until chicken is heated through. Remove to serving dish, sprinkle with cheese, and serve immediately.

Chicken Noodle Hotdish

Ruth Ann Collins
Waseca, MN
*Biblical Blocks
Christmas Quilt*

Makes 8-10 servings

Chicken:
5-6-lb. whole chicken
1 tsp. whole allspice
1 tsp. salt
1 tsp. pepper
1 1/2 cups milk
1 1/2 cups chicken broth

Homemade Noodles:
4 eggs, beaten
1 tsp. salt
2 Tbsp. warm water
2 1/4 cups flour

1. Cook whole chicken in large saucepan with water. Bring to a boil and cook 30-40 minutes until done.
2. While chicken cooks, prepare homemade noodles by combining ingredients in order given. Roll out dough into thin sheet and cut 1/2" x 6" strips of noodles. Let dry.
3. Remove chicken from saucepan, cool slightly, debone, and cut into pieces. Skim fat from broth and reserve 1 1/2 cups chicken broth.
4. In a roasting pan, combine noodles, chicken, allspice, salt, pepper, milk, and chicken broth.
5. Bake at 350° for 45-60 minutes.

Chicken Casserole

Dorothy Dyer
Lee's Summit, MO
*Dance by the
Light of the Moon*

Makes 6 servings

4 chicken breasts
10 3/4-oz. can cream of
  celery soup
3 cups herb-seasoned
  stuffing mix
1 1/2 cups margarine or
  butter
1 cup chicken broth
5-oz. can water chestnuts
salt and pepper to taste

1. Stew chicken breast in water until done. Reserve 1 cup broth, skimming fat. Cut stewed chicken into pieces.
2. Combine chicken, celery soup, stuffing mix, margarine, broth, water chestnuts, salt, and pepper. Pour into greased casserole dish. Refrigerate for at least 8 hours.
3. Bake at 350° for 1 hour or until done.

Chicken Strips in Wine Sauce
Rhondalee Schmidt
Scranton, PA
Three Little Pumpkins

Makes 4-6 servings

1-1¹/₂ cups flour
salt and pepper to taste
1 tsp. curry powder
2-3 lbs. boneless, skinless chicken strips
2-3 Tbsp. cooking oil
10³/₄-oz. can chicken broth
¹/₄ cup margarine, melted
¹/₄ cup white wine
1 clove garlic, minced
1 tsp. lemon juice
parsley

1. In a plastic bag, mix together flour, salt, pepper, and curry powder. Shake to mix.
2. Wash and dry chicken strips. Place in bag and shake to coat evenly. Brown in cooking oil. Drain well.
3. Place cooked chicken in single layer in 9" x 13" baking pan. Pour in chicken broth, margarine, and wine. On top of each slice of chicken sprinkle garlic, lemon juice, and parsley.
4. Bake at 350° for 1 hour.
5. Serve with rice.

Edisto Beach Chicken Casserole
Mary Ann Calhoun
Johns Island, SC
Michael's Quilt

Makes 8-10 servings

2 3-lb. chicken fryers, cooked, deboned
2 cups chopped celery
2 8-oz. cans water chestnuts, sliced
1¹/₂ cups mayonnaise
2 heaping cups cooked rice
2 medium onions, chopped
2 10³/₄-oz. cans cream of chicken soup
2-oz. jar pimientos (optional)
2 cups crushed cheese crackers
¹/₂ cup margarine, melted

1. Mix together chicken, celery, water chestnuts, mayonnaise, rice, onions, soup, and pimentos. Pour into two greased medium baking dishes.
2. Mix together crackers and margarine. Sprinkle over casserole.
3. Bake at 350° for 35-40 minutes or until bubbly.

Note: Some years ago, the Cobblestone Quilters Guild, Charleston, SC arranged several weekend retreats to Edisto Beach. Our host and beach house owner, Kaye Evans, always prepared wonderful food. Whenever I prepare this casserole, I remember quilting by the sea.

Mom's Super Chicken Bake
Jean Harris Robinson
Cinnaminson, NJ
My Secret Garden

Makes 12 servings

6 large chicken breasts, cooked, cut into bite-sized pieces
2 10-oz. pkgs. chopped, frozen broccoli or spinach
2 10³/₄-oz. cans cream of chicken soup
1 cup mayonnaise
³/₄-1 tsp. curry powder (optional)
3 Tbsp. lemon juice
8-ozs. cheddar or Swiss cheese, grated
4-oz. jar mushrooms (optional)
1 cup bread crumbs

1. Mix together chicken, broccoli, chicken soup, mayonnaise, curry powder, and lemon juice until blended. Pour into greased 9" x 13" baking pan.
2. Sprinkle cheese on top and spread with mushrooms, if desired. Sprinkle bread crumbs on top. Cover with foil. Refrigerate for up to 48 hours.
3. Bake uncovered at 350° for 45 minutes.
4. Serve with chinese noodles, wide noodles, or rice.

Chicken Enchiladas

Janie Steele
Moore, OK
Mary Ann England
Rosamond, CA
Cindy Ewert
Salem, OR

Makes 8-10 servings

8-10 tortillas
1/2 cup chopped onion
1 clove garlic, minced
2 Tbsp. margarine
1/2 cup sliced black olives
4-oz. can green chilies, drained
1/2 cup sour cream
10 3/4-oz. can cream of chicken soup
1 1/2 cups cubed chicken or turkey
1 cup grated cheese
1/4 cup milk

1. In saucepan sauté onion and garlic in margarine. Stir in 1/4 cup olives, chilies, sour cream, and chicken soup. Mix well. Set aside 3/4 cup of mixture. Fold in chicken and 1/2 cup cheese.
2. Fill warm tortillas with mixture, roll, and place seam down in greased 8" x 12" baking pan.
3. Combine milk with reserved sauce and pour over the top. Garnish, using 1/4 cup olives and 1/2 cup cheese.
4. Bake at 350° for 20-30 minutes.

Chicken Tortilla Casserole

Christine Weaver
Reinholds, PA
Lone Star

Makes 8-10 servings

2 Tbsp. chicken broth or water
8-oz. carton sour cream or plain yogurt
10 3/4-oz. can cream of mushroom soup
16-oz. jar mild, medium, or hot chunky salsa
12 flour tortillas, cut into strips
4 cups diced, cooked chicken or turkey
4 cups shredded cheddar cheese

1. Grease a 9" x 13" baking pan. Spoon broth into baking pan.
2. Mix together sour cream, mushroom soup, and salsa.
3. Layer 1/3 of tortilla strips, 1/3 of chicken, 1/3 of soup mixture, and 1/3 of cheese in baking pan. Repeat 2 times.
4. Bake at 350° for 40 minutes. Let stand 10-15 minutes before serving.

Turkey Enchiladas

Sharon Easter
Yuba City, CA
Scrappy Nine Patch
Bobbie Jean Weidner
Muscarella
State College, PA
State College Centennial Quilt

Makes 6 servings

2 4-oz. cans diced green chilies, chopped
1 large onion, chopped
2 Tbsp. olive oil
1/4 tsp. garlic powder
1 tsp. salt
1/2 tsp. oregano
28-oz. can stewed tomatoes
2 cups chopped, cooked turkey
1 cup sour cream
2 cups grated cheddar cheese
12 corn or flour tortillas

1. Sauté chilies and onion in olive oil. Add garlic powder, salt, oregano, and stewed tomatoes and simmer for 30 minutes.
2. Mix together turkey, sour cream, and cheddar cheese. Set aside.
3. Soften tortillas in microwave oven (or dip in hot oil). Fill with turkey mixture and roll up.
4. Place in 9" x 13" baking pan, seam side down. Pour chile sauce over top.
5. Bake at 350° for 20 minutes. Serve.

Holiday Enchiladas

Cora J. Peterson
Frederic, WI
Wagon Tracks

Makes 8-10 servings

Tortillas:
3 eggs
1 1/2 cups milk
1 cup flour
1 tsp. salt
1/2 cup cornmeal
2 Tbsp. butter

Filling:
2 lbs. ground beef
1/2 tsp. oregano
1/2 tsp. salt
1/2 tsp. pepper
1/4 tsp. garlic powder
16-oz. can refried beans
32-oz. jar tomato sauce

Garnish:
sour cream
green onions, chopped
olives, sliced
tomato, chopped

1. Mix together eggs, milk, flour, salt, and cornmeal. Melt butter on hot griddle. Pour desired amount of batter onto griddle and fry until light brown. (If batter is too thick, add more milk.) Repeat to make 8-10 tortillas. Set aside.
2. Brown ground beef in skillet. Add oregano, salt, pepper, garlic powder, beans, and 1/2 cup tomato sauce.
3. Pour enough tomato sauce into 9" x 13" pan to lightly cover bottom of pan.

Place 2-3 Tbsp. hamburger mixture on each tortilla. Roll up and place in pan. When all the rolls are in pan, cover with remaining sauce.
4. Bake at 350° for 20-30 minutes.
5. Garnish with sour cream, chopped green onions, olives, or chopped tomato.

Enchiladas Rancheras

Bobbie Jean Weidner
Muscarella
State College, PA
State College Centennial Quilt

Makes 12 servings

Enchiladas:
1/4 lb. cheddar cheese, grated
1 lb. Monterey Jack cheese, grated
2 scallions, finely chopped
1/4-1/3 cup butter, softened
12 flour tortillas

Ranchera Sauce:
1/4 cup oil
1/2 cup chopped onion
1 1/2 stalks celery, chopped
1 green pepper, chopped
4-oz. can green chilies, chopped
1/4 cup flour
1/2 tsp. marjoram
3/4 tsp. pepper
1 1/2 tsp. garlic powder
1/2 tsp. dried oregano
2 1/2 cups water

3 tsp. chicken stock base
28-oz. can whole tomatoes, undrained

Garnish:
1 cup grated Monterey Jack cheese
sour cream
guacamole
sliced scallions
sliced ripe olives

1. Mix together cheeses, scallions, and butter until well blended. Divide mixture into 4 equal portions, then form each portion into 3 individual sticks the length of a tortilla, making 12 cheese sticks.
2. Place a cheese stick on each tortilla. Roll up and place seam down in 9" x 13" baking pan.
3. To prepare sauce heat oil in skillet over medium heat. Sauté onion, celery, green pepper, and green chilies until soft.
4. Mix together flour, marjoram, pepper, garlic powder, and oregano. Slowly add water and mix until smooth.
5. Pour the flour mixture into vegetables. Stir in chicken stock and tomatoes. Cook over medium heat, stirring occasionally until mixture boils and thickens. Reduce heat and simmer for 1 hour.
6. Pour sauce over tortillas. Garnish with Jack cheese.
7. Bake at 450° for about 15 minutes, until sauce is bubbly and cheese has melted.
8. Garnish with choice of sour cream, guacamole, scallions, and ripe olives.

Wet Burrito Casserole

Elizabeth Chupp
Arthur, IL
Nine Patch

Makes 10-12 servings

1 1/2 cups sour cream
10 3/4-oz. can cream of mushroom soup
1 lb. ground beef
1 medium onion, chopped
1 medium green or red pepper, chopped (optional)
1 pkg. taco seasoning mix
4-oz. jar mushrooms, diced
16-oz. can refried beans
1 pkg. (10) soft tortillas
4 cups shredded cheddar cheese

1. Mix together sour cream and soup. Put 1/2 of mixture in bottom of 9" x 13" baking pan.
2. Fry ground beef, onion, and pepper. Add taco seasoning, mushrooms, and refried beans.
3. Divide mixture onto tortillas. Roll up tortillas and place on top of sour cream mixture in pan. Spread remaining sour cream and mushroom soup mixture on top.
4. Sprinkle with cheese.
5. Bake at 350° for 30-35 minutes.

Border Casserole

Joan Lemmler
Albuquerque, NM
Marissa

Makes 8 servings

6-oz. jar sliced mushrooms
1 lb. ground beef
1 large clove garlic, minced
2 onions, finely chopped
2-oz. jar chopped pimiento
2 8-oz. cans tomato sauce
1 Tbsp. chili powder
dash Tabasco
1 Tbsp. flour
1 medium green pepper, chopped
1/2 tsp. salt
2 cups shredded longhorn cheddar cheese
2 cups crushed corn chips

1. Drain mushrooms, reserving liquid.
2. Brown meat with garlic. Add mushrooms, 1/4 cup mushroom liquid, onions, pimiento, tomato sauce, chili powder, and Tabasco. Heat well.
3. Blend flour with remaining mushroom liquid. Stir into meat. Add green pepper and salt. Heat to boiling.
4. In a 2 1/2-quart casserole dish, alternate layers of meat mixture, cheese, and chips, ending with chips.
5. Bake at 300° for 1 1/2 hours.

Western Tamale Pie

Alyce C. Kauffman
Gridley, CA
Sailing Away

Makes 8-10 servings

Cornmeal:
4 1/2 cups boiling water
1 1/2 cups cornmeal
1 1/2 tsp. salt
2 Tbsp. butter
1 cup grated cheese

Filling:
2 Tbsp. oil
1 lb. ground beef
1 garlic clove, minced
3/4 cup chopped onion
1 1/2 cups sliced celery
2 1/2 cups tomatoes
2 cups whole kernel corn, drained
1 tsp. salt
1 Tbsp. chili powder
1 Tbsp. Worcestershire sauce
1 1/2 cups black olives, drained

1. Slowly stir cornmeal and salt into boiling water. Cover. Cook over very low heat for 30 minutes. Remove from heat.
2. Blend in butter and 3/4 cup cheese. Cool slightly.
3. Cook ground beef slightly in oil. Add garlic and onion. Cook until onions are tender.
4. Add celery, tomatoes, corn, salt, chili powder, and Worcestershire sauce.
5. Slowly stir in 1/2 cup cornmeal. Cover and cook slowly for 10 minutes.

6. Cut olives into large pieces. Stir into meat mixture.
7. Line 9" x 13" baking pan with 3/4 of cornmeal mixture. Pour in filling. Top with remaining cornmeal mixture and remaining 1/4 cup cheese.
8. Bake at 350° for 45-60 minutes.

Taco-Stuffed Pasta Shells
Sharon Shadburn
Ft. Leavenworth, KS
Northern Stars

Makes 6-8 servings

12-oz box jumbo pasta shells
2 Tbsp. margarine, melted
1 1/2 lbs. ground beef
4-oz. pkg. cream cheese, cubed
1 Tbsp. chives
1 tsp. chili powder
1/4 tsp. salt
2 1/2 cups taco sauce
1 cup shredded cheddar cheese
1 cup shredded Monterey Jack cheese
1 1/2 cups crushed tortilla chips
green onion, chopped

1. Cook pasta shells according to package directions. Drain and toss with margarine.
2. Brown ground beef, stirring to crumble. Drain.
3. Stir in cream cheese, chives, chili powder, and salt until cream cheese is

melted. Simmer 5 minutes.
4. Spoon a tablespoon or so of beef mixture into each pasta shell. Arrange in a greased 9" x 13" baking dish. Spoon taco sauce over shells.
5. Cover and bake at 350° for 15 minutes.
6. Uncover and top with cheeses and tortilla chips. Bake 15 minutes longer.
7. Sprinkle with chopped green onions and serve.

Note: This is great to make ahead of time, keeping it in the refrigerator until just before baking time. My daughters always save one or two shells immediately for the next day's after-school snack.

Grandmother Muscarella's Ravioli
Bobbie Jean Weidner
Muscarella
State College, PA
State College Centennial Quilt

Pasta:
4 cups flour
3 eggs, slightly beaten
1 Tbsp. olive oil
1/3-1/2 cup warm water

Filling:
2 lbs. ricotta cheese
2 eggs, beaten
1/4 cup grated Romano or Parmesan cheese

1. Make well in flour and add eggs and olive oil. Mix

with palms of hands, adding water slowly. Use only as much water as needed to make a slightly moist, but not wet texture. Knead with heal of hand until smooth. Make ball, cover, and allow to stand for 15 minutes.
2. Cut off piece of dough the size of golf ball. Roll through pasta machine twice at each setting (at least 8 times), making sheet of pasta progressively thinner. (The 8th time through the machine should be at the second to the last setting.) Repeat this step with remaining pasta. When ready for the ravioli press, the pasta should feel like baby skin.
3. Stir together filling ingredients. Lay 1 sheet of pasta across ravioli form press. Dollop filling into wells created by ravioli press. Lay second sheet of pasta on top and roll with rolling pin, sealing filling into center of pasta pillows. Cut off extra pasta with knife.
4. Ravioli should be frozen on sheets of wax paper, then transferred to plastic bags. They can be stored up to 3 months in the freezer for use at any time.
5. To prepare ravioli drop into rolling, boiling water and allow to boil until tender, about 4-6 minutes. Serve with your favorite sauce.

Turkey Lasagna
Mary Rogers
Waseca, MN
Sarah's Stars

Makes 10-12 servings

8-oz. pkg. lasagna
noodles
2 10³/4-oz. cans cream of
chicken soup
1/2 cup milk
1/3 cup chopped onion
1/2 tsp. bouillon
1/2 tsp. seasoned salt
1/4 tsp. pepper
1 cup sour cream
16-ozs. ricotta cheese
1 egg, beaten
1/2 tsp. salt
3 cups chopped turkey
2 cups shredded cheddar
cheese
2 cups shredded
mozzarella

1. Cook lasagna noodles
according to package directions, drain, and set aside.
2. In saucepan mix together
soup, milk, onion, bouillon,
salt, and pepper. Heat thoroughly. Stir in sour cream.
3. Blend together ricotta
cheese, egg, and salt.
4. In a 9" x 13" baking pan,
layer lasagna noodles, soup
mixture, ricotta mixture,
turkey, and cheeses.
5. Bake covered at 375° for
50 minutes. Uncover and
bake for another 10 min-
utes.

Chicken Lasagna Bake
Susan Orleman
Pittsburgh, PA
Hilton Head Memories

Makes 8-10 servings

8-oz. pkg. lasagna
noodles
1¹/2 cups cottage cheese
2 cups shredded
American cheese
1/2 cup chopped onion
1/2 cup chopped green
pepper
3 Tbsp. butter or
margarine
10³/4-oz. can cream of
chicken soup
1/2 cup milk
6-oz. jar sliced
mushrooms, drained
1/4 cup pimiento
(optional)
1/4 tsp. basil
3 cups diced, cooked
chicken
grated Parmesan cheese

1. Prepare noodles according to package directions.
Drain and set aside.
2. Line greased 9" x 13"
baking pan with cooked
noodles.
3. Mix together cottage
cheese and American
cheese. Set aside.
4. Sauté onion and green
pepper in butter until tender. Stir in soup, milk,
mushrooms, pimiento, basil,
and chicken.
5. Layer 1/2 of chicken mixture on top of noodles in
casserole. Add cheeses and

follow with remaining
chicken mixture. Top with
Parmesan cheese.
6. Bake at 350° for 45 minutes.

Seafood Lasagna
Eileen B. Jarvis
Wexford, PA
Snowball

Makes 8-10 servings

2 Tbsp. olive oil
1 medium leek
28-oz. can Italian-style
plum tomatoes,
undrained
1 Tbsp. tomato paste
salt and pepper to taste
8-ozs. shrimp, shelled,
deveined, and coarsely
chopped
8-ozs. medium-sized
scallops, thinly sliced
1 lb. boneless and
skinless filet of fish,
cut in 1" pieces
12 fresh basil leaves, torn
in half
15 plain or spinach
lasagna noodles,
cooked and drained
6 cups shredded
mozzarella cheese

1. Use white part of leek
only, rinsed and finely
chopped.
2. In skillet sauté leek in oil
until tender, about 10 minutes. Stir in tomatoes and
tomato paste. Cook, stirring
and breaking the tomatoes
until the mixture boils.
Simmer uncovered for

about 20 minutes or until the sauce is slightly thickened. Stir in salt and pepper.

3. Stir in shrimp, scallops, and fish. Stir in a few pieces of basil leaves. Cover and cook over low heat for 10 minutes. Do not boil or overcook.

4. Spoon 1/2 cup of seafood sauce into 9" x 13" baking pan. Arrange a single layer of 5 overlapping noodles on top of the sauce. Spoon 1/3 of sauce over the noodles. Sprinkle with 1/3 of the basil and 1/3 of the mozzarella cheese. Repeat with the next two layers.

5. Bake at 350° for 50 minutes or until the cheese is bubbly and the edges are browned. Let stand 15 minutes before cutting and serving.

Vegetable Cheese Lasagna
Cathy Kowalsky
Woodinville, WA
Christmas Sampler

Makes 6-8 servings

1 Tbsp. margarine
3 cups thinly sliced
  mushrooms
1 Tbsp. olive oil
1 cup chopped onion
6 garlic cloves, minced
1 1/2 cups tomato sauce
2 16-oz. cans Italian
  tomatoes, drained and
  diced
3/4 tsp. salt
1 tsp. oregano
1 tsp. basil
1/4 tsp. pepper
1 bay leaf
2 10-oz. pkgs. frozen,
  chopped spinach,
  thawed and drained
2 cups ricotta cheese
1 egg, slightly beaten
1/4 tsp. pepper
8-oz. pkg. lasagna
  noodles
12 ozs. Monterey Jack
  cheese, shredded

1. In skillet heat margarine over medium heat until bubbly and hot. Stir in mushrooms and sauté until mushrooms are lightly browned and cooked through, 2-3 minutes. Remove from heat and set aside.

2. In saucepan heat olive oil over medium heat. Add onion and garlic and sauté until onions are softened.

Add tomato sauce, tomatoes, salt, oregano, basil, 1/4 tsp. pepper, and bay leaf. Mix well. Reduce heat to low, cover, and simmer for 25-30 minutes, stirring occasionally. Remove and discard bay leaf.

3. Mix together spinach, ricotta cheese, egg, and 1/4 tsp. pepper. Mix well.

4. Prepare noodles according to package directions. Drain.

5. In bottom of greased 9" x 13" baking pan, spread 1/2 cup tomato mixture. Cover with lasagna noodles, arranging half lengthwise in dish, overlapping edges slightly. Spread 1/2 of spinach mixture over noodles. Spread 1/2 of mushrooms over spinach. Spread 1/2 cup of tomato mixture over mushrooms and sprinkle with 1/2 of Monterey Jack cheese. Arrange 1/2 the remaining lasagna crosswise in dish, overlapping edges slightly. Repeat layers as before ending with Monterey Jack cheese.

6. Bake at 350° for 40 minutes.

One-Step Lasagna
Joyce B. Suiter
Garysburg, NC
Pieced Tulip

Makes 10-12 servings

12-ozs. ricotta cheese or
   cottage cheese
2 cups shredded
   mozzarella
2 eggs, slightly beaten
1/3 cup dried parsley
1/2 tsp. basil leaves
1/8 tsp. black pepper
10-oz. pkg. frozen,
   chopped spinach,
   drained
1 lb. lean ground beef
1/2 lb. mild Italian
   sausage, removed from
   casing
32-oz. jar spaghetti sauce
1/2 cup water
1/4 cup sugar
mushrooms to taste
16-oz. pkg. lasagna
   noodles
2 cups shredded
   mozzarella cheese
8 ozs. sliced mozzarella
   cheese
Parmesan cheese

1. Combine ricotta cheese, 2
cups mozzarella, eggs, parsley, basil, pepper, and
spinach in food processor.
Process until smooth.
2. In saucepan cook beef
and sausage. Drain. Add
spaghetti sauce, water, sugar,
and mushrooms to meat.
3. In greased 9" x 13"
baking pan, pour 3/4 cup
spaghetti sauce on bottom.
Cover with layer of
uncooked noodles, sides
touching. Spread on 1/2
ricotta cheese mixture.
Sprinkle with 1 cup shredded mozzarella. Spread with
1/2 of sauce. Cover with
more noodles. Spread with
remaining ricotta cheese
mixture and shredded moz-
zarella. Cover with more
noodles. Spread with
remaining sauce. Cover
tightly with foil.
4. Bake at 375° for 45
minutes. Uncover and bake
for 15 minutes more. Cover
with sliced mozzarella.
Return to oven until moz-
zarella slices have melted.
5. Let stand for 10 minutes.
Cut into squares. Sprinkle
with Parmesan cheese.

Baked Ziti
Nicolina G. Emmi
Downey, CA
Picket Fences
Trudy Kutter
Corfu, NY
Cathedral Window

Makes 12-15 servings

1 1/2 lbs. ziti
2 quarts Italian sauce
2 16-oz. cartons ricotta
   cheese
1 cup grated Parmesan
   cheese
1 lb. mozzarella cheese,
   shredded

1. Cook ziti according to
directions on package. Drain.
2. Grease two 9" x 13" baking
pans. Pour 1/4 of Italian sauce
into each pan. Layer 1/4 of
pasta and 1/4 of each of the
cheeses over sauce in each
pan. Repeat layers, finishing
with mozzarella cheese on
top of each.
3. Bake at 400° for 15-20
minutes or until hot and bubbly.

Light Fettuccine Alfredo

Linda K. Taylor
Tucson, AZ
Milady's Fan

Makes 4 servings

1 1/3 cups skim milk
2 small cloves garlic, minced
2 Tbsp. flour
2 Tbsp. fat-free cream cheese
1 cup grated Parmesan cheese
5 tsp. butter substitute
4 cups hot, cooked fettuccine
1 tsp. fresh or dried parsley
1/8 tsp. pepper

1. In saucepan over medium heat, whisk together milk, garlic, flour, and cream cheese. Bring to a boil, whisking constantly. Reduce heat and simmer for 2 minutes or until thickened. Stir in Parmesan cheese and whisk until blended. Remove from heat and stir in butter substitute.
2. Pour sauce over hot fettuccine. Sprinkle with parsley and pepper and serve.

Angel Hair Pasta with Scallop Sauté

Dana Braden
Seattle, WA
May Baskets

Makes 2 servings

2 Tbsp. margarine
6-8 mushrooms, sliced
1 small clove garlic, minced
1 lb. scallops
3 Tbsp. cream cheese
1/2 cup lowfat milk
pepper to taste
16-oz. can asparagus, drained
1 oz. grated Parmesan cheese
1 cup angel hair pasta

1. Sauté mushrooms and garlic in margarine. Add scallops and sauté for about 5 minutes until scallops turn opaque.
2. Stir in cream cheese, milk, and pepper. Add asparagus and Parmesan cheese. Stir constantly until heated through.
3. Cook pasta according to package directions. Drain and serve pasta with scallop sauté.

Three-Cheese Manicotti

Joyce Cox
Port Angeles, WA
Amish Star

Makes 6-8 servings

32-oz. jar spaghetti sauce
1 cup water
2 cups ricotta cheese
2 cups mozzarella cheese, shredded
1/2 cup Parmesan cheese, grated
2 Tbsp. chopped parsley
1/2 tsp. salt
1/4 tsp. pepper
8-oz. pkg. manicotti

1. Mix together spaghetti sauce and water.
2. Mix together ricotta cheese, mozzarella cheese, 1/4 cup Parmesan cheese, parsley, salt, and pepper. Spoon into uncooked manicotti.
3. Pour 1 cup sauce on bottom of greased 9" x 13" baking pan. Place filled manicotti in a single layer over sauce. Pour remaining sauce over pasta. Cover with aluminum foil.
4. Bake at 400° for 40 minutes or until hot and bubbly. Remove foil. Bake for 10 minutes longer.
5. Sprinkle remaining 1/4 cup Parmesan cheese over top and serve.

Main Dishes

Manicotti
Bobbie Jean Weidner Muscarella
State College, PA
Stage College Centennial Quilt

Makes 10-12 servings

Tomato Sauce:
1/4 cup olive oil
1 cup finely chopped onion
1 clove garlic, crushed
35-oz. can Italian-style plum tomatoes
6-oz. can tomato paste
1 1/2 cups water
2 Tbsp. chopped, fresh parsley
2 tsp. sugar
1 tsp. dried oregano
1/2 tsp. dried basil
1/4 tsp. pepper

Pasta Shells:
5 eggs
1 1/4 cups flour
1/4 tsp. salt
1 1/4 cups water
1/3 cup cooking oil

Manicotti Filling:
2 lbs. ricotta cheese
8 ozs. mozzarella cheese, grated
1/3 cup grated Parmesan cheese
2 eggs
1 Tbsp. chopped, fresh parsley
1 tsp. salt
1/4 tsp. pepper
3 Tbsp. Parmesan cheese

1. To prepare sauce pour oil into 6-quart saucepan. Over medium heat sauté onion and garlic until brown, about 5 minutes. Add tomatoes including the juice, tomato paste, water, parsley, sugar, oregano, basil, and pepper. Mash tomatoes and mix well. Bring to a boil over high heat. Reduce heat and simmer covered for 1 hour, stirring occasionally.
2. To prepare shells combine eggs, flour, salt, and water. Beat until smooth. Pour oil into skillet over medium heat. Pour in scant 1/4 cup batter, rotating pan quickly, and cook until the top is dry, but the bottom is not brown. Turn the shells out on a wire rack to cool. Continue, adding more oil to skillet if needed, until all batter has been used.
3. To prepare filling combine ricotta, mozzarella, Parmesan, eggs, parsley, salt, and pepper, beating with wooden spoon until well blended.
4. To assemble spoon a layer of tomato sauce on bottom of each of two 9" x 13" baking pans. In center of each shell place about 1/4 cup filling and roll up. Place shells, seam side down, in a single layer in the baking dishes. Cover with remaining sauce and sprinkle with Parmesan.
5. Bake uncovered at 350° for 30 minutes. Serve with green salad and bread sticks.

Mexican Manicotti
Kathy Evenson
Fergus Falls, MN
Midnight Sky

Makes 8 servings

1 lb. ground beef
12-oz. can fat-free refried beans
2 tsp. crushed oregano
8-oz. pkg. manicotti
1 1/2 cups water
8-oz. jar taco sauce
8-oz. carton sour cream
1/4 cup chopped green onion
1/2 cup sliced black olives, pitted
1 cup shredded, mild cheddar cheese

1. Brown ground beef. Drain. Stir in refried beans and oregano.
2. Fill uncooked shells and arrange in 9" x 13" microwave dish.
3. Mix together water and taco sauce and pour over manicotti shells. Refrigerate for at least 8 hours.
4. Cover with plastic wrap and microwave on medium-high for 10 minutes.
5. Mix together sour cream, onion, and olives. Spread on top of shells. Top with cheese.
6. Microwave on high for 1-2 minutes, or until cheese melts. Serve.

130

Turkey Tetrazzini
Julie McKenzie
Punxsutawney, PA
Tumbling Blocks

Makes 16-20 servings

7-8 cups turkey broth
5-6 cups chopped, cooked turkey
1 lb. spaghetti, broken into pieces
3/4 cup butter
3/4 cup flour
2 cups milk or light cream
salt to taste
1/4 tsp. pepper
2 6-oz. cans mushrooms, sliced
2 cups buttered bread crumbs
1/2 cup Parmesan cheese
1/2 tsp. paprika

1. Bring turkey broth to a boil. Add spaghetti and cook until barely tender.
2. Melt butter over medium heat. Add flour and stir until smooth. Gradually add milk or cream and stir until smooth.
3. Add salt and pepper and a small amount of the hot turkey broth. Stir this mixture into the remaining broth and spaghetti. Cook, stirring constantly, until thickened.
4. Add chopped turkey and mushrooms.
5. Pour into 2 greased 9" x 13" baking pans. Sprinkle tops with buttered bread crumbs, Parmesan cheese, and paprika.

6. Bake at 350° for 30 minutes until browned and crusty on top.

Old-Fashioned Macaroni and Cheese
Claire Amick
Pine Grove Mills, PA
Autumn Stars

Makes 6 servings

4 cups cooked macaroni
2 Tbsp. butter
1 1/4 cups cubed sharp cheese
1/4 tsp. pepper
1/2 tsp. salt
3 cups milk
2 eggs, beaten
1/2 tsp. paprika

1. Mix together macaroni, butter, cheese, pepper, and salt. Spoon into greased 1 1/2-quart casserole dish.
2. Combine milk and eggs. Pour over macaroni. Sprinkle with paprika.
3. Bake at 350° for 40-50 minutes.

Spaghetti Pie
Diann J. Dunham
State College, PA
Jane's Quilt

Makes 6 servings

6-oz. pkg. spaghetti, cooked and drained
2 Tbsp. olive oil or butter
1 large egg, beaten
3/4 cup grated Parmesan cheese
1 cup ricotta cheese
1 cup spaghetti sauce
1/2 cup shredded mozzarella cheese
fresh basil

1. Toss hot spaghetti with olive oil or butter.
2. Mix together egg and 1/2 cup Parmesan cheese. Stir into spaghetti.
3. Pour spaghetti mixture into greased 10" pie pan. Form into a "crust."
4. Spread ricotta cheese over bottom of spaghetti crust. Add spaghetti sauce.
5. Bake uncovered at 350° for 25 minutes. Top with mozzarella cheese. Bake another 5 minutes or until cheese melts.
6. Remove from oven. Sprinkle with remaining 1/4 cup Parmesan cheese. Cool for 10 minutes before cutting into wedges.
7. Garnish with fresh basil and serve.

Taglarini Casserole

Linda Everly
Terre Haute, IN
Grandmother's Flower Garden

Makes 12 servings

1 Tbsp. cooking oil
3 small onions, diced
3 cloves garlic, minced
1 bell pepper, diced
1/2 tsp. salt
1 tsp. pepper
3 tsp. chili powder
1 tsp. paprika
2 lbs. ground beef
16-oz. pkg. egg noodles
16-oz. can whole kernel corn
4 ozs. grated Parmesan cheese
6-oz. jar ripe olives, sliced
2 10³/4-oz. cans mushroom soup
2 cups shredded cheddar cheese
1/2 cup green olives, sliced
1 1/2-2 cups tomato or V-8 juice

1. Sauté onions, garlic, bell pepper, salt, pepper, chili powder, and paprika in oil. When half done, add ground beef. Brown well. Drain.
2. Prepare egg noodles according to package directions. Drain.
3. Mix together meat and noodles. Add corn, Parmesan cheese, olives, and mushroom soup.
4. Spoon into casserole dish and top with cheddar cheese and green olives. Add enough tomato juice or V-8 to moisten.
5. Bake at 350° for 1 hour.

Easy Spinach Stromboli

Carlene Horne
Bedford, NH
Wild Irish Rose

Makes 6-8 servings

10-oz. pkg. frozen, chopped spinach
8-oz. pkg. feta cheese
1 frozen bread dough, thawed

1. Defrost spinach and bread dough. Squeeze all liquid out of spinach.
2. Mix together spinach and cheese. Set aside.
3. Roll out thawed bread dough into 12" x 18" rectangle.
4. Spread spinach mixture over center of rectangle. Fold edges over and pinch together.
5. Bake at 350° for 30-40 minutes.

Vegetables

Cranberry-Apple Sweet Potatoes
Dorothy McClure
Milliken, CO
Western Sunbonnet Sue
Elaine Patton
West Middletown, PA
Puss in the Corner

Makes 6-8 servings

**5-6 medium sweet
potatoes, peeled,
or 2 16-oz. cans sweet
potatoes, drained and
cut into bite-sized pieces
21-oz. can apple pie
filling
8-oz. can whole cranberry
sauce
2 Tbsp. apricot preserves
2 Tbsp. orange
marmalade**

1. If using fresh potatoes, cover with boiling water and cook until tender, about 15 minutes. Drain and set aside. When cooled, cut into bite-sized pieces.

2. Spread pie filling in an 8" x 8" baking dish. Arrange cooked or canned sweet potatoes on top.
3. In small mixing bowl, stir together cranberry sauce, apricot preserves, and orange marmalade. Spoon over sweet potatoes.
4. Bake, uncovered, at 350° for 20-25 minutes or until heated through.

Baked Sweet Potatoes and Cranberries
Dorothy Horst
Tiskilwa, IL
Ohio Star

Makes 8 servings

**8 medium sweet
potatoes, enough to
make 3 cups when
mashed
16-oz. can whole
cranberries**

**3/4-1 cup crushed
pineapple, drained
1 cup miniature
marshmallows
1/2 cup chopped nuts
1 1/2 tsp. salt
1/4 cup brown sugar
2 egg whites, stiffly
beaten**

1. Cook sweet potatoes until tender. Drain, cool, and peel. Mash sweet potatoes to make 3 cups.
2. Mix together all ingredients except egg whites. Fold in egg whites.
3. Pour into greased mold and bake at 350° for 1/2 hour or into greased casserole dish and bake at 350° for 1 hour.
4. Serve either hot or cold.

Baked Sweet Potatoes with Bourbon Sauce

Linda Gruhlkey Pond
Los Alamos, NM
Fields of Purple

Makes 6 servings

6-8 sweet potatoes,
  baked, sliced
2 cups brown sugar
1/4 cup orange juice
1/4 cup bourbon
8 Tbsp. butter
large marshmallows
  (optional)

1. Bake sweet potatoes and let cool slightly. Peel, slice, and place in casserole dish.
2. In saucepan mix together brown sugar, orange juice, bourbon, and butter. Bring to a boil and cook for 3 minutes.
3. Pour sauce over potatoes.
4. Bake at 350° about 15 minutes or until mixture is heated through.
5. If desired, cover with large marshmallows and bake until marshmallows have turned light brown.

Praline Yams

Pamela R. Kerschner
Stevensville, MD
The Chesapeake

Makes 10 servings

2 40-oz. cans yams, cut
  and drained
1/2 cup chopped pecans
1/2 cup coconut
1/2 cup firmly packed
  brown sugar
1/4 cup flour
1/4 cup butter, melted

1. Place yams in large ungreased casserole or baking dish.
2. In small bowl combine pecans, coconut, brown sugar, flour, and butter. Blend well and sprinkle over yams.
3. Bake at 350° for 35 to 40 minutes or until bubbly.

Carameled Sweet Potatoes

Patricia Snow
Lane, KS

Makes 10 servings

6 medium sweet potatoes
1 tsp. salt
1 cup brown sugar
3 Tbsp. flour
2 Tbsp. margarine
1 cup small
  marshmallows
1/2 cup nuts
12-oz. can evaporated
  milk

1. Cook sweet potatoes until tender. Drain, cool, and peel. Cut in half lengthwise. Arrange in greased shallow baking dish.
2. Mix together salt, sugar, and flour. Sprinkle over potatoes. Dot with margarine.
3. Sprinkle marshmallows and nuts over top. Pour milk over all.
4. Bake at 350° for 45-50 minutes.

Sweet Potato Bake

Mary Ann Mazur
Dublin, OH
ABC Quilt

Makes 6-8 servings

Sweet Potatoes:
3 cups cooked and
  mashed sweet potatoes
1/2 tsp. salt
2 2/3 Tbsp. margarine
1 tsp. vanilla
2 eggs, lightly beaten
1/2 cup brown sugar

Topping:
1/2 cup self-rising flour
4 Tbsp. margarine
1 cup chopped nuts
1 cup coconut
1 cup brown sugar

1. Mix together sweet potatoes, salt, margarine, vanilla, eggs, and brown sugar. Pour into 8" x 8" casserole dish.
2. Mix together all topping ingredients. Spread over potato mixture.
3. Bake at 350° for 30 minutes, or until top is brown.

Sweet Potato Casserole

Bonnie Moore
Pinckney, MI
Happy Cat Baby Quilt

Makes 10 servings

3 large sweet potatoes
1/2 cup milk
1/2 cup brown sugar
1 cup chopped nuts
1 egg yolk, beaten
1 egg white
1 Tbsp. sugar

1. Cook sweet potatoes until soft. Drain and cool slightly. Peel and mash sweet potatoes.
2. Add milk, brown sugar, and nuts and mix well. Stir in egg yolk.
3. Pour into casserole dish.
4. Beat egg white until stiff. Stir in 1 Tbsp. sugar, lightly. Spread over potato mixture.
5. Bake at 300° for 40 minutes.

Smashing Sweets

Brenda Joy Sonnie
Newtown, PA
Nine Patch Baby Quilt

Makes 10 servings

4 large sweet potatoes
1/4 cup margarine
1/4-1/2 cup milk
1 cup miniature marshmallows

1. Peel and cut sweet potatoes into pieces. Boil in water to cover until fork tender.
2. Mash and beat potatoes with an electric mixer. Add margarine and milk until smooth.
3. Add marshmallows and continue beating. Serve at once.

Maple-Pecan Sweet Potatoes

Joyce Bowman
Lady Lake, FL
Single Wedding Ring

Makes 8 servings

3 1/2 lbs. sweet potatoes
1/4 cup butter or margarine
1/2 cup firmly packed light brown sugar
1/3 cup maple syrup
1/4 tsp. salt
1/4 cup chopped pecans

1. Cook sweet potatoes in water until tender. Cool slightly, peel, and set aside.
2. In saucepan combine butter, brown sugar, maple syrup, and salt. Heat over medium heat until boiling. Reduce heat to low and cook, stirring until syrup mixture is clear and thick, about 2 minutes.
3. Cut sweet potatoes into large pieces and arrange in serving dish. Top with pecans and syrup mixture. Serve.

Sweet Potato Medley

Lois Mae E. Kuh
Penfield, NY
Fan-To-See

Makes 8-10 servings

4 large sweet potatoes, peeled and cut into large pieces
3 tart apples, peeled and sliced thickly
1 lb. carrots, cut into chunks
1 small Hubbard squash, peeled and cut into pieces
1 large onion, sliced
12-oz. can concentrated apple juice
1 cup orange juice
3/4 Tbsp. cinnamon
1/4 tsp. nutmeg
1 Tbsp. butter

1. Mix together sweet potatoes, apples, carrots, squash, and onion. Pour vegetables into greased 4-quart casserole dish.
2. Mix together apple juice, orange juice, cinnamon, and nutmeg. Pour over vegetables. Dot with butter.
3. Bake at 300° for 2-3 hours or until vegetables are fork tender.

Orange Sweet Potato Casserole

Janice Muller
Derwood, MD
Canadian Geese

Makes 6-8 servings

1/4 cup brown sugar
2 tsp. orange juice
2 tsp. margarine, melted
2 1-lb. cans sweet
   potatoes, drained
2 eggs
1/4 cup brown sugar
2/3 cup orange juice
1/3 cup margarine, melted
2 Tbsp. milk
1 tsp. salt
1/4 tsp. cloves
1 tsp. vanilla
1 tsp. ground cinnamon
1 cup chopped pecans

1. Mix together first three ingredients and set aside to use for glaze topping.
2. Whip sweet potatoes until smooth. Beat in eggs. Add 1/4 cup brown sugar, 2/3 cup orange juice, 1/3 cup margarine, milk, salt, cloves, vanilla, and cinnamon. Mix well.
3. Pour into a greased 1 1/2-quart casserole dish. Sprinkle with pecans. Pour glaze over pecans.
4. Bake at 350° for 40-45 minutes.

Orange Sweet Potatoes

Sally A. Price
Reston, VA
Jewel Box

Makes 6 servings

3 large sweet potatoes
3 small to medium
   oranges
1/4 cup juice from oranges
1 Tbsp. margarine
1/8 tsp. salt
1/4 tsp. pepper
1/4 tsp. ground ginger
2-oz. bag toasted slivered
   almonds (optional)

1. Bake sweet potatoes at 400° for 45-60 minutes or until tender. Cut potatoes in half lengthwise and scoop out pulp. Set the shells aside.
2. Squeeze 1/4 cup juice from oranges. Peel oranges and cut into small pieces.
2. Mash together sweet potatoes, orange juice, margarine, salt, pepper, and ginger. Stir orange pieces into potato mixture.
3. Scoop mixture back into sweet potato shells. Top with almonds.
4. Bake at 400° for 15 minutes.

Variations: Add 1/2 cup raisins. Use pineapple juice instead of orange juice.

Holiday Sweet Potatoes

Eunice B. Heyman
Baltimore, MD
William's Clown Parade

Makes 8 servings

10 carrots, scraped and
   sliced into thick pieces
4 medium sweet
   potatoes, peeled and
   cut into small pieces
1/4 cup honey
1 cup orange juice
2 tsp. grated orange peel
1/2 tsp. cinnamon
1/4 tsp. ginger
1 Tbsp. butter

1. Cook together carrots and sweet potatoes until just tender. Drain and place in a shallow baking pan.
2. Mix together honey, orange juice, orange peel, cinnamon, and ginger. Pour over carrots and sweet potatoes. Dot with butter.
3. Bake at 350° for 30 minutes, or until heated through.

Candied Sweet Potatoes

Alyce C. Kauffman
Gridley, CA
Sailing Away

Makes 6-8 servings

6-8 sweet potatoes, cooked, peeled, and cut into bite-sized pieces
4 Tbsp. margarine or butter
1 cup brown sugar
2 Tbsp. grated orange peel
1 tsp. nutmeg
2 tsp. cinnamon
6-8 large marshmallows

1. Place one layer of sweet potatoes in bottom of casserole dish. Dot with margarine.
2. Mix together brown sugar, orange peel, nutmeg, and cinnamon. Sprinkle thin layer over sweet potatoes.
3. Add another layer of sweet potatoes, followed by layer of brown sugar mixture. Continue layering until all ingredients are used.
4. Bake at 350° for 30 minutes.
5. Top with marshmallows. Return to oven and bake until marshmallows are melted and tops are slightly browned.

Sweet Potato Pudding

Anna Musser
Manheim, PA
PA Dutch Sampler

Makes 6 servings

2 cups mashed sweet potatoes
6 Tbsp. brown sugar
1 tsp. salt
2 tsp. butter, melted
1 cup milk
2 eggs
1 cup mini marshmallows

1. Beat together sweet potatoes, brown sugar, salt, butter, milk, and eggs.
2. Pour into greased casserole dish. Sprinkle marshmallows on top.
3. Bake at 350° for 45 minutes.

Fluffy Sweet Potato Casserole

Michele Manos
West Islip, NY
Friends

Makes 12 servings

9 medium sweet potatoes
3 eggs, separated
1/4 cup milk
4 Tbsp. butter, softened
3 Tbsp. cooking sherry
1 1/4 tsp. salt
1/4 tsp. pepper
1/4 cup packed light brown sugar
1/4 cup walnuts, chopped

1. In saucepan cover sweet potatoes with water. Heat to boiling. Reduce heat to low, cover and simmer for 30 minutes, or until sweet potatoes are tender. Drain. Cool sweet potatoes until easy to handle. Peel and set aside.
2. Beat egg whites until stiff peaks form. Set aside.
3. Beat together sweet potatoes, egg yolks, milk, butter, sherry, salt, and pepper until mixture is smooth.
4. Gently fold egg whites into sweet potato mixture.
5. Spoon mixture into greased casserole. Bake at 325° for 40 minutes. Remove casserole from oven. Sprinkle top with brown sugar and walnuts. Return to oven and bake for 15-20 minutes, until knife inserted in center comes out clean.

Scalloped Potatoes
Ida Schrock
Haven, KS
Flower Garden

Makes 65-70 servings

15 lbs. potatoes, peeled
and cut thin
9-10 lbs. ham, diced
2 cups butter or
margarine
2 cups flour
2¹/₂ quarts milk or cream
2 10³/₄-oz. cans cheddar
cheese soup
1¹/₂ Tbsp. salt
1¹/₂ tsp. pepper

1. Put potatoes in a large
roaster. Add diced ham.
2. In saucepan mix together
butter, flour, and milk. Cook
until thickened. Add soup,
salt, and pepper. Pour over
potatoes and ham.
3. Bake at 300° for 2¹/₂-3
hours.

*Note: This can be put in
smaller casseroles and frozen.*

Mom's Scalloped Potatoes
Lynne Fritz
Bel Air, MD
Mom's Star

Makes 6 servings

6 medium potatoes,
peeled and sliced
3 Tbsp. butter
3 Tbsp. flour
2¹/₂ cups milk
¹/₄ cup finely chopped
onions
³/₄ tsp. salt
³/₈ tsp. pepper
³/₈ tsp. onion salt
³/₄ tsp. celery salt

1. In saucepan melt butter.
Add flour and milk and stir
until thickened.
2. Arrange potatoes and
sauce in three layers in
greased casserole dish,
spicing each layer to taste.
3. Cover and bake at 350° for
30 minutes. Uncover and
continue to bake for 60-70
minutes, or until potatoes are
tender. Let stand for 5-10
minutes before serving.

Parmesan Potatoes
Marianne J. Miller
Millersburg, OH

Makes 8 servings

¹/₃ cup butter
¹/₄ cup flour
¹/₄ cup Parmesan cheese
salt to taste
seasoned salt to taste
6 medium potatoes,
peeled
sour cream

1. Melt butter on cookie
sheet in oven.
2. Combine flour, cheese,
and salts.
3. Cut potatoes into wedges
and soak briefly in water.
Dip each wedge into flour
mixture and arrange on
cookie sheet.
4. Bake at 375° for 1 hour
or until golden, turning
once.
5. Serve with sour cream.

Potatoes Augratin
Betty J. Hunter
Trenton, MI
Hollyhocks

Makes 12 servings

10 medium potatoes,
boiled and diced
1 cup salad dressing
¹/₂ cup olive juice
6-oz. jar olives
1 cup medium strong
cheese, grated

Being a quilter, I think I understand the true con-
cept of recycling. Quilters have been recycling fabric
for years. So this past year I added recycling to our
family Christmas traditions. Everyone was required
to find one recycled gift for each person on their list.
This gift could be fixed, refinished, or washed, but it
had to come from a garage sale, a secondhand store,
the Salvation Army, or in some way be a used gift.
We decided to open those gifts on Christmas Eve and
what a success! We now have a new tradition—recycled Christmas Eve gifts.
—*F. Elaine Asper, Stroudsburg, PA*

1 medium onion,
    chopped
1/4 tsp. salt
1/8 tsp. pepper
1/2 lb. bacon

1. Mix together salad dressing and olive juice.
2. Reserve 1/4 cup olives for garnish. Stir remaining olives, cheese, onion, salt, and pepper into salad dressing mixture.
3. Pour mixture over potatoes. Mix well. Pour into 9" x 13" baking dish.
4. Garnish with bacon slices and olives.
5. Bake at 350° for 30-40 minutes or until bacon is browned.

Grandma Britts Lefse
Ruth Liebelt
Rapid City, SD
Woven Heart

Makes 18-20 servings

8-10 potatoes in skins,
    cooked and riced
8 Tbsp. margarine
1/2 tsp. salt
1 Tbsp. sugar
2 Tbsp. cream
2 cups flour

1. Mix together riced potatoes, margarine, and salt. Stir in sugar and cream. Let set for 8 hours to cool.
2. Add 1 cup flour. Mix well.
3. Wrap a lefse rolling pin with a cloth and roll out lefse onto a cloth on the counter, adding flour as needed. Use as little flour as possible. Roll each lefse into a 10"-12" circle.
4. Fry on hot griddle until golden brown. Store immediately between 2 cloths and cover with plastic wrap to keep lefse moist. Serve.

Sour Cream Potato Casserole
Lois Stoltzfus
Honey Brook, PA
Colonial Star

Makes 10-12 servings

10-12 large potatoes
16-oz. carton sour cream
1 cup grated cheddar
    cheese
1/2 cup chopped onion
1/2 cup butter
1 tsp. salt
1/8 tsp. pepper
1 tsp. garlic salt

1. Cook potatoes in skins. Cool, peel, and shred. Pour into greased casserole dish.
2. In saucepan mix together sour cream, cheddar cheese, onion, and butter. Heat over low heat until melted. Pour over potatoes. Sprinkle salt, pepper, and garlic salt over the top.
3. Bake at 325° for 1 hour. Stir well before serving.

Variation: Reduce fat in recipe by substituting 1 cup milk for the butter.

Party Potatoes
Sandra Fulton Day
Oxford, PA
Road to Oklahoma
Denise Kuebler
St. James, MN

Makes 8-10 servings

6-8 large potatoes, boiled
    and mashed
8-oz. pkg. cream cheese
8 ozs. sour cream
dash salt
2 Tbsp. butter
dash paprika
1/2 cup grated cheese

1. Beat together potatoes, cream cheese, and sour cream until smooth. Stir in salt.
2. Pour into greased baking dish and bake at 325° for 1 hour.
3. Remove from oven. Dot with butter. Sprinkle with paprika and grated cheese. Serve.

Cheesy Potato Bake

Stephanie Yerger
Mechanicsburg, PA
Log Cabin

Makes 4-6 servings

2 lbs. potatoes, peeled
6 Tbsp. butter
6 Tbsp. heavy cream
1/2 tsp. salt
1/4 tsp. pepper
1/4 tsp. nutmeg
2 eggs, lightly beaten
1 cup cubed mozzarella
  cheese
1/4 cup grated Parmesan
  cheese
1 cup fresh bread crumbs
2 Tbsp. butter

1. Boil potatoes until tender.
Drain and mash with 6
Tbsp. butter and cream. Stir
in salt, pepper, and nutmeg.
2. Fold in eggs, mozzarella
cheese, and Parmesan
cheese, blending well.
3. Spoon into greased 2-
quart casserole dish.
4. Sauté bread crumbs in 2
Tbsp. butter over medium
heat until lightly browned,
about 5 minutes. Sprinkle
over potatoes.
5. Bake, uncovered, at 350°
for 20 minutes, until sizzling
around the edges and
browned on top. Serve in
pie-shaped wedges.

Special Mashed Potatoes

Loann Haegele
Woodland Hills, CA
Pink Tidings

Makes 6-8 servings

6-7 large potatoes, peeled
  and diced
1 1/4 cups butter
3/4-1 cup milk
8-oz. pkg. cream cheese,
  softened
1 pkg. dry ranch dressing

1. Boil potatoes until tender.
Drain.
2. Add butter and milk and
mash.
3. Stir in cream cheese and
ranch dressing. Serve immediately.

Potato Pierogi

Lillian McAninch
Leesburg, FL

Makes 4-5 dozen pierogi

Potato Filling:
5 lbs. potatoes
water to cover
1 lb. brick or Muenster
  cheese, cubed
1 tsp. salt

Pierogi:
4 cups flour
1 tsp. salt
1/4 cup sour cream
1 egg, slightly beaten
water

Bed for Pierogi:
1 large onion, chopped
1/2 lb. butter or margarine
sour cream

1. Peel and cut potatoes.
Place in cool water to cover
and bring to a boil. Boil
until soft. Drain.
2. Stir in cheese and salt.
Mash potatoes. Set aside to
cool.
3. To prepare pierogi mix
together flour, salt, sour
cream, egg, and enough
water to make dough, starting with 2/3 cup water. When
dough no longer sticks to
hands, form ball. Place in
bowl and cover with towel.
Let rest for 15 minutes.
3. Roll out onto floured
board until very thin. Cut
into rounds with biscuit cutter or water glass.
4. Fill each center with
potato filling. Fold in half
and pinch edges tightly
together.
5. Drop into boiling salted
water. Boil about 5 minutes
or until they rise to top. Boil
2 minutes more. Remove
with slotted spoon.
6. Sauté onion in butter.
Arrange pierogi over onion
on a serving platter. Serve
with sour cream.

Campfire Potatoes
Laura Troyer
Sugarcreek, OH
Alabama Star

Makes 4-6 servings

5 medium potatoes,
    peeled and thinly
    sliced
1 medium onion, sliced
6 Tbsp. butter or
    margarine
1/3 cup shredded cheddar
    cheese
2 Tbsp. minced fresh
    parsley
1 Tbsp. Worcestershire
    sauce
1/4 tsp. salt
1/2 tsp. pepper
1/3 cup chicken broth

1. Place the potatoes and
onion slices on a large piece
of heavy duty foil, about
20" x 20". Dot with butter.
2. Mix together cheese,
parsley, Worcestershire
sauce, salt, and pepper.
Sprinkle over potatoes.
3. Fold foil up around potatoes. Add broth. Seal the
edges of the foil well.
4. Grill, covered, over
medium coals for 35-40
minutes or until potatoes
are tender

Potatoes and Spinach
Sally A. Price
Reston, VA
Jewel Box

Makes 4 servings

4 medium red potatoes
1 Tbsp. margarine
1/2 cup chicken broth
1 large bunch spinach,
    washed and torn
1 Tbsp. red wine vinegar
1/4 tsp. pepper
1/2 tsp. salt

1. Microwave or bake potatoes until tender. Chop
coarsely with skins on.
2. Sauté chopped potatoes
in margarine for 3 minutes.
Stir in chicken broth and
spinach. Cover and simmer
for 3 minutes or until
spinach is limp.
3. Stir in vinegar, pepper,
and salt and heat through
before serving.

Spinach Souffle
Jacqueline E. Deininger
Bethlehem, PA
Jacob's Ladder

Makes 8 servings

10-oz. pkg. frozen,
    chopped spinach
3 Tbsp. butter
3 Tbsp. cornstarch
1/2 tsp. salt
1/8 tsp. pepper
1 cup milk
4 eggs, separated
3-oz. can mushrooms,
    drained

1. Cook spinach according
to package directions. Drain
well and set aside.
2. In a heavy saucepan melt
butter. Stir in cornstarch,
salt, and pepper. Add milk
and continue stirring until
smooth and creamy.
Remove from heat.
3. Combine egg yolks,
spinach, and mushrooms.
Add white sauce and mix
together.
4. Beat egg whites until
stiff. Fold into spinach mixture and spoon into greased
2-quart soufflé dish.
5. Bake at 375° for 30-35
minutes or until knife
inserted in center comes out
clean.

Spinach Casserole
Janice Way
Warrington, PA
Appliqué

Makes 6 servings

10-oz. pkg. frozen,
chopped spinach
1 egg, beaten
1/2 cup grated cheese
1 onion, chopped
1/4 cup margarine, melted
1 cup mushroom soup
1/4 tsp. pepper
1 cup stuffing mix
1 Tbsp. butter

1. Cook spinach according to package directions and drain well.
2. Stir in egg, cheese, onion, margarine, mushroom soup, and pepper. Mix well. Add 3/4 cup stuffing mix.
3. Pour into greased casserole dish. Top with remaining stuffing mix. Dot with butter.
4. Bake at 350° for 30 minutes.

Spinach with Artichokes
Barbara Nolan
Pleasant Valley, NY
Feedsack Quilt

Makes 12 servings

1/4 cup olive oil
2 Tbsp. chopped garlic
4 10-oz. pkgs. frozen, chopped spinach
3/4 cup margarine or butter
2 8-oz. pkgs. cream cheese
2 15-oz. cans artichoke hearts, drained and halved
1 cup crushed Ritz crackers
1/3 cup Parmesan cheese

1. In saucepan cook garlic in olive oil until soft. Set aside.
2. Cook spinach. Drain well. Stir in garlic and olive oil. Mix well.
3. Pour mixture into a greased 3-quart baking dish.
4. Melt together margarine and cream cheese over double boiler or put in bowl and microwave on medium for 3-4 minutes. Spread cheese mixture over spinach.
5. Arrange artichoke hearts over cheese.
6. Combine crackers and Parmesan cheese and sprinkle over spinach.
7. Bake at 350° for 25-30 minutes or until bubbly.

Note: This dish may be prepared ahead of time and refrigerated for a day.

Spinach Balls
Leigh Booth
Kintnersville, PA
Sampler
M. Jeanne Osborne
Wells, ME
Pansies for Florida

Makes 12-15 servings

4 large eggs, beaten
2 10-oz. pkgs. frozen spinach, thawed and drained
1 cup minced onion
3/4 cup Parmesan cheese
3/4 cup butter, melted
1/2 tsp. salt
1/2 tsp. thyme
1/4 tsp. pepper
1/4 tsp. nutmeg
21/2 cups herb-seasoned stuffing mix

1. Mix together eggs, spinach, onion, Parmesan cheese, butter, salt, thyme, pepper, and nutmeg.
2. Stir in stuffing mix and let stand for 20 minutes.
3. Shape into 1-inch balls and place on lightly greased cookie sheet.
4. Bake at 350° for 20 minutes until lightly browned.

Spiced Carrots
Nancy Jo Marsden
Glen Mills, PA
Tumbling Blocks Charm

Makes 8 servings

2 lbs. carrots
$1/4$ cup margarine
$1/4$ cup brown sugar
$1/4$ cup apple jelly
$1/2$ tsp. salt
1 tsp. lemon juice
$1/2$ tsp. nutmeg
$1/4$ tsp. cinnamon
$1/4$ cup slivered almonds

1. Boil small whole carrots until crisp-tender. Drain.
2. In saucepan combine all other ingredients and heat until melted and blended.
3. Pour carrots into a greased 2-quart baking dish. Cover with sauce. Refrigerate overnight.
4. Turn carrots to coat with sauce. Bake at 350° for 20-25 minutes.

Note: Instead of small carrots, larger ones may be cut diagonally into 2-inch pieces.

Copper Penny Carrots
Alyce C. Kauffman
Gridley, CA
Sailing Away
Carol L. O'Neill
Reston, VA
Remembering Mrs. Johnson

Makes 10-12 servings

2 lbs. carrots, sliced
1 green pepper, thinly sliced
1 medium onion, thinly sliced
$10^{3/4}$-oz. can tomato soup
1 tsp. salt
$1/4$ tsp. pepper
$1/2$ cup cooking oil
$3/4$ cup vinegar
1 cup sugar
1 tsp. dry mustard
1 tsp. Worcestershire sauce

1. Cook carrots in salted water until medium done. Rinse in ice water.
2. Arrange layers of carrots, green peppers, and onion in a bowl.
3. In saucepan mix together tomato soup, salt, pepper, oil, vinegar, sugar, mustard, and Worcestershire sauce.
4. Bring to a boil, stirring until thoroughly blended. Pour marinade over vegetables and refrigerate for at least 1 hour. Drain off marinade and serve.

Festive Carrot Ring
Jaclyn Ferrell
Carlisle, PA
Sisters' Choice

Makes 8-10 servings

2 cups cooked, mashed carrots
1 cup fine, dry bread crumbs
1 cup milk
$3/4$ cup shredded sharp cheddar cheese
$1/3$ cup butter, melted
1 small onion, grated
1 tsp. salt
$1/4$ tsp. pepper
3 eggs
10-oz. pkg. frozen green peas, cooked
leaf lettuce
parsley

1. Mix together carrots, bread crumbs, milk, cheese, butter, onion, salt, and pepper. Mix well.
2. Beat eggs at high speed until frothy and thickened. Gently fold into carrot mixture.
3. Spoon mixture into a greased $1^{1/2}$-quart aluminum or metal ring mold.
4. Bake at 350° for 45 minutes. Remove from oven; cool on wire rack for 20 minutes.
5. Invert carrot ring onto platter. Fill center with cooked peas. Garnish with leaf lettuce and parsley and serve.

Baked Carrot Casserole
Barbara J. Hill
Basalt, CO
The Maze

Makes 8-10 servings

3 cups finely shredded carrots
10-14 saltines, crushed
2 eggs, beaten
1¹/₂ cups diced mild cheddar cheese
16-oz. can cream-style corn
1/4 cup light cream
2 Tbsp. butter, melted
2 Tbsp. dried or fresh minced onion (optional)
1¹/₂ tsp. salt
1/4 tsp. pepper
fresh parsley

1. Mix together all ingredients and pour into a 2-quart baking dish.
2. Bake uncovered at 350° for 40 minutes or until set.
3. Garnish with fresh parsley and serve.

Corn Casserole
Jeanne Allen
Los Alamos, NM
Best Friends

Makes 4-6 servings

2 cups creamed corn
1/2 cup chopped ripe olives
1/2 cup cream
1 cup diced celery
1/4 cup bread crumbs
1 tsp. salt or less
1 tsp. pepper
1/2 cup chopped pimiento
1/2 cup grated cheese (optional)

1. Mix together all ingredients except cheese. Pour into a lightly greased baking dish. Sprinkle cheese over top of dish, if desired.
2. Bake at 350°. for 30 minutes. Let stand a few minutes before serving.

Crispy Scalloped Corn
Mary Helen Wade
Sterling, IL
Embroidered Blocks

Makes 6-10 servings

2 eggs, slightly beaten
1/2 cup milk
1 tsp. sugar
1 tsp. salt
1/8 tsp. pepper
1/3 cup diced onion
2 cups cubed bread
16-oz. can cream-style corn
1 cup crushed, crisp rice cereal
3 Tbsp. butter, melted

1. Mix together eggs and milk. Stir in sugar, salt, pepper, onion, bread, and corn.
2. Pour into medium casserole dish.
3. Mix together cereal and butter. Sprinkle over top.
4. Bake at 350° for 40-45 minutes.

Baked Corn
Jane S. Lippincott
Wynnewood, PA
Trip Around the World

Makes 8 servings

1/2 cup butter
2 Tbsp. sugar
1 Tbsp. flour
1/2 cup milk
2 eggs, well beaten
1¹/₂ tsp. baking powder
1/4 tsp. salt
2 10-oz. pkg. white corn, defrosted

1. In saucepan mix together butter and sugar. Heat until melted. Stir in flour. Remove from heat.
2. Slowly stir in milk, eggs, baking powder, and salt. Fold in corn.
3. Pour into greased casserole dish.
4. Bake at 350° for 35-40 minutes until golden brown.

Corn Chili Casserole

Mary Riha
Antigo, WI
Plaid Angel

Makes 6 servings

Corn:
2 cups cream-style corn
2 Tbsp. melted butter
4-oz. can green chilies, chopped
1 Tbsp. Parmesan cheese
1/3 cup grated sharp cheddar cheese
1/4 cup cracker crumbs
1/4 cup milk
1 tsp. salt
1/4 tsp. pepper

Topping:
1/4 cup grated sharp cheddar cheese
1/4 cup cracker crumbs
1 Tbsp. Parmesan cheese

1. Mix together all ingredients for corn casserole.
2. Pour into greased casserole dish.
3. Mix together all topping ingredients. Sprinkle over corn mixture.
4. Bake uncovered at 375° for 35 minutes.

Corn Scallop

Mary Jane Wackford
Oxford, NY
Log Cabin
Anna Tompkins
Greenfield, OH
Irish Chain

Makes 6-8 servings

2 16-oz. cans cream-style corn
2 1/2 cups milk
2 eggs, slightly beaten
44 saltines, crumbled
1/2 cup butter or margarine, melted
1 tsp. salt
1/2 tsp. paprika

1. Combine all ingredients and mix well. Turn into greased 9" x 13" baking dish.
2. Bake at 425° for 35-40 minutes.

Nebraska Corn Pudding

Evelyn L. Ward
Greeley, CO
Watercolor Quilt

Makes 8 servings

2 eggs, slightly beaten
16-oz. can cream-style corn
1 cup corn muffin mix
3/4 cup milk
1/4 cup cooking oil
1 1/2 cups grated cheddar cheese
1/2 tsp. salt
1/2 cup diced ham (optional)

1. Mix together all ingredients. Pour into greased 9" x 13" baking pan.
2. Bake at 375° for 45 minutes.

The oldest of our three very young sons recently helped our family establish a new Christmas tradition. I had a custom of preparing a big Christmas Eve dinner, which required working in the kitchen most of the day. By the time dinner was served, we often had only about a half hour to eat before we had to be out the door for our church's Christmas Eve service. I was exhausted. The boys usually didn't eat much of the meal anyway, so I got wise and asked my oldest what he would rather have for Christmas Eve dinner. His answer—a frozen Salisbury Steak dinner! And his brothers chimed in, as did my husband. Now we spend the entire day with our sons, eat a relaxed TV dinner together, and go to church for the evening service.
—Lynne Fritz, Bel Air, MD

Scalloped Corn

Lauren Eberhard
Seneca, IL
Around the Twist
Blanche Cahill
Willow Grove, PA
Tumbling Packages

Makes 10-12 servings

16-oz. can cream-style
corn
16-oz. can whole kernel
corn, undrained
8 Tbsp. margarine,
softened
1 cup sour cream
1 pkg. cornbread mix
2 eggs, slightly beaten
1 small onion, chopped
1 Tbsp. parsley

1. Mix together all ingredients and pour into greased 9" x 13" baking dish.
2. Bake at 350° for 1 hour.

*Variations: Substitute 16-oz.
can peas for whole corn. Add
chopped green pepper.*

Indian Corn

Jeanne Allen
Los Alamos, NM
Baltimore Beauty

Makes 8 servings

2 slices bacon, chopped
1 large onion, chopped
fine
1 egg, well beaten
2 16-oz. cans cream-style
corn
2 Tbsp. flour
1 Tbsp. sugar
1/4 cup milk

1. Brown bacon and onion
in skillet.
2. Mix together egg and
corn. Stir into onion mixture.
3. Blend together flour,
sugar, and milk. Stir into
corn mixture.
4. Pour into greased casserole dish.
5. Bake at 350° for 1 hour.

Corn Pie
with a Lid

Georgia Ann Egge
St. Paul, MN
Log Cabin

Makes 6-8 servings

4 eggs, beaten
1/2 tsp. salt
2 Tbsp. cornstarch
2 Tbsp. sugar
2 Tbsp. butter, melted
2 cups skim milk
3 16-oz. cans corn, drained
1 unbaked pie shell

1. Mix together eggs, salt,
cornstarch, sugar, and butter. Stir in milk and corn.
2. Pour into greased 2-quart
soufflé dish.
3. Cover with pie shell,
rolling the extra dough to
the inside of the soufflé
dish. Prick pastry with a
fork several times.
4. Bake at 350° for 50 minutes. If pastry turns too
dark, cover dish with a lid
for the last 15 minutes of
baking time.

Corn and
Broccoli Casserole

Sharon Easter
Yuba City, CA
Joyce Kaut
Rochester, NY
Glenna Keefer Smith
Punxsutawney, PA

Makes 6 servings

10-oz. pkg. frozen,
chopped broccoli
16-oz. can cream-style
corn
1 Tbsp. grated onion
8 Tbsp. butter or
margarine, melted
1 egg, slightly beaten
1 tsp. salt or less
1/4 tsp. pepper
1 cup herb-seasoned
stuffing mix
2 slices bacon, cut into 1"
pieces (optional)

1. Mix together broccoli,
corn, onion, 4 Tbsp. butter,
egg, salt, and pepper.
2. Pour into greased casserole.

3. Toss stuffing mix with remaining butter. Stir 3/4 of mix into corn and broccoli mixture. Use remaining stuffing as a topping. Top with bacon pieces, if desired.

4. Bake uncovered at 350° for 40-45 minutes or until done.

Broccoli Casserole

Shirley Hedman
Schenectady, NY
Stars for Many Mornings

Makes 6 servings

2 10-oz. pkgs. frozen, chopped broccoli
1/4 cup grated cheddar cheese
10³/4-oz. can cream of mushroom soup
1/2 cup mayonnaise or sour cream
1 Tbsp. lemon juice
1/4 cup chopped roasted red peppers
1/2 cup seasoned bread crumbs
1 Tbsp. Parmesan cheese

1. Partially cook broccoli. Drain well.
2. Mix together broccoli, cheddar cheese, mushroom soup, mayonnaise, lemon juice, and red peppers.
3. Pour into greased casserole dish.
4. Mix together bread crumbs and Parmesan cheese and spread over casserole.
5. Bake uncovered at 350° for 30 minutes.

Variations:
1. Omit lemon juice and red peppers. Substitute 1 egg, beaten and 1 Tbsp. chopped onion.
Bethel T. Moore
Fairfax, VA
Lucille Amos
Greensboro, NC

2. Substitute 1 small pkg. slivered almonds for red peppers.
Margaret A. Papuga
Prospect Heights, IL

Crumb-Topped Broccoli Casserole

Irene J. Dewar
Pickering, Ontario
Yesterday's Charm

Makes 4 servings

1 head broccoli, cut up with stalk
10³/4-oz. can cream of chicken soup
2 Tbsp. mayonnaise
1/4 cup shredded cheddar cheese
1/4 cup dry bread crumbs
1/4 cup Parmesan cheese
2 Tbsp. butter, melted

1. Parboil broccoli until partially cooked. Drain. Pour into greased casserole dish.
2. Mix together chicken soup, mayonnaise, and cheddar cheese. Pour over broccoli.
3. Mix together bread crumbs, Parmesan cheese, and butter. Sprinkle over broccoli mixture.
4. Bake at 350° for 40 minutes.

Cheesy Broccoli Casserole

Kay Miller
Mitchell, SD
Kathy Eagle
Charleston, SC
Theresa Leppert
Schellsburg, PA
Shelly Phillips
Ellsworth AFB, SD

Makes 8-10 servings

10-oz. pkg. frozen, chopped broccoli
1 cup cooked rice
1/4 cup chopped celery (optional)
10³/4-oz. can cream of chicken soup
4-ozs. Cheez Whiz
4-oz. jar mushrooms
1/8 tsp. garlic powder
1/8 tsp. pepper
buttered Ritz cracker crumbs

1. Thaw broccoli just enough to separate.
2. Mix together broccoli, rice, celery, soup, Cheez Whiz, mushrooms, garlic powder, and pepper.
3. Pour into greased casserole. Cover with cracker crumbs.
4. Bake at 350° for 45 minutes.

Broccoli Mornay
Jeanne Allen
Los Alamos, NM

Makes 4 servings

2 10-oz. pkgs. frozen,
  chopped broccoli
10³/4-oz. can cream of
  mushroom soup
2-oz. jar pimientos
3-oz. pkg. cream cheese,
  softened
5-oz. can water chestnuts,
  thinly sliced
1/2 tsp. salt
1/2 cup grated cheese

1. Cook broccoli until
nearly done. Drain.
2. Mix together soup,
pimientos, and cream
cheese. Add broccoli.
3. Stir in water chestnuts,
salt, and grated cheese.
4. Bake at 350° for 45 minutes.

Broccoli Joy
Carolyn W. Carmichael
Berkeley Heights, NJ

Makes 8-10 servings

2 10-oz. pkgs. frozen,
  chopped broccoli,
  thawed
3 eggs
1 cup cottage cheese
1 cup grated sharp
  cheddar cheese
2 Tbsp. flour
1/4 tsp. pepper

1. Mix together all ingredients.
2. Pour into greased 1¹/2-
quart casserole dish.
3. Bake at 350° for 30-35
minutes.

Broccoli Gratinee
Gwen Oberg
Albuquerque, NM
Fin and Fir

Makes 10 servings

2 lbs. fresh broccoli
  spears
  or 3 10-oz. pkgs. frozen
  broccoli
1 tsp. salt
1 tsp. pepper
1/4 cup butter
1/4 cup flour
2 cups half-and-half
1 cup chicken broth
1/2 tsp. salt
1/4 tsp. nutmeg
3/4 cup grated medium
  cheddar cheese
1/2 cup sliced almonds
1/2 cup crushed corn
  chips
2 Tbsp. chopped
  pimiento

1. Separate broccoli spears
into serving size portions.
Cook until stem portion is
barely tender. Do not overcook.
2. Arrange broccoli in
greased 2-quart casserole
dish. Sprinkle with salt and
pepper.
3. To prepare cream sauce,
melt butter in saucepan. Stir
in flour. Cook slowly for 5
minutes, stirring constantly.
(A honeycomb look will
form on bottom of pan.) Stir
in half-and-half. Increase
heat and add chicken broth,
salt, and nutmeg, stirring
constantly. Cook until thick
and creamy. Pour over broc-

I made a special Christmas quilt. Beginning at
Thanksgiving, the quilt passes from bed to bed in
our home until everyone has had a turn to sleep
under it. When we travel to visit parents and grandparents over the holidays, the quilt goes with us.
Each year I write the date on a new heart-shaped
label, and everyone who sleeps under the quilt signs
their name on the label. After the holiday season, I
stitch it to the back of the quilt. Hopefully, in fifty
years there will be fifty labels, supplying a family
history and story as well as a tradition.
—*Nancy Wagner Graves, Manhattan, KS*

coli. Sprinkle with 1/2 cup cheese and almonds.

4. Combine remaining 1/4 cup cheese, corn chips, and pimientos and arrange over top of casserole.

5. Bake at 350° for 20-30 minutes or until cheese is melted and sauce is bubbly.

Ricotta Broccoli Casserole

Jacqueline E. Deininger
Bethlehem, PA
Cathedral Window

Makes 8-10 servings

1 large bunch broccoli, cut into pieces
1 medium onion, diced
1/2 tsp. salt
1 cup ricotta cheese
3 eggs
1/2 tsp. salt
1/2 cup grated cheese

1. Boil broccoli, onion, and salt in water for 3 minutes. Remove from heat.

2. Mix together cheese, eggs, and salt. Stir into broccoli mixture.

3. Pour into a greased 2-quart casserole. Sprinkle cheese over top.

4. Bake at 350° for 40 minutes.

Cauliflower Gratin

Barbara Riley
Elk Grove, CA
Vase of Flowers

Makes 6 servings

4 slices bacon, chopped
4 cloves garlic, minced
1 large head cauliflower, sliced thin
2 Tbsp. flour
1 1/2 cups cream
1/8 tsp. cayenne pepper
1/4 tsp. black pepper
1 1/2 cups grated Swiss cheese
chopped parsley

1. Sauté bacon until brown. Add garlic and sauté for 2 minutes.

2. Add cauliflower to skillet and cook until it begins to soften. Stir in flour and mix well. Stir in cream, cayenne, and pepper. Heat to boiling.

3. Pour into shallow casserole dish and top with cheese and parsley.

4. Bake at 350° for 30 minutes.

Spiced Cabbage

Jean Turner
Williams Lake, BC
Weaver Fever

Makes 4-6 servings

1/4 cup butter
1 cup water
1 tsp. salt
1 small head red cabbage, finely shredded
2 cooking apples, peeled and sliced
3 cloves
1 Tbsp. sugar
dash vinegar

1. In saucepan place 1 Tbsp. butter, water, and salt. Stir in red cabbage, apples, and cloves. Simmer for 45 minutes.

2. Stir in remaining butter, sugar, and vinegar. Simmer another 5 minutes. Remove cloves before serving.

Meatless Stuffed Cabbage
Lillian McAninch
Leesburg, FL
Ohio Rose Applique

Makes 10-12 servings

4 cups water
2 cups rice
1 tsp. salt
3 large chopped onions
1 Tbsp. cooking oil
1 medium head cabbage
16-oz. can whole
    tomatoes
6-oz. can tomato paste
3/4 cup water
2 Tbsp. brown sugar

1. In saucepan bring water to a boil. Stir in rice and salt. Return to boil. Reduce heat, cover, and cook for about 20 minutes.
2. Sauté onions in oil until tender. Mix sautéed onion into cooked rice.
3. Parboil cabbage for about 5 minutes. Remove leaves from core. Cool cabbage. Pare off thick ribs of cabbage to the same thickness as rest of leaves. Place cabbage leaf in palm of hand. Place heaping tablespoon of rice filling close to end of leaf. Roll firmly, tucking in sides. Place close together in heavy roastpan. Cover top with leftover leaves.
4. Combine tomatoes, tomato paste, water, and brown sugar. Pour over stuffed cabbage rolls. Cover tightly.
5. Bake at 350° for 2 hours.

Cabbage Casserole
Eldeen Carter
Charleston, SC
A Charleston Basket

Makes 10-12 servings

1 medium head cabbage,
    shredded
4 ribs celery, chopped
1-2 cups water
salt to taste
1 small onion, chopped
2 Tbsp. butter
2 Tbsp. flour
1 cup milk
1 cup mayonnaise
1/2 tsp. curry
1 cup slivered almonds

1. Cook cabbage and celery in salted water for 8 minutes. Drain. Add onion.
2. In saucepan melt butter and stir flour into butter to make a smooth paste. Stir in milk until well mixed. Cook over low heat, stirring constantly until thickened. Stir into cabbage mixture. Fold in curry, mayonnaise, and almonds.
3. Pour into 2-quart casserole and bake at 350° for 30 minutes.

German-Style Cabbage
Joyce Kaut
Rochester, NY

Makes 8 servings

3 Tbsp. butter
1 onion, chopped
1 medium head (about 1
    lb.) red cabbage, finely
    shredded
1/2 cup water
2 tsp. wine vinegar
4 apples, peeled and
    sliced
4 whole cloves
1 bay leaf
1 tsp. salt
1 Tbsp. sugar
3 Tbsp. dry red wine

1. In a large skillet melt butter and cook onion until golden brown.
2. Add cabbage and continue to cook until cabbage is light brown.
3. Stir in water, vinegar, apples, cloves, bay leaf, and salt.
4. Cover and simmer until cabbage is tender, about 30-45 minutes.
5. Add sugar and wine and simmer 5 minutes longer.

Karen's Zucchini Casserole
Marge Reeder
State College, PA
Sara's Log Cabin

Makes 8-10 servings

1/2 cup margarine
1 cup seasoned bread crumbs
4 cups chunked zucchini
2 carrots, diced
1 onion, diced
1/2 cup sour cream
10 3/4-oz. can cream of chicken soup
1/4 cup milk

1. Melt margarine and stir bread crumbs into margarine. Set aside.
2. Boil zucchini chunks for 5 minutes. Drain.
3. Stir in carrots, onion, sour cream, chicken soup, and milk. Mix well, then add 1/2 of the bread crumb mixture. Mix well.
4. Pour into greased 9" x 13" casserole dish and top with remaining bread crumb mixture.
5. Bake at 350° for 25 minutes.

Zucchini Bake
Maxine Cooper
Danville, IL
Maple Leaf

Makes 6 servings

4 cups shredded zucchini
3 eggs, beaten slightly
1/2 cup cooking oil
1 small onion, grated
1 cup biscuit mix
1/2 cup grated Parmesan cheese

1. Mix together zucchini, eggs, oil, onion, and biscuit mix.
2. Pour into greased 9" x 13" baking dish. Top with grated cheese.
3. Bake at 350° for 45 minutes or until brown on top.

Zucchini Fritters
Katie Esh
Ronks, PA

Makes 8 servings

4 cups grated zucchini
3 eggs
1 cup flour
1 tsp. baking powder
1/2 tsp. salt
dash pepper

1. Mix together all ingredients.
2. Drop by large tablespoonfuls into a pan with hot oil. Fry until golden brown and serve.

Sylvia's Butternut Squash
Irene P. Dietlin
Winsted, CT
Pineapple Madness

Makes 8 servings

2 medium butternut squash, peeled and cut into 1" pieces
salt and pepper to taste
1 Tbsp. butter
1/2 cup heavy cream
1/2 cup maple syrup

1. Cook squash in boiling water until tender. Mash, stirring in salt, pepper, and butter.
2. Gently stir in remaining ingredients.
3. Pour into greased 1 1/2-quart casserole dish.
4. Bake at 425° for 20 minutes.

Vegetables

Squash Carrot Casserole
Eldeen Carter
Charleston, SC
A Charleston Basket

Makes 10-12 servings

3 lbs. squash, cut in
  pieces (approx. 8 cups)
3 carrots, cut in pieces
2 onions, cut in pieces
1/2 cup butter
16-oz. pkg. herb-seasoned
  stuffing mix
2 10³/4-oz. cans cream of
  chicken soup
4-oz. jar pimiento,
  chopped (optional)
1/2 cup sour cream
1 tsp. salt
1/8 tsp. pepper

1. Cook together squash,
carrots, and onions in a
small amount of water.
Drain well and mash.
2. In saucepan sauté dressing mix in butter. Pour 1/2 of
mixture into bottom of
greased 3-quart casserole.
3. Mix together chicken
soup, pimiento, sour cream,
salt, and pepper. Add to
mashed vegetables. Pour
into casserole on top of
dressing. Spread remaining
dressing mixture over top of
casserole.
4. Bake at 350° for 45 minutes.

Squash and Apple Bake
Sharon Leali
Jackson, OH

Makes 6 servings

2 lbs. butternut or
  buttercup squash
2 baking apples
1/2 cup brown sugar,
  packed
1/4 cup butter or
  margarine, melted
1 Tbsp. flour
1 tsp. salt
1/2 tsp. mace

1. Cut squash in half.
Remove seeds and fibers.
Cut squash into 1/2" slices.
Arrange in ungreased bak-
ing dish.
2. Core and cut apples into
1/2" slices. Place apples over
squash in dish.
3. Stir together brown sugar,
butter, flour, salt, and mace.
Sprinkle sugar mixture over
apples. Cover with foil.
4. Bake at 350° for 50-60
minutes or until squash is
tender.

Asparagus AuGratin
Charmaine Caesar
Lancaster, PA
Bits and Pieces

2 lbs. asparagus
4 Tbsp. butter
4 Tbsp. flour
dash salt
2 cups milk
1/2 tsp. lemon juice
6 egg yolks
4 Tbsp. grated Romano
  cheese
3 Tbsp. buttered bread
  crumbs

1. Trim tough stem bottoms
of asparagus. Cook whole,
just barely covered in boiling salted water for 10-15
minutes. Drain and arrange
in a flat baking dish.
2. In saucepan melt butter.
Stir in flour and salt.
Gradually stir in milk, stirring constantly. Remove
from heat. Mix together
lemon juice and egg yolks.
Stir 3 Tbsp. white sauce
into egg mixture. Stir egg
mixture into white sauce.
Heat over medium heat for
about 5 minutes or until
thickened.
3. Pour sauce over asparagus in baking dish. Sprinkle
with cheese and bread
crumbs. Lightly brown
under the broiler until the
sauce is bubbly.

Asparagus Casserole

Barbara L. McGinnis
Ocean City, NJ

Makes 6 servings

2 10-oz. pkgs. asparagus, cooked and drained
10³/4-oz. can mushroom soup
3 hard-boiled eggs, cut up
1 tsp. salt
1/4 tsp. pepper
1/2 cup grated cheese
1/2 cup bread crumbs
1 Tbsp. butter

1. Layer ingredients in greased casserole dish in order given. Dot with butter.
2. Bake at 350° for 30 minutes.

Italian Green Beans

Karen Bryant
Corrales, NM
Thimbleberry Pines

Makes 8 servings

1 lb. frozen green beans
1/4-1/2 cup blanched almonds or roasted pine nuts
1/4 cup olive oil
1/4 cup wine vinegar
1 tsp. basil
1/2 tsp. oregano
1/2 tsp. garlic salt
1/4 cup grated Parmesan cheese

1. Steam green beans until tender. Toast nuts in a 350° oven for about 5 minutes, until light golden toast.
2. In saucepan heat olive oil, vinegar, basil, oregano, and garlic salt on low.
3. Lightly toss the green beans, nuts, and oil and spice mixture with Parmesan cheese.
4. Serve warm or chilled.

Green Beans Casserole

Alice Kennedy
Dallas, TX
Ye Olde Bow Tie

Makes 8 servings

1/2 cup sliced onion
2 Tbsp. butter, melted
1¹/2 tsp. parsley
2 Tbsp. flour
salt to taste
pepper to taste
1/2 tsp. grated lemon rind
1 cup sour cream
5 cups frozen green beans
1/2 cup dry bread crumbs
1/4 cup grated Parmesan cheese

1. In large saucepan sauté onion in butter. Stir in parsley, flour, salt, pepper, and lemon rind. Mix well.
2. Add sour cream and mix well. Stir in beans and heat through.
3. Pour into casserole dish. Sprinkle with bread crumbs and cheese.
4. Bake at 350° for 30 minutes.

Green Beans Amandine

Laura M. Rohwedder
Pittsburgh, PA
Garden Path

Makes 6 servings

1 lb. fresh green beans
2 Tbsp. slivered almonds
2 Tbsp. butter
1 tsp. lemon juice
salt and pepper to taste

1. Remove ends of beans and slice lengthwise. Cook in salted water until tender. Drain.
2. Cook almonds in butter over low heat, stirring occasionally until golden. Remove from heat.
3. Stir in lemon juice and salt and pepper to taste. Pour over beans. Serve.

Ozark Baked Beans

Suzie Humphries
Fort Smith, AR
Around the World

Makes 20 servings

1 lb. ground beef
1/2 lb. bacon, cut into 2" strips
1/2 cup diced onions
1/2 tsp. salt
1/2 tsp. pepper
2 21-oz. cans pork and beans, undrained
16-oz. can red kidney beans, undrained
15-oz. can butter beans, undrained
1/2 cup brown sugar
1 1/4 cups ketchup
2 Tbsp. vinegar
2 tsp. prepared mustard
1/2 tsp. garlic powder

1. Cook bacon until crisp. Drain.
2. Brown ground beef, onion, salt, pepper, and garlic powder. Stir well to crumble meat. Drain.
3. Combine bacon and ground beef mixture. Stir in all remaining ingredients and mix well.
4. Pour into casserole dish. Bake at 325° for 1 hour.

Bunnell's Bean Casserole

Cathie Favret
Tillamook, OR
Puppy Love

Makes 12-15 servings

6 slices bacon
1 cup onion, chopped coarsely
53-oz. can pork and beans, not drained
16-oz. can red kidney beans, drained
16-oz. can white lima beans, drained
16-oz. can garbanzo beans, drained
1/2 cup ketchup
1/2 cup brown sugar
1 Tbsp. Worcestershire sauce
1/2 lb. cheddar cheese, cut into 1/2" cubes
1/2 cup Parmesan cheese

1. Cook bacon and onion together until onion is soft. Crumble bacon into pieces and drain some of fat, if desired.
2. Mix together bacon mixture, all beans, ketchup, brown sugar, Worcestershire sauce, and cheddar cheese. Pour into greased casserole dish. Sprinkle Parmesan cheese over top.
3. Bake at 350° for 1 hour.

Creamed Peas and Potatoes

Amanda Schlabach
Millersburg, OH
Lancaster Rose

Makes 6-8 servings

4 medium red potatoes, cubed
dash salt
10-oz. pkg. frozen peas
1 tsp. sugar
2 Tbsp. butter or margarine
2 Tbsp. flour
1/2 tsp. salt
1/4 tsp. pepper
1 1/2 cups milk
2 Tbsp. minced fresh dill

1. Place potatoes in a saucepan. Cover with water, add salt, and cook until tender.
2. Cook peas according to package directions, adding the sugar.
3. Melt butter in a saucepan. Add flour, salt, and pepper to form paste. Gradually stir in milk. Bring to a boil. Boil 1 minute.
4. Add dill. Cook until thick and bubbly.
5. Drain potatoes and peas. Place in serving bowl.
6. Pour sauce over potatoes and peas and stir to coat. Serve immediately.

Sarah's Christmas Peas

Abbie Christie
Berkeley Heights, NJ
Double Wedding Ring

Makes 4-6 servings

10-oz. pkg. frozen small peas
1/2 cup chopped celery
1 Tbsp. chopped onion
2 Tbsp. pimiento
4-oz. can sliced mushrooms
1 Tbsp. butter
1/2 tsp. winter savory

1. Cook peas according to package directions.
2. Sauté celery, onion, pimiento, and mushrooms in butter. Combine peas and savory with other ingredients. Serve in a clear glass bowl.

Bow Ties and Peppers

Carolyn D. Burkett
Punxsutawney, PA
Tulip

Makes 6 servings

12-oz. pkg. large bow pasta
1 small onion, chopped
1 clove garlic, minced
1/2 cup margarine or butter
1 medium red pepper, cut in thin strips
1 medium green pepper, cut in thin strips
1 small can dried tomatoes (optional)
1/3 cup olive oil
2 Tbsp. parsley

1. Boil pasta in water for 9 minutes.
2. Sauté onion and garlic in butter for 3-4 minutes. Add peppers and dried tomatoes and continue to sauté over low heat until tender.
3. Stir in pasta, olive oil, and parsley. Remove from heat and serve.

Scalloped Parsnips

Pauline Morrison
St. Marys, Ontario
Cinderella

Makes 6 servings

2 1/2 cups peeled, cubed
   parsnips
2 Tbsp. chopped onion
3 Tbsp. butter
1/2 tsp. salt
1/8 tsp pepper
1 tsp. sugar
1 1/2 Tbsp. cornstarch
1 1/2 cups tomato juice
1 1/4 cups soft bread
   crumbs

1. Cut parsnips into 1/2"
cubes and cook until tender.
2. Sauté onion in 2 Tbsp.
butter until golden. Add
salt, pepper, sugar, and
cornstarch. Blend in tomato
juice. Cook until smooth.
Add parsnips. Place in
casserole.
3. Melt remaining 1 Tbsp.
butter and toss with bread
crumbs. Pour over top of
casserole.
4. Bake at 400° for 15 minutes, until brown and bubbly.

Holiday Turnip

Phyllis Brokaw
North Plainfield, NJ
Doll Quilt

Makes 4 servings

1 large turnip, cooked
   and mashed
1/2 cup applesauce
3 Tbsp. butter
3 Tbsp. brown sugar
1 egg, slightly beaten
1/2 cup bread crumbs
2 Tbsp. butter

1. Mix together mashed
turnip, applesauce, butter,
brown sugar, and egg.
2. Pour into greased casserole. Cover with bread
crumbs and dribble with
butter. Cover and refrigerate
for 8 hours.
3. Bake at 350° for 30 minutes.

Christmas Company Beets

Ruth L. Welch
Jefferson, NY
Burgoyne Surrounded

Makes 4 servings

1 Tbsp. cornstarch
2 Tbsp. sugar
1/4 tsp. salt
8-oz. can pineapple
   chunks, undrained
1 Tbsp. butter
1 Tbsp. lemon juice
15-oz. can sliced beets,
   drained

1. In saucepan mix together
cornstarch, sugar, and salt.
Add pineapple and pineap-
ple juice to syrup. Cook
until syrup is thick and
clear, stirring constantly.
2. Add butter, lemon juice,
and beets. Heat thoroughly.
Serve.

> For as long as I can remember, it has been a
> tradition for my grandmother to bless everyone
> before our traditional Christmas Eve seafood dinner
> by making the sign of the cross on each person's
> forehead with honey. The honey is to make you
> sweet all year long. It's great fun to see who she
> decides needs a double dose of honey for the
> upcoming year. As our family circle has grown with
> boyfriends, girlfriends, and in-laws, we've also
> developed the tradition of keeping the newest
> member in suspense about the honey tradition.
> —*Christine Heuser, Farmingdale, NJ*

Baked Celery with Almonds
Jeanne Allen
Los Alamos, NM
Scrap-a-holic

Makes 6-8 servings

4 cups celery, cut into 1"
  pieces
5-oz. can water chestnuts,
  sliced
1/2 cup sliced almonds
2 Tbsp. butter
2 Tbsp. flour
1/2 tsp. salt
2/3 cup chicken broth
2/3 cup half-and-half
1/2 cup buttered bread
  crumbs

1. Cook celery for 5 minutes
in boiling water. Drain.
2. Mix together celery, chestnuts, and almonds. Pour into
a greased casserole dish.
3. In saucepan melt butter.
Stir in flour and salt.
Gradually add chicken broth
and half-and-half. Heat until
thickened, stirring constantly
4. Pour over the vegetables
and top with buttered
crumbs.
5. Bake at 350° until hot
and bubbling.

Onion Cheese Casserole
Jean Reistle
Mickleton, NJ
Ohio Star

Makes 6-8 servings

3 Bermuda onions, thinly
  sliced
1 Tbsp. butter
1/2 lb. grated Swiss cheese
2 10 3/4-oz. cans cream of
  chicken soup
6-8 slices Italian or
  French bread
1 Tbsp. butter, softened

1. Sauté onions in 1 Tbsp.
butter. Arrange across bottom of greased 9" x 13" baking pan.
2. Sprinkle cheese over
onions. Pour soup over
cheese. Place slices of bread
on top. Dot bread with
lumps of softened butter.
3. Cover and bake at 350°
for 25 minutes. Uncover
and bake 10 minutes longer.

Much-More-Than Mushrooms
Tillie Helmer
Oakhurst, CA
SMQA's Opportunity Quilt

Makes 6 servings

1 lb. fresh mushrooms,
  sliced
4 Tbsp. butter
3/4 cup chopped green
  onions

3/4 cup chopped celery
1 tsp. salt
1/4 tsp. pepper
2 Tbsp. chopped parsley
1/2 cup mayonnaise
8 slices firm white bread
3 eggs, slightly beaten
2 cups milk
1/4 cup grated Parmesan
  cheese

1. Sauté mushrooms in butter for 5 minutes. Add green
onions, celery, salt, pepper,
and parsley. Cook for 3 minutes. Remove from heat. Stir
in mayonnaise and set aside.
Cool.
2. Remove crust from bread
and cut into squares. Place
half of bread cubes in
greased casserole dish.
Spoon vegetable mixture
over bread. Cover with
remaining bread.
3. Beat together eggs and
milk. Pour over casserole.
4. Cover and refrigerate for
at least 1 hour.
5. Bake covered at 350° for
50 minutes. Sprinkle
Parmesan cheese over top
and return to oven for 10
more minutes or until golden
brown.

Mushroom Casserole

Susan Tjon
Austin, TX
Doll-Sized Pinwheel

Makes 10-12 servings

3 lbs. fresh mushrooms
1/2 cup margarine
1 large onion, chopped
8-oz. brick cheddar, shredded
16-oz. pkg. chicken-flavored stuffing mix
1 pint half-and-half

1. If mushrooms are large, cut in half. Place margarine, chopped onion, and mushrooms in 5-quart Dutch oven. Cover and cook over low heat for about 30 minutes or until mushrooms are tender and have made their own juice.
2. In a large casserole dish, place 1/3 mushroom and onions, 1/3 cheese, and 1/2 stuffing mix. Repeat layers, topping with remaining mushrooms and cheese. (When spooning mushrooms into casserole dish, use some juice, but not all of it.)
3. Pour half-and-half over casserole.
4. Bake at 350° for 30 minutes until set and cheese has melted.

Stuffed Mushrooms

Janice Deel
Paducah, KY

Makes 4-6 servings

1 lb. mushrooms
1/4 lb. ground beef
1 clove garlic, minced
1/4 cup minced onion
1 Tbsp. parsley
1/2 tsp. salt
2 Tbsp. lemon juice
1/2 cup sour cream or mayonnaise

1. Wash mushrooms thoroughly. Wipe with damp paper towel and remove stems.
2. Mix together ground beef, garlic, onion, parsley, and salt. Cook until brown.
3. Dip mushrooms in lemon juice. Fill mushroom cap with meat mixture.
4. Place on cookie sheet and bake at 350° for 12 minutes. Remove to serving dish and top with sour cream or mayonnaise.

Tomatoes with Stuffed Mushrooms

Charmaine Caesar
Lancaster, PA
Bits and Pieces

Makes 4 servings

4 large firm tomatoes
1/4 lb. fresh mushrooms, cleaned and chopped
1 small onion, chopped
2 Tbsp. butter
2 Tbsp. bread crumbs
2 Tbsp. sour cream
salt to taste
white pepper to taste

1. Cut tops off tomatoes and scoop out seeds, leaving fruit of tomato intact.
2. Sauté mushrooms and onion in butter for 5-10 minutes.
3. Mix together mushroom mixture, bread crumbs, sour cream, salt, and pepper. Stuff the tomatoes.
4. Place in a shallow, lightly greased 8" square casserole dish. Bake at 350° for 25-30 minutes.

Mushroom Pastry
Jeanne Allen
Los Alamos, NM
Baltimore Beauty

Makes 6-8 servings

1/3 cup butter
2 medium onions
1 lb. mushrooms, sliced
1/3 cup flour
1/2 cup light cream
2 Tbsp. sweet sherry
salt to taste
pepper to taste
12" x 14" puff pastry

1. Sauté onions in butter until transparent. Stir in mushrooms and sauté until golden and liquid has evaporated.
2. Sprinkle flour over the mushrooms and stir thoroughly until blended. Remove from heat and stir in cream and sherry, stirring until smooth. Return to heat and cook until thickened. Season with salt and pepper. Allow to cool.
3. Roll out puff pastry to a rectangle about 12" x 14". Spoon the mushroom filling down the center. Fold the edges over and secure the seams by wetting the edges of the dough with a bit of water. Press to seal. Make several small cuts across the top.
4. Bake at 450° for 15-20 minutes or until pastry is golden brown. Slice to serve.

Irish Colcannon on Bubble and Squeak
Blanche Cahill
Willow Grove, PA
Tumbling Packages

Makes 6-8 servings

8 potatoes
1/3 pint milk, heated
6 scallions, chopped
1 Tbsp. butter
1 1/2 cups boiled cabbage, chopped and drained
1 lb. chopped parsley
salt to taste
pepper to taste

1. Boil and mash potatoes. Stir in milk and scallions. Beat until fluffy.
2. In large saucepan melt butter. Stir in cabbage, potatoes, and parsley. Season with salt and pepper and heat through before serving.

Vegetable Medley
Dorothy Reise
Severna Park, MD
Appliqué Poinsettia

Makes 8 servings

2 10-oz. pkgs. frozen, chopped spinach
10-oz. pkg. frozen, chopped broccoli
10-oz. pkg. frozen limas
10 3/4-oz. can cream of mushroom soup
2 tomatoes, thinly sliced
1/2 cup grated sharp cheddar cheese
1 Tbsp. chopped fresh dill
2.8-oz. can French-style onions

1. Cook spinach, broccoli, and limas until almost tender. Drain.
2. Add mushroom soup to vegetables and mix well. Pour into greased shallow casserole.
3. Layer tomatoes over vegetables in casserole. Sprinkle grated cheese on top of tomatoes. Sprinkle dill on top. Scatter a few onion rings over the top.
4. Bake at 350° for 30 minutes.

Vegetable Bake
Rhondalee Schmidt
Scranton, PA
*Three Little Pumpkins
Sitting On My Wall*

Makes 6-8 servings

1 medium head
  cauliflower
1 medium bunch broccoli
2 cups sliced carrots
5 Tbsp. butter
2 Tbsp. flour
1/2 tsp. salt
1 1/2 cups milk
1 cup grated American
  cheese
3/4 cup fine dry bread
  crumbs

1. Cook cauliflower, broccoli, and carrots until tender. Drain. Place in greased casserole.
2. In saucepan melt 2 Tbsp. butter. Stir in flour and salt until bubbly. Add milk and cook until thickened, stirring constantly. Stir in cheese. Pour cheese sauce over vegetables.
3. Combine remaining butter with bread crumbs to make a crumb topping. Sprinkle over casserole.
4. Bake at 350° for 25 minutes.

Onion-Potato Stuffing
Joyce Valley
Pelican Rapids, NM
Apple Quilt

Makes 12 cups

20 medium potatoes,
  pared and diced
3 cups chopped onion
1 cup coarsely chopped
  celery
3/4 cup butter
3 tsp. salt or less
1/2 tsp. pepper
4 cups small bread cubes
1/2 cup milk
4 eggs, lightly beaten
1/2 cup chopped parsley

1. In a large frying pan, cook onion and celery in butter until soft. Sprinkle with salt and pepper. Stir in potatoes and cook for 20 minutes until tender.
2. Mix together bread cubes and milk in a large bowl. Stir in eggs. Blend into potato mixture. Add parsley. Cook slowly until eggs are solidified.
3. Stuff into turkey which has been baking for several hours.

Note: As we always have such a large turkey, we bake it for a couple of hours before stuffing. Then, we use some of the drippings from the turkey or broth from boiling giblets to stir into the stuffing. This makes the stuffing more moist.

Vegetarian Bread Stuffing
Denise Scandone Rominger
Bel Air, MD
Life I—Woodburning

Makes 8 servings

12 cups cubed white
  bread
2 Tbsp. margarine
1 1/2 cups chopped celery
1 cup chopped onion
2 Tbsp. water
1 Tbsp. sugar
2 1/2 tsp. poultry
  seasoning
3/4 tsp. dried basil
1/4 tsp. salt
1/4 tsp. ground nutmeg
1/4 tsp. pepper
1 cup vegetable broth
1 egg, lightly beaten

1. Place bread cubes on a jelly roll pan. Bake at 325° for 20 minutes or until lightly toasted. Set aside.
2. Melt margarine in a large skillet over medium heat. Add celery, onion, and water. Cover. Reduce heat and cook 15 minutes or until tender. Remove from heat.
3. Stir in sugar, poultry seasoning, basil, salt, nutmeg, and pepper.
4. In a large bowl mix together bread cubes, celery mixture, vegetable broth, and egg. Stir well.
5. Spoon mixture into a greased 2-quart casserole dish.
6. Bake uncovered at 325° for 35 minutes.

Cornbread Stuffing

Janice Muller
Derwood, MD
Canadian Geese

Makes 8-10 servings

1 cup chopped onion
1 cup chopped celery
8 Tbsp. butter or
   margarine
8-oz. pkg. cornbread
   stuffing
16-oz. jar applesauce
1/2 tsp. thyme
1/2 tsp. marjoram
1/4 tsp. lemon-pepper
   seasoning
1/3 cup boiling water

1. In a large skillet sauté onion and celery in butter until soft.
2. Stir in cornbread stuffing, applesauce, thyme, marjoram, lemon-pepper seasoning, and boiling water. Toss lightly until evenly moist.
3. Spoon into a buttered 2-quart baking dish and cover with foil. Or use to stuff turkey.
4. If preparing separately from turkey, bake at 325° for 30 minutes.

Crockpot Sage Stuffing

Carma Popp
Mitchell, SD
Four-Block Sampler

Makes 10-12 servings

1 cup celery, chopped
1 onion, chopped
3/4 cup margarine
4 eggs, beaten
10 3/4-oz. can cream of
   chicken soup
1 tsp. baking powder
3 tsp. sage
1/2 tsp. pepper
1 1/2 lbs. loaf bread, cubed
10 3/4-oz. can chicken
   broth

1. Sauté celery and onions in margarine for 15 minutes.
2. Mix together eggs, soup, baking powder, sage, pepper, and cubed bread.
3. Stir in chicken broth, celery, and onion. Stir until bread is coated. Mixture will be very moist.
4. Pour into greased crockpot. Cook on high for 1 hour, turn to low for 4-5 hours. Stir often to prevent sticking.

Chestnut Filling

Flossie Sultzaberger
Mechanicsburg, PA
Christmas Scene

Makes 12 servings

1/2 cup margarine or
   butter
1 medium onion,
   chopped
2 large stalks celery and
   leaves
1 egg
1 large loaf white bread,
   torn into small pieces
1 lb. chestnuts
1/4 cup milk
1/2 tsp. salt
1/4 tsp. pepper
2 Tbsp. dried parsley

1. Sauté onion and celery in butter until transparent. Remove from heat and stir in egg. Pour mixture over bread and mix well.
2. Clean chestnuts and break into large pieces.
3. Add chestnuts and all remaining ingredients to bread mixture and stir together. Spoon into lightly greased 9" x 13" baking dish.
4. Cover and bake at 350° for 30-35 minutes. Uncover and bake another 10 minutes.

Holiday Apple Stuffing
Jean Turner
Williams Lake, BC
Attic Window

Makes 6-8 servings

1 cup chopped onion
2 Tbsp. butter
2 cups chopped apple
5-oz. can water chestnuts, drained and sliced
3 Tbsp. chopped parsley
3/4 tsp. ground sage
1/2 tsp. salt
1/8 tsp. pepper
2 eggs, beaten
1/2 cup chicken broth
4 cups dry bread cubes

1. In skillet sauté onion in butter until tender but not brown. Stir in apple, water chestnuts, parsley, sage, salt, and pepper. Stir in eggs and chicken broth.
2. Pour egg and apple mixture over bread cubes. Toss lightly to mix. Use to stuff poultry or spoon into 1 1/2-quart casserole dish.
3. Bake at 375° for 30-35 minutes.

Baked Pineapple Dressing
Janet Derstine
Telford, PA
Double Wedding Ring

Makes 8 servings

1/2 cup butter or margarine
1 cup sugar
4 eggs
20-oz. can crushed pineapple, undrained
pinch salt
6-8 slices stale bread, cubed

1. Cream together butter and sugar. Add eggs, one at a time, beating well after each addition. Add undrained pineapple and salt and mix well.
2. Stir in bread cubes and spoon into well greased casserole dish.
3. Bake at 350° for 45 minutes.

Note: Delicious when served with a ham dinner.

Cranberry Rice
Marlene Fonken
Upland, CA
Crazy Patch

Makes 4 servings

1/4 cup diced onion
1 1/4 cups water
1 cup quick brown rice
1/2 cup dried cranberries

1/4 tsp. nutmeg
1 Tbsp. chopped fresh parsley

1. Sauté onion in a little water to soften. Stir in 1 1/4 cups water and bring to a boil.
2. Stir in rice, cranberries, and nutmeg. Cover and cook 10 minutes or until rice is done. Remove from heat, stir in parsley, and serve.

Rice Casserole
Eldeen Carter
Charleston, SC
A Charleston Basket
Barbara G. Winiarski
South Dennis, MA
Sunbonnet Sue
All Through the Year

Makes 4-6 servings

8 Tbsp. margarine, melted
1 cup uncooked rice
10 3/4-oz. can onion soup
4-oz. can mushrooms, sliced
8-oz. can water chestnuts, drained and cut up

1. Stir together all ingredients in casserole dish.
2. Bake uncovered at 300° for 1 to 1 1/2 hours. (Add water if needed.)

Almond Rice
Leila Orr Gormley
Van Nuys, CA
Double Irish Chain

Makes 4-6 servings

3 cups water
1 tsp. salt
1 cup long grain white
  rice
1 cup grated Parmesan
  cheese
3/4 cup slivered almonds
  with skins
1 1/3 cups whipping cream
1 Tbsp. butter

1. Bring salted water to a
boil. Add rice and simmer
uncovered for 20 minutes.
Drain well.
2. Mix together rice,
Parmesan cheese, almonds,
and whipping cream
(unwhipped).
3. Pour into greased 1 1/2-
quart shallow baking dish.
Dot with butter.
4. Bake at 350° for 40 minutes until golden and crispy
on top.

Wild Rice
with Pecans
Pamela R. Kerschner
Stevensville, MD
The Chesapeake

Makes 10-12 servings

2 Tbsp. butter
2 6-oz. pkgs. long grain
  and wild rice, with
  seasoning
4 cups chicken broth
8 spring onions with
  green tops, chopped
1 lb. fresh mushrooms,
  sliced
1 1/2 cups pecans, coarsley
  chopped and toasted
few parsley springs
  (optional)

1. In skillet or Dutch oven
melt butter. Add rice. Cook
over medium heat until
lightly browned, stirring frequently. Stir in chicken
broth, seasoning packets
from rice, green onions, and
mushrooms. Bring to a boil.
Remove from heat.
2. While preparing rice,
spread pecans in a single
layer on large baking pan.
Toast at 300° for 15 minutes
or until lightly browned,
stirring every 5 minutes.
3. Transfer rice mixture to a
lightly buttered, 3-quart
casserole.
4. Cover and bake at 350°
for 30 minutes. Remove
cover and bake an additional
30 minutes until rice is tender and liquid is absorbed,
stirring once about 15 minutes into baking time.

5. Stir in the toasted pecans.
Garnish with parsley.

Fruited Rice Mix
Jan Steffy Mast
Lancaster, PA
Bow Tie Doll Quilt

Makes 6 cups mix

4 cups long grain rice
1 cup chopped dried
  apples
1/3 cup golden raisins
1/3 cup slivered almonds
1/4 cup instant chicken
  bouillon powder
1/4 cup dried onion
4 tsp. curry powder

1. Mix together all ingredients and seal in an airtight
container.
2. To serve combine 1 cup
mix, 2 cups water, and 2
Tbsp. butter. Bring to a boil.
Reduce heat. Cover tightly
and simmer for 1/2 hour or
until water is absorbed.
3. Stir and serve.

*Note: This tasty rice is espe-
cially delicious when served
with chicken.*

Pies

Famous Pumpkin Pie

Judy Steiner Buller
Beatrice, NE
Shifting Mountains
Beverly Roberts Kessler
Marietta, SC

Makes 1 9" pie

2 eggs, slightly beaten
2 cups pumpkin (16-oz. can)
3/4 cup brown sugar
1/2 tsp. salt
1 tsp. cinnamon
1/2 tsp. ginger
1/4 tsp. cloves
12-oz. can evaporated milk
1 9" unbaked pie shell

1. Combine eggs, pumpkin, brown sugar, salt cinnamon, ginger, cloves, and milk. Pour into pie shell.
2. Bake at 425° for 15 minutes. Reduce temperature to 350° and bake for 45 minutes or until knife inserted in center comes out clean.
3. Cool and serve.

Pie in the Sky

Jean Reistle
Mickleton, NJ
Ohio Star

Makes 1 9" pie

8 ozs. cream cheese
1/4 cup sugar
1/2 tsp. vanilla
1 egg
1 1/4 cups pumpkin
1/2 cup sugar
1 tsp. cinnamon
1/4 tsp. ginger
1/4 tsp. nutmeg
1/8 tsp. salt
1 cup evaporated milk
2 eggs, beaten
1 9" unbaked pie shell

1. Mix together cream cheese and 1/4 cup sugar. Add vanilla and 1 egg. Mix well. Spread on bottom of pie crust.
2. Mix together pumpkin, 1/2 cup sugar, cinnamon, ginger, nutmeg, salt, and milk. Add 2 eggs. Pour over cream cheese mixture.

3. Bake at 350° for 60-70 minutes.

Brandy Pumpkin Pie

Carol A. Findling
Princeton, IL
Pinwheel Medallion

Makes 2 9" pies

3 eggs, beaten
28-oz. can pumpkin
2 cups half-and-half
1/2 cup milk
6 Tbsp. brown sugar
2 Tbsp. white sugar
1/2 tsp. salt
1 tsp. cinnamon
1/2 tsp. ginger
1/8 tsp. cloves
1/2 cup molasses
1/4 cup brandy or rum
2 9" unbaked pie shells

1. Mix together all ingredients except pie crust. Mix thoroughly.

2. Pour into pie shells.
3. Bake at 425° for 15 minutes. Reduce temperature to 350° for 45 minutes or until knife inserted 1 inch from edge comes out clean.
4. Chill and serve with dollop of whipped cream or ice cream.

Nana's Pumpkin Custard Pie

Debbie Chisholm
Fallston, MD
Whole Cloth Quilt

Makes 1 9" pie

2 eggs
1 cup pumpkin
3/4 cup brown sugar
1 tsp. cinnamon
1 Tbsp. flour
1 1/4 cups milk
1 9" unbaked pie shell

1. Beat 2 eggs until fluffy. Add pumpkin, brown sugar, cinnamon, and flour and beat 1 minute.
2. Add milk and mix thoroughly. Spoon into pie crust.
3. Bake at 425° for 15 minutes. Reduce temperature to 350° and bake for 40-45 minutes or until knife inserted in center comes out clean.

Pumpkin Chiffon Pie

Barbara F. Shie
Colorado Springs, CO
Picket Fences

Makes 1 9" pie

1/3 cup brown sugar
1/2 cup butter or margarine
1/3 cup chopped walnuts or pecans
3/4 cup white sugar
1 pkg. unflavored gelatin
1 1/2 tsp. pumpkin pie spice
1/2 tsp. salt
4 egg yolks, slightly beaten
16-oz. can pumpkin
3/4 cup milk
4 egg whites
1/4 cup sugar
1 9" unbaked pie shell

1. Bake pie shell at 425° for 10 minutes.
2. While pie shell is baking, cream together brown sugar and butter. Remove pie shell from oven and spread mixture over partially baked shell. Return to oven and bake for 5 minutes. Cool.
3. Combine white sugar, gelatin, spice, and salt in top of double boiler. Stir in egg yolks, pumpkin, and milk. Cook for 15 minutes over hot, not boiling, water and stir constantly until gelatin is completely dissolved. Chill just until mixture starts to set.
4. Beat egg whites until foamy. Beat in sugar, a

tablespoon at a time.
5. Beat chilled pumpkin mixture until fluffy. Fold in egg whites. Spoon into pie shell and chill before serving.

Impossible Pumpkin Pie

Frieda Weisz
Aberdeen, SC
Baskets

Makes 1 9" pie

3/4 cup sugar
1/2 cup biscuit mix
2 Tbsp. margarine or butter
12-oz. can evaporated milk
2 eggs
16-oz. can pumpkin
2 1/2 tsp. pumpkin pie spice
2 tsp. vanilla

1. Beat together all ingredients until smooth.
2. Pour into greased 9" pie pan.
3. Bake at 350° for 50-55 minutes, or until knife inserted in center comes out clean.
4. Chill, top with whipped cream, and serve.

Sweet Potato Pie
Janice Muller
Derwood, MD
Canadian Geese

Makes 2 9" pies

6-8 large sweet potatoes
1½ cups sugar
1½ tsp. nutmeg
1 tsp. cinnamon
½-¾ tsp. cloves
12-oz. can evaporated milk
1½ cups water
1½ tsp. lemon extract
1½ tsp. vanilla
6 eggs, beaten
12 Tbsp. butter
2 9" unbaked pie shells

1. Boil sweet potatoes in jackets until tender. Peel and mash or purée in blender or food processor.
2. Add sugar, nutmeg, cinnamon, cloves, milk, water, lemon extract, vanilla, eggs, and butter.
3. Pour into pie shells.
4. Bake at 450° for 15 minutes. Reduce oven temperature to 350° and bake another 45 minutes.

Cherry Pie with Streusel Crumb Topping
Janet Groff
Stevens, PA
Medallion

Makes 1 9" pie

Pie Filling:
3-4 cups canned cherries, reserve liquid
¾-1 cup sugar
3 Tbsp. cornstarch or clear gel
⅛ tsp. salt
1 Tbsp. butter, melted (optional)
⅛ tsp. almond extract
¼ tsp. red food coloring
1 9" unbaked pie shell

Streusel Crumb Topping:
1 cup biscuit mix
⅓ cup packed brown sugar
3 tsp. firm butter or margarine

1. To prepare pie filling, combine sugar, cornstarch, and salt in saucepan. Add cherry juice and stir with whisk over medium heat until thickened.
2. Add cherries, butter, almond extract, and food coloring. Set aside to cool slightly.
3. To prepare crumb topping, combine all ingredients to make fine crumbs.
4. Pour cherry mixture into unbaked pie shell and top with crumbs.
5. Bake at 425° for 10 minutes. Reduce oven tempera-

ture to 375° and bake another 30 minutes.

Mom's Cottage Cheese Pie
Dorothy Reise
Severna Park, MD
Log Cabin

Makes 1 9" pie

16-oz. carton cottage cheese
⅔ cup plus 2 Tbsp. sugar
½ cup milk
2 eggs, beaten
2 Tbsp. flour
pinch salt
1 Tbsp. butter, melted
1 Tbsp. lemon juice
1 9" unbaked pie shell
½ tsp. cinnamon

1. Cream cottage cheese by blending it quickly in a blender.
2. Mix together cottage cheese, sugar, milk, eggs, flour, salt, butter, and lemon juice.
3. Pour into unbaked pie shell. Sprinkle top with cinnamon.
3. Bake at 425° for 10 minutes. Reduce oven temperature to 375° and bake for another 30 minutes.
4. Cool completely before serving.

Strawberry Rhubarb Pie
Betty J. Smith
Punxsutawney, PA
Country Bride

Makes 1 9" pie

1¹/2 cups fresh or frozen rhubarb, cut in pieces
1 cup fresh or frozen strawberries
1 cup sugar
2 Tbsp. flour
2 Tbsp. butter
1 Tbsp. milk
1 9" unbaked pie shell
pastry for lattice top

1. Mix together rhubarb, strawberries, sugar, flour, 1 Tbsp. butter, and milk.
2. Pour into unbaked pie shell. Dot top with remaining 1 Tbsp. butter.
3. Cover top of pie with lattice made from pastry.
4. Bake at 450° for 10 minutes. Reduce oven temperature to 350° and bake another 20-30 minutes.

Strawberry Pie
Janie Canupp
Millersville, MD
Double Wedding Ring
Ann L. Boyer
Baltimore, MD
Scraps in My Attic

Makes 1 9" pie

1 quart strawberries, washed and drained
3/4 cup sugar
2 heaping Tbsp. cornstarch
2 heaping Tbsp. white corn syrup
2 cups water
3 heaping Tbsp. strawberry gelatin
1 9" graham cracker crust or baked pie shell

1. In saucepan cook together sugar, cornstarch, corn syrup, and water until thick and clear. Stir in gelatin and mix well. Cool.
2. Place strawberries into graham cracker crust or baked pie shell. Pour thickened mixture over strawberries in pie shell. Refrigerate and chill until firm. Serve with whipped topping.

Grape Pie
Alma Ranck
Lancaster, PA

Makes 1 9" pie

3 cups concord grapes
1 cup sugar
3 Tbsp. flour
1 Tbsp. lemon juice
1 Tbsp. butter, melted
2 9" unbaked pie shells

1. Wash, drain, and stem grapes.
2. Remove skins and simmer pulp for 5 minutes. Do not add any water to pulp.
3. While hot, press pulp through a sieve to remove seeds.
4. Combine strained pulp with skins.
5. Combine sugar and flour and add to grapes.
6. Blend in lemon juice and melted butter.
7. Pour into crust.
8. Cover with top crust or strips.
9. Bake at 425° for 10 minutes, reduce oven temperature to 350° and bake for another 30 minutes.
10. Serve with whipped topping.

In 1993 my mother was in a serious automobile accident, and she remained in a coma through the Christmas season. In late winter she had come out of the coma and was able to be home on weekends. So while everyone else was celebrating Easter, our family celebrated Christmas. Forty-three of us sat down to an early spring Christmas dinner and declared it was the happiest one we had ever had.
—*Judy Newman, St. Marys, Ontario*

Raisin Custard Pie
Alma Ranck
Lancaster, PA

Makes 1 9" pie

1 cup raisins
1/2 cup water
1/2 cup white sugar
2 Tbsp. flour
1 1/2 cups milk
2 egg yolks, beaten
1 Tbsp. butter
1 tsp. vanilla
1 9" baked pie shell

1. In a saucepan combine raisins and water and bring to a boil. Reduce heat and cook until raisins are soft and puffy. Remove from heat and drain well.
2. In another saucepan combine sugar and flour. Gradually add milk, stirring gently.
3. Add egg yolks. Boil until thickened, then boil a few minutes longer, stirring constantly. Remove from heat and add butter, vanilla, and raisins.
4. Pour into baked pie shell. Cool before serving.

Key Lime Pie
Patricia Fielding
Stone Mountain, GA
Georgia on My Mind

Makes 1 9" pie

3 jumbo or 4 large eggs, separated
14-oz. can sweetened condensed milk
1/2 cup key lime juice
1/2 tsp. cream of tartar
4 Tbsp. sugar
1 9" baked pie shell or graham cracker crust

1. Mix together egg yolks and milk. Stir in key lime juice. Set aside.
2. Beat egg whites. Gradually add cream of tarter and sugar until egg whites peak.
3. Fold 1/4 of the meringue into key lime pie filling.
4. Fill baked pie shell with key lime mixture and top with remaining meringue.
5. Bake at 350° for 10-15 minutes until meringue turns golden brown. Cool and serve.

Lemon Sponge Pie
Dorothy Reise
Severna Park, MD
Log Cabin

Makes 1 9" pie

Pie Shell:
1/2 cup less 1 Tbsp. shortening
3 Tbsp. boiling water
1 tsp. milk
1 1/4 cups flour, sifted
1/2 tsp. salt

Pie Filling:
3 Tbsp. margarine, softened
1 1/4 cups sugar
4 eggs, separated
3 Tbsp. flour
1/8 tsp. salt
1 1/4 cups milk
grated rind of 2 lemons
1/3 cup fresh lemon juice

1. To prepare pie shell, combine shortening, boiling water, and milk and whip with a fork until smooth.
2. In separate bowl mix flour and salt quickly with a fork. Add to shortening mixture and stir until pastry becomes manageable. Roll out between 2 pieces of waxed paper.
3. Bake at 400° for 10-15 minutes.
4. To prepare pie filling, cream together margarine and sugar until fluffy. Beat in egg yolks, flour, salt, milk, lemon rind, and lemon juice.
5. In separate bowl beat egg whites until stiff, but not

dry. Fold into pie filling mixture.

6. Remove pie shell from oven, cool slightly, and pour pie filling into shell.

7. Reduce oven temperature to 300° and bake for 35-40 minutes or until toothpick inserted in center comes out clean and top is golden brown.

8. Cool and serve.

Coconut Butternut Pie
Janie Canupp
Millersville, MD
Double Wedding Ring

Makes 1 9" pie

3/4 cup sugar
4 Tbsp. margarine
2 cups evaporated milk
1/4 cup biscuit mix
4 eggs
1 tsp. vanilla butternut
    flavoring
7-oz. pkg. coconut
1 9" unbaked pie shell

1. Mix together sugar, margarine, milk, biscuit mix, eggs, vanilla, and butternut flavoring.

2. Fill pie shell 2/3 full with coconut. Pour blended batter over coconut.

3. Bake at 350° for 40 minutes or until firm in the middle.

Coconut Orange Pie
Barbara R. Zitzmann
Metairie, LA
Illusion

Makes 1 8" pie

2 eggs
1 heaping Tbsp. butter
1 cup sugar
grated orange rind of 1
    orange
juice of 1 orange
1 cup shredded coconut
1 8" unbaked pie shell

1. Beat together eggs, butter, and sugar until well mixed. Stir in orange rind, orange juice, and coconut.

2. Pour into pie shell.

3. Bake at 350° for 30-35 minutes or until knife inserted in center comes out clean.

Party Pie
Joyce B. Suiter
Garysburg, NC
Pieced Tulip

Makes 1 9" pie

Meringue:
4 egg whites
1/2 tsp. cream of tartar
1/8 tsp. salt
1/2 tsp. vanilla
1 cup sugar

Pie Filling:
4 egg yolks
1/2 cup sugar

few grains salt
grated rind of 1 lemon
2 Tbsp. lemon juice
1/4 cup crushed
    pineapple, undrained

Topping:
3/4 cup whipping cream
2 Tbsp. sugar
1/2 tsp. vanilla
1/2 cup long, shredded
    coconut

1. To prepare meringue combine egg whites, cream of tartar, salt, and vanilla. Beat until stiff. Gradually beat in sugar. When very stiff, spread in well-buttered deep glass pie pan.

2. Bake at 275° for 1 hour. (Meringue will not brown.) Set aside to cool.

3. To prepare pie filling, combine egg yolks, sugar, salt, lemon rind, lemon juice, and pineapple in double boiler. Cook over hot water until thick and smooth. Cool, then spread over center of meringue.

4. To prepare topping beat cream until stiff. Stir in sugar and vanilla. Spread over pineapple filling. Sprinkle with coconut.

5. Place in airtight container and refrigerate for at least 8 hours.

Irresistible Apple Pie

Gertrude W. Miller
Smicksburg, PA
Broken Star

Makes 1 9" pie

6 cups sliced apples
2 Tbsp. orange juice
1/3 cup packed brown
  sugar
1/3 cup white sugar
3 Tbsp. flour
1 tsp. cinnamon
1/4 tsp. salt
1/4 tsp. nutmeg
2 Tbsp. butter or
  margarine
2 9" unbaked pie shells

1. Toss apples with orange juice.
2. Mix together sugars, flour, cinnamon, salt, and nutmeg. Toss with apples until coated.
3. Spoon into 1 unbaked pie shell and dot with butter. Add top pie shell and prick top so air can escape.
4. Bake at 400° for 50-70 minutes.

Apple Mince Crumb Pie

Carol Jensen
Watchung, NJ
Morning Star

Makes 1 10" pie

2 cups prepared
  mincemeat
3 medium apples, pared,
  cored, and sliced
1/2 cup white sugar
1 1/2 Tbsp. lemon juice
1/2 cup flour
1/2 cup firmly packed
  brown sugar
1/4 cup butter or
  margarine
1 10" unbaked pie shell

1. Spread mincemeat evenly in pie shell.
2. Toss together apples, white sugar, and lemon juice. Spread over mincemeat.
3. Mix together flour and brown sugar. Cut in butter until coarse crumbs form. Sprinkle evenly over apples.
4. Bake at 425° for 40 minutes.

Mincemeat

Julie McKenzie
Punxsutawney, PA
Sunshine and Shadows

Makes 6 quarts

2 1/2-3-lb. chuck roast,
  with fat
3 quarts peeled, chopped
  apples
2 large oranges, with peel
1/4 cup lemon juice
2 lbs. currants
3 lbs. raisins
6 ozs. candied orange
  peel
4 1/2 cups brown sugar,
  packed
1 Tbsp. salt
1 Tbsp. cinnamon
1 Tbsp. ground allspice
2 tsp. nutmeg
1 tsp. ground cloves
1/4 tsp. ginger
1 quart cider or grape juice

1. Cook roast in water until tender. Drain. Chop meat and fat together in food processor or meat grinder.
2. Grind or chop oranges with peel.
3. In large kettle combine all ingredients. Simmer 1 hour, stirring frequently.
4. Freeze in quart containers or pressure can in hot jars for 20 minutes at 10 lbs. pressure.
5. To use pour 1 quart of mincemeat into 9" unbaked pie shell. Sprinkle with sugar and bake at 450° for 15 minutes, reduce oven temperature to 350° and bake another 30-45 minutes.

Mincemeat Pie
Elizabeth M. Bivin
Sterling, IL
Nine Patch Scrap

Makes 2 9" pies

1 lb. lean pork
8-9 apples, peeled and
  chopped
9-oz. box raisins
10-oz. box currants
16-oz. can red tart pie
  cherries
2 whole oranges, ground
1/2 cup white vinegar
1 tsp. salt
1 1/2 cups sugar
1 tsp. ground cloves
1 Tbsp. cinnamon
1 tsp. nutmeg
1 tsp. allspice
3 Tbsp. sherry or brandy
2 9" unbaked pie shells

1. Cut pork into small
pieces and bring to a boil,
cooking for about 20
minutes or until done.
Drain, cool, and chop into
very fine pieces.
2. In 5-quart saucepan mix
together all ingredients
except sherry and pie shells.
Simmer for 1 hour. (May

need to add a bit of water
so it doesn't stick.) Stir in
sherry. Remove from heat.
3. May be refrigerated
overnight. When ready to
use, spoon into pie shells.
4. Bake at 400° for 35
minutes.

*Note: This mixture also
freezes well. I put mincemeat
in an aluminum pie pan and
cover. When ready to bake,
remove from freezer and slip
right onto pie shell.*

Pecan Pie
Rhonda Yoder
Goshen, IN
Tracey B. Stenger
Gretna, LA
Eleanor Botelho
Falmouth, MA
Linda V. Caldwell
Lockeford, PA

Makes 1 9" pie

3 eggs, beaten
3/4-1 cup sugar
1 cup light corn syrup
1/8 tsp. salt
1 Tbsp. butter

1 tsp. vanilla
1/2 tsp. almond flavoring
3/4 cup pecans
1 9" unbaked pie shell

1. Mix together all
ingredients except pecans.
Pour into unbaked pie shell.
2. Spread pecans evenly
over top of filling.
3. Bake at 400° for 15
minutes. Reduce oven
temperature to 300° and
bake another 30 minutes.

Brandy Pecan Pie
Nancy Jo Marsden
Glen Mills, PA
Plaid School House Quilt

Makes 1 9" pie

3 eggs
1 cup sugar
1/2 tsp. salt
2 Tbsp. margarine,
  melted
1/2 cup dark corn syrup
1/2 cup whipping cream
  or half-and-half
1 tsp. vanilla
1/4 cup brandy
1 cup pecan halves
1 9" unbaked pie shell

1. Beat together eggs, sugar,
salt, margarine, corn syrup,
and cream. Stir in vanilla,
brandy, and pecans. Pour
into pie crust.
2. Bake at 375° for 40-45
minutes until filling is set
and pastry is golden brown.
3. Cool before serving. Or
bake ahead of time and
freeze until ready to use.

Each year in October, our local quilt guild has a
mini-quilt auction. My first contribution to the event
was a small red and green Nine Patch. During the
pre-auction viewing, I overheard two women com-
menting on my quilt, "What a cute Christmas
potholder," one said to the other.
  Potholder! Why the very nerve, I thought. When
the auction began, I decided rather quickly to buy
my "potholder" back.
  —*Debbie Divine, Salina, KS*

Oatmeal Pecan Pie

Pat Unternahrer
Wayland, IA
Dahlia

Makes 1 9" pie

1/4 cup margarine or
butter, melted
1 cup dark brown sugar
2 eggs, slightly beaten
dash of salt
1 tsp. vanilla
3/4 cup milk
3/4 cup light corn syrup
1/2 cup flaked coconut
3/4 cup quick oatmeal
1/4 cup pecans
1 9" unbaked pie shell

1. Mix together margarine,
sugar, eggs, salt, and vanilla.
Add remaining ingredients
in the order given. Mix
well.
2. Pour into unbaked pie
shell.
3. Bake at 350° for 50 minutes. Cool and serve with
whipped topping or ice
cream.

Walnut Pie

Mary Jane Wackford
Oxford, NY
Log Cabin

Makes 8 servings

1/2 cup white sugar
1 cup light brown sugar,
firmly packed
1 Tbsp. flour
2 eggs, beaten
1 tsp. vanilla
1/2 cup butter, melted
1 cup chopped walnuts
several walnut halves for
garnish
1 9" unbaked pie crust

1. Mix together sugar,
brown sugar, and flour.
2. In separate bowl combine
eggs, vanilla, butter, and
chopped nuts. Add sugar
mixture to egg mixture and
blend well.
3. Pour into unbaked pie
crust. Arrange walnut halves
in single layer over filling.
4. Bake at 375° for 45-50
minutes, until knife inserted
1" from edge comes out
clean. Cool.

Peanut Butter Meringue Pie

Dorothy McClure
Milliken, CO
A Patriotic Quilt
Linda V. Caldwell
Lockeford, CA
Ships-at-Sea

Makes 1 9" pie

Peanut Butter Filling:
3/4 cup powdered sugar
1/2 cup creamy peanut
butter
1/2 cup white sugar
3 Tbsp. cornstarch
1 Tbsp. flour
1/4 tsp. salt
3 large egg yolks
3 cups milk
2 tsp. butter
1 tsp. vanilla
1 deep 9" baked pie shell

Meringue:
3 large eggs whites
1/4 tsp. cream of tartar
1/4 cup sugar

1. To prepare peanut butter
filling, mix together
powdered sugar and peanut
butter to make coarse
crumbs. Set aside.
2. In saucepan mix together
white sugar, cornstarch,
flour, and salt. Add egg
yolks and milk, stirring with
whisk until well combined.
Heat to boiling over
medium heat. Cook for two
minutes, stirring constantly.
3. Remove from heat and
stir in butter and vanilla.
4. Sprinkle 1/3 of peanut
butter mixture over bottom

of pie shell. Spoon half of pudding over crumbs. Sprinkle with another 1/3 of crumbs and top with remaining pudding.

5. To prepare meringue add cream of tartar to egg whites and beat until soft peaks form. Gradually sprinkle sugar over egg whites, beating until meringue forms stiff peaks.

6. Spread meringue over pudding in pie shell, being sure to touch edge of shell to seal. With spatula or back of spoon, swirl top of meringue. Sprinkle remaining 1/3 of peanut butter crumbs around edge of pie to make a border.

7. Bake at 375° for 8-10 minutes. Cool completely before cutting to serve.

Chocolate Peanut Butter Pie
Janie Canupp
Millersville, MD
Double Wedding Ring

Makes 1 9" pie

8-oz. pkg. cream cheese
14-oz. can sweetened condensed milk
1 Tbsp. lemon juice
1 tsp. vanilla
3/4 cup chunky peanut butter
2 Tbsp. chocolate syrup
1 9" chocolate graham cracker crust

1. Cream together cream cheese and condensed milk.

Mix well. Add lemon juice and vanilla. Mix well.

2. Stir in peanut butter until well blended. Pour into crust. Freeze. Immediately before serving, remove from freezer, and drizzle chocolate over top.

Banana-Chocolate Cream Pie
Betty Wilson
Pinckney, MI

Makes 1 9" pie

2 cups sliced bananas
1 large pkg. sugar-free instant chocolate pudding
2/3 cup nonfat dry milk
1 cup water
1/4 cup low-calorie maple syrup
3/4 cup light whipped topping
2 Tbsp. chopped pecans
1 9" graham cracker crust

1. Line graham cracker crust with sliced bananas.

2. Mix together dry pudding mix and dry milk. Combine water and maple syrup. Add liquid mixture to dry mixture. Mix well with wire whisk. Blend in 1/4 cup whipped topping. Spread mixture evenly over bananas.

3. Refrigerate for about 15 minutes. Spread remaining whipped topping over top. Garnish with pecans.

Note: This is truly a low-fat pie and very delicious!

Coffee, Cookies & Cream Pie
Christine H. Weaver
Reinholds, PA
Lone Star

Makes 1 9" pie

1 1/2 cups cold milk
1 small pkg. instant vanilla pudding
1 Tbsp. prepared instant coffee
3 1/2 cups whipped topping
1 cup crushed Oreo cookies
1 9" graham cracker crust

1. Whisk together milk, pudding mix, and coffee until well blended, about 1 minute. Let stand for 5 minutes.

2. Fold in thawed whipped topping and cookies.

3. Spoon into crust and freeze for 6 hours.

4. Let stand for 10 minutes to soften prior to serving.

Mud Pie

Pat Segal
Woodbury, NY
Mariners Compass in Space

Makes 1 9" pie

1/2 pkg. chocolate wafers,
    crushed
1/4 cup butter
1 quart coffee ice cream
    or frozen yogurt,
    softened
1 1/2 cups fudge sauce
chopped pecans or
    chocolate shavings

1. Mix together chocolate
wafers and butter. Press
into 9" pie pan.
2. Cover with ice cream and
freeze until firm, at least 1
hour.
3. Top with fudge sauce and
return to freezer.
4. Immediately before serving, remove from freezer and
sprinkle with chopped
pecans or chocolate shavings.

Brownie Pie

Frani Shaffer
Coatesville, PA
*All Hearts Come Home
at Christmas*

Makes 1 9" pie

1 cup sugar
1/4 tsp. flour
1/2 cup evaporated milk
2 eggs, slightly beaten
1/2 cup butter, melted
1 cup pecans

1 cup semisweet
    chocolate chips
1 tsp. vanilla
1 9" graham cracker crust

1. Mix together sugar and
flour. Add milk, eggs and
butter. Mix well.
2. Gently stir in pecans and
chocolate chips. Add vanilla.
Pour into graham cracker
crust.
3. Bake at 350° for 40 minutes. Middle should be
slightly soft when removed
from oven.
4. Cool completely. Serve
with whipped topping.

Fudge Sundae Pie

Jeanne Sanson
Chatham, IL
*Sunbonnet Sue
All Through the Seasons*

Makes 9" x 13" pan

1 cup evaporated milk
6-oz. pkg. chocolate chips
1/4 tsp. salt
3 cups marshmallows
1 pkg. vanilla wafers
1/2 gallon vanilla ice
    cream, softened
1 1/4 cups pecans halves
4 Tbsp. butter, melted
1/8 tsp. salt

1. In saucepan mix together
milk, chocolate chips, salt,
and marshmallows. Stir over
low heat until melted and
thickened. Cool to room
temperature.
2. Line bottom of 9" x 13"
pan with vanilla wafers.

Layer 1/2 of ice cream over
wafers, then 1/2 of sauce.
Repeat ice cream and sauce
to make another layer. Put
in freezer.
3. Spread pecan halves on
cookie sheet. Pour on
melted butter and salt. Bake
at 300° for 15 minutes, stirring occasionally.
4. Remove fudge sundae pie
from freezer and spread
pecans on top of pie. Freeze
overnight before serving.

Crisco Pie Crust

Elsie Schlabach
Millersburg, OH
Log Cabin

Makes 4 9" pie shells

4 cups flour
1 tsp. salt
1 Tbsp. sugar
1 2/3 cups Crisco
1 egg, beaten
1/2 cup water
1 Tbsp. vinegar

1. Blend together flour, salt,
and sugar. Cut in Crisco.
2. Mix together egg, water,
and vinegar. Add to flour
and mix well.
3. Chill dough before
rolling.

*Note: This will keep soft in
refrigerator for several days. It
is always flaky and has never
failed for me.*

Cakes

Creamy Cranberry Cake

Nicole Koloski
East Sandwich, MA
Piecemakers 1995
Calendar Quilt

Makes 12-16 servings

Cake:
3 egg whites, room temperature
1 cup sugar
1/2 cup butter
1 1/2 cups flour
2 tsp. baking powder
1/4 tsp. salt
1/2 cup milk
1/2 tsp. vanilla
1/2 tsp. almond extract

Cranberry Filling:
16-oz. can whole cranberry sauce
1/2 cup cranberry juice
1/2 cup sugar

Whipped Cream Filling:
1 cup heavy cream
1/4 cup sugar
1 tsp. vanilla

1. To prepare cake beat egg whites until frothy. Stir in 1/2 cup sugar and beat until soft peaks form.
2. Cream together butter and remaining 1/2 cup sugar until light and fluffy.
3. Sift together flour, baking powder, and salt. Add alternately with milk to butter mixture, ending with flour.
4. Fold in egg whites, vanilla, and almond extract. Spoon batter into 2 greased and floured 9" round cake pans.
5. Bake at 350° for 25 minutes or until done. Cool completely.
6. To prepare cranberry filling, combine cranberry sauce, juice, and sugar in a saucepan. Bring to a boil over medium high heat, stirring constantly. Boil for 3 minutes.

7. To prepare whipped cream filling, beat together cream, sugar, and vanilla until frothy.
8. Slice two pieces of cooled cake in half horizontally to get 4 layers. Alternate cranberry filling and whipped cream between layers. Frost top and sides with whipped cream. Refrigerate until ready to serve. Present on fancy cake platter.

Cranberry Cake
Patricia Andreas
Wausau, WI
Ohio Star Table Runner

Makes 2 loaves

8-oz. pkg. cream cheese,
　softened
1 cup butter
1¹/₂ cups sugar
4 eggs
1¹/₂ tsp. vanilla
2¹/₄ cups flour
1¹/₂ tsp. baking powder
1 cup chopped walnuts
1 cup cranberries

1. Cream together cream cheese, butter, and sugar. Add eggs and vanilla. Mix well.
2. Sift together flour and baking powder. Add to creamed mixture.
3. Fold in walnuts and cranberries.
4. Pour into 2 greased and floured loaf pans.
5. Bake at 325° for 80-90 minutes.

Cherry Spiral Cake
Annabelle Unternahrer
Shipshewana, IN
Round Robin

Makes 20-24 servings

5 eggs, separated
1 cup white sugar
2 Tbsp. lemon juice
1 Tbsp. water
1 cup flour
1/4 tsp. salt
sifted powdered sugar
2 large pkgs. vanilla
　pudding or ice cream
21-oz. can cherry pie
　filling

1. Beat egg yolks until thick and lemon colored. Beat in 1/2 cup white sugar, lemon juice, and water. Add flour and salt. Mix well.
2. Beat egg whites until soft peaks form. Gradually add remaining 1/2 cup white sugar, beating until stiff peaks form. Fold yolk mixture into egg whites.
3. Pour batter into 10" x 15" baking pan which has been lined with greased and floured waxed paper.
4. Bake at 350° for 15 minutes or until cake springs back when touched in center. Immediately loosen edges of cake from pan and turn cake out onto a towel sprinkled with powdered sugar. Roll towel and cake jelly-roll style, beginning at one of cake's short ends. Cool on wire rack.
5. Unroll cake. Remove towel. Spread cake with pudding (prepared according to package directions) or softened ice cream. Roll up cake. Freeze if using ice cream, chill if using pudding.
6. Serve, topping each slice with heaping spoonful of cherry filling.

The year my oldest son was born, I decided our family needed a special tree skirt to wrap our tree in. I chose lots of lovely holiday prints and set out to make a scrap patchwork skirt. I have always been a fast sewer and was sure I could put it together in several weeks.

My son, however, occupied more of my time than I expected, and the fabric slowly began to collect dust. With only a few days left before family was to arrive for Christmas, I finally finished piecing the skirt, but I did not have enough time to quilt it and decided it would have to be tied. My husband was so thrilled with what I had accomplished that he sat up with me the night before everyone arrived and helped me tie the skirt with bits of yarn. That night together is one of my favorite holiday memories.
—*Mary K. Mitchell, Battle Creek, MI*

Apple Walnut Cake

Jeanne Allen
Los Alamos, NM
Clams in the Cabin

Makes 16-20 servings

Cake:
21-oz. can apple filling
2 cups flour
1 1/2 tsp. baking soda
1 tsp. salt
1 cup sugar
2 eggs, beaten
1 tsp. vanilla
2/3 cup cooking oil or
  melted butter
3/4 cup walnuts

Topping:
1/4 cup cake batter
1/4 cup evaporated milk
1/2 tsp. vanilla
1/2 cup walnuts

1. Spread apple filling in greased 9" x 13" pan.
2. Combine flour, baking soda, salt, and sugar. Sprinkle over filling in pan.
3. Combine eggs, vanilla, cooking oil, and 3/4 cup walnuts. Mix well. Pour into pan. Stir contents of pan until lightly blended. Smooth the batter. Save 1/4 cup of batter for topping.
4. Bake at 350° for 40-45 minutes.
5. To prepare topping combine reserved cake batter and milk in saucepan. Cook for 2 minutes, stirring constantly. Remove from heat. Stir in vanilla.
6. Prick hot cake with fork.

Pour hot topping over hot cake. Prick again with fork. Sprinkle 1/2 cup walnuts over top.
7. Serve with whipped topping or ice cream.

German Apple Cake

Fanny Naught
Quincy, IL
Dogwood

Makes 20-24 servings

2 cups sugar
1 cup vegetable oil
2 eggs, beaten
2 cups flour
2 tsp. cinnamon
1 tsp. salt
1 tsp. baking soda
1 tsp. vanilla
4 cups sliced apples
1/2 cups chopped walnuts

1. Cream together sugar and vegetable oil. Add beaten eggs.
2. Mix in all remaining ingredients, saving apples and nuts until last. Spoon batter into greased and floured 9" x 13" pan.
3. Bake at 350° for 40-50 minutes.
4. Serve with whipped topping or vanilla ice cream.

Apple Pie Cake

Tracy Supcoe
Barclay, MD
Patience Corner

Makes 6-8 servings

1 cup sugar
1/8 tsp. salt
1/2 cup margarine
1 egg
1 cup flour
2 tsp. cinnamon
1/2 tsp. nutmeg
1 tsp. baking powder
2 Tbsp. boiling water
2 tsp. vanilla
1/2 cup chopped nuts
2 cups diced apples, unpeeled

1. Cream together sugar, salt, margarine, and egg.
2. Sift together flour, cinnamon, and nutmeg. Add to creamed mixture.
3. Dissolve baking powder in boiling water. Add to batter.
4. Stir in vanilla, nuts, and apples. Mix well. Spoon into greased pie pan.
5. Bake at 350° for 45 minutes.

Applesauce Cake-in-a-Jar
Dede Peterson
Rapid City, SD

Maks 8 1-pint cakes

2/3 **cup shortening**
22/3 **cups sugar**
4 **eggs**
2 **cups applesauce**
2/3 **cup water**
31/3 **cups flour**
2 **tsp. baking soda**
1 **tsp. cinnamon**
1/2 **tsp. baking powder**
11/2 **tsp. salt**
2 **tsp. ground cloves**
2/3 **cup chopped nuts**

1. Cream together shortening and sugar. Beat in eggs, applesauce, and water.
2. Sift together flour, baking soda, cinnamon, baking powder, salt, and cloves. Blend into applesauce mixture. Stir in nuts.
3. Prepare 8 1-pint tapered canning jars with widemouth lids by greasing them thoroughly on the inside. Pour batter into each jar, filling 1/2 full. Place jars in oven.
4. Bake at 325° for 45 minutes. Remove 1 jar at a time. Wipe seal edge clean and put on dry canning lid and ring. If cake has risen higher than the jar, slice off the top of the cake so you have a headspace of 1/4" to 1/2". Screw tightly. Jar will seal as cake cools. May be stored as canned goods for six months.
5. To serve remove from jar and slice. Serve plain or gar-

nish with a dollop of whipped topping.

Note: This recipe makes a wonderful gift. Make a little cap of fabric to decorate the jar and include directions for how to serve the cake.

Apricot Gift Cake
Sharon Easter
Yuba City, CA

Makes 12-16 servings

Cake:
11/2 **cups white sugar**
8-oz. **pkg. cream cheese, softened**
1 **cup butter or margarine**
11/2 **tsp. vanilla**
4 **eggs**
21/4 **cups sifted cake flour**
11/2 **tsp. baking powder**
3/4 **cup chopped, dried apricots**
1/2 **cup coarsely chopped pecans**
1/2 **cup finely chopped pecans**

Glaze:
11/2 **cups sifted powdered sugar**
2 **Tbsp. orange juice**
1 **tsp. grated orange peel**

1. Cream together white sugar, cream cheese, butter, and vanilla, mixing until well blended. Add eggs, one at a time, mixing well after each addition.
2. Sift together 2 cups flour and baking powder.

Gradually stir into cream cheese mixture.
3. Toss apricots and coarsely chopped pecans with remaining flour. Fold into batter.
4. Sprinkle greased 10" tube pan with finely chopped pecans. Pour batter into pan.
5. Bake at 325° for 70 minutes. Cool 5 minutes. Remove from pan and cool completely on wire rack.
6. Combine powdered sugar, orange juice, and orange peel. Mix well. Drizzle over cake and garnish with additional chopped dried apricots and nuts, if desired. Cut into 6-8 thick slices. Wrap in clear plastic and tie with bows to give as gifts.

Cajun Cake
Sylvia Netterville
Metairie, LA
Maple Leaf

Makes 16-20 servings

21/2 **cups crushed pineapple with juice**
11/2 **cups sugar**
2 **large eggs**
1/2 **tsp. salt**
21/2 **cups flour**
2 **tsp. baking soda**

1. Blend together all ingredients. Mix well.
2. Grease the bottom of 8" x 12" pan. Pour batter into pan.
3. Bake at 350° for 30 minutes. Serve warm with ice cream.

Apricot Brandy Cake

Eleanor Fabiszak
Columbia, MD
Paddington Bear

Makes 16-20 servings

3 cups sugar
1 cup butter
6 eggs
3 cups flour
1/4 tsp. baking soda
1 cup sour cream
1/2 cup apricot brandy
1 Tbsp. bourbon
1/2 tsp. rum flavoring
1 tsp. orange extract
1/4 tsp. almond extract
1/4 tsp. lemon extract
1 tsp. vanilla
dash nutmeg
powdered sugar

1. Bring all ingredients to room temperature.
2. Cream together butter and suggar. Add eggs, one at a time, beating thoroughly after each egg.
3. Sift together flour and baking soda.
4. Combine sour cream, brandy, bourbon, rum flavoring, orange extract, almond extract, lemon extract, vanilla, and nutmeg.
5. Add flour and sour cream mixture alternately to creamed ingredients and mix well until blended.
6. Pour into large greased and floured tube pan.
7. Bake at 325° for 70 minutes. Cool.
8. Dust with powdered sugar.

Orange Slice Cake

Donna M. Mulkey
Oregon City, OR
Bow Tie
Doris H. Blue
Mechanicsburg, PA

Makes 12-16 servings

Cake:
4 cups flour
1/2 tsp. salt
1 lb. orange slice candy, chopped
1 lb. pitted dates, chopped
2 cups chopped walnuts
31/2-oz. can flaked coconut
1 Tbsp. grated orange rind
1 cup margarine
2 cups sugar
4 eggs
1 tsp. baking soda
1/2 cup buttermilk

Glaze:
2 cups powdered sugar
1 cup orange juice

1. Sift together 31/2 cups flour and salt.
2. Combine remaining flour with candy, dates, nuts, coconut, and orange rind.
3. Cream together margarine and sugar. Add eggs, one at a time, beating well after each addition.
4. Combine baking soda and buttermilk. Add alternately with flour to creamed mixture. Mix well. Stir in candy mixture. Mix well. Pour into greased 10" tube pan.
5. Bake at 250-300° for 11/2

to 13/4 hours. Place pan of water under rack to keep moist.
6. Poke holes in warm cake with a toothpick. Mix together powdered sugar and orange juice and pour over top of cake. Cool. Refrigerate overnight before removing from pan.

Obstkuchen

Irma H. Schoen
Windsor, CT
Log Cabin

Makes 8 servings

1/4 cup butter
1 egg
3/4 cup sugar
1 tsp. vanilla
1 cup flour
1/4 tsp. salt
1 tsp. baking powder
1 cup sliced apples, blueberries, peaches, or bananas
1 Tbsp. sugar
1 tsp. cinnamon

1. Cream together butter, egg, sugar, and vanilla. Add flour, salt, and baking powder and mix well. Spread into a 9" springform pan. Top with sliced apples or choice of fruit. Sprinkle with sugar and cinnamon.
2. Bake at 375° for 35-40 minutes. Serve warm with whipped topping or ice cream.

Ribbon of Fruit Teacake

Elizabeth Miller
Walnut Creek, OH
Rose Trellis

Makes 12-16 servings

Cake:
2¼ cups flour
¾ cup sugar
¾ cup margarine or butter
½ tsp. baking powder
½ tsp. baking soda
¼ tsp. nutmeg
⅛ tsp. salt
1 egg, beaten
⅔ cup sour milk or
   buttermilk
1 tsp. vanilla
1¼ cups canned fruit pie
   filling

Frosting:
½ cup powdered sugar
½ tsp. vanilla
1-2 tsp. milk

1. Mix together flour and sugar. Cut in margarine until mixture resembles coarse crumbs. Reserve ½ cup for topping.
2. Add baking powder, baking soda, nutmeg, and salt to flour mixture.
3. Mix together egg, sour milk, and vanilla. Add to flour mixture. Stir until moistened. Reserve 1 cup batter.
4. Spread remaining batter on bottom and 1" up sides of a greased and floured 2-quart rectangular baking dish. Spread desired flavor pie filling on top. Spoon reserved 1 cup batter on top of filling. Sprinkle with reserved ½ cup crumbs.
5. Bake at 350° for 40 minutes or until golden. Cool.
6. To prepare frosting mix together powdered sugar, vanilla, and milk. Drizzle over cake. Serve.

Christmas M&M Cake

Iola L. Sugg
Akron, NY
Amish Bars

Makes 12-16 servings

Cake:
1 cup butter, softened
1 cup sugar
½ cup light brown sugar
3 eggs
1 cup milk
1 tsp. vanilla
2½ cups flour
2 tsp. baking powder
⅛ tsp. salt
16-oz. pkg. red and green
   M&Ms

Frosting:
1 cup powdered sugar
juice of 1 lemon
1-2 tsp. water

1. Cream together butter and sugars until light. Add eggs, 1 at a time, beating well after each addition.
2. Stir together milk and vanilla.
3. Mix together flour, baking powder, and salt. Alternately add flour and milk to creamed mixture.
4. Reserve ½ cup M&Ms for topping. Stir remaining M&Ms into batter. Pour into greased and floured 12-cup bundt or tube pan.
5. Bake at 350° for 40-50 minutes. Cool 15 minutes before removing from pan.
6. Mix together frosting ingredients to make spreadable glaze. Drizzle over top and decorate with reserved ¼ cup M&Ms.

Note: The chocolate from the M&Ms melts and goes to bottom of cake pan (top when turned out of pan) and the red and green candies leave colorful trails throughout the cake.

Holiday Chip Cake

Nicole Koloski
East Sandwich, MA
Piecemakers 1995
Calendar Quilt

Makes 16-18 servings

2 cups candied fruits
2 cups raisins
1½ cups chopped
   walnuts
1 cup chocolate chips
4 Tbsp. butter
1 cup sugar
3 eggs
¼ cup applesauce
¼ cup water
1½ cups flour, sifted
¼ tsp. baking soda
⅛ tsp. allspice
⅛ tsp. cinnamon
⅛ tsp. nutmeg
⅛ tsp. instant coffee
   granules

1. Combine fruits, raisins, nuts, and chocolate chips.
2. Cream together butter and sugar until light and fluffy. Add eggs, one at a time, mixing well after each addition.
3. Stir in applesauce and water and mix well.
4. Mix together flour, baking soda, allspice, cinnamon, nutmeg, and coffee. Add to batter. Gently fold in fruit.
5. Spoon into greased and floured 7-cup ring mold.
6. Bake at 275° for 2 hours and 45 minutes. Check after 2 hours for doneness. Allow to cool in pan. Unmold onto cake platter and serve.

Black Walnut Pound Cake
Janie Canupp
Millersville, MD
Double Wedding Ring

Makes 20-24 servings

1 cup butter
1/2 cup shortening
3 cups sugar
6 eggs
1 tsp. vanilla
1/2 tsp. black walnut extract
3 cups flour
1 tsp. baking powder
1 cup evaporated milk
1 cup chopped black walnuts

1. Cream together butter and shortening. Add sugar. Beat until light and fluffy.

Add eggs, one at a time, beating well after each addition. Add flavoring.
2. Reserve 1/4 cup flour. Sift remaining flour and baking powder together. Alternately add flour and milk to creamed mixture, beating well after each addition.
3. Mix together walnuts and 1/4 cup flour. Fold into batter.
4. Pour into greased and floured 10" tube pan.
5. Bake at 325° for 80 minutes.

Sour Cream Pound Cake
Melissa Hess
Bellingham, WA
Pumpkin Vine

Makes 16-20 servings

1 cup butter
2 3/4 cups sugar
6 eggs, separated
3 cups sifted flour
1/2 tsp. salt
1/4 tsp. baking soda
1 cup sour cream
1 tsp. vanilla
1 tsp. almond extract

1. Cream butter. Gradually beat in sugar until light and fluffy. Add egg yolks, one at a time, beating well after each addition.
2. Sift together flour, salt, and baking soda. Alternately add flour mixture and sour cream to creamed mixture. Stir in almond and vanilla extracts.

3. Beat egg whites until stiff peaks form. Fold into batter.
4. Pour into greased and floured 10" bundt pan.
5. Bake at 350° for 70-80 minutes or until done. Cool for 15 minutes, then remove from pan.

Chocolate Apple Bundt Cake
Carol Ambrose
Napa, CA
Kittens in the Attic

Makes 12-16 servings

2 cups sugar
1 cup margarine
3 eggs
1/2 cup water
2 1/2 cups flour
2 Tbsp. cocoa
1 tsp. cinnamon
1 tsp. allspice
1 tsp. baking soda
1/2 cup chocolate chips
1/2 cup chopped nuts
2 cups grated apples
1 Tbsp. vanilla

1. Cream together sugar and margarine. Add eggs and water and mix well.
2. Mix together flour, cocoa, cinnamon, allspice, and baking soda. Add to creamed mixture.
3. Fold in chocolate chips, nuts, apples, and vanilla. Spoon into greased and floured bundt cake pan.
4. Bake at 325° for 65-70 minutes. Let cool for 5 minutes before removing from pan. Cool and serve.

Dr. Bird Cake

Audrey L. Couvillon
Dallas, TX
Friendship

Makes 12-16 serving

1/4 cup soy flour
3/4 cup whole wheat flour
2 cups white flour
1 cup honey
1 1/2 cups olive oil
3 eggs
1 1/2 tsp. vanilla
1 tsp. baking soda
1 tsp. salt
1 tsp. cinnamon
1 tsp. cardamom
1 tsp. coriander
1 tsp. nutmeg
1 cup chopped nuts
2 cups diced bananas
8-oz. can crushed
    pineapple, undrained

1. Mix together all ingredients, except nuts, bananas, and pineapple. Mix well. Fold in nuts, bananas, and pineapple with juice.
2. Pour into greased bundt pan.
3. Bake at 350° for 75 minutes.
4. Serve with whipped topping, if desired.

Variation: Use 3 cups regular flour, 2 cups sugar instead of honey, and omit cardamom, coriander, and nutmeg.
    Betty B. Dennison
    Grove City, PA
    Sampler

Toffee Treasure Cake

Jeanne Allen
Los Alamos, NM
Clams in the Cabin

Makes 12-16 servings

1/4 cup sugar
1 tsp. cinnamon
2 cups flour
1 cup sugar
1 1/2 tsp. baking powder
1 tsp. baking soda
1/4 tsp. salt
1 tsp. vanilla
8-oz. carton sour cream
1/2 cup butter or
    margarine, softened
2 eggs

1/4 cup chopped nuts
6 5/8-oz. chocolate toffee
    candy bars, coarsely
    crushed
1/4 cup butter or
    margarine, melted

1. Combine sugar and cinnamon. Set aside.
2. Combine flour, sugar, baking powder, baking soda, salt, vanilla, sour cream, butter, and eggs. Blend at low speed until moistened. Beat 3 minutes at medium speed, scraping the bowl occasionally.
3. Spoon half of batter into greased and floured bundt pan. Sprinkle wtih cinnamon-sugar mixture, then with nuts and crushed

My grandparents on my mother's side were born in Czechoslovakia so we always celebrated the holidays as they did in the old country. As many family members as could would come to Chicago and my grandparent's house would be full of excited grandchildren and wonderful smells. Gram and Bumps, as we called them, never cared who was underfoot and always had lots of activities planned and things for us to see and do.

On Christmas Eve everyone gathered around the huge dining room table, set with Gram's special china. Bumps always put a coin under each plate. The amount of the coin signified how many years of good luck each person would have. The candles were lit, the lights turned off, and a prayer of thanksgiving was offered. A glass of wine was passed around the table, and everyone took a small sip.

During the night St. Nicholas came and filled our stockings with wonderful surprises. My favorite gift from that time in my life was a doll bed which my grandfather made for me. I'm fifty-four years old now; my daughter played with it, my son fell asleep in it, and I hope someday to have grandchildren who will also enjoy it.

—*Cyndie Marrara, Port Matilda, PA*

candy bars. Top with remaining batter. Pour melted butter over batter.
4. Bake at 325° for 45-50 minutes or until top springs back when touched lightly in center. Cool upright in pan for 15 minutes. Remove from pan. If desired, sprinkle with powdered sugar.

Christmas Cake
Betty B. Dennison
Grove City, PA
Sampler

Makes 8-10 servings

1 1/2 cups sugar
1/2 cup shortening
4 egg whites, unbeaten
1 cup milk
1 1/2 tsp. vanilla
2 1/4 cups flour
3 1/4 tsp. baking powder
1 tsp. salt
4 Tbsp. finely chopped
   maraschino cherries
3/4 cup chopped nuts

1. Cream together sugar and shortening. Stir in unbeaten egg whites, milk, and vanilla.
2. Blend in flour, baking powder, and salt. Stir in cherries and nuts and mix well.
3. Pour into greased and floured tube pan.
4. Bake at 350° for 25-30 minutes.

Angel Dream Cake
Emilie Kimpel
Arcadia, MI
Cherry Wreath

Makes 8-10 servings

5 eggs, separated
1 1/2 cups sugar
1 1/2 cups flour
1 tsp. baking powder
1 tsp. salt
1/2 cup water
1 tsp. vanilla

1. Beat egg whites until stiffened and peaks form. Gradually add 1/2 cup sugar. Set aside.
2. Beat egg yolks until thick. Add remaining 1 cup sugar and mix well.
3. Mix together flour, baking powder, and salt.
4. Combine water and vanilla.
5. Alternating with water, stir flour mixture into egg yolk mixture. Beat until smooth. Carefully fold in egg white mixture. Spoon batter into greased and floured tube pan.
6. Bake at 350° for 1 hour. Invert and cool in pan. Frost with a favorite butter frosting and serve.

Ma's Brown Cake
Donna Conto
Saylorsburg, PA

Makes 16-20 servings

1/2 of 15-oz. box raisins
2 cups cold water
2 tsp. baking soda
1 cup cold prepared
   coffee
1 tsp. salt
1/2 cup cooking oil
1 cup white sugar
1 cup brown sugar
1 tsp. cloves
1 tsp. allspice
1 tsp. nutmeg
1 tsp. cinnamon
2 tsp. baking powder
4 cups flour
1 tsp. vanilla
powdered sugar

1. Pour water over raisins and cook for 15 minutes. Set aside to cool.
2. Mix together baking soda, coffee, and salt in a large bowl.
3. Stir in cooking oil, sugars, cloves, allspice, nutmeg, cinnamon, baking powder, and flour. Mix until smooth. Fold in raisin mixture. Pour into greased and floured 9" x 13" baking pan.
4. Bake at 350° for 45 minutes or until toothpick inserted in center comes out clean.
5. Cool cake, sprinkle with powdered sugar, and serve.

Special Spice Cake
Barbara Sparks
Glen Burnie, MD
Study in Blue and White

Makes 16-20 servings

1 cup corn oil
1¹/₂ cups sugar
3 eggs
1 tsp. vanilla
2 cups flour
1 tsp. baking soda
¹/₄ tsp. salt
1 Tbsp. cinnamon
1 Tbsp. nutmeg
1 Tbsp. allspice
1 cup buttermilk
2 Tbsp. flour
¹/₂ cup chopped, cooked
    prunes
1 cup chopped nuts

1. Cream together corn oil
and sugar. Add eggs and
vanilla.
2. Sift together 2 cups flour,
baking soda, salt, and
spices. Alternately add dry
ingredients with buttermilk
to creamed mixture.
3. Stir 2 Tbsp. flour into
prunes and nuts. Fold into
cake batter.
4. Pour into ungreased tube
pan or 2 4" x 8" loaf pans.
5. Bake at 350° for 1 hour.

*Note: Try making this
delicious, moist cake with a
large bowl and spoon. It's
easy and fun, and I think it
tastes better in the end!*

Georgie's Washday Cake
Shirley Odell
Manteca, CA
Dresden Plate

Makes 12-16 servings

2 cups cold prepared
    coffee
1 cup shortening
2 cups sugar
2 cups raisins
1 tsp. cinnamon
1 tsp. nutmeg
1 tsp allspice
¹/₄-¹/₂ tsp. powdered
    cloves
4 cups flour
1 tsp. salt
2 tsp. baking soda
1 cup chopped nuts

1. In heavy saucepan
combine coffee, shortening,
sugar, raisins, cinnamon, nutmeg, allspice, and cloves.
Bring to a boil and let simmer
for 5-10 minutes. Cool. Place
in refrigerator overnight.
2. In the morning mix
together flour, salt, baking
soda, and nuts. Add to
mixture from refrigerator.
3. Spoon mixture into a
greased angel food or bundt
cake pan.
4. Bake at 350° for 1 hour.
Cool and remove cake from
pan. Serve.

*Note: Washday Cake is so
named because after a busy
day of washing, you need only
put it together, boil it, then
cool overnight and bake the
next day.*

Norwegian Honey Cake
Dorothy Van Deest
Memphis, TN
A Tisket—A Tasket

Makes 12-16 servings

4 cups sifted flour
1 cup raisins
1 tsp. baking soda
¹/₂ tsp. ground cloves
¹/₂ tsp. ground cinnamon
3 eggs
2¹/₃ cups sugar
1¹/₂ cups sour cream
2 Tbsp. honey
3 Tbsp. grated orange
    rind
powdered sugar

1. Sprinkle 1 Tbsp. flour over
raisins in bowl. Toss to coat.
2. Sift together remaining
flour, baking soda, cloves,
and cinnamon.
3. Beat eggs and sugar in a
bowl until fluffy. Beat in
sour cream and honey. Add
flour mixture and mix until
blended. Stir in raisins and
orange rind.
4. Pour into greased and
floured 10" angel cake tube
pan.
5. Bake at 325° for 75
minutes or until cake pulls
away from sides of pan and
top springs back when
lightly pressed. Cool in pan
on wire rack for 5 minutes.
Run knife around inner and
outer edges of cake. Turn
onto wire rack. Cool com-
pletely.
6. Store covered at room
temperature overnight or

for at least 8 hours before cutting. Sprinkle top with powdered sugar and serve.

Note: I often place a large paper doily over top of cake before sprinkling with powdered sugar. This gives the cake a festive appearance.

Black Cloud Honey Cake
Audrey L. Couvillon
Dallas, TX
Friendship

Makes 12-16 servings

8 plain chocolate bars
1 cup butter or
   margarine, softened
1 cup honey
1 cup sugar
4 eggs
2 5¹/2-oz. cans chocolate
   syrup
2¹/2 cups flour
¹/4 tsp. salt
¹/2 tsp. baking soda
¹/4 cup buttermilk

1. Melt chocolate bars in top of double boiler.
2. Cream together butter, honey, and sugar until the butter absorbs the honey and sugar. Stir in eggs, one at a time, beating vigorously after each addition. Gradually add chocolate syrup.
3. Sift together flour, salt, and baking soda. Alternately add dry ingredients and buttermilk to creamed mixture.

4. Add melted chocolate bars to cake batter. Beat well. Spoon into greased tube pan.
5. Bake at 350° for 60 minutes or until cake tester comes out clean from the middle of pan.

Lemon Nut Cake
Carol Price
Los Lunas, NM
Celtic Rose

Makes 2 loaves

2 cups butter, softened
2 cups sugar
2 ozs. lemon extract
1 lb. shelled pecans
6 eggs
1 lb. golden, bleached
   raisins
3³/4 cups flour, sifted
2 tsp. baking powder
pinch salt

1. Cream together butter and sugar. Add lemon extract, pecans, eggs, and raisins and mix well. Add dry ingredients and mix well.
2. Spoon into 2 large loaf pans lined with waxed paper.

3. Bake at 325° for 1¹/2 hours. Cool on wire rack and serve.

Kirsten Kake
Joan Kowalsky
Shelton, WA
Trip Around the World

Makes 8-10 servings

4 eggs, room temperature
1 cup sugar
1 Tbsp. almond extract
¹/2 cup cooking oil
1 cup flour
¹/4 tsp. salt
¹/2 tsp. baking powder
¹/2 cup slivered almonds

1. Beat eggs until thick and lemon colored, about 10 minutes. Gradually add sugar.
2. Slowly add almond extract and cooking oil. Stir in flour, salt, and baking powder. Mix well.
3. Pour into greased 8" square baking pan or 12" Pyrex pie pan. Sprinkle with slivered almonds.
4. Bake at 350° for 25-30 minutes.

We have four children who love to get into the act when I'm baking. Each year around the holidays, I mix up a large batch of sugar cookies, put all the supplies on the kitchen table, and turn them loose. While the children begin with great enthusiasm, they usually tire out before the job is done. That's where I come in. I finish what needs to be decorated and clean up. For our family this is a tradition as important as having a Christmas tree.
—*Sharon Leali, Jackson, OH*

Walnut Christmas Cake with Comfort Icing

Mary Evangeline Dillon
Tucson, AZ
Bunnies and Bows

Makes 12-16 servings

Cake:
2/3 cup shortening
1 1/2 cups sugar
1 tsp. vanilla
1 tsp. almond extract
2 1/2 cups cake flour
2 1/2 tsp. baking powder
1/2 tsp. salt
3/4 cup milk
4 egg whites
1 cup finely chopped
   walnuts

Comfort Frosting:
1 cup white sugar
1/3 cup water
1/3 tsp. cream of tartar
2 egg whites
1 1/2 tsp. vanilla

1. To prepare cake cream shortening. Gradually add sugar and beat until light and fluffy. Stir in vanilla and almond extract.
2. Reserve 2 Tbsp. flour for the walnuts. Sift together remaining flour, baking powder, and salt. Alternately add flour and milk to creamed mixture. Beat until smooth. (This will be a very thick batter.)
3. Beat egg whites until stiff, but not dry, and fold into the batter. Mix together nuts and 2 Tbsp. flour. Fold into cake batter.

4. Spoon into 2 greased and floured 9" round cake pans.
5. Bake at 350° for 30-35 minutes. This cake improves in flavor when stored unfrosted in refrigerator or cake box for several days.
6. To prepare frosting mix together sugar, water, and cream of tartar in a saucepan. Boil slowly without stirring until syrup spins a 6"-8" thread or reaches 242° on candy thermometer. Cover saucepan for first 3 minutes to prevent crystals from forming on sides of pan. While syrup is cooking, beat egg whites stiff enough to hold a point. Pour hot syrup very slowly into stiffly beaten whites, beating constantly. Add vanilla. Beat until frosting holds its shape. Frost cake and serve.

Esther's Nut Cake

Geraldine A. Ebersole
Hershey, PA
Old Maid's Puzzle

Makes 16-20 servings

1 lb. ripe dates
1 cup flour
2 rounded Tbsp. baking
   powder
1 cup sugar
10-oz. jar maraschino
   cherries
4 egg yolks, well beaten
4 egg whites, stiffly
   beaten
1 lb. English walnuts
orange juice or sherry

1. Mix together whole dates, flour, and baking powder.
2. Drain juice from maraschino cherries and beat into egg yolks.
3. Stir sugar, maraschino cherries, and egg yolk mixture into date mixture and mix well.
4. Stir in egg whites and mix well. Fold in whole English walnuts.
5. Grease 10" tube pan. Place brown paper ring onto bottom of tube pan and grease it also. Pour cake batter on top of the brown paper in the tube pan.
6. Bake at 350° for 60-75 minutes. Remove cake from pan and cool.
7. Wrap in moist cloth which has been dampened with orange juice or sherry. Wrap plastic bag around cake and moist cloth. Refrigerate for at least 24 hours. Add more orange juice to dampen cloth as needed.
8. When ready to serve, slice with an electric knife.

Note: This cake also freezes well.

Mama's Nut Cake

Shirley Taylor
Yuba City, CA
*Four Patch
Plus Christmas Quilt*

Makes 16-20 servings

1 cup margarine
1 Tbsp. shortening
2 cups sugar
5 eggs
1 tsp. black walnut
 flavoring
1 tsp. vanilla
1/4 cup milk
1 1/2 cups self-rising flour
1 1/2 cups cake flour
2 cups walnuts
2 cups pecans
1/2 cup black walnuts

1. Flour the nuts with a small amount of flour. Set aside.
2. Cream together margarine, shortening, and sugar. Add eggs, walnut flavoring and vanilla and mix well. Alternately add flours and milk to creamed mixture and mix well. Fold in nuts.
3. Spoon into greased and floured tube pan.
4. Bake at 325° for 1 hour. If not done, cover with a circle cut from a brown paper bag and bake at 200° for 30 minutes. Test for doneness with a toothpick.

Chipmunk Cake

Jeanne Allen
Los Alamos, NM
Chimneys and Cornerstones

Makes 16-20 servings

1 cup boiling water
1 cup diced dates
1 cup butter or
 shortening
1 cup sugar
2 eggs, beaten
1 tsp. vanilla
1 3/4 cups sifted flour
1/4 cup cocoa
1 tsp. baking soda
1/2 tsp. salt
1/2 cup chopped walnuts
 or pecans
1 cup semi-sweet
 chocolate chips

1. Combine water and dates. Cool to room temperature.
2. Cream together butter and sugar until fluffy. Stir in eggs and vanilla. Mix well.
3. Sift together flour, cocoa, baking soda, and salt. Alternately add flour mixture and date mixture to creamed ingredients, mixing well after each addition.
4. Spoon batter into greased and floured 9" x 13" pan. Sprinkle walnuts and chocolate chips on top, pressing them lightly into the batter.
5. Bake at 350° for 45 minutes or until wooden pick inserted in center comes out clean. Cut into squares and serve.

Date Cake

Doris Roberts
Fairbank, IA
Trip Around the World
Mildred Duley
Yates City, IL
Woven Hearts

Makes 12-16 servings

2 cups dates, chopped
2 tsp. baking soda
2 cups boiling water
2 cups sugar
2 Tbsp. butter
2 eggs
1/4 tsp. salt
3 cups flour
whipped topping

1. Combine dates, baking soda, and boiling water. Set aside to cool.
2. Cream together sugar and butter. Beat in eggs. Add salt and flour and mix well. Stir in date mixture. Pour into greased and floured 9" x 13" pan.
3. Bake at 350° for 25-30 minutes or until toothpick inserted in center comes out clean. Cool cake completely
4. Serve on individual plates with whipped topping.

Cakes

Amazing Raisin Cake

Doris J. Collier
Annapolis, MD
Trip Around the World

Makes 8-10 servings

3 cups flour
1 cup mayonnaise
2 eggs
1 1/2 tsp. cinnamon
1/2 tsp. salt
2 cups sugar
1/3 cup milk
2 tsp. baking soda
1/2 tsp. nutmeg
1/4 tsp. ground cloves
3 cups chopped, peeled apples
1/2 cup coarsely chopped nuts
1 cup raisins
2 cups whipped topping

1. Mix together flour, mayonnaise, eggs, cinnamon, salt, sugar, milk, baking soda, nutmeg, and ground cloves. Beat for 2 minutes.
2. Stir in apples, nuts, and raisins. Pour into 2 greased and floured 9" round pans.
3. Bake at 350° for 45 minutes. Cool in pans for 10 minutes. Remove. Cool completely.
4. Frost with whipped topping and serve.

Note: At Christmas time I often decorate the edges of the plate with holly leaves and berries.

Mix-in-Pan Carrot Cake

Janet Miller
Princeton, IL

Makes 8-10 servings

1 cup flour
3/4 cup sugar
1 tsp. cinnamon
1/2 tsp. salt
1/2 tsp. baking soda
1/2 tsp. baking powder
1/4 tsp. nutmeg
1 1/2 cups shredded carrots
2 eggs, slightly beaten
1/2 cup cooking oil
1/4 cup water
1/2 tsp. vanilla
powdered sugar

1. In an 8" square pan, mix together flour, sugar, cinnamon, salt, baking soda, baking powder, and nutmeg. Stir in carrots, eggs, oil, water, and vanilla. Mix briefly with a fork until thoroughly blended.
2. Bake at 350° for 30 minutes or until toothpick comes out clean and cake pulls away from pan. Cool. Sprinkle with powdered sugar and serve.

Low-Fat Carrot Snacking Cake

Kimberly Davison
Coral Gables, FL
Nine Patch Garden Quillow

Makes 16-20 servings

3/4 cup sugar
1 cup raisins
2 cups finely grated carrots
1 1/4 cups water
1 Tbsp. margarine
1 tsp. ground cloves
1 tsp. cinnamon
1/2 tsp. nutmeg
1 cup chopped nuts or sunflower seeds
1 1/4 cups whole wheat flour
1 1/8 cups all-purpose flour
2 tsp. baking powder
1 tsp. baking soda
1/2 tsp. salt

1. In large saucepan combine sugar, raisins, carrots, water, margarine, cloves, cinnamon, and nutmeg. Bring to boil over moderately high heat. Simmer for 5 minutes. Cover and set aside for 12 hours. Do not refrigerate.
2. Combine nuts, flours, baking powder, baking soda, and salt. Stir by hand into cooked mixture.
3. Pour into 2 greased 5" x 9" loaf pans.
4. Bake at 275° for 70 minutes.

Carrot Cake
Rosaria Strachan
Old Greenwich, CT
Friendship

Makes 12-16 servings

Cake:
1 cup white sugar
1 cup brown sugar
2 cups flour
1 tsp. baking powder
1 tsp. baking soda
1 tsp. salt
1 tsp. cinnamon
3 cups shredded carrots
1 1/2 cups vegetable oil
4 large eggs
2 tsp. vanilla
1/2 cup chopped nuts
1/2 cup raisins (optional)

Cream Cheese Frosting:
8-oz. pkg. cream cheese,
    softened
1/4 cup margarine or
    butter, softened
1 tsp. vanilla
1 1/2 cups powdered sugar
1 tsp. orange or lemon
    rind

1. Combine sugars, flour,
baking powder, baking soda,
salt, and cinnamon.
2. Mix in carrots, oil, eggs,
and vanilla. Beat 2-3
minutes.
3. Stir in nuts and raisins.
Spoon into greased and
floured bundt pan.
4. Bake at 325° for 50-60
minutes. Remove from pan
and cool completely.
5. To prepare frosting beat
together cream cheese, margarine, and vanilla.

Gradually add sugar and
rind until desired consistency.
6. Frost cake and serve.

Mom's Rhubarb Cake
Margaret M. Sherman
Pompano Beach, FL
Family History Sampler
Dolly Jansen
DePere, WI
Victorian Hearts

Makes 16-20 servings

Cake:
1 1/2 cups brown sugar,
    packed
1/2 cup margarine or
    butter
1 egg
2 cups flour
1/4 tsp. salt
1 tsp. baking soda
1 cup sour milk or
    buttermilk
1 tsp. vanilla
2 1/2 cups rhubarb, cut
    into 1" pieces

Topping:
1 cup chopped nuts
1/4 cup sugar
1 tsp. cinnamon

1. Cream together brown
sugar and margarine until
fluffy. Beat in egg.
2. Mix together flour, salt,
and baking soda. Add
alternately with sour milk
to creamed mixture, beginning and ending with flour.
3. Stir in vanilla and
rhubarb. Pour into greased

and floured 9" x 13" baking
pan.
4. Mix together topping
ingredients. Sprinkle over
batter in pan.
5. Bake at 375° for 40-50
minutes or until cake
springs back when lightly
pressed with finger.

Pumpkin Cake
Dorothy Reise
Severna Park, MD
Dimensional Rose

Makes 12-16 servings

2 cups sugar
1 1/4 cups shortening
4 eggs
3 cups self-rising flour
3 tsp. cinnamon
1 tsp. allspice
1 tsp. nutmeg
1 3/4 cups canned
    pumpkin
1/2 cup chopped pecans

1. Cream together sugar,
shortening, and eggs.
2. Sift together flour, cinnamon, allspice, and nutmeg.
Add to creamed ingredients.
(Mixture will be dry until
pumpkin is added.)
3. Add pumpkin and mix
well. Fold in pecans. Spoon
into ungreased tube pan.
4. Bake at 300° for 1 to 1 1/2
hours.
5. Serve with whipped topping or frost with cream
cheese frosting.

Delicious Dark Chocolate Cake

Flossie Sultzaberger
Mechanicsburg, PA
Christmas Scene

Makes 16-20 servings

Cake:
2 cups flour
1 tsp. salt
1 tsp. baking powder
2 tsp. baking soda
1/2 cup unsweetened cocoa
2 cups sugar
1/2 cup vegetable oil
1 cup hot prepared coffee
1 cup buttermilk
2 eggs
1 tsp. vanilla

Frosting:
2/3 cup margarine or butter
1/2 cup peanut butter
4 cups powdered sugar
1/4 cup milk

1. To prepare cake sift together all dry ingredients, including sugar, in a large mixer bowl. Add vegetable oil, coffee, and milk and mix at medium speed for 2 minutes. Add eggs and vanilla and beat 2 more minutes. (This batter will be thin.)
2. Pour into a 9" x 13" baking pan.
3. Bake at 325° for 30-35 minutes.
4. To prepare frosting cream together margarine and peanut butter. Gradually add powdered sugar and milk. Beat until smooth and nice spreading consistency. If frosting is too stiff, add more milk, 1 tsp. at a time.
5. Let cake cool before spreading it with frosting.

Classic Chocolate Cake

Ashlene Drake
Salem, OR

Makes 16-20 servings

Cake:
3 cups brown sugar, packed
1 cup butter, softened
4 eggs
2 tsp. vanilla
3 cups cake flour
3/4 cup cocoa
1 Tbsp. baking soda
1/2 tsp. salt
1 1/3 cups sour cream
1 1/3 cups boiling water

Frosting:
1/2 cup butter
3 1-oz. squares unsweetened chocolate
3 1-oz. squares semi-sweet chocolate
5 cups powdered sugar
1 cup sour cream
2 tsp. vanilla

1. To prepare cake cream together brown sugar and butter. Add eggs, one at a time, beating well after each addition. Stir in vanilla.
2. Sift together flour, cocoa, baking soda, and salt. Alternately add dry ingredients and sour cream to creamed mixture, beginning and ending with flour. Stir in water until well blended.
3. Grease 3 9" round cake pans. Line with waxed paper and grease the paper. Pour batter into pans.
4. Bake at 350° for 30-35 minutes. Cool for 10 minutes. Remove from pans. Remove paper and cool completely.
5. To prepare frosting melt butter and chocolate in a saucepan over low heat. Cool slightly. Sift powdered sugar. Stir sour cream and vanilla into sugar. Add chocolate mixture and beat until smooth.
6. When cake has cooled, frost each layer and put layers together on a fancy cake platter. Serve.

Old Joe's Chocolate Cake

Chris Poeller Kaczynski
Schenectady, NY
Wyoming Valley Star

Makes 8-10 servings

2 cups brown sugar
1/2 cup butter or margarine
2 eggs
2 1-oz. squares chocolate
6 tsp. vinegar
1 tsp. baking soda
2 cups flour
1 tsp. vanilla
1 tsp. salt
1 cup cold water

1. Cream together sugar and butter. Add eggs.

2. In a small saucepan, melt chocolate with vinegar and stir into creamed mixture.
3. Sift together baking soda and flour. Add to mixture. Stir in vanilla, salt, and water. Beat for 2 minutes.
4. Pour into 2 9" round cake pans.
5. Bake at 350° for 30-35 minutes.
6. Cool and frost each layer with favorite frosting.

One-Layer Chocolate Cake
Susanne Troise
West Hills, CA
Amish Love

Makes 8-10 servings

1 cup flour
1 cup sugar
1/4 cup unsweetened cocoa
1 tsp. baking powder
1/4 tsp. baking soda
1/4 tsp. salt
3/4 cup milk
21/2-oz. jar baby food prunes
1/2 tsp. vanilla
2 egg whites
powdered sugar

1. Combine flour, sugar, cocoa, baking powder, baking soda, and salt in large mixer bowl.
2. Add milk, prunes, and vanilla. Beat on low speed until combined. Beat on medium speed for 2 minutes. Add egg whites and beat for 2 more minutes.

Pour into a greased and floured 9" round cake pan.
3. Bake at 325° for 30-35 minutes or until toothpick inserted in center comes out clean. Cool on wire rack for 10 minues. Remove cake from pan.
4. Dust with powdered sugar and serve.

Secret Cake
Linda V. Caldwell
Lockeford, CA
Grandmother's Flower Garden

Makes 16-20 servings

Cake:
2 cups flour
2 cups sugar
1/2 tsp. salt
1/2 cup margarine
1/2 cup shortening
1 cup water
31/2 Tbsp. cocoa
1/2 cup buttermilk
2 eggs, unbeaten
1 tsp. vanilla
1 tsp. baking soda

Frosting:
1/2 cup margarine
31/2 Tbsp. cocoa
1/2 cup buttermilk
1 lb. powdered sugar
1 tsp. vanilla
1 cup chopped black walnuts

1. Sift together flour, sugar, and salt.
2. In saucepan bring margarine, shortening, water, and cocoa to a boil. Pour over dry mixture and mix well.
3. Stir in buttermilk, eggs, vanilla, and baking soda. Mix well. (Batter will be thin.)
4. Pour into greased and floured 11" x 16" baking pan.
5. Bake at 350° for 20-25 minutes.
6. To prepare frosting combine margarine, cocoa, and buttermilk in a saucepan. Bring to a boil and cook until slightly thickened, stirring occasionally. Remove from heat. Add sugar, vanilla, and walnuts and mix until smooth and spreadable.. Frost cake while hot.

When I was nine years old, I desperately wanted a Shirley Temple doll for Christmas. About three weeks before the big day, I was playing upstairs with a friend, and we went snooping under the eaves in a closet. There inside a trunk was a long pink box. I peeked. It was Shirley, all decked out in a red polka dot dress! I was excited, but also guilty and went through several weeks of agony, wondering how in the world I could fake a surprised look when opening my gifts. Somehow I pulled it off, and my parents never knew that I had actually discovered Shirley before Christmas.

—*Dorothy Van Deest, Memphis, TN*

Raspberry Chocolate Cake
Barbara Riley
Elk Grove, CA
Vase of Flowers

Makes 8-10 servings

Cake:
3/4 cup butter, softened
2 cups sugar
2 eggs
2 1/2 cups flour
2 tsp. baking soda
1/2 cup cocoa
1 cup milk
2 Tbsp. vinegar
1 cup boiling water
1/2 cup raspberries, puréed

Frosting:
1/2 cup butter
5 Tbsp. milk
1/4 cup cocoa
1 tsp. vanilla
1 lb. powdered sugar

1. To prepare cake cream together butter, sugar, and eggs.
2. Mix together flour, baking soda, and cocoa.
3. Mix together milk and vinegar.
4. Alternately add flour mixture and soured milk to creamed mixture. Add boiling water and mix well.
5. Pour into 2 greased and floured 9" round cake pans.
6. Bake at 375° for 35 minutes. Cool and remove from pans.
7. Spread puréed raspberries between layers.
8. To prepare frosting combine butter, milk, and cocoa in a saucepan and heat until well mixed, stirring frequently. Remove from heat and beat in vanilla and powdered sugar. Stir until smooth and spreadable.
9. Spread frosting over outside of cake and serve.

Poor Man's Chocolate Cake
Claire Amick
Pine Grove Mills, PA
Autumn Stars

Makes 16-20 servings

3 cups flour
2 scant cups sugar
8 Tbsp. cocoa
1 tsp. salt
2 tsp. baking soda
2 cups water
2 tsp. vanilla
2/3 cup vegetable oil
2 Tbsp. vinegar

1. Sift together flour, sugar, cocoa, salt, and baking soda. Stir in remaining ingredients and mix well.
2. Pour into lightly greased 9" x 13" baking pan.
3. Bake at 350° for 30 minutes.
4. Cool and frost with favorite cream cheese frosting.

Red Party Cake
Faye Meyers
San Jose, CA
Grandmother's Fan

Makes 8-10 servings

Cake:
1/2 cup shortening
1 1/2 cups sugar
2 eggs
2 ozs. red food coloring
2-3 Tbsp. cocoa
2 1/4 cups cake flour
1 tsp. salt
1 tsp. baking soda
1 cup buttermilk
1 tsp. vanilla
1 tsp. vinegar

Cream Frosting:
1 cup milk
3 Tbsp. flour
pinch salt
1 cup butter
1 cup sugar
1 tsp. vanilla

1. To prepare cake cream together shortening, sugar, and eggs.
2. Make a paste of the food coloring and cocoa and add to creamed mixture.
3. Sift together flour, salt, and baking soda and add alternately with buttermilk to creamed mixture.
4. Stir in vinegar and vanilla. Do not beat.
5. Pour into 2 greased and floured 9" round cake pans.
6. Bake at 350° for 20-25 mintues.
7. To prepare frosting combine milk, flour, and salt. Cook until thickened,

stirring constantly. Cool thoroughly. Cream together butter and sugar with mixer for 7 minutes. Gradually add milk mixture, beating constantly. Continue beating for 5 minutes or until fluffy. Stir in vanilla.

8. Cool cake, frost between each layer and over top and sides.

Coca Cola Cake
Linda V. Caldwell
Lockeford, CA
Mystery Quilt

Makes 16-20 servings

Cake:
1/2 cup butter
1/2 cup shortening
1 cup Coca Cola
1/2 tsp. salt
1 1/2 cups miniature
   marshmallows
2 eggs
2 tsp. vanilla
1/4 cup buttermilk
1 tsp. baking soda
2 cups sugar
2 cups flour
3/8 cup cocoa

Frosting:
1/2 cup butter
1/4 cup cocoa
3/8 cup Coca Cola
1 lb. powdered sugar
1 cup chopped nuts

1. In a saucepan combine butter, shortening, Coca Cola, and salt. Bring to boil. Remove from heat and stir in marshmallows. Cool.

2. Beat together eggs and vanilla. Add buttermilk and baking soda.

3. Sift together sugar, flour, and cocoa. Stir in Coca Cola mixture and egg mixture. Mix well.

4. Pour into greased and floured 9" x 13" cake pan.

5. Bake at 350° for 30-35 minutes.

6. To prepare frosting combine butter, cocoa, and Coca Cola in a saucepan. Bring to boil. Remove from heat and stir in sugar and nuts. Spread over hot cake. Cool and serve.

Buttermilk Fudge Cake
Sharon Easter
Yuba City, CA

Makes 24-30 servings

Cake:
2 cups flour
2 cups sugar
1/2 cup margarine
1/2 cup shortening
1 cup water
4 Tbsp. cocoa
2 eggs, slightly beaten
1/2 cup buttermilk
1 tsp. cinnamon
1 tsp. baking soda
1 tsp. vanilla

Frosting:
1/2 cup margarine
4 Tbsp. cocoa
1/3 cup buttermilk
1 lb. powdered sugar
1 tsp. vanilla
1 cup chopped nuts

1. Mix together flour and sugar. Set aside.

2. In saucepan combine margarine, shortening, water, and cocoa. Bring to a boil. Pour into the flour mixture. Mix well. Add all remaining cake ingredients and mix well.

3. Pour into greased and floured 11" x 17" cookie sheet that has 1" sides.

4. Bake at 350° for 20 minutes.

5. To prepare frosting melt margarine with cocoa and buttermilk in a saucepan. Bring to a boil. Stir in powdered sugar and stir until mixture appears smooth. Stir in vanilla and nuts. Mix well and spoon frosting over hot cake just after it comes out of oven. Cool and serve.

Fruitcakes and Christmas Puddings

Applesauce Fruitcake
Ruth L. Welch
Jefferson, NY
Burgoyne Surrounded

Makes 12 servings

1 cup brown sugar
1/2 cup shortening
1 1/2 cups unsweetened
   applesauce
2 tsp. baking soda
1 tsp. cinnamon
1 tsp. nutmeg
1 tsp. cloves
1 cup raisins
1 1/2 cups mixed candied
   fruit
1 cup chopped nuts
2 cups flour

1. Cream together brown
sugar and shortening. Add
applesauce, baking soda,
cinnamon, nutmeg, and
cloves.

2. Add raisins, fruit, nuts,
and flour and mix well.
3. Pour into greased and
floured tube pan.
4. Bake at 325° for 60-70
minutes. Remove from pan
and let cool.

Applesauce Fruitcake Variation
Kareen Armstrong
Rockaway Beach, OR
White on White Heirloom

Makes 2 loaves

2 cups applesauce
1/2 cup warm water
2 tsp. baking soda
2 cups white sugar
4 cups flour
1 tsp. salt
1 tsp. cinnamon
1 tsp. nutmeg
1 tsp. ground cloves

1 tsp. allspice
1 cup raisins
1 cup chopped nuts
1 cup diced, candied
   cherries
1 cup diced, candied
   pineapple
1/3 cup cooking oil

1. Mix together applesauce,
water, and baking soda in
small bowl and set aside.
2. Mix together sugar, flour,
salt, cinnamon, nutmeg,
cloves, allspice, raisins, nuts,
cherries, and pineapple.
Combine with applesauce
mixture. Stir in oil. Mix
well.
3. Spoon into 2 waxed
paper-lined 5" x 9" loaf
pans.
4. Bake at 325° for 1 hour
or more until the cakes
shrink from sides of pans.

Christmas Fruitcake

Cora J. Peterson
Frederic, WI
*Wagon Tracks
Through the Blueberry Patch*

Makes 3 loaves

Fruitcake:
1/2 cup brown sugar
1 cup white sugar
1/2 cup margarine
2 eggs, slightly beaten
1/2 cup molasses
1 cup applesauce
1 cup sweet red wine
31/2 cups flour
1 tsp. cloves
11/2 tsp. cinnamon
1/8 tsp. salt
1 tsp. ginger
1 tsp. baking soda
3 tsp. baking powder
1/4 lb. raisins
1 lb. mixed candied fruits
1/2 lb. red candied cherries
1/2 lb. whole walnut halves
1/2 lb. whole shelled Brazil nuts

Glaze:
1 cup maple syrup
1/2 cup sweet red wine

1. Cream together sugars and margarine. Mix in eggs until creamy.
2. Add molasses, applesauce, and wine and mix well.
3. Mix together flour, cloves, cinnamon, salt, ginger, baking soda, and baking powder. Add to creamed ingredients and mix well. (This makes a very thick batter.)
4. By hand fold in raisins, candied fruits, candied cherries, walnut halves, and Brazil nuts.
5. Fill 3 well greased loaf pans 3/4 full of batter.
6. Bake at 350° for 1 hour and 25 minutes. Cool.
7. To prepare glaze combine maple syrup and red wine in a saucepan. Bring to a rolling boil.
8. Remove from heat and cool to lukewarm.
9. Dip all sides and top of each fruitcake loaf in glaze. Allow to cool on rack for 30 minutes before wrapping in plastic wrap or aluminum foil. Store in cool place or freeze.

Incredibly Edible Fruitcake

Beverly Simmons
Boulder, CO
*Spirit of the Carousel
1895-1995*

Makes 3 loaves

Fruitcake:
1 lb. dates, chopped
8 ozs. dried cranberries, cherries, or papaya
8 ozs. red and green candied pineapple, chopped
1 cup sugar
1/4 cup brandy
4 eggs
1 tsp. vanilla
1 lb. chopped pecans
1 cup flour
2 tsp. baking powder
1/8 tsp. salt

Topping Decorations:
candied cherries
half pecans
candied pineapple slices

1. Combine dates, cranberries, pineapple, sugar, brandy, eggs, and vanilla in a large bowl and set aside.
2. Combine pecans, flour, baking powder, and salt. Mix well. Add to fruit mixture and mix thoroughly by hand.
3. Pack into 3 greased loaf pans. Decorate tops with candied cherries, half pecans, and candied pineapple slices.
4. Bake at 300° for 11/4-11/2 hours.

Note: I usually make this recipe in mini loaf pans and give the fruitcake to friends and neighbors at Christmas time. Makes 10 mini loaves.

Best-Ever Fruitcake
Lucille Amos
Greensboro, NC
Ohio Star

Makes 12-16 servings

1 cup butter, room temperature
1 cup sugar
5 eggs
1 1/2 cups flour
1/2 tsp. baking powder
1/2 tsp. salt
1 Tbsp. vanilla
1 Tbsp. lemon extract
1 lb. candied pineapple
3/4 cup candied cherries
1/4 cup flour
3 cups pecans
1 cup white raisins

1. Cream together butter and sugar. Beat in eggs, one at a time.
2. Stir in flour, baking powder, salt, vanilla, and lemon extract.
3. Mix together pineapple, cherries, and flour. Stir pineapple mixture, pecans, and white raisins into batter.
4. Pour into greased and floured tube pan.
5. Starting in a cold oven, bake at 250° for 3 hours.

Aunt Thelma's Lemon Fruitcake
Janice Muller
Derwood, MD
Canadian Geese

Makes 4 small loaves

1 lb. butter, melted
4 cups flour
2 cups white sugar
6 eggs
1 lb. pecans
1 lb. cherries
1 lb. pineapple
2-oz. bottle lemon extract
1 tsp. salt
1 heaping tsp. baking powder

1. Mix together all ingredients.
2. Spoon into 4 small, greased loaf pans.
3. Bake at 250° for 2 hours.

White Fruitcake
Iva L. Schmidt
McConnellsburg, PA
Single Irish Chain

Makes 12-16 servings

4 cups shelled pecans
3/4 lb. candied cherries
1 lb. candied pineapple
1 3/4 cups flour
1 cup butter or margerine
1 cup white sugar
5 eggs, beaten
1/2 tsp. baking powder
1 Tbsp. vanilla
1 Tbsp. lemon extract

1. Chop pecans, candied cherries, and pineapple into medium-sized pieces. Dredge with 1/4 cup flour.
2. Cream together butter and sugar until light and fluffy. Beat in eggs until well blended.
3. Sift together remaining 1 1/2 cups flour and baking powder. Fold into egg and butter mixture.
4. Add vanilla and lemon extract. Mix well. Blend in nuts and fruits.
5. Grease a 10-inch tube pan. Line with heavy brown paper and grease again.
6. Spoon batter into prepared pan.
7. Starting in a cold oven, bake at 250° for 3 hours. Cool.

My favorite food memory is of going to my grandpa and grandma's on Christmas morning and having shrimp cocktail and lobster tail at 10:00 in the morning. We did this every year from the time we were kids until Grandpa died in the early 1980s. Believe me, Christmas morning is not the same without Grandpa cooking his shrimp and lobster.
—*Suzanne S. Nobrega, Duxbury, MA*

Light Fruitcake
Millie Hohimer
Independence, MO
Heart of Roses

Makes 20-24 servings

4 cups pecan halves
2 cups English walnut halves
2 cups whole candied cherries
2 cups diced candied pineapple
1 1/2 cups white raisins
1 cup flour, sifted
1 1/2 cups butter or margarine
1 1/2 cups sugar
3 eggs
1-oz. bottle lemon extract
2 cups flour
3/4 tsp. baking powder
light corn syrup
red and green candied cherries

1. In large mixing bowl, combine pecans, walnuts, cherries, pineapple, and raisins.
2. Toss with 1 cup flour and set aside.
3. Cream together butter and sugar until light and fluffy. Add eggs, one at a time, beating well after each addition. Stir in lemon extract.
4. Sift together 2 cups flour and baking powder. Add to the creamed ingredients, 1/3 of mixture at a time, and mix well.
5. Add batter to fruit, mixing well to coat all fruits and nuts.
6. Pour batter into a well-greased 10-inch tube pan. Cover tightly with foil.
7. Place a pan of hot water on bottom oven rack. Bake cake on shelf above water at 300° for 2 1/2 hours.
8. Remove foil. Bake 3-5 minutes or until top is slightly dry.
9. Remove cake from pan when thoroughly cooled. Store in tightly covered container.
10. Immediately before serving, brush with light corn syrup and garnish with poinsettias cut from candied cherries.

Fruitcake
Marie Fuller
Ashfield, MA
Jennifer's Cat Family

Makes 4 small loaves

1 1/2 cups raisins
1 1/2 cups dates, chopped
2 cups sugar
2 cups boiling water
5 Tbsp. shortening
3 cups flour
2 tsp. baking soda
1 tsp. cinnamon
1 tsp. cloves
1 tsp. salt
1 cup chopped walnuts
1 lb. mixed candied fruit

1. In saucepan mix together raisins, dates, sugar, boiling water, and shortening. Simmer on stove for 20 minutes. Cool to lukewarm.
2. Add flour, baking soda, cinnamon, cloves, and salt. Mix well. Stir in chopped walnuts and fruit. Mix well.
3. Pour into 4 greased and floured small loaf pans.
4. Bake at 325° for 90 minutes.

Note: Every year during the weekend after Thanksgiving, I make my fruitcakes. I give some away as Christmas gifts, and my husband enjoys the two I give him throughout January and February. Homemade fruitcake is very different than storebought fruitcake.

Brazil Nut Fruitcake

Janet L. Haver
Punxsutawney, PA
Windblown Tulips
Ruth Liebelt
Rapid City, SD
Woven Heart

Makes 1 large loaf

1¹/2 cups shelled Brazil nuts
1¹/2 cups walnut halves
1/2 lb. pitted dates
1/2 cup red maraschino cherries, drained
1/2 cup green maraschino cherries, drained
3/4 cup flour
3/4 cup sugar
1/2 tsp. baking powder
1/2 tsp. salt
3 eggs
1 tsp. vanilla

1. Mix together nuts, dates, and cherries.
2. Sift together flour, sugar, baking powder, and salt. Pour over nuts and fruit and mix well.
3. Beat eggs until light and fluffy. Stir in vanilla. Blend into nut mixture. Batter will be stiff.
4. Spoon mixture into 5" x 9" loaf pan.
5. Bake at 300° for 1³/4 hours. Cool in pan for 10 minutes. Turn out onto wire rack. Cool before slicing.

Brandied Plum Pudding

Mary E. Wheatley
Mashpee, MA
Mariner's Compass

Makes 12 servings

1 cup dried currants
1 cup seedless raisins
1 cup golden raisins
1/2 cup candied cherries
1/4 cup chopped, candied lemon peel
1/4 cup chopped, candied orange peel
1/4 cup finely chopped citron
2 Tbsp. finely chopped, crystallized ginger
1 medium apple, chopped
1 small carrot, grated
1/2 cup blanched slivered almonds
1 cup finely ground beef suet
juice and rind of 1 lemon
juice and rind of 1 orange
1/2 cup brandy
1 cup flour
1/2 tsp. salt
1/2 tsp. cinnamon
1/2 tsp. allspice
1/4 tsp. nutmeg
1/8 tsp. ground cloves
1¹/2 cups fresh bread crumbs
6 eggs
1/2 cup packed brown sugar

1. In large non-corrosive bowl, mix together currants, raisins, golden raisins, cherries, lemon peel, orange peel, citron, ginger, apple, carrot, and almonds. Stir in suet, lemon juice and rind, and orange juice and rind. Add brandy and mix to moisten all ingredients with brandy. Cover and refrigerate overnight or up to one week, stirring occasionally.
2. Sift together flour, salt, cinnamon, allspice, nutmeg, and cloves. Add to brandy-soaked fruit mixture. Sprinkle with bread crumbs. Stir to distribute well.
3. Beat eggs until light. Add brown sugar, continuing to beat until eggs are thick and smooth. Pour over fruit mixture. Mix with hands or wooden spoon until well blended.
4. Spoon into well greased

Each year for the past twenty-five years, I have enjoyed making a small handmade ornament for each member of my family as well as several special friends. I start early and always make the same ornament for everyone. In our own home, we have a special tree decorated with these handmade ornaments, and friends and family eagerly await their ornaments each year, reminding me periodically not to forget this holiday tradition.
—*Patricia Fielding, Stone Mountain, GA*

and sugared 3-4 quart pudding mold with tight-fitting cover. (If you don't have a mold, use an oven-proof bowl covered with heavy foil. Drape a damp towel over top and secure with string around bowl rim. Draw corners of towel back up and over top of bowl and tie.)

5. Set pudding mold in large pot on stove. Pour boiling water around sides of mold to 3/4 full. Bring to boil. Lower heat to maintain gentle simmer. Cover and steam for eight hours, replenishing water as needed.

6. Cool on wire rack for 3 hours. Remove pudding from mold gently. Wrap in plastic bag and store in refrigerator for at least 3 weeks or up to one year. Serve with favorite hard sauce.

Christmas Plum Pudding
Joyce Clark
East Amherst, NY
Amish Bars

Makes 20 servings

Plum Pudding:
1/2 cup flour
1/2 tsp. ground cloves
1/2 tsp. cinnamon
1/2 tsp. allspice
1/2 tsp. mace
1/2 tsp. nutmeg
1/2 tsp. baking soda
3/4 cup bread crumbs
1/2 cup butter
3/4 cup firmly packed brown sugar

3 eggs
1 can canned purple plums, drained, pitted, and chopped
1 cup pitted chopped, dates
1 cup seedless raisins
1 cup chopped, candied fruits
1 cup chopped pecans or almonds
1/2 cup currants

Hard Sauce:
1 cup butter
3 cups powdered sugar
2 Tbsp. vanilla

1. Sift together flour, spices, and baking soda. Stir in bread crumbs.

2. Cream together butter and sugar until light. Beat in eggs, one at a time. Stir in plums. Add dry ingredients and mix until blended. Fold in all remaining ingredients. Spoon into greased 8-10 cup mold. Cover tightly.

3. Place tightly covered mold on a rack or trivet in a large pot or steamer. Pour boiling water to half the depth of pudding mold. Cover tightly. Keep water boiling gently during entire cooking time, adding more boiling water as needed. Steam for 4 1/2 hours.

4. To prepare hard sauce, beat together all ingredients and mix until smooth and creamy.

5. Serve plum pudding hot with hard sauce. Or place pudding on fancy dish which has been heated. Pour 1/2 cup warmed brandy or rum over and

around the pudding. Ignite and bring flaming to table.

Note: Traditionally, this steamed pudding is wrapped in a cloth. It is then hung from a hook in a cold cellar for two weeks prior to Christmas in order for it to attain perfection.

Hard Sauce for Plum Pudding
Shan D. Lear
Middleton, MA
Country Bride

Makes 1 1/2 cups sauce

1/2-lb. box powdered sugar
1 Tbsp. milk
1/2 cup butter, softened

1. Beat together all ingredients until smooth and creamy.

2. Serve with favorite Christmas Plum Pudding recipe.

Christmas Pudding

Margaret F. Moehl
Pinckney, MI
Christmas Treasures

Makes 10-12 servings

Pudding:
1 Tbsp. baking soda
1 Tbsp. warm water
1 cup sugar
1 1/2 cups flour
1 cup packed, chopped
   suet
4 carrots, shredded
1/2 tsp. cinnamon
1/2 tsp. nutmeg
1/4 tsp. cloves
1/2 tsp. salt
1 1/2 cups seedless raisins
1/2 cup blanched almonds
1/2 cup citron
1/2 cup candied orange peel

Vanilla Sauce:
1 cup sugar
2 Tbsp. cornstarch
1/8 tsp. salt
2 cups boiling water
4 Tbsp. butter
2 tsp. vanilla

1. Mix together baking soda and warm water in large bowl. Stir in remaining ingredients. Spoon into well greased large mold with tight fitting cover.
2. Place mold in large kettle. Pour boiling water around sides of mold and steam for 3 hours.
3. To prepare sauce combine sugar, cornstarch, and salt in a saucepan. Gradually add boiling water, stirring constantly. Cook for 5 minutes until thickened and clear. Stir in butter and vanilla and mix well. Remove from heat and serve with steamed Christmas pudding.

Grandma's Christmas Pudding

Brenda J. Marshall
St. Marys, Ontario
Sampler and the Ivy

Makes 10-12 servings

1 cup bread crumbs
1 cup milk
2 eggs
1 cup brown sugar
1 Tbsp. molasses
1/2 tsp. salt
1 tsp. cinnamon
1 tsp. allspice
1/2 tsp. nutmeg or mace
2 tsp. baking powder
2 1/2 cups flour
1/4 lb. mixed candied
   fruit
1 lb. seedless raisins
1/2 cup sliced almonds
1/2 cup candied cherries,
   halved
1/2 lb. fine suet

1. Soak bread crumbs in milk.
2. Beat eggs until light and fluffy. Add brown sugar, molasses, and soaked bread crumbs.
3. Sift together salt, cinnamon, allspice, nutmeg, baking powder, and flour. Add to bread crumb mixture.
4. Fold in candied fruit, raisins, almonds, cherries, and suet. Pour into mold or large oven-proof glass bowl. Cover tightly with aluminum foil or lid from mold.
5. Set mold in large kettle and pour boiling water

Several years ago I decided to make a Christmas quilt for our daughter. I collected worn flannel shirts from her father, grandfathers, and close friends and made Nine Patch blocks by combining the plaids of the shirts with solid flannel squares. The center square in each block was a shirt pocket, and at the intersection of each of the blocks, I placed a shirt label. I kept the quilt secret from both my husband and daughter, and on Christmas Day, my husband finally understood what had happened to his old flannel shirts. Our daughter was delighted with the warmth, memories, and love which the quilt evoked.
—*Elaine Patton, West Middletown, PA*

around sides of mold. Do not cover with water. Steam for 3-5 hours or until set and cooked through. Replenish water as needed.

Note: I like to make this at least 1 month ahead of time to let flavors combine. On Christmas Day steam to reheat or cover with plastic wrap and microwave for 10 minutes. Invert onto large platter and serve with favorite sauce.

Suet Pudding
Muriel B. Haley
Dexter, ME
Trip Around the World

Makes 8-10 servings

Pudding:
1 cup finely chopped, packed suet
1 cup molasses
1 cup sour milk
1 tsp. baking soda
3 cups flour
1 cup raisins
1 tsp. cinnamon
1 tsp. cloves
1/2 tsp. nutmeg
1 tsp. salt

Hard Sauce:
1/2 cup butter, softened
1 1/2 cups powdered sugar
1 tsp. vanilla

1. To prepare pudding mix ingredients in order given. Place in tightly covered, medium-sized mold.
2. Set mold into larger kettle. Pour boiling water

around sides of mold and steam for two hours.
3. To prepare sauce work butter into sugar. Stir in vanilla and refrigerate until ready to serve.
4. Serve warm pudding with hard sauce.

Grandmother's Pudding with Lemon Sauce
Bonita Ensenberger
Albuquerque, NM
Snowflake

Makes 8-10 servings

Pudding:
1/4 cup shortening
1 cup sugar
2 Tbsp. molasses
1/2 cup flour
1/2 tsp. salt
1/2 tsp. ground cloves
1/2 tsp. ground allspice
1 tsp. ground cinnamon
1 tsp. baking soda
1 cup fine bread crumbs
1/2 cup coarsely chopped nutmeats
1 cup milk

Lemon Sauce:
1 egg, beaten
1 cup sugar
2 Tbsp. butter
3 Tbsp. lemon juice
2 tsp. lemon zest
3 Tbsp. boiling water
1/8 tsp. nutmeg
whipped topping

1. Cream together shortening and sugar. Stir in

molasses and mix well.
2. Sift together flour, salt, cloves, allspice, cinnamon, and baking soda. Add to creamed ingredients and mix well. Mix in bread crumbs and nuts. Gradually blend in milk. Pour into a greased 2-quart rectangular casserole dish. Cover tightly with aluminum foil.
3. Bake at 350° for 45-55 minutes. Cool. Cut into squares.
4. To prepare lemon sauce, combine egg, sugar, butter, lemon juice, lemon zest, boiling water, and nutmeg in heavy saucepan. Cook over medium heat until smooth and slightly thickened, stirring constantly.
5. To serve put pudding squares on individual serving plates. Top with spoonful of hot lemon sauce and dollop of whipped topping.

Cookies and Bars

Christmas Cake Cookies

Mary E. Wheatley
Mashpee, MA
Mariner's Compass

Makes 12-14 dozen

1 cup butter
1 1/2 cups sugar
2 eggs
2 1/2 cups flour
1 tsp. baking soda
1 tsp. cinnamon
1 tsp. salt
2 lbs. dates
1/2 lb. candied cherries
1/2 lb. candied pineapple
1/2 lb. shelled almonds
1/2 lb. shelled Brazil nuts

1. Cream together butter and sugar, adding sugar gradually and mixing until smooth. Beat in eggs, one at a time.
2. Sift together flour, baking soda, cinnamon, and salt. Mix dry ingredients into creamed ingredients.

3. Cut dates into chunks, candied cherries into quarters, and candied pineapple into thin slivers.
4. Blanch almonds, chop coarsely, spread on cookie sheet, and toast at 400° until golden.
5. Chop Brazil nuts.
6. Stir all fruits and nuts into batter. Drop cookie batter by teaspoonfuls onto ungreased cookie sheets.
7. Bake at 400° for 10 minutes. Do not overbake.
8. Remove from oven. Cool slightly and remove from cookie sheet.

Note: Preparing and cutting the fruits and nuts as indicated in steps 3-5 is important to the final flavor of the cookies.

Fruitcake Cookies

Betty Ziegler
Bay City, OR
Pamela R. Kerschner
Stevensville, MD
Mary Helen Wade
Sterling, IL

Makes 5 dozen

1 cup butter or
  margarine
2 cups sugar
2 eggs
3 cups flour, sifted
1/2 tsp. salt
3 tsp. baking powder
1/2 tsp. nutmeg
1/2 tsp. cloves
2 tsp. cinnamon
3/4 cup milk
1 1/4 cups chopped
  walnuts
1 cup raisins, rinsed and
  drained
1 3/4 cups fruitcake fruit
  mix

1. Cream together butter and sugar. Add eggs and

continue creaming until light and fluffy.
2. Sift together flour, salt, baking powder, nutmeg, cloves, and cinnamon. Add to creamed mixture, alternating with milk.
3. Stir in walnuts, raisins, and fruitcake fruit mix.
4. Drop by heaping teaspoonfuls onto greased baking sheet.
5. Bake at 375° for about 12 minutes.

Holiday Fruit Cookies
Kathy Wheeler
Griffith, IN
Prairie Pines

Makes 4-5 dozen

1/2 cup margarine
1 cup sugar
2 eggs
1 3/4 cups flour
1/4 tsp. salt
1/2 tsp. cinnamon
1/2 tsp. nutmeg
1/2 tsp. orange extract
1/2 tsp. vanilla
1/2 cup chopped, pitted dates
3/4 cup currants
3/4 cup mixed candied fruit
2 cups chopped walnuts

1. Cream together margarine and sugar. Beat in eggs, one at a time.
2. Mix together flour, salt, cinnamon, and nutmeg. Stir into creamed mixture.
3. Stir in orange extract,

vanilla, dates, currants, candied fruit, and walnuts.
4. Drop by teaspoonfuls onto greased cookie sheets.
5. Bake at 350° for 10-12 minutes.

Christmas Date Cookies
Beverly Roberts Kessler
Marietta, SC
Teddy Bear and Bows

Makes 3-4 dozen

1 1/2 cups light brown sugar
1/2 cup sugar
16 Tbsp. butter
3 eggs
1 tsp. vanilla
4 cups flour
1/2 tsp. salt
1/2 tsp. baking soda
1/2 tsp. cinnamon
1/2 cup chopped dates
8-ozs. red candied cherries, chopped
3 slices candied pineapple, diced
2 cups chopped pecans
1/2 cup raisins

1. Cream together sugars, butter, eggs, and vanilla.
2. Mix together flour, salt, baking soda, and cinnamon. Add to creamed mixture. Mix well.
3. Stir in dates, cherries, pineapple, pecans, and raisins. Shape into logs and chill.
4. Slice into thin pieces. Bake at 325° for 12-15 minutes.

Holiday Nuggets
Alice Kennedy
Dallas, TX
Ye Olde Bow Tie

Makes 3 dozen

3/4 cup butter or margarine
3/4 cup sugar
1 egg
1 tsp. grated lemon rind
2 cups flour
1/2 tsp. salt
1 cup flaked coconut
3/4 cup raisins, rinsed and drained
1/4 cup chopped, candied cherries

1. Cream together butter and sugar, gradually adding sugar. Beat until light and fluffy. Stir in egg and lemon rind.
2. Sift together flour and salt. Add to mixture. Mix to form a stiff dough.
3. Stir in coconut, raisins, and cherries. Drop by teaspoonfuls onto greased cookie sheet.
4. Bake at 350° for 15-18 minutes.

Brilliant Candy Cookies

Cyndie Marrara
Port Matilda, PA
Sampler

Makes 7 dozen

1 cup butter
1 cup powdered sugar
1 egg, unbeaten
1 tsp. vanilla
2¹/₂ cups sifted flour
1 cup pecan halves
1 cup green candied
    cherries, cut in half
1 cup red candied
    cherries, cut in half

1. Cream together butter and sugar. Blend in egg. Add vanilla and flour and mix well. Fold in pecans and fruit.
2. Shape dough into 4 rolls. Wrap in plastic wrap and chill for at least 3 hours.
3. Slice off ¹/₈" pieces and arrange on ungreased cookie sheets.
4. Bake at 350° for 12-15 minutes.

Christmas Cookies

Scarlett von Bernuth
Canon City, CO
Postage Stamp

Makes 4-6 dozen

1 cup raisins
1 cup currants
1 cup pecans
3/4 cup water
2 cups sugar
1 cup margarine
2 eggs
1 tsp. vanilla
1/2 tsp. almond extract
4¹/₂ cups flour
1 tsp. baking powder
1 cup coconut (optional)

1. In saucepan mix together raisins, currants, pecans, and water. Bring to a boil. Cool. Drain water and reserve.
2. Cream together sugar and margarine. Stir in eggs, vanilla, and almond extract. Add water that has been drained from fruit.
3. Sift together flour and baking powder. Stir into creamed mixture to make a stiff dough. Fold in fruit and coconut, if desired. Drop by teaspoonfuls onto greased cookie sheet.
4. Bake at 350° for 12-15 minutes.

Special K Fruit Cookies

Lucille Reagan
Salem, OR

Makes 5 dozen

1 cup butter or margarine,
    softened
2 cups firmly packed
    brown sugar
2 eggs
1 tsp. vanilla
2 cups flour
1 tsp. baking soda
1 tsp. baking powder
1/2 tsp. salt or less
1/2 cup raisins
1 cup flaked coconut
1 cup broken walnuts
1 cup citrus fruit mix
4 cups Special K cereal

1. Cream together butter and sugar until fluffy. Stir in eggs and vanilla and mix well.
2. Sift together flour, baking soda, baking powder, and salt. Add to creamed mixture.
3. Stir in raisins, coconut, walnuts, and fruit mix. Stir in Special K cereal.
4. Drop by tablespoonfuls onto greased cookie sheets.
5. Bake at 350° for 10 minutes or until lightly browned.

My mother died with cancer several years ago. Because the holidays are especially difficult, my sisters and I decided to make enough Spinning Star wallhangings so each of us could have one. We are using scraps of fabric from our mother's dresses for these holiday memory quilts. And we have begun to take turns hosting our annual family Christmas dinner.

—*Ilene Bontrager, Arlington, KS*

Sandtarts
Emma S. Byler
Paradise, PA
Heart of Roses

Makes 5-6 dozen

1 cup brown sugar
1/2 cup butter
1 egg
1 tsp. vanilla
2 1/2 cups flour
1/4 tsp. salt
2 tsp. baking powder
1 egg, beaten
colored sugar or
  cinnamon

1. Cream together sugar and butter. Add 1 egg and vanilla. Mix well.
2. Sift together flour, salt, and baking powder. Add to creamed mixture.
3. On lightly floured board, roll dough until very thin. Cut with 2" cookie cutter. Place on lightly greased cookie sheet. Brush with beaten egg and top with colored sugar or cinnamon.
4. Bake at 350° for 10-15 minutes, until light brown.

Anise Peppernuts
Ruth Ann Penner
Hillsboro, KS
Sunflower Appliqué Jacket

Makes many dozen

3/4 cup lard
1 cup sugar
1/4 cup brown sugar
1 cup dark corn syrup
1 tsp. baking soda
1 Tbsp. hot water
1 egg
4 1/4 cups flour
1 tsp. ground cloves
1 tsp. cinnamon
1 tsp. ground anise

1. Cream together lard, sugars, corn syrup, baking soda, and hot water. Stir in egg and mix well.
2. Mix together flour, cloves, cinnamon, and anise. Add to creamed mixture. Mix well. Chill dough in refrigerator several hours or overnight.
3. Roll dough into pencil-sized sticks. Cut each piece dough into 1/4" pieces. Arrange on greased baking sheets.
4. Bake at 350° for 8-10 minutes. May be stored several weeks in airtight container.

Peppernuts
Marilyn Maurstad
Beatrice, NE
Crosses and Losses

Makes 8 dozen

1/2 cup sugar
1/2 cup shortening
1/2 cup dark corn syrup
1/4 cup cold prepared
  coffee
1/4 tsp. baking soda
1/4 tsp. salt
1/4 tsp. nutmeg
1/4 tsp. ginger
1/4 tsp. ground cloves
1/4 tsp. pepper
2 tsp. freshly ground
  anise seed
2 1/2 cups flour

1. Cream together sugar and shortening. Stir in corn syrup and coffee.
2. Mix together baking soda, salt, nutmeg, ginger, cloves, pepper, anise, and flour. Stir into creamed mixture. Mix well. Chill dough in refrigerator at least 2 hours.
3. Take small sections of dough and roll into pencil-sized rolls. Cut into 1/2" slices.
4. Bake on lightly greased cookie sheets at 350-375° for 8 minutes or until golden brown. Remove immediately from cookie sheet. Cool. Will keep for weeks in airtight container.

Sour Cream Peppernuts
E. Ann Warkentin
Enid, OK
Baskets, Bottles, and Bowls

Makes many dozen

3 cups brown sugar
1 cup shortening
2 eggs, beaten
1 cup thick sour cream
1 tsp. baking soda
1 tsp. salt
1 tsp. star anise, rolled
　　fine, or 2 tsp. ground
　　anise seed
1 cup finely chopped
　　nuts
5-6 cups flour

1. Cream together sugar and shortening. Add eggs. Stir in sour cream, baking soda, salt, anise, and nuts. Add enough flour to make a stiff dough.
2. On a floured board, roll dough into small rolls. Lay out on waxed paper-covered cookie sheets and refrigerate overnight.
3. Cut into small pieces, using a string. Place on lightly greased cookie sheet.
4. Bake at 375° for 8-10 minutes, until they turn light brown.

Molasses Peppernuts
Evelyn L. Ward
Greeley, CO
Watercolor Quilt

Makes 10 dozen

1/2 cup sugar
1 tsp. ground cloves
1 tsp. cinnamon
1/4 cup finely chopped,
　　black walnuts
1/2 cup finely chopped,
　　candied fruit
3-4 cups flour
1 1/2 cups light corn syrup
1/2 cup butter
2 Tbsp. sorghum or
　　molasses
1 tsp. baking soda
1 Tbsp. hot water

1. Mix together sugar, cloves, cinnamon, walnuts, candied fruit, and flour.
2. In a saucepan bring corn syrup to a boil. Add butter and bring to boil again. Cool slightly. Stir in sorghum and baking soda. Mix well. Stir into dry ingredients to make a very stiff dough. Add more flour if needed. Chill dough for at least 8 hours.
3. Shape 1/4 of dough into long roll, 1/2" thick. Cut into 1/4" slices. Place, cut side down, on lightly greased baking sheet. Repeat until dough has been used.
4. Bake at 325° for 8-10 minutes or until light brown.

Christmas Cherries
Phyllis Hadley
Inverness, FL
Charm

Makes 3-4 dozen

1/2 cup butter or
　　margarine
1/4 cup sugar
1 egg yolk
1/2 tsp. vanilla
1 Tbsp. grated orange
　　peel
1 1/2 tsp. grated lemon
　　peel
1 Tbsp. lemon juice
1 cup cake flour
1 egg white, beaten
1/2 cup chopped nuts
6 candied cherries,
　　chopped

1. Cream together butter and sugar. Add egg yolk, vanilla, orange peel, lemon peel, lemon juice, and cake flour. Mix well.
2. Drop by teaspoonfuls onto lightly greased cookie sheet. Brush with egg white, sprinkle with chopped nuts, and top with small piece of cherry.
3. Bake at 350° for 10 minutes.

Cranberry Drop Cookies
Lois Stoltzfus
Honey Brook, PA
Colonial Star
Shan D. Lear
Middleton, MA
Cake Stand

Makes 6 dozen

1/2 cup butter
1 cup sugar
3/4 cup brown sugar
1/4 cup milk
2 Tbsp. orange juice
1 egg
2 1/3 cups flour
1 tsp. baking powder
1/4 tsp. baking soda
1/2 tsp. salt
1 cup chopped nuts
2 1/2 cups coarsely
  chopped cranberries

1. Cream together butter and sugars. Add milk, orange juice, and egg and mix well.
2. Mix together flour, baking powder, baking soda, and salt. Stir into creamed mixture. Mix well. Stir in nuts and cranberries.
3. Drop by teaspoonfuls onto greased baking sheet.
4. Bake at 375° for 10-12 minutes. Store in refrigerator.

Hannukah Apricot Cookies
Patty Arnold
Medina, NY
Cats Cradle

Makes 4 dozen

2 2/3 cups flour
1 cup butter
8-oz. pkg. cream cheese, softened
4-ozs. apricot preserves

1. Cut butter into flour. Stir in softened cream cheese.
2. On floured board roll out dough to 1/4" thickness. Cut with 2-3" diameter glass. Arrange on ungreased cookie sheet. Dab center of each cookie with apricot preserves.
3. Bake at 350° for 12 minutes.

Pumpkin Cookies
Shirley Odell
Manteca, CA
Dresden Plate

Makes 4-5 dozen

Cookie Dough:
1 cup brown sugar
1/4 cup cooking oil
1 cup mashed pumpkin
1 tsp. vanilla
2 cups flour
1 tsp. cinnamon
1/2 tsp. nutmeg
1/4 tsp. ginger
1/2 tsp. salt
1 tsp. baking soda

1 tsp. baking powder
1/2 cup chopped nuts

Frosting:
3 Tbsp. margarine
3 Tbsp. milk
1/2 cup brown sugar
1/2 tsp. vanilla
1 cup powdered sugar

1. To prepare cookie dough, cream together sugar, oil, pumpkin, and vanilla.
2. Mix together flour, cinnamon, nutmeg, ginger, salt, baking soda, baking powder, and nuts. Stir into creamed mixture and mix well. Drop onto greased cookie sheet.
3. Bake at 400° for 8-10 minutes. Cool before frosting.
4. To prepare frosting mix together margarine, milk, and brown sugar. Boil for 2 minutes until mixture coats a spoon. Remove from heat and stir in vanilla and powdered sugar. Cool and chill frosting.

Spirited Raisin Cookies

Barbara Hooley
Shipshewana, IN
Victorian Elegance

Makes 2-3 dozen

1 cup raisins
1/2 cup rum or 3 Tbsp.
   rum extract in 1/2 cup
   warm water
1 cup butter, softened
1/2 cup powdered sugar,
   sifted
2 cups flour
1/4 tsp. salt
1/4 tsp. baking powder

1. In saucepan combine raisins and rum and bring to a boil. Remove from heat. Cover and let stand for 30 minutes. Drain.
2. Cream together butter and sugar.
3. Sift together flour, salt, and baking powder. Gradually add to creamed mixture. Add raisins and mix well.
4. On floured board roll out dough to 1/2" thickness. Cut with cookie cutters.
5. Bake at 375° for 20 minutes.

Date Pinwheels

Rita I. Friesen
Paoli, IN
Rosebud

Makes 4-6 dozen

Pinwheel Dough:
1/2 cup butter, softened
1/2 cup light brown sugar
1/2 cup white sugar
1/2 tsp. vanilla
1 egg
2 cups flour
1/8 tsp. salt
1/4 tsp. baking soda

Filling:
8-oz. pkg. dates, finely
   chopped
1/4 cup white sugar
dash salt
1/3 cup water
1 cup finely chopped
   nuts

1. Cream together butter and sugars. Add vanilla and egg and beat until light and fluffy.
2. Sift together flour, salt, and baking soda. Add to creamed ingredients and mix well. Chill until firm, about 1 1/2 hours.
3. Meanwhile, prepare filling by combining dates, sugar, salt, and water in a saucepan. Bring to a boil, reduce heat, and simmer about 5 minutes, stirring often. Remove from heat, fold in nuts, and set aside to cool.
4. When dough is firm, divide in half. Roll each half onto a floured piece of

waxed paper to 9" x 12" rectangle. Spread 1/2 of filling over each half of dough. Roll tightly from one end. Wrap and chill overnight.
5. Slice into 1/8" pieces and bake on lightly greased cookie sheets at 375° for 10 minutes. Store in airtight container.

Variation: Substitute 1/2 tsp. cinnamon for vanilla. Proceed as above.

Shirley Sears
Tiskilwa, IL
Autumn Glory

Rainbow Walnut Slices

Shirley Taylor
Yuba City, CA

Makes 5-6 dozen

1/2 cup shortening
1/2 cup butter
1 3/4 cups sugar
2 eggs
2 tsp. vanilla
3 cups flour
1 1/4 tsp. salt
1/2 tsp. baking powder
red and green food
   coloring
1/4 cup chopped, candied
   red cherries
1 1/2 cups chopped
   walnuts
1 oz. unsweetened
   chocolate, melted
2 Tbsp. finely chopped,
   candied ginger
   (optional)
1/4 cup chopped, candied
   green cherries

1. Cream together shortening, butter, sugar, eggs, and vanilla.
2. Sift together flour, salt, and baking powder. Combine with creamed mixture and mix well. Divide dough into thirds.
3. Tint 1/3 of dough pink with red food coloring. Blend in red cherries and 1/2 cup walnuts. Pack into an even layer in lined loaf pan.
4. Blend melted chocolate, 1/2 cup nuts, and ginger into another 1/3 of dough. Pack on top of pink dough.
5. Tint remaining 1/3 of dough light green and add 1/2 cup nuts and green cherries. Pack into pan on top of chocolate dough. Cover pan and chill in freezer.
6. Cut frozen dough into thin slices and cut each slice in half. Place on greased cookie sheets.
7. Bake at 350° for 8-10 minutes. Do not brown.

Note: This dough will keep indefinitely in freezer. It is important to slice dough while still frozen.

Nut Cookies
Theresa Leppert
Schellsburg, PA
Grandmother's Flower Garden

Makes 8 dozen

1 lb. margarine
4 cups flour
4 eggs
1/8 tsp. salt
sugar for coating
1 lb. ground walnuts
3/4 cup sugar
1 Tbsp. butter
1/4 cup hot milk

1. Mix together margarine, flour, eggs, and salt. Form into walnut-sized pieces of dough and roll in sugar. Flatten.
2. Mix together walnuts, 3/4 cup sugar, butter, and enough milk to make it hold together. Fill middle of dough with a teaspoon of filling. Fold both ends of dough over filling. Place seam side down on cookie sheet.
3. Bake at 375° for 20-25 minutes.

Pecan Delights
Irene P. Dietlin
Winsted, CT
Pineapple Madness

Makes 6-8 dozen

1 cup butter
1/2 cup sugar
1 Tbsp. water
1 tsp. vanilla
2 cups flour
2 cups chopped pecans
sugar to coat

1. Cream together butter and 1/2 cup sugar until light and fluffy. Blend in water and vanilla. Stir in flour and pecans and mix well.
2. Flour hands, break off pieces of dough, and shape like dates. Place one inch apart on ungreased cookie sheet.
3. Bake at 325° for 25-30 minutes until very light brown. While still warm, roll cookies in sugar and place on rack to cool.

Teatime Pecan Tassies

Shirley Sears
Tiskilwa, IL
Karen Ferebee
Hastings, NE
Anne Townsend
Albuquerque, NM

Makes 4 dozen

Crust:
2 3-oz. pkgs. cream
    cheese, room
    temperature
1 cup butter or
    margarine, room
    temperature
2 cups flour

Filling:
4 eggs
1 lb. brown sugar
4 Tbsp. soft butter
1 tsp. vanilla
1/4 tsp. salt
2 cups chopped pecans

1. Blend together cream cheese and butter. Stir in flour. Chill about 1 hour.
2. Shape cookie crust into 4 dozen 1" balls. Place in tiny ungreased 1 3/4" muffin tins. Press dough on bottom and up the sides of each muffin tin, using a small wooden mallet.
3. To prepare filling beat together eggs, brown sugar, butter, vanilla, and salt until smooth. Blend in 1/2 cup pecans. Divide mixture evenly among pastry-lined muffin tins. Top with remaining 1/2 cup pecans.
4. Bake at 325° for 25 min-

utes. Cool before removing from muffin tins.

Tea Cakes

Violette Harris Denney
Carrollton, GA
Birds of Paradise

Makes 2-3 dozen

2 cups margarine
2 Tbsp. shortening
2 cups sugar
2 eggs
1 tsp. baking soda
1 tsp. salt
2 tsp. vanilla
5 1/2 cups flour

1. Cream together margarine, shortening, and sugar. Add eggs and mix well. Stir in baking soda, salt, and vanilla. Mix well. Gradually add flour, kneading until it is firm enough to roll.
2. On lightly floured surface, roll out dough to 1/4" thickness. Cut with floured cookie cutters. Place on greased cookie sheet.
3. Bake at 325° for 15-20 minutes or until brown on edges.

Coconut Cookies

Lola Kennel
Strange, NE
Log Cabin Star

Makes 6 dozen

1 cup white sugar
1 cup brown sugar
1 cup margarine
2 eggs, slightly beaten
1 cup coconut
3 cups oatmeal
2 cups flour
1 tsp. baking powder
1 tsp. baking soda
1 tsp. vanilla

1. Cream together sugars, margarine, and eggs. Stir in all remaining ingredients and mix well.
2. Roll mixture into small balls and flatten with spoon. (Mixture will be dry.)
3. Bake at 375° for 8-10 minutes.

Thumbprints

Carolyn Shank
Dayton, VA
Laurie Rott
Fargo, ND
Geraldine A. Ebersole
Hershey, PA

Makes 8 dozen

1 cup margarine,
    softened
1 cup butter, softened
1 cup brown sugar
4 egg yolks
2 tsp. vanilla

4 cups flour
1 tsp. salt
4 egg whites, slightly
  beaten
3 cups finely chopped
  pecans

1. Mix together margarine, butter, brown sugar, egg yolks, and vanilla thoroughly.
2. Stir in flour and salt. Roll dough into 1" balls. Dip balls in egg whites and roll in pecans. Place on ungreased cookie sheet.
3. Bake at 350° for 5 minutes. Remove from oven and quickly press thumb gently on top of each cookie. Return to oven and bake 8-10 minutes more until done. Cool.
4. Fill thumbprint with candied fruit, jelly, or frosting.

Note: At Christmas time fill the thumbprint with vanilla frosting and a red or green M&M.

Pistachio Thumbprints
Rhondalee Schmidt
Scranton, PA
Three Little Pumpkins

Makes 3-4 dozen

Cookie Dough:
1/3 cup powdered sugar
1 cup margarine or
  butter, softened
1 tsp. vanilla
3/4 tsp. almond extract
1 small pkg. instant
  pistachio pudding
1 egg
2 cups flour
1/2 cup miniature semi-
  sweet chocolate chips
1 1/4 cups finely chopped
  walnuts

Filling:
1 1/2 cups powdered sugar
2 Tbsp. margarine or
  butter, softened
1 tsp. vanilla
1-3 Tbsp. milk

Glaze:
2 tsp. shortening
1/2 cup miniature semi-
  sweet chocolate chips

1. Cream together powdered sugar, margarine, vanilla, almond extract, pudding mix, and egg until well blended.
2. Stir in flour and chocolate chips. Mix well. Shape into 1" balls and roll into walnuts. Place 2 inches apart on cookie sheets. Make imprint in center of each cookie with thumb.
3. Bake at 350° for 10-14 minutes or until light golden brown. Cool 1 minute before removing from cookie sheets.
4. Combine all filling ingredients until smooth. Spoon scant teaspoonful of filling on center of each cookie.
5. To prepare glaze combine chocolate chips and shortening in a saucepan. Heat, stirring constantly until dissolved. Drizzle about 1/2 tsp. glaze over each filled cookie. Allow filling and glaze to set before storing cookies.

Many New Mexico cities, towns, and pueblos are truly wondrous places at Christmas time. Each pueblo has its own religious festival, revolving aroung customs that go back hundreds of years. Often the public is invited to observe the ceremonies and to share in the hospitality of its residents.

Old Town Albuquerque holds a walk-along sing-along called La Posada (The Pilgrimage). Mary and Joseph lead the procession through this beautiful section of the city, stopping at various homes and asking for shelter. They are welcomed at a pre-planned location where there is music and food for the walkers. Luminarias light the streets and sidewalks.
—*Joan Lemmler, Albuquerque, NM*

Bird's Nest Cookies

Esther Lantz
Leola, PA
Broken Star
Patricia Andreas
Wausau, WI
Ohio Star Table Runner

Makes 3-4 servings

1 cup butter
1 cup sugar
1 tsp. vanilla
1/2 tsp. salt
2 egg yolks
2 1/2 cups flour
2 egg whites
chopped nuts
red or green jelly

1. Cream together butter, sugar, vanilla, and salt. Add egg yolks and flour. Mix well.
2. Form into 1" balls. Dip in slightly beaten egg whites, then roll in nuts. Place on greased cookie sheet.
3. Push thumb into center of each cookie. Fill with red or green jelly.
4. Bake at 375° for 8-10 minutes or until light brown.

Split Seconds

Mary Ann Potenta
Bridgewater, NJ
Double Irish Chain

Makes 3-4 dozen

2/3 cup sugar
3/4 cup butter, softened
2 tsp. vanilla
1 egg
2 cups flour
1/2 tsp. baking powder
1/2-1 cup red or green preserves

1. Cream together sugar and butter. Add vanilla and egg and mix well.
2. Mix together flour and baking powder. Stir into creamed mixture. Mix well.
3. Divide dough into 4 pieces. Roll each piece out to a 3/4" x 12" rectangle. Place the four 12" rectangles on ungreased cookie sheet. Make indentations on each rectangle 1/4" deep and 1/2" apart. Fill each indentation with preserves.
4. Bake at 350° for 15-20 minutes. While still warm, cut the four large cookie rectangles apart into individual cookies. Cut on the diagonal with preserves in middle of each cookie.

Butterfly Cookies

Barbara Hummel
Punxsutawney, PA
Challenge Quilt

Makes 2-3 dozen

1 3/4 cups flour
1 cup butter, chilled
1/2 cup sour cream
1 tsp. grated lemon peel
10-12 Tbsp. sugar

1. Cut butter into flour with pastry blender until mixture resembles coarse crumbs. Stir in sour cream and lemon peel until blended. Mold dough into a 4 1/2" square. Wrap and chill for at least 2 hours.
2. Cut dough into 4 pieces. Work with one piece at a time and keep remaining dough in the refrigerator.
3. Sprinkle 2 Tbsp. sugar on work surface. Coat cookie dough piece with sugar. On sugared surface roll out, turning often, into a 5" x 12" rectangle. On the 12" side, score dough down the center. (Do not cut through.) From the 5" side, roll up jelly roll fashion toward center. Wrap and place in freezer for 20 minutes. Repeat with remaining dough and sugar.
4. Place 1/4 cup sugar on waxed paper. Cut each roll of dough into 1/2" slices and dip slices into sugar. Place on baking sheet, 2" apart.
5. Bake at 375° for 15 minutes until golden. Turn and bake 5 minutes more. Cool on wire rack.

Poinsettias
Inez E. Dillon
Tucson, AZ
Crazy Quilt

Makes 4-5 dozen

1/2 **cup shortening,**
   softened
1 **cup sugar**
2 **eggs**
2 **Tbsp. thick cream**
1 **tsp. vanilla**
2 1/2 **cups flour**
1/4 **tsp. baking soda**
1/2 **tsp. salt**
2-3 **drops yellow food**
   coloring
2-3 **drops red food**
   coloring
3/4-1 **cup mincemeat**

1. Cream together shortening, sugar, and eggs. Stir in cream and vanilla and mix well.
2. Sift together flour, baking soda, and salt. Stir into creamed mixture. Mix well.
3. Reserve a small amount of dough and color with yellow food coloring. Color remaining dough with red food coloring. Chill dough.
4. Roll out chilled red dough to 1/8" thickness and cut into 3" squares. Place on lightly greased baking sheet. With a sharp knife, cut from the corners of each square almost to the center, making 4 triangular sections in each square. Place 1 tsp. of mincemeat in center. Pick up and fold the point of each triangle over the center filling. Press gently

in center to hold 4 points together.
5. Using reserved yellow dough, roll small balls and flatten. Place small piece of flattened yellow dough in center of each poinsettia.
5. Bake at 400° for 8-10 minutes.

Spellbinders
Cheryl P. Owens
Hattiesburg, MS
The Heart Quilt

Makes 4 dozen

Cookie Dough:
1 **cup butter or**
   margarine, softened
1 **cup firmly packed**
   brown sugar
1 **egg**
1 1/2 **cups self-rising flour**
1 **cup quick oats**
1 **cup shredded coconut**
1/2-1 **cup chopped pecans**
1/2 **cup crushed bran**
   flakes

Frosting:
1 **Tbsp. margarine,**
   melted
1 **cup powdered sugar**
1 **tsp. vanilla**
hot water

1. Cream together butter and brown sugar. Beat in egg.
2. Add flour gradually, mixing well. Stir in oats, coconut, pecans, and bran flakes.
3. Drop by teaspoonfuls onto ungreased cookie sheet.

4. Bake at 350° for 10-12 minutes or until light brown. Cool.
5. To prepare frosting mix together margarine, powdered sugar, and vanilla. Add hot water until you have desired consistency for drizzling frosting on cookies.

Cinnamon Snowballs
Charlotte Shaffer
Ephrata, PA
Irish Chain

Makes 4 dozen

1 **cup margarine**
1 1/4 **cups powdered sugar**
1 1/2 **cups flour**
1/4 **tsp. salt**
1/2 **tsp. cinnamon**
3/4 **cup quick oats**
1 **Tbsp. vanilla**
3/4 **cup ground walnuts**
3/4 **cup ground pecans**

1. Beat margarine until creamy.
2. Sift together 3/4 cup powdered sugar, flour, salt, and cinnamon. Gradually add to margarine, beating well.
3. Stir in oats, vanilla, walnuts, and pecans. Mix well. Shape to form small balls and place on ungreased cookie sheets.
4. Bake at 350° for 25 minutes.
5. Remove cookies from sheets while hot. Using reserved 1/2 cup, sprinkle with powdered sugar. Cool and sprinkle again.

Katelyn's Chocolate Chip Cookies
Katelyn Potenta
Oxford, NJ
Trevor's Nine Patch

Makes 3¹/2 dozen

1 cup firmly packed dark
   brown sugar
¹/2 cup white sugar
1 cup butter, softened
2 large eggs
2 tsp. vanilla
2¹/2 cups flour
¹/2 tsp. baking soda
¹/4 tsp. salt
2 cups semi-sweet
   chocolate chips

1. Cream together sugars
and butter. Stir in eggs and
vanilla. Mix well, but do not
over mix.
2. Combine flour, baking
soda, and salt. Mix into
creamed mixture. Stir in
chocolate chips.
3. Drop by rounded table-
spoonfuls onto an ungreased
cookie sheet, 2" apart.
4. Bake at 300° for 22-24
minutes or until golden
brown. Transfer cookies to
cool surface with spatula
immediately.

Giant Chocolate Chip Cookies
Nancy Vance
Carterville, IL
Scrap Quilt

Makes 1¹/2-2 dozen

1 cup butter, softened
1¹/2 cups sugar
1 egg
1 tsp. vanilla
2 cups flour
1 tsp. baking soda
dash salt
12-oz. pkg. chocolate
   chips
1 cup chopped nuts

1. Cream butter until fluffy.
Gradually beat in sugar
until light. Beat in egg and
vanilla.
2. Mix together flour, baking soda, and salt. Stir into
creamed mixture. Mix well.
Stir in chocolate chips and
nuts.
3. Shape dough into large 2"
balls (makes a 4" cookie).
Place 3" apart on ungreased
cookie sheet.
4. Bake in middle rack at
350° for 20-24 minutes.
Cool on cookie sheet.

*Note: Put five or six of these
cookies together, wrap them
in cellophane wrap, and tie a
ribbon around them. They
make wonderful gifts for co-
workers or other special people.*

Fudgy Cookies
Sharleen White
Arnold, MD
Quilted Christening Coat

Makes 2-3 dozen

12-oz. pkg. chocolate
   chips
2 Tbsp. butter
14-oz. can sweetened
   condensed milk
1 cup flour
1 tsp. vanilla
¹/2 cup chopped walnuts

1. In saucepan over low
heat, mix together chocolate
chips, butter, and condensed
milk until melted and
smooth. Stir in flour,
vanilla, and walnuts.
Remove from heat.
2. Drop by teaspoonfuls on
greased cookie sheet.
3. Bake at 325° for 10-12
minutes.

Fudge Puddles
Rebecca Meyerkorth
Wamego, KS
Challenge Quilt

Makes 4 dozen cookies

Cookie Dough:
1/2 cup butter or
   margarine, softened
1/2 cup creamy peanut
   butter
1/2 cup white sugar
1/2 cup light brown sugar
1 egg
1 tsp. vanilla
11/4 cups flour
3/4 tsp. baking soda
1/2 tsp. salt

Fudge Filling:
6-oz. pkg. milk chocolate
   chips
6-oz. pkg. semi-sweet
   chocolate chips
14-oz. can sweetened
   condensed milk
1 tsp. vanilla extract
1 cup chopped nuts

1. Cream together butter,
peanut butter, and sugars.
Add egg and vanilla. Mix
well.
2. Stir together flour, baking
soda, and salt. Add to
creamed ingredients and
mix well. Chill for 1 hour.
3. Shape into 48 1" balls.
Place in lightly greased
mini-muffin tins.
4. Bake at 325° for 14-16
minutes or until lightly
brown. Remove from oven
and immediately make
wells in center by pressing
lightly with a melon baller.

Cool in pans for 5 minutes,
then carefully remove to
wire racks.
5. For filling melt chocolate
chips in double boiler over
simmering water. Stir in
milk and vanilla. Mix well.
Using a small pitcher or
pastry bag, fill each shell
with chocolate. Sprinkle
with nuts.

Mocha Truffle Cookies
Sharon Easter
Yuba City, CA

Makes 21/2 dozen

1/2 cup margarine or
   butter
1/2 cup chocolate chips
1 Tbsp. instant coffee
   granules
3/4 cup sugar
3/4 cup packed brown
   sugar
2 eggs
2 tsp. vanilla
2 cups flour
1/3 cup cocoa
1/2 tsp. baking powder
1/4 tsp. salt
1 cup chocolate chips

1. In large saucepan melt
margarine and chocolate
chips over low heat.
Remove from heat and stir
in coffee granules. Cool 5
minutes. Stir in sugars,
eggs, and vanilla.
2. Combine flour, cocoa,
baking powder, and salt. Stir
into coffee mixture. Add
chocolate chips and stir.

3. Drop by rounded table-
spoonfuls onto lightly
greased cookie sheet.
4. Bake at 350° for 10 minutes. Let cool 1 minute
before removing from sheet.

Chipped Meringue Cookies
Lois Mae E. Kuh
Penfield, NY

Makes 3 dozen

2 egg whites
1/2 cup sugar
1 tsp. vanilla
1 cup chopped nuts
1 cup chocolate chips

1. Preheat oven to 400°.
2. Beat egg whites until stiff
peaks form. Gradually add
sugar and continue beating.
Add vanilla. Stir in nuts and
chocolate chips.
3. Drop by teaspoonfuls
onto foil-lined cookie sheet.
4. Place in oven and turn
off oven. Check in two
hours. Cookie should be dry
and ready to eat.

Chewy Chocolate Cookies
Christine Heuser
Farmingdale, NJ
Double Wedding Ring

Makes 4 dozen

1¹/4 cups butter, softened
2 cups sugar
2 eggs
2 tsp. vanilla
2 cups flour
³/4 cup cocoa
1 tsp. baking soda
¹/2 tsp. salt

1. Cream together butter and sugar. Add eggs and vanilla. Blend well.
2. Stir in flour, cocoa, baking soda, and salt. Mix well.
3. Drop by teaspoonfuls onto lightly greased cookie sheet.
4. Bake at 350° for 8-9 minutes.

Chocolate Crinkles
Mary Jane Musser
Manheim, PA
Friendship Quilt

Makes 5 dozen cookies

¹/2 cup vegetable oil
4-ozs. unsweetened chocolate, melted
2 cups sugar
4 eggs
2 tsp. vanilla
2 cups flour
2 tsp. baking powder
¹/2 tsp. salt
1 cup powdered sugar

1. Mix together oil, chocolate, and sugar. Blend in eggs until well mixed. Add vanilla.
2. Stir together flour, baking powder, and salt. Add to chocolate mixture. Chill dough for several hours.
3. Drop by teaspoonfuls into powdered sugar. Roll in sugar and roll into balls. Place balls 2" apart on greased baking sheet.
4. Bake at 350° for 10 minutes.

Caramel-Filled Chocolate Cookies
Bobbie Jean Weidner
Muscarella
State College, PA
State College Centennial Quilt
Jo Haberkamp
Fairbank, IA
Card Tricks

Makes 4-5 dozen

1 cup white sugar
1 cup packed brown sugar
1 cup butter, softened
2 tsp. vanilla
2 eggs
2¹/2 cups flour
³/4 cup cocoa
1 tsp. baking soda
1 cup pecans
48-60 Rolo candies
1 Tbsp. sugar

1. Cream together 1 cup white sugar, 1 cup brown sugar, and butter until light and fluffy. Add vanilla and eggs and mix well.
2. Sift together flour, cocoa, and baking soda. Add to creamed ingredients and mix well. Blend in ¹/2 cup pecans.
3. Shape about a tablespoon of dough around each Rolo candy.
4. In small bowl combine remaining ¹/2 cup pecans with 1 Tbsp. sugar. Press one side of each ball in pecan mixture. Place nut side up on ungreased cookie sheet.
5. Bake at 375° for 7-10 minutes. Cool 2 minutes before removing from cookie sheet. Cool on wire racks.

Chocolate Peppermint Rounds
Phyllis Hadley
Inverness, FL
Charm

Makes 2¹/2 dozen

Cookie Dough:
1/2 cup butter
1 cup sugar
1 egg, beaten well
3 ozs. chocolate, melted
2¹/3 cups flour
2 tsp. baking powder
1/4 tsp. salt
1/4 cup evaporated milk.

Peppermint Frosting:
1 cup powdered sugar
milk
1-2 drops peppermint
  extract
1 drop green food
  coloring

1. Cream together butter and sugar. Add egg and beat well. Stir in chocolate.
2. Sift together flour, baking powder, and salt. Add alternately with evaporated milk to creamed ingredients and mix well. Form into long roll. Chill.
3. Slice into thin pieces and place on greased cookie sheet.
4. Bake at 400° for 5-8 minutes. Cool.
5. To prepare frosting mix together powdered sugar and milk until desired consistency. Stir in peppermint extract and green food coloring.

6. Fill cookies with frosting to make cookie sandwiches.

Chocolate Sandwich Cookies
Anna Oberholtzer
Lititz, PA
Improved Nine Patch

Makes 4-5 dozen

Cookie Dough:
4 cups brown sugar
1 cup margarine
3/4 cup cocoa
4 eggs, beaten
1 tsp. baking soda
1 Tbsp. water
4 cups flour

Frosting:
3 cups powdered sugar
1/2 cup shortening
1 tsp. vanilla
milk

1. Cream together brown sugar and margarine. Add cocoa and mix well. Stir in eggs.
2. Mix together baking soda and water. Add to creamed mixture. Stir in flour. Mix well. Shape into log and chill for at least 8 hours.
3. Slice very thin and place on cookie sheet.
4. Bake at 350° for 8-10 minutes. Cool.
5. To prepare frosting beat together powdered sugar, shortening, and vanilla. Add milk gradually until fluffy and desired consistency.
6. Fill cookies with frosting to make cookie sandwiches.

Butterscotch Chip Cookies
Janie Steele
Moore, OK
Sunbonnet Sue

Makes 5-6 dozen

1 cup white sugar
1 cup brown sugar
1 cup margarine
1 cup cooking oil
1 egg
1 tsp. vanilla
3 cups flour
1/4 tsp. salt
1 tsp. baking soda
1 cup quick oats
1 cup cornflakes
1/2 cup coconut (optional)
1/2 cup chopped nuts
16-oz. pkg. butterscotch
  chips

1. Cream together sugars, margarine, and oil. Add egg and vanilla and mix well.
2. Mix together flour, salt, and baking soda. Add to creamed mixture and mix well.
3. Add oats, cornflakes, coconut, nuts, and butterscotch chips. Mix well.
4. Roll into balls and place 1" apart on greased cookie sheet.
5. Bake at 350° for 8-10 minutes or until light golden brown.

Peanut Butter Cup Cookies
Julie McKenzie
Punxsutawney, PA
Floral Applique

Makes 3 dozen

1 egg, beaten
1 cup sugar
1 cup peanut butter
14-oz. pkg. miniature
    peanut butter cups

1. Mix together egg and sugar. Stir in peanut butter. Drop by teaspoonfuls into greased miniature muffin tins.
2. Bake cookies at 350° for 10 minutes. (The tips of the rough edges will just be starting to brown when cookie is done.)
3. Immediately upon removing cookies from oven, push a peanut butter cup into each cookie. Let cool completely before removing from muffin tins.

Peanut Butter and Jelly Posies
Tracy Supcoe
Barclay, MD
Patience Corner

Makes 3 dozen

1/2 cup margarine or
    butter
1/2 cup peanut butter
1/3 cup white sugar
1/3 cup packed brown
    sugar
3 Tbsp. orange juice
1 1/2 cups flour
1/2 tsp. baking powder
1/2 tsp. baking soda
1/4 tsp. salt
red and/or green jelly

1. Cream together margarine and peanut butter. Add sugars and beat until fluffy. Add orange juice. Mix well.
2. Stir together flour, baking powder, baking soda, and salt. Gradually add to creamed mixture, beating until well mixed.
3. Shape dough into 1" balls. Place 1" apart on ungreased cookie sheet. Press down the center of each ball with thumb.
4. Bake at 350° for 8-10 minutes or until golden. Cool on cookie sheet for 2 minutes. Remove to wire rack and cool completely.
5. Spoon about 1/4 tsp. jelly into center of each cookie.

Peanut Whirls
M. Jeanne Osborne
Wells, ME
Snail's Trail

Makes 3 dozen

1/2 cup shortening
1/2 cup peanut butter
1 cup sugar
1 egg
1 tsp. vanilla
1 1/4 cups flour
1/2 tsp. baking soda
1/2 tsp. salt
2 Tbsp. milk
6-oz. pkg. chocolate chips

1. Beat together shortening, peanut butter, and sugar. Add egg and vanilla.
2. Sift together flour, baking soda, and salt. Add to creamed mixture. Add milk and beat well.
3. Turn onto lightly floured board. Roll out to 1/4" inch thickness.
4. Melt chocolate chips in double boiler over hot water and cool slightly. Spread onto rolled out cookie dough. Roll up like a jelly roll. Chill for 1/2 hour.
5. Cut into 1/4" slices. Place slices on baking sheet.
6. Bake at 350° for 10 minutes.

Old-Fashioned Butter Cookies

Geri Sherwood
Schererville, IN
Family Album

Makes 5 dozen

Cookie Dough:
3 cups flour
1 tsp. baking powder
1/2 tsp. salt
1 cup butter
3/4 cup sugar
1 egg
2 Tbsp. cream or milk
11/2 tsp. vanilla extract

Frosting:
2 Tbsp. butter
1/2 tsp. vanilla
13/4 cups powdered sugar
4 Tbsp. milk

1. Sift together flour, baking powder, and salt.
2. Cream butter. Gradually add sugar and cream well.
3. Stir in egg, cream, and vanilla. Add dry ingredients gradually and mix well. Chill in refrigerator.
4. Divide dough into three parts. Roll out onto floured surface to 1/4" thickness. Cut with cookie cutters. Place on ungreased cookie sheet.
5. Bake at 400° for 5-8 minutes until delicately brown.
6. To prepare frosting cream together butter, vanilla, and powdered sugar. Add milk and beat until light and fluffy. Frost each cookie and store in airtight container.

Half Moon Cookies

Doris H. Perkins
Mashpee, MA
Card Tricks

Makes 3 dozen

3/4 cup margarine or butter
11/2 cups sugar
2 eggs, well beaten
1 tsp. vanilla
3 cups flour
1 tsp. baking powder
1 tsp. baking soda
1/2 tsp. salt
1 cup sour milk

1. Cream together margarine and sugar until fluffy. Stir in eggs and vanilla.
2. Sift together flour, baking powder, baking soda, and salt. Add alternately with sour milk to creamed mixture. Mix well.
3. Drop by tablespoonfuls far apart on lightly greased cookie sheet.
4. Bake at 375° for 10-12 minutes. Cool on rack.
5. Frost flat side of each cookie with favorite vanilla and chocolate frostings. Frost 1/2 of cookie with vanilla and 1/2 with chocolate to create the half moon look.

I grew up on the typical American holiday fare, turkey and stuffing for Thanksgiving and ham or turkey with all the trimmings for Christmas. When I married a military man from Michigan, I thought our holiday food traditions would probably continue to the next generation. But on our first Christmas together, we were stationed in Korea. Our apartment had no oven, and the commissary had no turkeys. So we ate at a hotel restaurant and dined on smoked salmon and caviar. Our next assignment was in Hawaii where we enjoyed a pork luau for our Christmas meal.

By the time we had moved to Charlottesville, Virginia, we had two children and decided to establish some of our own family traditions. We had received a gourmet recipe book as a wedding gift and in looking through that decided on Peking duck for Christmas. It was an incredible amount of work, and we soon decided to leave that tradition to others. In the ten years since, we have made Peking duck only one more time.

—*Dianna Milhizer, Springfield, VA*

Great-Grandmother Haines Molasses Cookies

Joy Reistle
Mickleton, NJ
Grandmother's Fan

Makes 3 dozen large cookies

1 cup sugar
1 scant cup shortening
1 cup molasses
2 eggs
2 cups flour
1 tsp. salt
1 tsp. ginger
1 tsp. cinnamon
2 1/2 cups flour
1 1/2 tsp. baking powder

1. Cream together sugar and shortening. Add molasses, eggs, and 2 cups flour. Mix well.
2. Stir in salt, ginger, cinnamon, and 1 cup flour. Add baking powder and remaining 1 1/2 cups flour. Mix well. Chill for several hours or overnight
3. Roll golf ball-sized balls and place on lightly greased cookie sheet 2" apart. Flatten with floured spatula.
4. Bake at 400° for 6-8 minutes or until done.

Molasses Spice Cutouts

Gloria R. Yoder
Dundee, OH

Makes 7-8 dozen

Cookie Dough:
1 cup butter or margarine, softened
1 1/2 cups sugar
1 cup light molasses
1/2 cup cold prepared coffee
6 cups flour
2 tsp. baking soda
1 tsp. salt
1/2 tsp. ground nutmeg
1/4 tsp. ground cloves

Frosting:
1 pkg. unflavored gelatin
3/4 cup cold water
3/4 cup sugar
3/4 cup powdered sugar
3/4 tsp. baking powder
1/2 tsp. vanilla
colored sugar or nonpareils

1. Cream together butter and sugar. Beat in molasses and coffee.
2. Stir together flour, baking soda, salt, nutmeg, and cloves. Add to molasses mixture and mix well. Chill dough for several hours or until easy to handle. If needed, add a little additional flour before rolling.
3. On lightly floured surface, roll out dough to 1/4" thickness. Cut with 2 1/2" cookie cutter dipped in flour. Place on ungreased baking sheets.
4. Bake at 350° for 12-15 minutes. Cool on wire racks.
5. To prepare frosting combine gelatin and water in saucepan. Let stand for 5 minutes to soften. Add sugar. Heat and stir over low heat until gelatin and sugar dissolve. Transfer to mixing bowl.
6. Stir in powdered sugar, beating until foamy. Add baking powder and vanilla and beat until very thick, about 10 minutes. Frost cookies by inverting them and quickly swirling the tops in the frosting. Decorate with colored sugar and nonpareils.

Variation: From cookie dough ingredients, omit coffee. Substitute 1 cup honey for the 1 cup molasses. Proceed as given.

Kathy Evenson
Fergus Falls, MN
Dresden Flower

Ginger Cookies
Cathy Kowalsky
Woodinville, WA
Christmas Sampler
Bonita Ensenberger
Albuquerque, NM
Snowflake

Makes 4-5 dozen

3/4 **cup butter-flavored**
  shortening
1 **cup sugar**
1/4 **cup dark molasses**
1 **egg**
2 **cups flour**
1/2 **tsp. salt**
2 **tsp. cinnamon**
1 **tsp. ground ginger**
1 **tsp. ground cloves**
2 **tsp. baking soda**
sugar

1. Cream together shortening, sugar, molasses, and egg.
2. Sift together flour, salt, cinnamon, ground ginger, ground cloves, and baking soda. Add to creamed mixture.
3. Shape into small balls and roll in bowl of sugar. Place on greased cookie sheet.
4. Bake at 350° for 10-12 minutes. Cool on sheet for 1 minute, then remove to cooling racks.

Note: To keep cookies soft, put several pieces of apple peel into storage container with cookies.

Variation: After step 2 above, chill dough for 15 minutes.

Roll out to 1/4" thickness. Cut out gingerbread boys and let the small children use raisins to create eyes, mouth, and buttons. Bake as directed, but be careful not to overbake. Makes 2-3 dozen gingerbread boys.

Joan Kowalsky
Shelton, WA
Trip Around the World
Martha Bender
New Paris, IN
Boston Common

Gingerbread Boys
Leona Cook
Falmouth, MA
Mariner's Compass

Makes 1 1/2-2 dozen

Cookie Dough:
2/3 **cup shortening**
1 **cup sugar**
1/4 **cup molasses**
1 **egg yolk**
2 **cups flour**
1/4 **tsp. salt**
1 **tsp. baking soda**
1 **tsp. cinnamon**
1 **tsp. ginger**
1 **tsp. ground cloves**
1/2 **tsp. nutmeg**
1 **tsp. vanilla**

Frosting:
1 1/4 **cups powdered sugar**
1/8 **tsp. cream of tartar**
1 **egg white**
1/4 **tsp vanilla**

1. Cream together shortening and sugar until fluffy. Add molasses and egg yolk and beat well.

2. Sift together flour, salt, baking soda, cinnamon, ginger, cloves, and nutmeg. Add to sugar and egg mixture. Add vanilla and beat well.
3. Chill for 15 minutes. Roll out to 1/4" thickness. Using floured gingerbread boy cutter, cut out cookies. Decorate with raisins for eyes, mouth, and buttons.
4. Bake at 350° for 10 minutes until set. Do not overbake.
5. To prepare frosting sift together powdered sugar and cream of tartar. Stir in egg white and vanilla. Beat at high speed until frosting holds its shape. Cover with damp cloth.
6. When gingerbread boys are cool, decorate with frosting.

Gingerbread Teddy Bear Cookies

Bobbie Jean Weidner
Muscarella
State College, PA
State College Centennial Quilt

Makes 2 dozen

1 cup butter or
  margarine
1 1/2 cups sugar
1 egg
4 tsp. grated orange peel
2 Tbsp. dark corn syrup
3 cups flour
2 tsp. baking soda
2 tsp. cinnamon
1 tsp. ginger
1/2 tsp. ground cloves
1/2 tsp. salt

1. Cream together butter and sugar. Add egg. Beat until light and fluffy.
2. Add orange peel and corn syrup. Mix well.
3. Sift together flour, baking soda, cinnamon, ginger, cloves, and salt. Stir into creamed mixture. Chill thoroughly.
4. On lightly floured surface, roll out to 1/4" thickness. Cut with teddy bear cookie cutter. Place 1" apart on ungreased pan.
5. Bake at 375° for 8-10 minutes. Decorate with frosting when cool.

Oatmeal Persimmon Cookies

Sharon Easter
Yuba City, CA

Makes 5-6 dozen cookies

1 cup shortening or
  margarine
1 cup brown sugar
1 cup white sugar
1 cup persimmon pulp
1 egg
1 tsp. salt
1 tsp. vanilla
2 cups flour
1 tsp. baking soda
1 tsp. cinnamon
1 cup chopped nuts
1 cup raisins
1 1/2 cups quick oats

1. Cream together shortening, sugars, persimmon pulp, egg, salt, and vanilla. Mix well.
2. Sift together flour, baking soda, and cinnamon. Stir into creamed mixture. Add nuts, raisins, and oats and mix well.
3. Drop by teaspoonfuls onto ungreased cookie sheet.
4. Bake at 350° for 18 minutes.

Self-Frosting Oatmeal Cookies

Lola Kennel
Strang, NE
Log Cabin Star

Makes 4-5 dozen

1 cup brown sugar
1 cup white sugar
1 cup cooking oil
1 tsp. vanilla
2 eggs
1 1/2 cups flour
1 tsp. salt
1/2 tsp. baking soda
1 tsp. baking powder
2 1/2 cups oatmeal
powdered sugar

1. Cream together sugars, oil, and vanilla. Add eggs and mix well.
2. Sift together flour, salt, baking soda, and baking powder. Add to creamed mixture. Stir in oatmeal.
3. Chill dough for 2 hours. Roll into walnut-sized balls and roll in powdered sugar. Place 2" apart on greased cookie sheet.
4. Bake at 350° for 8-10 minutes.

Oatmeal Lace Cookies
Karen Harer
Fort Hood, TX
Scrap Tulip Circle
Carol L. O'Neill
Reston, VA
Remembering Mrs. Johnson

Makes 4-5 dozen

1 cup butter
2¹/4 cups packed light brown sugar
1 Tbsp. sugar
2¹/4 cups old-fashioned oats
1 Tbsp. flour
1 large egg, slightly beaten
1 tsp. vanilla

1. In saucepan melt butter over low heat. Add both sugars, stirring constantly until sugar melts. Remove from heat. Stir in oats and flour. Stir in beaten egg and vanilla. Mix well. Refrigerate for 10 minutes.
2. Line cookie sheets with lightly greased aluminum foil. Drop scant tablespoonfuls batter onto 1 sheet, leaving plenty of space for the cookies to spread. Bake one sheet at a time.
3. Bake at 375° for 7 minutes, watching carefully, until cookies are a deep golden brown around the edges. Remove from oven and slide foil onto wire rack. Cool cookie sheet completely before adding next batch of cookies.
4. Cool cookies completely and peel aluminum foil off cooled cookies. Store cookies tightly covered with waxed paper between layers.

Delicious Oatmeal Cookies
Robin Schrock
Millersburg, OH
Irish Chain

Makes 3 dozen

Cookie Dough:
3 cups brown sugar
1¹/2 cups butter
3 eggs
1¹/4 tsp. vanilla
1¹/4 tsp. baking soda
1¹/4 tsp. baking powder
3/4 tsp. salt
2¹/4 cups flour
4¹/4 cups oatmeal

Filling:
2 egg whites
2 Tbsp. vanilla
1/4 cup milk
1 cup butter-flavored shortening
4-5 cups powdered sugar

1. Cream together sugar, butter, eggs, and vanilla.
2. Sift together baking soda, baking powder, salt, and flour. Add to creamed ingredients and mix well. Stir in oatmeal.
3. Form balls and roll in powdered sugar. Place on greased cookie sheet.
4. Bake at 350° for 10 minutes or until cookies are just starting to brown. Cool.

5. To prepare filling beat egg whites. Add vanilla, milk, and 2 cups powdered sugar. Beat thoroughly. Add shortening and remaining powdered sugar to achieve desired consistency, beating well after each addition.
6. Frost flat side of cookie to make oatmeal cookie sandwich.

Monster Cookies
Pat Wojciechowski
Lake Orion, MI
Take Your Pick

Makes 2-3 dozen

1/2 cup brown sugar
1/4 cup white sugar
1/2 cup margarine
1 cup peanut butter
3 eggs
2 tsp. vanilla
4¹/2 cups rolled oats
2 tsp. baking soda
4-ozs. chocolate chips
4-ozs. M&M candy
1/2 cup chopped walnuts

1. Cream together sugars, margarine, and peanut butter. Add eggs and vanilla. Beat well.
2. Mix together oats and baking soda. Add to creamed mixture. Stir in chocolate chips, candy, and walnuts. Mix thoroughly.
3. Drop by teaspoonfuls onto greased cookie sheet.
4. Bake at 350° for 10 minutes.

Sugar Cookies
Joyce Cox
Port Angeles, WA
Amish Star

Makes 4 dozen

1/2 cup butter
1/4 cup shortening
1 cup white sugar
2 eggs
1 tsp. vanilla
2 1/2 cups flour
1 tsp. baking powder
3/4 tsp. salt
1 1/2 cups powdered sugar

1. Mix together butter, shortening, sugar, eggs and vanilla.
2. Sift together flour, baking powder, and salt. Blend into creamed ingredients and mix well.
3. Chill dough for at least 1 hour.
4. Roll out to 1/8" thickness on board sprinkled with powdered sugar. Cut with 3" cookie cutter. Place on ungreased baking sheet.
5. Bake at 400° for 6-8 minutes or until cookies are golden color.
6. Sprinkle with powdered sugar while cooling.

My Favorite Sugar Cookies
Marie Fuller
Ashfield, MA
Jennifer's Cat Family
Claudia Keith Nelson
Columbia, MO
Grandmother's Flower Garden

Makes 3-4 dozen

1 1/2 cups powdered sugar
1 cup butter or margarine
1 egg
1/2 tsp. almond flavoring
1 tsp. vanilla
2 1/2 cups flour
1 tsp. baking soda
1 tsp. cream of tartar

1. Mix together sugar and butter. Add egg, almond flavoring, and vanilla and mix thoroughly.
2. Mix together flour, baking soda, and cream of tartar. Blend into creamed ingredients and mix well.
3. Refrigerate for 2 or 3 hours.
4. Divide dough in half and roll out to 1/4" thickness on lightly floured surface. Cut with cookie cutters and sprinkle lightly with additional powdered sugar. Place on lightly greased baking sheets.
5. Bake at 375° for 7 to 8 minutes or until delicately golden.

Grandma's Sugar Cookies
Cindy Dorzab
Fort Smith, AR
Flying Geese
Marlene Fonken
Upland, CA
Crazy Patch

Makes 8-9 dozen

1 cup margarine
1 cup shortening
1 cup sugar
1 cup powdered sugar
2 eggs
1 tsp. vanilla
1 tsp. baking soda
1 tsp. cream of tartar
4 cups sifted flour

1. Cream together margarine, shortening, sugar, and powdered sugar. Add eggs and vanilla. Stir in remaining ingredients and mix well. Chill dough for 15-20 minutes.
2. Roll dough into walnut-sized balls and place on greased cookie sheet. Flatten with bottom of damp glass. Sprinkle with colored sugar.
3. Bake at 375° for 12 minutes.

Molasses Sugar Cookies

Bobbie Jean Weidner
Muscarella
State College, PA
State College Centennial Quilt

Makes 3-4 dozen

3/4 cup shortening
1 cup sugar
1/4 cup molasses
1 egg
2 cups flour
2 tsp. baking soda
1/2 tsp. ground cloves
1/2 tsp. ground ginger
1 tsp. ground cinnamon
1/2 tsp. salt
1/2 cup sugar

1. Melt shortening in saucepan over low heat. Remove from heat. Cool.
2. Stir in 1 cup sugar, molasses, and egg. Mix well.
3. Sift together flour, baking soda, cloves, ginger, cinnamon, and salt. Stir into molasses mixture and mix well. Chill for at least one hour.
4. Form dough into 1" balls. Roll in sugar and place 2" apart on greased cookie sheets.
5. Bake at 375° for 8-10 minutes.

Chocolate Sugar Cookies

Stacy Petersheim
Mechanicsburg, PA

Makes 2-3 dozen

1/4 cup butter
1 cup sugar
2 eggs
1 cup flour
1 tsp. baking powder
1 tsp. vanilla
2 squares baking chocolate, melted
powdered sugar

1. Beat together butter and sugar. Add eggs.
2. Stir in flour and baking powder. Mix well. Stir in vanilla and chocolate.
3. Roll into small balls and coat with powdered sugar.
4. Bake at 350° for 8-10 minutes.

Brown Sugar Cookies

Katie Stoltzfus
Leola, PA
Log Cabin

Makes 9-10 dozen

Cookie Dough:
1 1/2 cups lard
2 cups brown sugar
2 eggs, beaten
5 cups flour
3/4 cup milk
3/4 cup evaporated milk
1 tsp. baking powder
2 tsp. baking soda
1 Tbsp. vanilla

Butter Frosting:
3 cups powdered sugar
1 heaping Tbsp. butter
milk

1. Cream together lard and brown sugar. Add eggs.
2. Alternately add flour and milk, mixing well. Stir in baking powder, baking soda, and vanilla.
3. Drop by teaspoonfuls onto greased cookie sheet.
4. Bake at 350° for 15-18 minutes. Cool.
5. To prepare frosting mix together powdered sugar and butter. Stir in milk until desired spreading consistency. Spread frosting on cookies.

Christmas Sugar Cookie Cut-Outs
Carol A. Findling
Princeton, IL
Pyramids

Makes 20-24 dozen

2 cups sugar
4 cups butter or
   margarine
5 tsp. baking powder
1/4 tsp. salt
2 cups milk
9 cups flour (approx.)

1. Cream together sugar and butter until fluffy. Stir in baking powder and salt. Alternately add milk and flour, adding only enough flour to handle. Chill dough at least 2 hours.
2. On well-floured cloth, roll out dough to 1/8-1/4" thickness. Cut into desired shapes. Place on ungreased cookie sheet.
3. Bake at 350° for 10-12 minutes or until edges are lightly browned. When cookies have cooled completely, frost and decorate as desired.

Biscochitos
Donna Barnitz
Rio Rancho, NM
Jane Talso
Albuquerque, NM
Jean Sinclair
Rio Rancho, NM
Dana Braden
Seattle, WA

Makes 6-7 dozen

1 lb. butter-flavored
   shortening
1 1/2 cups white sugar
2 tsp. anise seed
2 eggs, beaten
6 cups flour
3 tsp. baking powder
1 tsp. salt
1/2 cup orange juice
1/2 cup white sugar
1 tsp. cinnamon

1. Cream together shortening, 1 1/2 cups sugar, and anise seed. Add eggs and mix well.
2. Mix together flour, baking powder, and salt. Add alternately with orange juice to creamed mixture. Mix well.
3. Knead dough. Roll out to 1/4" thickness and cut into desired shapes.
4. Mix together 1/2 cup sugar and cinnamon and dust top of each cookie. Place on ungreased cookie sheet.
5. Bake at 350° for 8-10 minutes.

Note: This is a favorite Christmas cookie in New Mexico.

Holiday Cookies
Laura Ashby
Boulder Creek, CA
Leap Frog Baby Quilt

Makes 4-5 dozen

Cookie Dough:
1 cup butter, room
   temperature
8-oz. pkg. cream cheese,
   room temperature
1 1/2 cups sugar
1 egg
1 tsp. vanilla
1/2 tsp. almond extract
3 1/2 cups flour
1 tsp. baking powder

Frosting:
3 cups powdered sugar
3 Tbsp. softened butter
1/2 tsp. vanilla
5-6 Tbsp. milk
food coloring

1. Cream together butter, cream cheese, and sugar until fluffy. Add egg, vanilla, and almond extract. Beat until smooth.
2. Mix together flour and baking powder. Stir into creamed mixture and mix well. Chill covered for at least 8 hours.
3. On lightly floured surface, roll dough to 1/8" thickness. Cut into assorted shapes with cookie cutters. Place on ungreased cookie sheet.
4. Bake at 375° for 8-10 minutes. Remove from cookie sheet and cool on wire rack. Frost.
5. To prepare frosting cream

together powdered sugar, butter, and vanilla. Add milk until frosting is of spreading consistency. Tint with food coloring and sprinkle with colored sugars.

Christmas Cut-Out Cookies
Ruth Ann Collins
Waseca, MN
Biblical Blocks Christmas Quilt
Carol Huber
Austin, TX

Makes 7-8 dozen

Cookie Dough:
2 cups sugar
1 cup shortening
1/2 cup sour cream
2 eggs
1 tsp. vanilla or almond extract
41/2 cups flour
1 tsp. salt
1 tsp. baking soda

Frosting:
3 cups powdered sugar
3 Tbsp. milk
2 Tbsp. butter
1 drop food coloring of desired color

1. Cream together sugar and shortening.
2. Beat together sour cream and eggs. Add to creamed ingredients and mix well. Stir in extract, flour, salt, and baking soda. Mix well. Chill overnight.
3. Divide dough into three parts. On lightly floured sur-face, roll out to 1/4" thickness. Cut with floured cookie cutters.
4. Bake at 325° for 7-10 minutes. Cool.
5. To prepare frosting blend together all ingredients, adding more powdered sugar if mixture seems too thin. Frost cookies.

Ricotta Cookies
Denise Scandone Rominger
Bel Air, MD
Life I-Woodburning

Makes 10 dozen

Cookie Dough:
1/2 lb. butter
2 cups sugar
2 eggs
1 lb. ricotta cheese
1 tsp. almond extract
1 tsp. vanilla
4 cups flour
1 tsp. baking powder
1 tsp. baking soda

Frosting:
11/2 cups powdered sugar
4 Tbsp. milk

1. Cream together butter and sugar. Add eggs one at a time. Mix well. Add cheese, almond extract, and vanilla. Beat one minute.
2. Sift together flour, baking powder, and baking soda. Stir into creamed ingredients and mix well.
3. Drop by teaspoonfuls onto ungreased cookie sheet.
4. Bake at 350° for 10-12 minutes.

5. To prepare frosting beat together sugar and milk to desired consistency.
6. Frost cookies while still warm.

Rum and Coffee Cookies
Melissa Hess
Bellingham, WA
Pumpkin Vine

Makes 21/2 dozen

1 cup packed brown sugar
1/2 cup butter
2 eggs
1/2 tsp. rum extract
1 tsp. coffee granules
1 Tbsp. boiling water
11/2 cups flour
11/2 tsp. baking powder
1/4 tsp. salt
1 cup finely chopped nuts

1. Cream together butter and sugar. Beat in eggs one at a time. Add rum extract. Beat well.
2. Dissolve coffee in boiling water and stir into creamed ingredients. Stir in flour, baking powder, and salt and mix well.
3. Chill for several hours.
4. Drop by teaspoonfuls into nuts and place 2" apart on greased cookie sheet.
5. Bake at 350° for 8-10 minutes.

Coffee Cookies

Lorene P. Meyer
Wayland, IA
Sampler

Makes 10 dozen

Cookie Dough:
3 cups brown sugar
1 1/2 cups shortening
3 eggs, beaten
2 tsp. vanilla
4 1/2 tsp. baking powder
1 1/2 tsp. baking soda
1 1/2 cups prepared coffee
6 cups flour

Frosting:
1/2 cup butter or
    margarine
1/4 tsp. salt
1 cup brown sugar
6 Tbsp. milk
4 1/2 cups powdered sugar

1. Cream together brown sugar, shortening, eggs, vanilla, baking powder, and baking soda.
2. Alternately add coffee and flour to creamed mixture. Chill for at least 8 hours.
3. Drop by heaping teaspoonfuls onto greased cookie sheet.
4. Bake at 375° for 12-15 minutes. Touch top. If imprint stays, bake a little longer. Cool before frosting.
5. To prepare frosting cook together butter, salt, brown sugar, and milk until sugar is dissolved. Cool slightly. Add powdered sugar until desired consistency.

Cherry Butter Tarts

Janet Case
Rehoboth, MA
Ohio Star

Makes 1 1/2-2 dozen

Pastry Shells:
1 cup flour
1/2 cup butter or
    margarine, softened
1/4 cup powdered sugar

Filling:
3/4 cup brown sugar
1/4 cup butter, softened
1/4 cup honey
1 egg, slightly beaten
1/4 tsp. salt
1/4 cup chopped walnuts
1 cup whipped topping
20-24 cherries

1. Mix together flour, butter, and powdered sugar until it resembles cornmeal. Press into small muffin cups, making sure pastry doesn't extend over tops of cups.
2. Mix together brown sugar, butter, honey, egg, salt, and chopped walnuts. Pour into cups.
3. Bake at 350° for about 20 minutes, until crust is slightly brown and filling is set. Cool.
4. Top with whipped cream and a cherry when cool.

Butter Tarts

Janet Major
Pleasanton, CA
Muskoka Day

Makes 1 dozen

2 eggs, beaten
2 cups brown sugar
2 Tbsp. white vinegar
1 tsp. vanilla
1/2 cup butter, melted
1 1/3 cups raisins,
    currants, or chopped
    dates
2 9" unbaked pie shells

1. Beat together eggs and sugar. Stir in vinegar and vanilla. Add butter and

---

I am the oldest of eleven children, and each year at Christmas we would travel to Livingston, Wisconsin, to be with our Grandma Biddick. We slept upstairs in an old two-story frame house which received heat through the grates in the floor. It was always cold until you got settled under a wonderful pile of quilts. Unfortunately, I have no idea whether the quilts just wore out or what ever happened to them.

We would always be very still until the little children were asleep, then some of us older ones would sneak over to the floor registers and listen in on the adult conversations in the parlor below us.

—*Patricia Andreas, Wausau, WI*

dried fruit of choice. Mix well.
2. Line 12 3" muffin cups with pie dough. Fill 1/2-2/3 full with fruit mixture.
3. Bake at 450° for 10 minutes. Reduce heat to 350° and bake for 20-25 minutes or until filling is firm.

Kourabithies
Judi Manos
West Islip, NY
Garden of Love

Makes 5 dozen

1 lb. butter
1/2 cup powdered sugar
1 egg yolk
1 tsp. almond extract
1-oz. whiskey
4 cups flour
powdered sugar

1. Cream together butter and powdered sugar until creamy. Add egg yolk, almond extract, and whiskey. Mix well. Slowly stir in flour until well blended.
2. Shape a small ball of dough, about the size of a quarter, into a log about 1/2" thick. Place log on cookie sheet, turning each end in opposite directions, forming an "S" shape.
3. Bake at 350° for 16-20 minutes until lightly colored. Sprinkle with powdered sugar when cool or just before serving.

Jumbo Cookies
Carole Whaling
New Tripoli, PA
Drunkard's Path

Makes 3-4 dozen

1 cup boiling water
2 cups dark raisins
1 cup softened margarine
1 cup white sugar
1 cup dark brown sugar
3 eggs
1 tsp. vanilla
4 cups flour
1 tsp. baking powder
1 tsp. baking soda
2 tsp. salt
2 tsp. cinnamon
1/2 tsp. allspice
1/2 tsp. nutmeg
1 tsp. ground cloves
1 tsp. ginger
1 cup chopped nuts

1. In saucepan mix together boiling water and raisins and boil for five minutes. Remove from heat. Cool to room temperature.
2. Cream together margarine and sugars. Add eggs and vanilla. Mix well.
3. Sift together flour, baking powder, baking soda, salt, cinnamon, allspice, nutmeg, cloves, and ginger. Gradually add to creamed mixture. Mix in cooled raisins and nuts.
4. Drop by teaspoonfuls onto greased cookie sheet.
5. Bake at 350° for 10 minutes or until lightly browned. Allow to age at least one week before serving.

Raisin-Filled Cookies
Ruth N. Mellinger
Willow Street, PA
Log Cabin Star
Janet Derstine
Telford, PA
Nine Patch

Makes 3 dozen

Filling:
1 1/2 cups raisins
1 1/2 cups brown sugar
1/2 cup water
2 heaping Tbsp. flour

Cookie Dough:
1 scant cup butter or shortening
2 cups brown sugar
2 eggs, beaten
4 cups flour
pinch salt

1. To prepare filling mix together raisins, brown sugar, water, and flour. Cook until thickened.
2. To prepare cookie dough, mix together butter, brown sugar, and eggs. Gradually add flour and salt and mix well. Chill dough for several hours or overnight.
3. Roll out dough onto floured surface to 1/4" thickness. Cut with round cookie cutter.
4. Add 1 tsp. filling to center and cover with another cookie, sealing the edges.
5. Cook at 350° for 15 minutes or until browned.

Grandma Lynch's Filled Cookies

Scarlett von Bernuth
Canon City, CO
Sampler

Makes 2 dozen

Cookie Dough:
4 eggs
1¹/2 cups brown sugar
1¹/2 cups shortening
1 Tbsp. vanilla
4¹/2 cups flour
1 tsp. baking soda
1 tsp. baking powder
1 tsp. salt

Filling:
2 cups chopped apricots,
   dates, raisins, or figs
¹/2 cup chopped nuts
1 cup water
1 cup sugar
1 Tbsp. flour
1 tsp. diced grapefruit or
   orange rind

1. Cream together eggs, brown sugar, shortening, and vanilla until blended.
2. Sift together flour, baking soda, baking powder, and salt. Slowly stir into creamed mixture. Mix well. Dough will be soft. Refrigerate overnight.
3. To prepare filling combine all ingredients in saucepan and cook until thickened, stirring frequently.
4. Roll out ¹/4 of dough onto lightly floured surface. Cut into 4" circles. Drop 1 Tbsp. filling in center. Top with another circle. Using fork, press tines around edge.

Place on greased cookie sheet.
5. Bake at 375° for 12-15 minutes.

Fruit-Filled Cookies

Christine Novotny
Baden, PA
Alaskan Sampler

Makes 4 dozen

Filling:
1 cup dried apricots
2 cups diced apples
1 cup water
1 cup sugar
¹/2 tsp. salt
¹/2 tsp. cinnamon
2 Tbsp. lemon juice

Cookie Dough:
¹/2 cup shortening
1 cup sugar
1 egg
1 tsp. vanilla
2³/4 cups flour
¹/2 tsp. salt
¹/2 tsp. baking powder
¹/4 cup milk

1. To prepare filling cook apricots and apples in water until tender. Add sugar, salt, and cinnamon and cook until thickened. Add lemon juice and cool.
2. To prepare cookie dough, mix together shortening, sugar, egg, and vanilla.
3. Sift together flour, salt, and baking powder. Alternating with milk, add dry ingredients to creamed mixture.

4. Roll out to ¹/4" thickness onto floured board or pastry cloth and cut with round cookie cutter.
5. Place 1 rounded tsp. filling in center of cookie and cover with another cookie, pinching edges to seal. Place on ungreased cookie sheet.
6. Bake at 375° for 10-12 minutes.

Florentine Cookies

Pat Houle
Barnstead, NH
Log Cabin Scrap

Makes 3¹/2 dozen

²/3 cup butter
1 cup sugar
²/3 cup flour
2 cups quick oats
¹/4 cup milk
¹/4 cup light corn syrup
1 tsp. vanilla
¹/4 tsp salt
2 cups chocolate chips

1. In saucepan melt butter over medium heat.
2. Remove from heat and add sugar, flour, oats, milk, corn syrup, vanilla, and salt. Mix well.
3. Cover cookie sheets with baking paper or foil. Drop by teaspoonfuls, about 2¹/2-3 inch apart, onto cookie sheet. Press flat with spatula.
4. Bake at 375° for 5-7 minutes or until golden brown.
5. Cool completely before removing from paper or foil.

6. Meanwhile, melt chocolate in a double boiler over hot water. Stir until smooth and spread between two cookies to make sandwich.

Cornflake Kisses
June E. Hoffmann
Akron, NY
Picket Fence

Makes 2 dozen

2 egg whites
1 cup white sugar
1 tsp. vanilla
2 cups cornflakes
1 cup coconut (optional)

1. Beat egg whites until stiff and dry. Gradually add sugar and continue beating for 2 minutes. Add vanilla.
2. Mix together cornflakes and coconut. Add to previous mixture. Stir only enough to mix. Drop by tablespoonfuls onto greased cookie sheet.
3. Bake at 350° for 12-14 minutes.

Yuletide Kisses
Carol L. O'Neill
Reston, VA
Remembering Mrs. Johnson

Makes 5 dozen

1/8 tsp. salt
1/2 tsp. cream of tartar
3 egg whites
2 1/4 cups powdered sugar

1 tsp. vanilla
2 cups broken pecans, M&M's, or chocolate chips

1. Add salt and cream of tartar to egg whites and beat until egg whites form stiff peaks.
2. Add sugar gradually, beating constantly. Add vanilla and mix well. Fold in pecans.
3. Drop by slight teaspoonfuls onto lightly greased baking sheet.
4. Bake at 275° for 15-20 minutes, watching carefully.

Coconut Kisses
Michelle Harkins
Punxsutawney, PA
Log Cabin Barn Raising

Makes 2 dozen

3 cups grated coconut
1 cup firmly packed brown sugar
8 Tbsp. flour
1/4 tsp. salt
4 Tbsp. butter
4 egg yolks
1/2 tsp. vanilla or grated rind of 1 lime

1. Place grated coconut into large bowl. Add remaining ingredients in the order given and mix thoroughly. Choose vanilla or lime, depending on the flavor preferred.
2. Grease a 9" x 13" glass baking dish. Take mixture by tablespoonfuls, turn each

into a ball, and arrange on baking dish.
3. Bake at 350° for 30-40 minutes or until golden.
4. Remove from heat and allow to cool, upside down, on a platter. When cooled, turn right side up onto another platter. Store in single layer.

Linda's Macaroons
Gail Skiff
Clifton Park, NY
Swirling Peony

Makes 2-3 dozen

1 Tbsp. flour
1/2 cup sugar
1/4 tsp. salt
2 egg whites
1/2 tsp. vanilla
2 cups coconut
15-18 maraschino cherries

1. Combine flour, sugar, and salt and set aside.
2. Beat egg whites until stiffened. Stir in vanilla. Fold dry ingredients into egg whites. Add coconut and stir very gently.
3. Drop by teaspoonfuls onto greased and floured cookie sheet. Garnish each cookie with 1/2 of a maraschino cherry.
4. Bake at 325° for 20-25 minutes until edges are golden.

Norwegian Cookies

Karen Kay Tucker
Manteca, CA
Crazy Quilt

Makes 3¹/2-4 dozen

1 cup butter
1 cup sugar
1 egg, beaten
2 cups flour
1 tsp. almond flavoring
21-24 maraschino
   cherries, cut in half

1. Cream together butter and sugar. Add egg and mix well.
2. Stir in flour and almond flavoring. Chill dough for 1-2 hours.
3. Make balls the size of small walnuts. Flatten balls on cookie sheet with bottom of a drinking glass dipped in flour.
4. Press ¹/2 of maraschino cherry onto each cookie.
5. Bake at 350° for 15 minutes or until edge of cookie is light brown. Do not overbake.

Lebkuchen

Charlotte Fry
St. Charles, MO
Basket Quilt

Makes 5 dozen

Cookie Dough:
¹/2 cup honey
¹/2 cup molasses
³/4 cup packed brown
   sugar
1 egg
1 tsp. grated lemon peel
1 Tbsp. lemon juice
2³/4 cups flour
1 tsp. cinnamon
1 tsp. ground cloves
1 tsp. allspice
1 tsp. nutmeg
¹/2 tsp. baking soda
¹/3 cup chopped citron
¹/3 cup chopped nuts

Glaze:
1 cup white sugar
¹/2 cup water
¹/4 cup powdered sugar

1. In large saucepan mix together honey and molasses. Heat to boiling. Remove from heat and cool thoroughly.
2. Stir in brown sugar, egg, lemon peel, and juice. Stir in remaining ingredients. Mix well. Cover and chill for at least 8 hours.
3. On lightly floured board, roll out small amount of dough to ¹/4" thickness. Keep remaining dough in refrigerator. Cut into 2¹/2" x 1¹/2" rectangles. Place 1" apart on greased cookie sheet.

4. Bake at 400° for 10-12 minutes or until no imprint remains when touched lightly with finger.
5. To prepare glaze combine white sugar and water in a saucepan. Cook over medium heat until 230° on candy thermometer. Remove from heat and stir in powdered sugar. (If glaze becomes too sugary, add a little water and reheat slightly.)
6. Brush glaze lightly over cookies. Immediately remove from baking dish and cool. Store in airtight container with slice of apple or orange.

Mexican Wedding Balls

Sharleen White
Arnold, MD
Charlotte Fry
St. Charles, MO
Basket

Makes 4-5 dozen

1 cup butter
2 cups flour
¹/3 cup powdered sugar
¹/4 tsp. salt
2 tsp. vanilla
1 tsp. almond extract
2 cups pecans, chopped
powdered sugar

1. Mix together all ingredients except powdered sugar. Roll into very small balls, less than 1" in diameter.
2. Bake at 275° for 40 minutes. Remove from oven.

While still hot, roll in powdered sugar. Cool cookies and roll again in powdered sugar. Store in airtight container.

Easy Brownies
Mrs. Allan Bachman
Putnam, IL
Double Irish Chain
Barbara Tenney
Delta, PA
Sunbonnet Sue

Makes 16 large brownies

Brownies:
1 1/2 cups flour
2 cups sugar
1/2 cup plus 2 Tbsp. cocoa
1 tsp. salt
1 cup cooking oil
4 eggs
2 tsp. vanilla
1 cup chopped nuts
1/2 tsp. baking powder

Frosting:
2 cups powdered sugar
1 1/2 Tbsp. butter
1 Tbsp. vanilla
5 Tbsp. cocoa
1/2-1 cup milk
1/8 cup chopped nuts

1. To prepare brownies place all ingredients in mixing bowl and beat at medium speed for 3 minutes. Pour into greased 9" x 13" baking pan.
2. Bake at 350° for 40 minutes.
3. To prepare frosting mix together powdered sugar, butter, vanilla, and cocoa.

Add milk to desired consistency. Spread frosting over brownies in pan. Top with chopped nuts. Cut into 16 bars and serve.

Fudge Brownies
Jeanne Allen
Los Alamos, NM
Clams in the Cabin

Makes 36 brownies

Brownies:
16 Tbsp. butter or margarine
4 ozs. unsweetened chocolate
1 1/2 cups plus 2 Tbsp. flour
1/2 tsp. baking powder
1 tsp. salt
4 eggs, slightly beaten
2 cups sugar
1 tsp. vanilla
3/4 cup chopped nuts

Frosting:
2 ozs. unsweetened chocolate
3 Tbsp. butter
5 Tbsp. milk
dash salt
1/2 tsp. vanilla
2 cups powdered sugar, sifted

1. Melt together butter and chocolate over very low heat. Cool.
2. Sift together flour, baking powder, and salt.
3. Gradually add sugar to eggs, mixing thoroughly. Add vanilla and cooled chocolate mixture, blending

well. Stir in dry ingredients and blend in nuts.
4. Pour into greased and floured 9" x 13" baking pan.
5. Bake at 375° for 30-35 minutes or until toothpick inserted in center comes out clean. Cool completely.
6. Meanwhile, prepare frosting by combining chocolate, butter, and milk in top of double boiler. Cook over hot water until chocolate and butter melt. Stir to blend thoroughly. Add salt and vanilla and mix well. Remove from heat. Gradually stir in powdered sugar until frosting has desired spreading consistency.
7. Spread quickly over cooled brownies.

Brownies

Jeannine Dougherty
Tyler, TX
Joe's Cows

Makes 32 brownies

2 cups sugar
1 cup butter
4 eggs
1/3 cup unsweetened
   cocoa
1 cup flour
1 cup chopped pecans or
   walnuts
2 tsp. vanilla

1. Cream together sugar and butter. Blend in eggs, one at a time.
2. Add dry ingredients and blend well. Stir in nuts and vanilla.
3. Turn into greased 9" x 13" baking pan.
5. Bake at 350° for 30 minutes or until brownies start to pull away from the edges. Cut while still warm.

Note: Serve on individual glass serving plates with a scoop of ice cream. Top with a bit of whipped cream and a cherry.

Chocolate Caramel Brownies

Pat Unternahrer
Wayland, IA
Dahlia

Makes 24 brownies

Caramel Filling:
1 cup butter
2 cups light brown sugar
1 cup light corn syrup
14-oz. can sweetened
   condensed milk
1 tsp. vanilla

Brownies:
1 pkg. German chocolate
   cake mix
3/4 cup margarine, melted
1/3 cup milk
1 cup chocolate chips
1 cup pecans

1. In medium glass bowl, combine butter, sugar, corn syrup, and sweetened condensed milk. Mix and microwave on high for 15 minutes, stirring every 5 minutes. Stir in vanilla and pour into 8" square glass baking dish. Let cool until it can be divided into 3 equal pieces. Freeze 2 of the pieces for future use. Gently spoon remaining softened caramel into plastic bag with a tight seal.
2. To prepare brownies combine cake mix, melted margarine, and milk. Press 1/2 of mixture into greased 9" x 13" baking pan. Bake at 350° for 6 minutes.
3. Remove from oven and immediately cover with chocolate chips and pecans. Spread softened caramel filling over chips and nuts. (Cut one lower corner off plastic bag and squeeze caramel out of bag.)
4. Drop remaining cake mixture on top of caramel layer by teaspoonfuls.
5. Bake at 350° for 15-18 minutes. Do not overbake. (This will set up as it cools.) Cut into squares when cool.

When I was a child (many moons ago!), our family always spent Christmas at "the farm" with my grandparents, aunts, uncles, and cousins. After the gifts had been opened and the turkey dinner devoured, we would hear a strange noise in the basement. Here came Grandpa Santa wearing a strange looking Santa mask and costume. He would direct all the grandchildren into the formal sitting room where we encountered a tree laden with homemade cookies and small special gifts for each one. Though I am much older now, it is still a most precious memory.
—*Nancy W. Berger, Medina, NY*

Chocolate Mint Brownies

Naomi Stoltzfus
Leola, PA
Mary Ann Markano
Wilmington, DE
Sharon Wantland
Menomonee Falls, WI
Janet Case
Rehoboth, MA

Makes 36 brownies

Brownies:
1 cup flour
1/2 cup butter, softened
1/2 tsp. salt
4 eggs
1 tsp. vanilla
1 cup sugar
16-oz. can chocolate
  syrup

Frosting:
2 cups powdered sugar
1/2 cup butter
1 Tbsp. water
3 drops green food
  coloring
1/2 tsp. mint extract or
  2 Tbsp. creme de
  menthe

Topping:
10-oz. pkg. chocolate chips
9 Tbsp. butter

1. Combine all brownie ingredients and mix well. Pour batter into greased 9" x 13" baking pan.
2. Bake at 325° for 30 minutes. Cool.
3. To prepare frosting combine all ingredients and mix well. Spread over cooled cake.

4. In top of double boiler, melt together chocolate chips and butter. Spread over frosting layer. Cool.
5. Store in refrigerator.

Hershey Kiss Brownies

Susan Orleman
Pittsburgh, PA
Hilton Head Memories

Makes 48 brownies

1 cup butter
12-oz. pkg. semi-sweet
  chocolate chips
1 1/3 cups sugar
2 tsp. vanilla
4 eggs
1 cup flour
1 cup coarsely chopped
  pecans
48 Hershey Kisses

1. Melt butter in microwave or on top of stove over medium-low heat. Add chocolate chips, stirring until melted. Remove from heat.
2. Stir in sugar and vanilla and blend well. Add eggs, one at a time, stirring briskly after each addition.
3. Gradually stir in flour until blended. Fold in pecans.
4. Line 48 mini-muffin cups with foil muffin liners. (Paper liners will stick to brownie.) Fill each cup 3/4 full of batter.
5. Bake at 350° for 22-25 minutes. Do not overbake. Centers should be moist.

6. Remove from oven and immediately place 1 Hershey Kiss on top of each brownie. Remove brownies from pans and cool on racks.

Butterscotch Brownies

Anne Fiedler
Barrington, IL
Alaskan Sampler

Makes 24 brownies

6-oz pkg. butterscotch
  morsels
1/4 cup butter or
  margarine
1 cup brown sugar
2 eggs
1/2 tsp. vanilla
1 cup flour
1 tsp. baking powder
3/4 tsp salt (optional)
1/2 cup chopped walnuts
  or pecans

1. Melt together butterscotch morsels and butter (microwave on high for 1 1/2 minutes). Cool slightly. Stir in brown sugar, eggs, and vanilla.
2. Add flour, baking powder, salt, and walnuts and mix well.
3. Spread into greased and floured 9" x 13" baking pan.
5. Bake at 350° for 20-25 minutes. Cut into 2" squares and serve.

Coconut Brownies

Ashlene Drake
Salem, OR

Makes 36 brownies

Brownies:
1 cup butter, softened
3 eggs
3 heaping Tbsp. cocoa
1¼ cups sugar
1 cup flour
½ tsp. salt
1 cup chopped walnuts
2½ cups coconut
14-oz. can sweetened
    condensed milk

Frosting:
⅓ cup milk
¼ cup butter
6-oz. pkg. semi-sweet
    chocolate chips
2¼ cups powdered sugar
1 tsp. vanilla

1. Cream together butter and eggs. Stir in cocoa, sugar, flour, salt, and walnuts. Mix well.
2. Spread into greased 9" x 13" baking pan.
3. Bake at 350° for 20 minutes.
4. Mix together coconut and sweetened condensed milk. Spread over hot cake. Bake 15 minutes longer. Cool for 5 minutes.
5. Meanwhile, to prepare frosting heat together milk, butter, and chocolate chips until melted.
6. Sift powdered sugar into a bowl. Remove chocolate mixture from heat and pour into powdered sugar. Beat

well and stir in vanilla. Spread over warm cake. Cool and cut into squares.

Mom's Date Nut Bars

Debra Botelho Zeida
Mashpee, MA
Sunbonnet Sue

Makes 24 bars

2 eggs, beaten
1 cup sugar
8-oz. pkg. dates, chopped
1 cup chopped nuts
1 heaping cup self-rising
    flour
¾ cup Wesson oil
1 tsp. vanilla
powdered sugar

1. Beat together eggs and sugar until well blended.
2. Add dates, nuts, flour, Wesson oil, and vanilla and mix by hand until blended.
3. Pour into ungreased 9" x 13" baking pan.
4. Bake at 350° for 25 minutes.
5. When cool, sift powdered sugar over the top. Cut into bars and serve.

Soft Date Bars

Linda Nixon
Stewartstown, PA
*Piecemakers 1996
Calendar Quilt*
JoAnn Hussey
Milford, CT

Makes 42 bars

1 cup sugar
3 eggs
2 cups chopped dates
1 cup coarsely chopped
    nuts
1 cup bread flour
1 tsp. baking powder
⅛ tsp. salt
¼ tsp. cloves
¼ tsp. cinnamon
1 tsp. vanilla
powdered sugar

1. Mix together sugar and eggs and blend until mixture is very light. Add dates and nuts and set aside.
2. Sift together flour, baking powder, salt, cloves, and cinnamon. Add to egg mixture and beat well. Add vanilla.
3. Pour into 9" x 13" baking pan lined with greased waxed paper.
4. Bake at 325° for 25 minutes. Cool completely.
5. Cut into bars and roll generously in powdered sugar.

Note: This bar remains soft and fresh for a long time and keeps well when sent through the mail.

Raisin Mumble Bars
Mary Puterbaugh
Elwood, IN
Fan

Makes 24-36 bars

Filling:
2¹/₂ cups seedless raisins
¹/₂ cup white sugar
2 Tbsp. cornstarch
1 cup water
3 Tbsp. lemon juice

Bars:
³/₄ cup soft margarine
1 cup packed brown
   sugar
1³/₄ cups flour
¹/₂ tsp. salt
¹/₂ tsp. baking soda
1¹/₂ cups rolled oats

1. In saucepan mix together raisins, sugar, cornstarch, water, and lemon juice. Cook over low heat for about 5 minutes until thickened. Set aside to cool.
2. Cream together margarine and sugar. Stir in flour, salt, baking soda, and oats. Mix well.
3. Spread ¹/₂ of crumb mixture into greased 9" x 13" baking pan. Press down. Spread cooled filling over bottom crust. Sprinkle with remaining crumbs and press down lightly.
4. Bake at 400° for 20-30 minutes. Cut and serve.

Nordstrom's Nordy Bars
Dana Braden
Seattle, WA
May Baskets for Mother

Makes 36 bars

¹/₂ cup butter
12-oz. pkg. butterscotch
   chips
¹/₂ cup firmly packed
   sugar
2 eggs
1¹/₂ cups flour
2 tsp. baking powder
¹/₂ tsp. salt
2 tsp. vanilla
12-oz. pkg. chocolate
   chips
2 cups miniature
   marshmallows
1 cup chopped pecans

1. In saucepan melt butter over medium heat. Add butterscotch chips and brown sugar, stirring until melted. Remove from heat.
2. Stir in eggs. Add flour, baking powder, and salt. Mix well. Stir in vanilla. Cool completely.
3. When cooled, stir in chocolate chips, marshmallows, and pecans. Spread into greased 9" x 13" baking pan.
4. Bake at 350° for 25 minutes. Remove from oven and cool completely. Cut into squares and serve.

Marble Mellow Bars
Karen M. Rusten
Waseca, MN
Angela's Kitty Quilt

Makes 24 large bars

1 cup butter
²/₃ cup brown sugar
1 tsp. vanilla
2 cups flour
3 cups miniature
   marshmallows
6-oz. pkg. chocolate chips
3 Tbsp. butter
1 Tbsp. water

1. Cream together 1 cup butter, brown sugar, and vanilla. Add flour and mix well. Spread onto greased jelly roll pan.
2. Bake at 350° for 15 minutes. Sprinkle marshmallows over top and bake another 5 minutes.
3. Melt together chocolate chips and 1 Tbsp. butter. Add water, stirring until smooth. Remove from heat and drizzle over warm marshmallow layer. Cool before cutting.

Deluxe Chocolate Marshmallow Bars
Betty Wilson
Pinckney, MI

Makes 36 bars

Bars:
3/4 cup butter or
  margarine
1 1/2 cups sugar
3 eggs
1 tsp. vanilla
1 1/3 cups flour
1/2 tsp. baking powder
1/2 tsp. salt
3 Tbsp. baking cocoa
1/2 cup chopped nuts
4 cups miniature
  marshmallows

Topping:
1 1/3 cups chocolate chips
3 Tbsp. butter or
  margarine
1 cup peanut butter
2 cups crisp rice cereal

1. Cream together butter
and sugar. Add eggs and
vanilla and beat until fluffy.
2. Mix together flour, baking powder, salt, and cocoa.
Add to creamed mixture
and mix well. Stir in nuts.
Spread into greased jelly roll
pan.
3. Bake at 350° for 15-18
minutes. Sprinkle marsh-
mallows evenly over cake.
Cool.
4. To prepare topping combine chocolate chips, butter,
and peanut butter in a
saucepan. Cook over low
heat, stirring constantly

until melted and well
blended. Remove from heat.
Stir in cereal. Spread over
bars. Chill.

Brown Sugar Bars
Lois J. Cassidy
Willow Street, PA
Star Light

Makes 12-16 bars

2/3 cup flour
1 tsp. baking powder
1/4 tsp. salt
1/4 cup margarine, melted
1 cup dark brown sugar
1 egg
1 tsp. vanilla
1/2 cup chopped nuts

1. Mix together flour, baking powder, and salt. Set
aside.
2. Cream together mar-
garine and brown sugar.
Add egg and vanilla and
beat well. Stir in nuts and
dry ingredients. Spread into
greased 8" square pan.
3. Bake at 350° for 30 minutes. Cut into bars and cool.

Chocolate Cherry Bars
Karen Weber
Alexandria, SD
Applique Quilt in a Day
Chris Peterson
Green Bay, WI
Star Medallion

Makes 16-20 bars

Bars:
1 pkg. chocolate cake mix
21-oz. can cherry pie
  filling
1 tsp. almond flavoring
2 eggs, beaten

Frosting:
1 cup sugar
5 Tbsp. margarine
1/3 cup milk
1/2 cup chocolate chips

1. Mix together dry cake
mix, pie filling, almond flavoring, and eggs. Pour into
greased 10" x 15" baking
pan.
2. Bake at 325° for 20-25
minutes or until toothpick
inserted in center comes out
clean.
3. To prepare frosting combine sugar, margarine, and
milk in a saucepan. Bring to
boil and boil for 1 minute.
Remove from heat and add
chocolate chips. Beat until
smooth and creamy.
4. Frost bars while they are
still warm.

Banana Chocolate Chip Bars

Carol Huber
Austin, TX
Churn Dash

Makes 20-24 bars

3/4 cup butter or
  margarine
2/3 cup white sugar
2/3 cup brown sugar
2 eggs
1 tsp. vanilla
3 bananas, mashed
2 cups flour
2 tsp. baking powder
1/2 tsp. salt
12-oz. pkg. semi-sweet
  chocolate chips

1. Cream together butter
and sugars. Add eggs and
vanilla. Mix well. Stir in
mashed bananas.
2. Sift together flour, baking
powder, and salt and add to
creamed mixture.
3. Stir in chocolate chips.
Pour into greased 9" x 13"
baking pan.
4. Bake at 350° for 20-25
minutes.

Fruit Bars

Anna Stoltzfus
Honey Brook, PA

Makes 24 bars

1/2 cup butter
11/2 cups brown sugar
2 eggs
1 tsp. vanilla
1 cup flour
2 tsp. baking powder
1/2 tsp. salt
1 cup chopped nuts
1/2 lb. candied cherries
1/4 lb. candied pineapple

1. Cream together butter
and sugar. Add eggs and
vanilla and mix well.
2. Mix together flour, baking powder, and salt. Add to
creamed mixture and mix
well.
3. Stir in nuts, cherries, and
pineapple. Spread into
greased and floured 7" x 11"
baking pan.
4. Bake at 300° for 1 hour.

Apple Butterscotch Bars

Susan L. Schwarz
N. Bethesda, MD
Americana Hearts

Makes 24 bars

1 cup flour
1/2 cup whole wheat flour
1 tsp. baking soda
1 tsp. cinnamon
1/4 tsp. ground cloves
1/4 tsp. salt
1/4 cup butter
1/2 cup brown sugar
1 cup applesauce
1 tsp. vanilla
1 cup finely chopped
  apple
1 cup raisins
1/2 cup regular oats,
  uncooked
1/3 cup butterscotch
  morsels

1. Mix together flours, baking soda, cinnamon, cloves,
and salt. Stir well.
2. Cream butter. Gradually
add sugar, beating at medium
speed until light and fluffy.
3. Alternating with applesauce, add flour mixture to
creamed mixture, beginning
and ending with flour mixture. Stir in vanilla.
4. Fold in apple, raisins,
oats, and butterscotch
morsels. Mix well.
5. Pour batter into a greased
7" x 11" baking dish.
6. Bake at 350° for 40 minutes or until toothpick
inserted in center comes out
clean. Cool completely in
pan before cutting.

Applesauce Fudgy Bars

Jaclyn Ferrell
Carlisle, PA
Sisters' Choice

Makes 12-16 bars

2 1-oz. squares
  unsweetened chocolate
1/2 cup margarine
1/2 cup applesauce
2 eggs, beaten
1 cup brown sugar
1 tsp. vanilla
1 cup flour
1/2 tsp. baking powder
1/4 tsp. baking soda
1/4 tsp. salt
1/2 cup chopped nuts

1. Melt chocolate and margarine together. Remove from heat and stir in applesauce, eggs, sugar, and vanilla.
2. Sift together flour, baking powder, baking soda, and salt. Stir into chocolate mixture. Mix well.
3. Pour into greased 9" square baking pan. Sprinkle with nuts.
4. Bake at 350° for 30 minutes. Cool and cut into squares.

Aunt Sophie's Apricot Bars

Andrea O'Neil
Fairfield, CT
Irish Chain

Makes 24 bars

6-oz. pkg. dried apricots
3/4 cup water
2/3 cup sugar
1 cup shortening
1/2 tsp. salt
1 tsp. lemon or orange
  rind
1/3 cup sugar
4 eggs
2 1/2 tsp. baking powder
2 1/4 cups flour
1/2 tsp. cinnamon
1 Tbsp. sugar

1. Mix together apricots and water and cook over low heat for 35-40 minutes. Add 2/3 cup sugar and cook for 5-10 minutes longer.
2. Mix together shortening, salt, lemon rind, and 1/3 cup sugar. Beat in eggs, one at a time. Stir in baking powder and flour. Mix well.
3. Pour 1/2 of batter into greased 9" x 13" baking pan. Spread apricots over batter, then cover with remaining batter.
4. Mix together cinnamon and sugar and sprinkle on top.
5. Bake at 350° for 30-35 minutes.

Danish Pastry Bars

Clara Schrock
Millersburg, OH
Irish Chain

Makes 15 servings

Bars:
3/4 cup shortening
1/2 cup white sugar
2 1/2 cups flour
1/2 tsp. baking soda
1/2 tsp. baking powder
1/2 tsp. salt
1 egg, separated
milk, about 1/2 cup
1 tsp. vanilla
21-oz. can pie filling

Glaze:
1 cup powdered sugar
1/2 tsp. vanilla
water

1. Cream together shortening and white sugar.
2. Sift together flour, baking soda, baking powder, and salt.
3. Put beaten egg yolk in 1/2 cup measuring cup and fill with milk.
4. Mix together creamed mixture, dry mixture, and milk mixture.
5. To roll out this dough, take a piece of waxed paper the size of your jelly roll pan. Put a bit of water on the counter top so that paper will stick to the counter top. Put 1/2 of dough onto waxed paper. Take another piece of waxed paper (the same size) and spread over top of dough.

Roll out to the size you need. Pick up paper, peel off one side, slide dough into pan, and peel off other side.
6. Spread choice of pie filling over dough.
7. Repeat step 5 with remaining 1/2 of dough. Cut into strips and arrange, lattice like, on top of pie filling.
8. Bake at 375° for 30 minutes or until nice and brown.
9. To prepare glaze mix together powdered sugar, vanilla, and enough water so glaze is thin enough to drizzle. Drizzle over danish while still warm.

Pineapple Squares
Mary Ann Potenta
Bridgewater, NJ
Double Irish Chain
Betty Gresham
Trenton, MI
Friendship

Makes 36 squares

20 oz. can crushed pineapple
1 1/2 cups sugar
3 Tbsp. cornstarch
3 cups flour
2 tsp. baking powder
3 Tbsp. sugar
1 tsp. salt
1 cup shortening
1 egg yolk
3/4 cup milk
1 egg white
1/2 cup chopped walnuts

1. Drain pineapple and reserve 2 Tbsp. juice. Cook together drained pineapple and sugar for 10 minutes.
2. Mix together 2 Tbsp. pineapple juice and cornstarch. Add to hot pineapple mixture. Cook until thickened. Set aside to cool.
3. Mix together flour, baking powder, sugar, and salt. Cut in shortening.
4. Beat together egg yolk and milk. Stir into dry mixture and mix well.
5. Divide dough into two parts. Roll out 1/2 of dough and place in bottom of 9" x 13" baking pan. Pour pineapple mixture over crust. Roll out remaining dough and place on top.
6. Beat egg white until stiff. Spread on top of crust and sprinkle with walnuts.
7. Bake at 375° for 35-40 minutes. Cut into squares when cool.

Pumpkin Squares
Charlene Bement
Rancho Cucamonga, CA

Makes 24 squares

1 cup flour
1/2 cup quick oats
1/2 cup brown sugar
1/2 cup butter
2 cups mashed pumpkin
12-oz. can evaporated milk
2 eggs
3/4 cup sugar
1/2 tsp. salt
1/4 tsp. ground cloves
1/2 tsp. ginger
1/2 cup chopped pecans
1/2 cup brown sugar
2 Tbsp. butter
whipped topping

1. Mix together flour, oats, 1/2 cup brown sugar, and butter until crumbly. Press into ungreased 9" x 13" baking pan.
2. Bake at 350° for 15 minutes.
3. Beat together pumpkin, milk, eggs, sugar, salt, cloves, and ginger. Pour over crust.
4. Bake at 350° for 20 minutes.
5. Mix together pecans, 1/2 cup brown sugar, and butter until crumbly. Sprinkle over top.
6. Bake at 350 for 15-20 minutes. Cool. Cut into squares and top with whipped cream.

Dainty Date Squares

Mary Seielstad
Schenectady, NY
Stained Glass Wall Panel

Makes 12-16 squares

1 1/2 cups flour
1 3/4 cups uncooked
    oatmeal
1 cup sugar
1 tsp. baking soda
3/4 cup margarine
1 Tbsp. milk
3/4 cup pitted dates
3/4 cup sugar
3/4 cup water

1. Mix together flour, oatmeal, 1 cup sugar, baking soda, and margarine with hands until crumbly. Reserve 1 cup crumbs. Add milk to remaining crumb mixture and mix well.
2. In saucepan cook dates, 3/4 cup sugar, and water until soft and gooey, about 20 minutes.
3. Spread crumb mixture into 8" square pan. Cover with cooked date mixture and sprinkle with reserved 1 cup crumbs.
4. Bake at 350° for 25-30 minutes. (Will look bubbly, as though not done, when removed from the oven.) Cut into squares and serve.

Holiday Malt Chews

Bonnie Moore
Pinckney, MI
Happy Cat Baby Quilt

Makes 12-16 squares

Malt Chews:
6 Tbsp. butter or
    margarine, melted
3/4 cup brown sugar
2 eggs, slightly beaten
1/2 tsp. vanilla
3/4 cup flour
1/2 cup chocolate malted
    milk powder
1/2 tsp. baking powder
1 cup chopped dates
1/2 cup walnuts
1/2 cup coconut

Frosting:
1 Tbsp. soft margarine
1 cup powdered sugar
2 Tbsp. chocolate malted
    milk powder
1/4 tsp. vanilla
1 tsp. milk

1. Cream together butter and brown sugar. Beat in eggs and vanilla. Stir in flour, malt powder, and baking powder. Mix well. Fold in dates, nuts, and coconut.
2. Spread date mixture into greased 8" square baking pan.
3. Bake at 350° for 25-30 minutes. Cool completely.
4. Meanwhile, prepare frosting by combining margarine, powdered sugar, malt powder, vanilla, and milk. Mix until smooth and creamy. Frost cooled bars and serve.

Mom's Spiced Sheet Squares

Marge Reeder
State College, PA
Sara's Log Cabin

Makes 36 squares

1 tsp. baking soda
1/2 cup sour milk
1/2 cup shortening
1 egg
1 tsp. nutmeg
1 cup brown sugar
1 tsp. ground cloves
1 tsp. cinnamon
1/2 cup light molasses
3 cups flour
1/2 tsp. salt
1 cup finely chopped nuts
1 cup raisins
1 1/4 cups powdered sugar
4 tsp. water

1. Dissolve baking soda in sour milk in large bowl. Stir in all remaining ingredients except powdered sugar and water. Spread batter on greased jelly roll pan.
2. Bake at 375° for 15-20 minutes.
3. Moisten powdered sugar with water and drizzle over warm bars. Cool. Cut into squares.

Charleston Chews
Ann Mould
Mt. Pleasant, SC
Teacups

Makes 48 small squares

4 eggs
3 cups brown sugar
24 Tbsp. butter, melted
1 tsp. vanilla
2 1/4 cups flour
1 tsp. baking powder
1 1/4 cups pecans, chopped
   fine
powdered sugar

1. Beat together eggs and brown sugar. Add butter and vanilla and mix well.
2. Mix together flour and baking powder. Add to creamed mixture. Stir in pecans. Pour into greased 9" x 13" baking pan.
3. Bake at 350° for 30-35 minutes until firm in center. Cool. Dust with powdered sugar when cool. Cut into very small squares, as these are very rich.

Pizza Chocolate Chip Cookie
Janie Steele
Moore, OK
Winter Geese

Makes 1 large cookie

1/3 cup margarine
1 cup brown sugar
1 egg
1 Tbsp. hot water
1 cup flour
1/2 tsp. baking powder
1/8 tsp. baking soda
1/2 tsp. salt
1/2 cup chopped nuts
12-oz. pkg. chocolate chips

1. Cream together margarine and sugar. Stir in egg and hot water. Mix well.
2. Mix together flour, baking powder, baking soda, and salt. Add to creamed mixture and mix well. Stir in nuts and chocolate chips. Spread onto a greased round pizza pan.
3. Bake at 350° for 25 minutes. Cool. Decorate if desired.

Rockefeller Bars
Elinor L. Briggs
Eaton, IN
Devil's Puzzle

Makes 36 bars

3/4 cup margarine, melted
2 cups graham cracker
   crumbs
12-oz. jar peanut butter
2 cups powdered sugar
12-oz. pkg. chocolate chips

1. In a saucepan melt margarine. Remove from heat and stir in graham cracker crumbs. Set aside.
2. Cream together peanut butter and powdered sugar. Add graham cracker mixture and mix well. Press into greased 9" x 13" baking pan. Set aside.
3. In top of double boiler melt chocolate chips. Spread melted chocolate over peanut butter and graham cracker mixture. Let stand at room temperature until chocolate hardens. Cut into small squares and serve.

Granola Bars
Mrs. Lester J. Gingerich
Arthur, IL
Flower Garden

Makes 24 servings

1/2 cup brown sugar
1 cup corn syrup
pinch salt
2 cups peanut butter
2 cups quick oats
2 cups crispy rice cereal
1 cup chocolate chips

1. In saucepan combine brown sugar, corn syrup, and salt and bring to a boil. Remove from heat and add peanut butter, oats, cereal, and chocolate chips.
2. Press into 9" x 13" pan and cut into bars.

Scotch Toffee Shortbread
Margaret Clark
Lancaster, NY
Family History Quilt

Makes 25 servings

Shortbread:
3 cups flour
1 cup butter
1/2 cup sugar

Toffee:
1 cup butter
1 cup sugar
2 Tbsp. white corn syrup
14-oz. can sweetened
   condensed milk

Topping:
12-oz. semi-sweet
   chocolate chips

1. To prepare shortbread rub butter into flour. Add sugar. Press firmly into 9" x 13" pan.
2. Bake at 325° for 15-20 minutes.
3. In saucepan melt together butter, sugar, corn syrup, and milk over low heat. Boil for 10 minutes, stirring constantly. Pour over cooled shortbread. Cool.
4. Melt chocolate morsels. Pour over mixture in pan. Refrigerate to set. Cut into squares.

Scotch Shortbread
Janet Major
Pleasanton, CA
Muskoka Day

Makes 6 dozen

1 lb. butter, softened*
1 cup fine white sugar
1 cup cornstarch
5 cups flour, sifted

*Do not substitute margarine.

1. Using wooden spoon, cream butter. Gradually add sugar and beat until light.
2. Sift flour. Add cornstarch to flour and sift again. Gradually add flour to creamed mixture. Work into dough and knead with hands. Turn dough onto flat surface to finish kneading in the last of flour mixture. Knead at least 10 minutes.
3. Line a 9" x 13" cookie sheet with foil. Pat dough out on cookie sheet. Cover with waxed paper and roll with rolling pin to make smooth top. Remove waxed paper and mark or prick with a fork. Cover with fresh waxed paper and chill in refrigerator overnight.
4. Bake on middle rack at 275° for 1 to 1 1/2 hours. Watch carefully until very lightly browned. Remove from oven. Immediately mark into 1 1/2" x 1" pieces, using ruler and paring knife. Cut while still warm. Let cool completely on cookie sheet.
5. Store in airtight container.

Biscotti
Janet L. Haner
Punxsutawney, PA
Windblown Tulips

Makes 7-8 dozen

1/2 lb. shortening, part
  butter
13/4 cups sugar
6 eggs
2 tsp. anise oil
2 tsp. vanilla
6 cups flour
3 tsp. baking powder
1 tsp. salt
1 cup ground nuts

1. Cream together shortening and sugar. Add eggs, one at a time. Mix well. Stir in anise and vanilla.
2. Sift together flour, baking powder, and salt. Add to creamed mixture. Stir in nuts. Knead well.
3. On floured surface divide batter into 4 pieces. Roll each portion into a 11/2" wide log. Place on greased cookie sheet.
4. Bake at 350° for 30 minutes. Remove from oven and cool. Reduce oven temperature to 300°.
5. Cut biscotti into 1/2" slices. Stand upright on cookie sheet and bake for 20 minutes. Cool.

Almond Biscotti
Joyce Bowman
Lady Lake, FL
Single Wedding Ring

Makes 30 slices

1/3 cup margarine or
  butter
2 cups flour
2/3 cup sugar
2 eggs
2 tsp. baking powder
1 tsp. vanilla
11/2 cups sliced almonds
1 egg yolk
1 Tbsp. water

1. Cream margarine until soft. Add 1 cup flour, sugar, 2 eggs, baking powder, and vanilla. Mix well. Stir in remaining 1 cup flour and almonds. Divide dough in half. Shape each portion into 9" x 2" log. Place about 4" apart on lightly greased cookie sheet.
2. Mix together egg yolk and water. Brush onto logs.
3. Bake at 375° for 25 minutes. Cool on cookie sheet for one hour. Cut each log diagonally into 1/2" slices. Lay slices on ungreased cookie sheet.
4. Bake at 325° for 8 minutes. Turn over and bake 8-10 minutes more until dry and crisp. Cool on wire rack.

Cranberry Almond Biscotti
Peggy Gausepohl
Fallbrook, CA
Star for Mary

Makes 21/2 dozen

2 eggs
2 egg whites
1 Tbsp. almond extract
21/4 cups flour
1 cup sugar
1 tsp. baking powder
1/2 tsp. baking soda
1 tsp. cinnamon
1/2 tsp nutmeg
1/4 cup sliced almonds
1 cup sweetened
  cranberries

1. Whisk together eggs, egg whites, and almond extract.
2. Mix together flour, sugar, baking powder, baking soda, cinnamon, and nutmeg. Add egg mixture to dry ingredients. Mix well. Stir in almonds and cranberries.
3. On floured surface divide batter in half. Roll each half into a 14" x 11/2" log. Place on greased cookie sheet.
4. Bake at 325° for 30 minutes. Cool. Reduce oven temperature to 300°.
5. Cut biscotti into 1/2" slices. Stand upright on cookie sheet and bake for 20 minutes. Cool.
6. Store in loosely covered container such as a cookie jar.

Desserts

❖

Red Raspberry Mousse

Blanche M. Cahill
Willow Grove, PA
Tumbling Packages

Makes 6-8 servings

2 3-oz. pkgs. raspberry
   gelatin
2 cups boiling water
2 10-oz. pkgs. frozen red
   raspberries, partially
   thawed
1 pint heavy cream
1/8 tsp. peppermint
   extract
12 ladyfingers, split
whipped cream
fresh mint

1. Dissolve gelatin in boiling
water. Add raspberries, stirring until completely
thawed. Chill mixture until
thick and syrupy.
2. Whip cream with peppermint extract until soft peaks
form. Gently fold whipped
cream into gelatin mixture.

Chill at least 10 minutes.
3. Place ladyfingers around
the sides of an 8" springform pan. Pour gelatin mixture into center. Chill until
set. Remove sides of pan.
Decorate with puffs of
whipped cream and fresh
mint.

Raspberry Dessert

Donna Wright
Oxford, NY
Tulip Basket Pillow Top

Makes 12-16 servings

1 1/4 cups graham cracker
   crumbs
1/4 cup chopped nuts
1/4 cup butter or
   margarine, melted
50 large marshmallows
1 cup milk
2 cups heavy cream,
   whipped
1 tsp. vanilla
2 10-oz. pkg. frozen
   raspberries

1 cup water
1/2 cup sugar
2 tsp. lemon juice
4 Tbsp. cornstarch
1/4 cup cold water

1. Mix together graham
cracker crumbs, nuts, and
butter. Press firmly into
9" x 13" pan.
2. In double boiler combine
marshmallows and milk.
Heat until melted. Cool.
3. Whip heavy cream and
stir in vanilla. Fold into
marshmallow mixture.
Spread over graham cracker
crumbs.
4. In saucepan heat raspberries, 1 cup water, sugar, and
lemon juice. Dissolve cornstarch in 1/4 cup cold water
and stir into raspberries.
Cook until thickened and
clear. Cool. Pour over
marshmallow mixture in
pan. Refrigerate until firm.

Rok Gruetzl
Patty Arnold
Medina, NY
Cats Cradle

Makes 6 servings

10-oz. pkg. frozen red
  raspberries
1/4 cup red raspberry jam
1/4 cup sugar
1 1/4 cups plus 2 Tbsp.
  cold water
3 1/2 Tbsp. minute tapioca
1/2 pint heavy cream,
  whipped

1. In saucepan combine
raspberries, jam, sugar,
water, and tapioca. Bring to
boil over medium heat, stirring constantly.
2. Pour into glass serving
bowl. Let stand for 20 minutes. Stir thoroughly.
Refrigerate for at least 8
hours. Serve with whipped
cream.

Raspberry Pretzel Dessert
Nadine Martinitz
Salina, KS
Midnight Sky
Elaine Anderson
Mitchell, SD
Sampler

Makes 12-16 servings

2 cups finely crushed
  thin pretzels
2 Tbsp. sugar
1/3 cup chopped pecans
3/4 cup butter or
  margarine, softened
8-oz. pkg. cream cheese,
  softened
3/4 cup sugar
8-oz. carton frozen
  whipped topping
6-oz. pkg. raspberry
  flavored gelatin
2 cups boiling water
2 10-oz. pkgs.
  unsweetened frozen
  raspberries

1. Combine pretzels, sugar,
pecans, and butter. Press
into bottom of 9" x 13" pan.
2. Bake at 350° for 10 minutes. Cool.
3. Cream together cream
cheese and sugar until
smooth. Fold in whipped
topping. Spread over crust.
4. Dissolve gelatin in water.
Stir in frozen raspberries.
Chill until gelatin is almost
set, about 8-10 minutes.
Spread over cream cheese
filling. Chill several hours.

New England Cranberry Delight
Ada J. Miller
Sugarcreek, OH
Nancy J. Marsden
Glen Mills, PA
Carol Jensen
Watchung, NJ

Makes 6 servings

3 cups chopped apples
2 cups raw cranberries
1 1/4 cups sugar
1 1/2 cups oatmeal,
  uncooked
1/2 cup brown sugar
1/3 cup flour
3/4 tsp. salt
1/2 cup butter, melted
1/3 cup chopped nuts
  (optional)

1. Combine apples and
cranberries in 9" pie place.
Sprinkle sugar over fruit.
2. Mix together oats, brown
sugar, flour, and salt. Add
butter, mixing until
crumbly. Sprinkle over fruit
mixture. Top with nuts.
3. Bake at 350° for 1 hour.
Serve warm or cold with
whipped topping or vanilla
ice cream.

Cranberry Sherbet
Deanna E. Lybarger
Akron, OH
Hunter's Star Variation

Makes 8-10 servings

1 lb. cranberries
2 cups boiling water
1 tsp. unflavored gelatin
1/4 cup cold water
2 cups sugar
1 pint ginger ale

1. Cook cranberries in water until skins pop. Press through strainer.
2. Soften gelatin in cold water. In saucepan mix together cranberry juice, softened gelatin, and sugar. Cook over medium heat, stirring until sugar is dissolved. Stir in ginger ale. Fast freeze in automatic refrigerator tray to mushy consistency. Turn into mixing bowl and beat with electric beater.
3. Return to tray and freeze until firm.

Note: We now use an electric ice cream maker to prepare this sherbet. But the above method works very well. We did it this way for years.

Cranberry Fluff
Barbara Lucas
Fishers, IN

Makes 12-14 servings

2 cups fresh cranberries
3 cups miniature marshmallows
3/4 cup sugar
2 cups diced, unpeeled apples
1/2 cup seedless grapes (optional)
1/2 cup chopped nuts
1/4 tsp. salt
8-oz. carton whipped topping

1. Combine cranberries, marshmallows, and sugar. Cover and chill for at least 8 hours.
2. Stir in apples, grapes, nuts, and salt. Fold in whipped topping. Chill and serve.

Cranberry Pudding
Laurie Rott
Fargo, ND
Rose and Tulip Appliqué

Makes 8 servings

2 tsp. baking soda
1/2 cup molasses
1/2 cup boiling water
1 1/3 cups flour
1 tsp. baking powder
1 cup cranberries
1/2 cup sugar
1/2 cup cream
1/4 cup butter

1. Mix together baking soda, molasses, and boiling water.
2. Sift together flour and baking powder. Add to molasses mixture. Stir in cranberries.
3. Pour mixture into greased 1-lb. coffee can. Cover with aluminum foil and tie a string tightly around the edge of the can. Put can in a large kettle with about 3" boiling water and cover kettle with a tight lid. Steam the pudding for 2 hours.

Note: I often make this ahead of time and rewarm it by steaming again for a short time. Slices can also be warmed in the microwave.

Cranberry Mousse
Anna Petersheim
Paradise, PA
Noah's Ark
Donna Lantgen
Rapid City, SD
Interlock

Makes 16-20 servings

6-oz. pkg. strawberry
gelatin
1 cup boiling water
20-oz. can crushed
pineapple
16-oz. can whole berry
cranberry sauce
3 Tbsp. lemon juice
1 tsp. grated lemon peel
1/2 tsp. ground nutmeg
2 cups sour cream
1/2 cup chopped pecans
(optional)

1. Dissolve gelatin in boiling
water.
2. Drain pineapple. Add
pineapple juice to gelatin.
3. Stir in cranberry suace,
lemon juice, lemon peel,
and nutmeg. Chill until mixture thickens.
4. Fold in sour cream,
pineapple, and pecans. Pour
into glass serving bowl or a
greased 9-cup mold. Chill
until set.

Orange-Cranberry Gelatin
Betty Ziegler
Bay City, OR
Dresden Plate

Makes 8-10 servings

6-oz. pkg. orange gelatin
16-oz. can whole berry
cranberry sauce
1 cup chopped pecans
8-oz. can crushed
pineapple
8-oz. pkg. cream cheese

1. Prepare gelatin according
to package instructions,
using 1/2 cup less of the cold
water.
2. Break up cranberry sauce
with a fork. Add to gelatin
mixture. Stir in undrained
pineapple and nuts. Chill
until set.
3. Serve in individual dishes
with frosting of softened
cream cheese.

Strawberries in the Snow
Margaret Morris
Middle Village, NY
Noah's Ark

Makes 6-8 servings

1/2 large angel food cake
4-oz. pkg. cream cheese,
softened
1/2 cup sugar
2 cups whipping cream
1 pint strawberries, sliced
and sugared or 16-oz.
pkg. frozen, sliced
strawberries, thawed

1. Cut cake into 1" slices
and layer across bottom of
9" x 13" pan.
2. Cream together cream
cheese and sugar. Stir in
whipping cream. Beat until
mixture forms stiff peaks.
3. Pour some of strawberry
juice onto cake. Cover cake
with whipped topping.
Spread strawberries over
topping, letting some juice
penetrate the topping. Chill
and serve.

Following a relocation from New York state to
Texas just before the holidays one year, we realized
the missing element was going to be celebrating with
family. All our relatives remained in the northeast,
and we needed a new family.

Lucky for us, we had good friends in the Austin
area who were as anxious as we for family. Our
Chanukah celebrations grew to include our new family and we developed a tradition of sharing
Grandma's Latkes.

—*Sherri Lipman McCauley*

Strawberry Dessert

Joyce Shackelford
Green Bay, WI
Double Irish Chain

Makes 10-12 servings

8-oz. can crushed
  pineapple
6-oz. pkg. strawberry
  gelatin
20-oz. pkg. frozen
  strawberries, thawed
16-oz. pkg. sour cream

1. Drain and save juice from pineapple. Add water to juice to equal 1 cup. Bring juice to boil.
2. Dissolve gelatin in hot juice. Stir in strawberries and pineapple. Pour half of mixture into 9" x 13" pan. Chill until set.
3. Spread sour cream over gelatin. Gently pour remaining strawberry mixture over sour cream. Chill until firm.

Strawberry Layer Dessert

Mrs. Eli G. Kauffman
Arthur, IL
Mariner's Star

Makes 12-14 servings

1 cup flour
3/4 cup chopped pecans
1/2 cup butter
8-oz. pkg. cream cheese
1 cup powdered sugar
1 cup whipped topping

5 cups water
2 cups sugar
4 Tbsp. cornstarch
6-oz. pkg. strawberry
  gelatin
red food coloring
1 1/2-2 quarts chopped
  fresh strawberries

1. Mix together flour, pecans, and butter. Press into 9" x 13" pan.
2. Bake at 375° for 15 minutes. Cool.
3. Cream together cream cheese, powdered sugar, and whipped topping. Spread over baked crust. Refrigerate.
4. Cook together water, sugar, and cornstarch until thickened. Stir in gelatin and food coloring. Add strawberries. Spoon over top of cream cheese layer.
5. Chill and serve.

Cherry Berries on a Cloud

Rayann Rohrer
Allentown, PA
The Twist
Marion Matson
Bloomington, MN
Winding Ways

Makes 12-14 servings

6 egg whites
1/2 tsp. cream of tartar
1/4 tsp. salt
1 3/4 cups sugar
2 cups chilled whipping
  cream
2 3-oz. pkgs. cream
  cheese

1 cup sugar
1 tsp. vanilla
2 cups miniature
  marshmallows
21-oz. can cherry pie
  filling
1 tsp. lemon juice
2 cups sliced fresh
  strawberries or 16-oz.
  pkg. frozen
  strawberries, thawed

1. Beat egg whites, cream of tartar, and salt until foamy. Beat in sugar, 1 tablespoon at a time. Continue beating until stiff and glossy. Spread into greased 9" x 13" pan.
2. Bake at 275° for 1 hour. Turn off oven. Leave in oven with door closed for 12 hours or longer.
3. In chilled bowl beat whipping cream until stiff. Blend in cream cheese, sugar, and vanilla. Fold in marshmallows. Spread over meringue. Chill 12-24 hours.
4. Stir together pie filling, lemon juice, and strawberries. Pour over mixture in pan.

Baked Oranges

Tillie Aelmer
Oakhurst, CA
Drunkard's Path

Makes 12-14 servings

6 medium oranges
2¹/2 cups sugar
1 cup red hot candies
2 cups water

1. Place whole oranges in saucepan. Cover with water, bring to boil, and simmer for 45 minutes. Drain completely and cool. Cut each orange into eighths and place in 9" x 13" baking pan.
2. In saucepan combine sugar, candies, and water. Cook until sugar and candies are dissolved. Pour syrup over oranges.
3. Bake at 350° for 1¹/2 hours. Serve hot or cold.

Bumpy Apple Dessert

Jeanne Allen
Los Alamos, NM
Railroad Crossing

Makes 12 servings

Apple Mixture:
3 Tbsp. butter
1 cup sugar
1 egg
1 cup flour
1/2 tsp. cinnamon
1/2 tsp. nutmeg
1/2 tsp. salt
1 tsp. baking soda
1 tsp. vanilla
3 cups diced, tart apples
1/4 cup chopped walnuts or pecans

Syrup:
1/2 cup brown sugar
1/2 cup white sugar
1/2 cup butter
1/2 cup sour cream
1/2 tsp. vanilla or almond extract

1. To prepare apple mixture cream together butter and sugar. Stir in egg. Mix well.
2. Sift together flour, cinnamon, nutmeg, salt, and baking soda. Mix well into creamed mixture.
3. Stir in vanilla, apples, and nuts. Batter will be thick and lumpy. Pour into greased 9" square pan.
4. Bake at 350° for 40-45 minutes. Cut into squares and serve with syrup.
5. To prepare syrup mix together sugars, butter, sour cream, and vanilla in a saucepan. Bring to a boil. Boil until mixture forms a soft ball when tested in cold water, at least 15 minutes.
6. Serve hot over apple squares.

Carolyn's Apple Pandowdy

Ann Mather
Lansing, MI
Miniature Churn Dash

Makes 8 servings

5 cups sliced, pared apples
1 cup brown sugar
1/4 cup flour
1/4 tsp. salt
1 tsp. vinegar
1 cup water
1/4 tsp. cinnamon
dash nutmeg
1 tsp. lemon juice
1 tsp. vanilla
2 Tbsp. butter, melted
1 cup flour
2 tsp. baking powder
3/4 tsp. salt
3 Tbsp. shortening
3/4 cup milk

1. Arrange apples in greased 8" x 12" baking dish.
2. In saucepan mix together brown sugar, flour, and salt. Stir in vinegar and water. Cook, stirring constantly until thickened. Cool.
3. Stir in cinnamon, nutmeg, lemon juice, vanilla, and butter. Mix well. Pour over apples in baking dish.
4. Sift together flour, baking powder, and salt. Cut in shortening. Add milk. Mix well. Drop dough on top of apples.
5. Bake at 375° for 40 minutes. Serve with cream.

Apple Date Dessert

Dorothy Stickler
Moline, IL
Lindsay's Baby Quilt

Makes 12-15 servings

Apple Mixture:
2 cups flour
1 cup sugar
1 1/2 tsp. baking soda
1 tsp. salt
1 tsp. cinnamon
1/2 tsp. allspice
2 eggs, slightly beaten
21-oz. can apple pie
   filling
1/2 cup cooking oil
1 tsp. vanilla
1 cup chopped dates
1/4 cup chopped nuts

Rum Sauce:
1/2 cup flour
1 cup sugar
1/8 tsp. salt
2 Tbsp. margarine
1 cup water
2 tsp. vanilla
2 tsp. imitation rum
   extract
1/4 tsp. butter flavoring

1. To prepare apple mixture, sift together flour, sugar, baking soda, salt, cinnamon, and allspice.
2. Combine eggs, apple pie filling, oil, and vanilla. Stir into dry mixture. Mix well. Stir in dates and nuts. Spoon into greased 9" x 13" baking pan.
3. Bake at 350° for 40-45 minutes.
4. To prepare rum sauce, combine flour, sugar, salt, margarine, and water in a saucepan. Cook over medium heat, stirring constantly until it boils and thickens. Add vanilla, rum extract, and butter flavoring.
5. Serve rum sauce warm over apple date dessert.

Apple Crisp

Donna Holton
Green Bay, WI
Album Quilt

Makes 12 servings

6 cups apples, peeled and
   sliced
1 cup sugar
1 tsp. cinnamon
1/2 cup butter or
   margarine
3/4 cup sugar
1 cup flour

1. Mix together apples, sugar, and cinnamon. Place in greased 9" x 13" baking pan.
2. Cut butter into flour and sugar. Sprinkle over apples.
3. Bake at 350° for 1 hour.

Apple Mystery Dessert

Doris H. Perkins
Mashpee, MA
Friendship

Makes 12 servings

2 cups graham cracker
   crumbs
1/2 cup butter or
   margarine, melted
1/4 cup sugar
3 egg yolks, well beaten
14-oz. can sweetened
   condensed milk
1 cup thick applesauce
1/3 cup lemon juice
1 Tbsp. grated lemon
   rind
3 egg whites, stiffly
   beaten

1. Mix together graham cracker crumbs, butter, and sugar. Reserve 1/2 cup of mixture. Press remaining crumbs on bottom and sides of 8" x 12" greased pan.
2. Mix together egg yolks, milk, applesauce, lemon juice, and lemon rind. Fold in egg whites. Pour into crumb crust. Top with reserved crumbs. Chill for several hours or overnight.

Rhubarb Dessert
Kathi Rogge
Alexandria, IN
Beatrix Potter
Preprinted Baby Quilt

Makes 12-14 servings

1/2 cup shortening,
  melted
1/2 cup butter, melted
2 cups flour
2 Tbsp. sugar
5 cups rhubarb, peeled
  and diced
6 egg yolks
2 cups sweetened
  condensed milk
4 Tbsp. flour
1/2 tsp. salt
6 egg whites
3/4 cup sugar
1 tsp. vanilla
1/4 tsp. salt

1. Mix together shortening, butter, flour, and 2 Tbsp. sugar. Pat evenly into bottom and up sides of 9" x 13" baking pan. Bake at 350° for 15 minutes.

2. Spoon rhubarb over crust.
3. Mix together egg yolks, milk, flour, and salt. Pour over rhubarb. Bake at 350° for 1 hour.
4. Beat egg whites. Slowly add sugar, vanilla, and salt. Spread over rhubarb dessert.
7. Bake at 350° for 10 minutes or until meringue has browned.

Pinescotch Pudding
Lorene Diener
Arthur, IL
Dahlia

Makes 10-12 servings

Pineapple Mixture:
1 1/2 cups flour
1/2 tsp. salt
2 tsp. baking powder
4 eggs
2 cups sugar
2 tsp. vanilla
2 cups drained, crushed
  pineapple

1 cup chopped nuts
whipped topping

Butterscotch Sauce:
1/2 cup butter
1 1/3 Tbsp. cornstarch
2 cups brown sugar
1/2 cup pineapple juice
1/2 cup water
2 eggs, beaten
2 tsp. vanilla

1. Sift together flour, salt, and baking powder.
2. Beat eggs until fluffy. Gradually add sugar, beating until ivory colored. Add vanilla. Mix well. Fold in pineapple and nuts. Gently fold in dry ingredients. Pour into greased 9" x 13" baking pan.
3. Bake at 350° for 30 minutes. Cool. Cut into squares and serve with whipped topping and butterscotch sauce.
4. To prepare butterscotch sauce, melt butter in a saucepan. Blend in cornstarch, stirring constantly. Add brown sugar, pineapple juice, and water. Boil for 3 minutes, stirring frequently. Add a bit of hot mixture to eggs. Stir eggs into hot mixture. Cook for 1 minute. Stir in vanilla. Cool slightly before serving.

I grew up near extended family with lots of cousins, aunts, and uncles. When I married, my husband and I established our own family far away in another state. At first our Christmas celebrations seemed bland compared to my own memories.

Then I got the idea to have a Relative's Party on Christmas Eve. First, we have a casual dinner. Then we open all the gifts that have been shipped from our families back home. Finally, we put the kids on the phone with their grandparents, cousins, aunts, and uncles. Now, even if we are invited out for Christmas Eve, we hurry home for our long distance party with our own relatives.
—*Maricarol Magill, Freehold, NJ*

Heavenly Delight
Jacquelyn Kreitzer
Mechanicsburg, PA
Starlit Flower Garden

Makes 10-12 servings

2 Tbsp. pineapple juice
  or juice of 1 lemon
1 tsp. dry mustard
1/4 tsp. salt
2 Tbsp. sugar
4 egg yolks, beaten
2 Tbsp. vinegar
1 Tbsp. butter
1 cup yellow or red
  seeded grapes
20-oz. can pineapple
  chunks
1/4 cup chopped
  maraschino cherries
2 cups miniature
  marshmallows
1/2 cup chopped walnuts
  (optional)
12-oz. carton whipped
  topping

1. In saucepan combine
pineapple juice, dry mus-
tard, salt, sugar, egg yolks,
vinegar, and butter. Cook,
stirring constantly, until
slightly thickened. Cool to
room temperature.
2. Stir in fruit, marshmallows, and walnuts.
Refrigerate for at least 8
hours.
3. Immediately before serving, fold in whipped top-
ping.

Fresh Fruit Cobbler
Marilyn Chandler
Louisburg, KS
Double Wedding Ring

Makes 10-12 servings

2/3 cup sugar
1 Tbsp. cornstarch
1 cup water
3 cups fresh fruit
1 cup flour
1 Tbsp. sugar
1 1/2 tsp. baking powder
1/2 tsp. salt
3 Tbsp. margarine
1/2 cup milk

1. In saucepan mix together
2/3 cup sugar and corn-
starch. Gradually add water.
Bring to boil. Cook and stir
until thickened. Gently fold
in fruit. Pour into 2-quart
baking dish.
2. Mix together flour, sugar,
baking powder, and salt.
Cut in margarine until mixture turns into small
crumbs. Stir in milk. Drop
dough by tablespoonfuls
over fruit.
3. Bake at 400° for 25-30
minutes. Serve warm.

Make-Ahead Crockpot Cobbler
Lena Mae Janes
Lane, KS
Carpenter's Star

Makes 12-14 servings

1 batch drop biscuits
  (approx. 9 biscuits)
1/4 cup brown sugar
4 Tbsp. butter or
  margarine
1 tsp. cinnamon
2 21-oz. cans pie filling

1. Bake biscuits according to
package instructions. Set
aside to cool.
2. Mix together brown
sugar, butter, and cinnamon
in small bowl.
3. Crumble biscuits into
chunks. In large crockpot
alternate layers of biscuits,
pie filling, and sugar mixture.
4. Cook on high for 2 hours.
5. Serve warm with
whipped topping or ice
cream.

Hot Christmas Fruit

Eylene Egan
Babylon, NY
Drunkard's Path
Judi Manos
West Islip, NY
Garden of Love

Makes 12 servings

16-oz. can sliced peaches
16-oz. can pineapple
chunks
16-oz. can pear halves
16-oz. can plums
16-oz. can cherries
1/2 cup butter or
margarine, melted
16-oz. jar applesauce
3/4 cup light brown sugar
cinnamon

1. Drain fruit and place in large casserole dish.
2. Melt butter in a saucepan. Add applesauce and brown sugar and stir until sugar is dissolved.
3. Bake at 350° for 20-25 minutes until bubbly and browned. Sprinkle with cinnamon and serve.

Curried Fruit

Betty Gray
Ellicott City, MD
Log Cabin

Makes 4-6 servings

2 16-oz. cans mixed fruit
1/3 cup butter, melted
1 Tbsp. curry powder
2/3 cup brown sugar

1. Drain fruit and arrange in shallow casserole dish.
2. Melt butter and add curry powder, stirring until well mixed. Pour over fruit.
3. Sprinkle with brown sugar.
4. Bake at 325° for 45 minutes. Remove from oven and let stand for at least 2 hours for flavors to blend. Reheat for 15 minutes before serving.

Note: Excellent to serve with poultry, ham, or pork.

Glazed Fruit Compote

Trudy Kutter
Corfu, NY
Cathedral Window

Makes 10-12 servings

20-oz. can pineapple
chunks
1/3 cup orange juice
1 Tbsp. lemon juice
1/3 cup sugar
2 Tbsp. cornstarch
11-oz. can mandarin
oranges, drained
4 apples, cut up
2-3 bananas, sliced

1. Drain pineapple. Reserve 3/4 cup of juice.
2. In saucepan combine pineapple juice, orange juice, lemon juice, sugar, and cornstarch. Cook, stirring constantly until thick and bubbly. Simmer one minute more. Set aside.
3. Mix together oranges and apples. Pour warm sauce over fruit. Stir gently. Chill several hours.
4. Stir in bananas immediately before serving.

Karen's Fruit Pudding
Marge Reeder
State College, PA
Sara's Log Cabin

Makes 8-10 servings

20-oz. can pineapple chunks
16-oz. can sliced peaches
1 small pkg. non-instant vanilla pudding
16-oz. can dark sweet pitted cherries
2 medium bananas, sliced

1. Drain pineapple, reserving 3/4 cup juice. Drain peaches, reserving 3/4 cup juice.
2. In a microwave container, combine pineapple and peach juices with vanilla pudding. Microwave on high for 3 to 6 minutes or until boiling, stirring after the first 2 minutes, and then every minute.
3. Remove from microwave and cover with plastic wrap directly on pudding surface. Let stand for 1 hour.
2. Stir in pineapple, peaches, and cherries. Chill. Immediately before serving, add bananas.

Frozen Fruit Delight
Susan Stephani Smith
Monument, CO
May Baskets

Makes 12 servings

1 pint sour cream
1 cup sugar
1 Tbsp. vanilla
2 10-oz. pkgs. frozen strawberries
8-oz. can crushed pineapple
16-oz. can cherries, drained
1 cup miniature marshmallows
1/2 cup broken pecans or walnuts

1. Combine sour cream and sugar until sugar is dissolved. Add vanilla.
2. Break strawberries apart and fold into mixture. Fold in pineapple, cherries, marshmallows, and nuts.
3. Pour into individual molds or one large mold. Place in freezer. Remove from freezer about 15 minutes before serving.

Tropical Slush
Arlene Wengerd
Millersburg, OH
Double Wedding Ring

Makes 10 servings

12-oz. can frozen orange juice concentrate
juice of 2 lemons
2 cups sugar
3 cups water
12-oz. can lemon-lime soda
20-oz. can crushed pineapple
1 grapefruit, peeled and cut into bite-sized pieces
1 quart fresh or frozen peach slices, diced
1/4 cup maraschino cherries, well drained and halved

1. Mix together all ingredients, making sure all the sugar is dissolved. Freeze. When partially frozen, stir to blend all fruit evenly. Freeze again until ready to eat.
2. Thaw to slushy consistency and serve.

Frozen Fruit Slush
Elizabeth Chupp
Arthur, IL
Nine Patch

Makes 20 servings

1 pint fresh or frozen peaches, sliced
6-oz. can frozen orange juice concentrate, thawed
16-oz. can crushed pineapple, undrained
2 cups sugar
2 cups water
6 bananas, sliced and dipped in lemon juice

1. Mix together all ingredients. Pour into 9" x 13" pan and freeze.
2. Set out for a few minutes before serving.

Norwegian Fruit Soup
Mary K. Mitchell
Battle Creek, MI
Miniature Wild Goose Chase

Makes 6 servings

1/4 cup tapioca
pinch salt
5 whole cloves
2 cinnamon sticks
2/3 cup sugar
1 rounded cup tart red cherries
3/4 cup frozen red raspberries
3/4 cup frozen blueberries

1. Drain juice from tart red cherries. Add enough water to measure 1 quart.
2. In saucepan mix together cherry juice, tapioca, salt, cloves, and cinnamon sticks. Bring to a boil, stirring until thickened. Stir in sugar and cherries. Reduce heat to simmer and cook for 1-2 minutes. Stir in raspberries and blueberries. Serve warm or cold.

Note: Cloves and cinnamon sticks may be placed in a piece of cheesecloth for easy removal. But in our family the cinnamon sticks stay in the soup while serving, and the first person to find a clove gets a small gift.

Danish Fruit Soup
Evelyn L. Ward
Greeley, CA
Watercolor Quilt

Makes 15 servings

2 cups prunes
1 1/2 cups raisins
3/4 cups currants
2 sticks cinnamon
1/2 cup pearled barley
2 quarts water
1/4 tsp. salt
2 apples, peeled and thinly sliced
1/2 cup corn syrup
brown sugar to taste
1 cup apple, cranberry, or grape juice

1. Rinse prunes, raisins, and currants. Drain. Place in 6-8 quart kettle with cinnamon, barley, and water. Bring to a boil slowly. Reduce heat and simmer 2-3 hours.
2. Add salt and apples. Simmer until apples are tender. Stir in corn syrup and brown sugar. Add juice. Simmer until hot. Taste and add more sugar if necessary.
3. Serve with assorted crackers, breads, cheese, and cold cuts.

Chilled Blueberry Soup
Charmaine Caesar
Lancaster, PA
Bits and Pieces

Makes 2-4 servings

1 pint fresh blueberries
2 cups water
2 tsp. cooked rice or uncooked minute rice
1/4 tsp. cinnamon
1/8 tsp. ground cloves
1/4 cup sugar
1/2 cup sour cream

1. In saucepan mix together blueberries, water, rice, cinnamon, ground cloves, and sugar. Simmer over medium heat for about 10 minutes.
2. Swirl mixture in blender until smooth. Chill.
3. Pour into individual serving cups and garnish with sour cream. Serve.

Date Pudding
Juanita Marner
Shipshewana, IN
Grandmother's
Flower Garden

Makes 12-15 servings

2 cups boiling water
2 tsp. baking soda
2 cups chopped dates
2 Tbsp. butter
2 cups sugar
2 eggs
3 cups flour
2 tsp. baking powder
1 cup chopped nuts
1 tsp. vanilla
2 8-oz. cartons whipped
   topping

1. Combine boiling water, baking soda, dates, and butter and stir until smooth. Cool.
2. Add all remaining ingredients and mix to blend well. Spoon into greased 9" x 13" baking pan.
3. Bake at 350° for 30-40 minutes.

4. Cut into squares and serve warm, topped with whipped topping.

Variations: 1. Cut date pudding into small squares. Prepare 1 large pkg. instant vanilla pudding according to package directions. In large glass serving bowl, layer ingredients in the following order: date squares, vanilla pudding, sliced bananas. Repeat layers, ending with sliced bananas. Garnish with whipped topping and chill before serving. (Use only 1/2 cup whipped topping.)
Dorothy Farmwald
Sullivan, IL
Drunkard's Path

2. Prepare a butter sauce using the following ingredients: 1 Tbsp. butter, 1 cup brown sugar, 1 Tbsp. cornstarch, 2 cups water. Melt butter in saucepan. Stir in brown sugar and cornstarch until well blended. Add water and cook until smooth and slightly thickened. Cut date pudding into bite-sized squares. In large glass serving bowl, mix date pudding with whipped topping. Make three layers of date squares, pouring butter sauce on each layer, allowing date squares to absorb sauce. Serve warm.
Elizabeth Chupp
Arthur, IL
Nine Patch

Swedish Fruit Soup
Carol Armstrong
Winston, OR
Neon Garden

Makes 15-20 servings

2 11-oz. pkgs. mixed
   dried fruit, cut into
   small pieces
1 cup golden seedless or
   regular raisins
1 stick cinnamon
5 cups water
1 medium orange,
   unpeeled
48-oz. can pineapple juice
1/2 cup currant jelly
1/2 cup sugar
1/4 cup minute tapioca
1/4 tsp. salt

1. In large saucepan combine fruit, raisins, cinnamon, and water. Bring to boil. Simmer uncovered until fruits are tender, about 30 minutes.
2. Cut orange into 1/4" slices.
3. Stir all remaining ingredients into fruit mixture. Bring to a boil slowly. Cover and cook over low heat for 15 minutes, stirring occasionally. Serve warm or chilled.

When I was young, my mother always made sure my brother and I had a wonderful Christmas in spite of the fact that we had very little money. One year the only thing she could afford was a very scrawny tree. It was pretty pathetic, and I remember one of our friends making fun of it when he saw the tree before it was decorated.

Mother had a knack for making something from nothing, and she turned that tree into one of the most beautiful we ever had. People oohed and ahhed when they saw it. Christmas is still our favorite holiday and no matter how much we do or do not have; we share with each other and have a special family time.

—*Dana Braden, Seattle, WA*

Deep Dark Secret

Shirley Sears
Tiskilwa, IL
Autumn Glory

Makes 12-15 servings

4 eggs, separated
1 lb. dates, chopped
1 cup sugar
1 cup chopped walnuts
1/2 cup flour
1 tsp. baking powder
2 tsp. vanilla
1/4 tsp. salt
3-4 bananas, sliced
2 oranges, cut up
2 8-oz. cans crushed
  pineapple, undrained
1/2 pint whipping cream
pecan halves
maraschino cherries

1. Beat egg whites until
slightly stiff. Stir in dates,
sugar, walnuts, egg yolks,
flour, baking powder,
vanilla, and salt. Spread into
greased 9" x 13" baking pan.
2. Bake at 350° for 30 minutes.
3. One hour before serving,
break half of date cake into
pieces and arrange on large
serving platter. Top with
bananas and oranges. Break
other half of cake and pile
on top of fruit, mounding
and shaping. Over this
mound pour crushed
pineapple and juice.
4. Whip the cream until soft
and fluffy. Spread over date
cake. Decorate with
maraschino cherries and
pecan halves.

Baked Rice Custard

Bernice M. Guidovec
Streator, IL
Single Irish Chain

Makes 6 servings

2/3 cup minute rice
3 cups milk
2 eggs
2/3 cup sugar
3/4 tsp. salt
1/4 tsp. nutmeg
1 tsp. vanilla
1/2 cup raisins
1 tsp. cinnamon

1. In saucepan combine rice
and milk and bring to a
boil.
2. Mix together eggs, sugar,
salt, nutmeg, and vanilla.
Add hot rice and milk. Mix
well. Stir in raisins and mix
well. Pour into greased
casserole dish.
3. Bake at 375° for 35 minutes, stirring 4 times in first
20 minutes and not at all
during last 15 minutes.
Remove from oven and let
set 5 minutes.
4. Sprinkle with cinnamon
and serve.

Rice Pudding

Nancy Vance
Carterville, IL
Scrap Quilt

Makes 8-10 servings

1/2 gallon milk
1 cup raw rice
1 cup sugar
3/4 tsp. salt
3 eggs, beaten
1 tsp. vanilla
cinnamon
cream

1. In heavy saucepan mix
together milk, rice, sugar,
and salt. Simmer for 1-2
hours, stirring occassionally
until thickened.
2. Stir small amount of
beaten eggs into pudding
and slowly add the remaining eggs. Stir in vanilla and
mix well.
3. Spoon into serving bowl,
sprinkle with cinnamon,
and serve with cream.

Glorified Rice
Joan Brown
Warriors Mark, PA
Group Quilt with 6th Graders

Makes 8 servings

3-oz. pkg. lemon gelatin
1 cup boiling water
1 cup cooked rice
16-oz. can crushed
    pineapple
1/2 cup chopped walnuts
    or pecans
2 Tbsp. powdered sugar
6-oz. pkg. miniature
    marshmallows
8-oz. carton whipped
    topping

1. Dissolve gelatin in boiling water. Cool until gelatin begins to thicken.
2. Mix together rice, pineapple, nuts, sugar, and marshmallows. Add to gelatin. Fold in whipped topping.
3. Chill for 2-3 hours before serving.

Christmas Bread Pudding
Joyce Sczygelski
Merrill, WI
Stars of the Thirties

Makes 6-8 servings

4 eggs
1/2 cup sugar
1/8 tsp. salt
1/4 tsp. cinnamon
2 tsp. vanilla
1 Tbsp. butter, melted

4 cups cubed white bread
    (10 slices)
4 cups milk
1/4 cup sugar
1 cup apricot preserves
1/2 cup strawberry
    preserves

1. Separate 2 eggs and reserve egg whites for meringue. Combine 2 egg yolks, 2 eggs, 1/2 cup sugar, salt, cinnamon, vanilla, and butter.
2. Place bread cubes in greased 8-cup baking dish. Pour milk over bread and let stand for 15 minutes.
3. Set dish into a larger baking dish and pour boiling water around the edges to a depth of 1".
4. Bake at 350° for 50 minutes. Center will be set, but still soft.
5. Beat egg whites, adding 1/4 cup sugar, 1 Tbsp. at a time, until meringue stands in firm peaks.
6. Spoon 1/2 cup apricot preserves over hot pudding. Spread meringue over pudding so no pudding shows through. Make peaks on top of meringue. Place pudding and pan of hot water back into oven for 10 more minutes, or until peaks turn golden. Cool 2 hours.
7. Immediately before serving, melt 1/2 cup apricot and 1/2 cup strawberry preserves in separate dishes. Drizzle over and around the meringue peaks.

Bread Pudding
Amy Picard
Leesburg, FL

Makes 12 servings

1-lb. loaf cinnamon-raisin
    bread
1 quart milk
3 eggs, slightly beaten
1 cup sugar
2 tsp. vanilla
1/8 tsp. ground nutmeg
3 Tbsp. butter or
    margarine, melted
whipped topping

1. Break bread into small chunks. Place in a large bowl. Add milk and soak for 10 minutes. Work mixture with hands until milk is absorbed.
2. Combine eggs, sugar, vanilla, nutmeg, and butter. Stir into bread mixture. Pour into greased 9" x 13" baking pan.
3. Bake at 350° for 50 minutes or until knife inserted in center comes out clean. Serve with whipped topping.

Cracker Pudding

Lizzie Weaver
Ephrata, PA
Medallion

Makes 6-8 servings

5 cups milk
1 cup sugar
1 cup cracker crumbs
1/2 cup coconut
2 eggs, beaten
1 tsp. vanilla

1. In saucepan combine 3 cups milk, sugar, crumbs, and coconut. Add eggs and a little milk until blended. Stir in remaining milk and vanilla.
2. Stir over medium heat until thickened. Chill and serve plain or with whipped topping.

Baked Indian Pudding

Myrtle Mansfield
Alfred, ME
Good Wishes

Makes 4-6 servings

3 Tbsp. cornmeal
1 pint milk
3 Tbsp. molasses
1/4 tsp. salt
1/4 tsp. nutmeg
1/4 cup sugar
2 Tbsp. butter
1/4 tsp. ginger
1/4 tsp. cinnamon
2 eggs, beaten

1. Heat milk in double boiler until hot to the finger or almost to boiling point. Add cornmeal and cook for 15 minutes, stirring constantly. Stir in all remaining ingredients and mix well.
2. Pour into greased casserole dish. Bake uncovered at 400° for 30 minutes or until set in middle. Serve warm.

Pumpkin Bread Pudding

Nanci C. Keatley
Salem, OR
Brian's Sea of Cabins

Makes 6-8 servings

4 cups cubed day-old bread
1/2 cup chopped dates or raisins
1/2 cup chopped pecans
2 cups milk
1 cup cooked pumpkin
2 eggs, separated
2/3 cup brown sugar
1 1/2 tsp. ground cinnamon
3/4 tsp. ground nutmeg
1/4 tsp. salt
1/8 tsp. ground cloves
whipped topping (optional)

1. Mix together bread cubes, dates, and 1/3 cup pecans. Pour into greased 2-quart baking dish.
2. Combine milk, pumpkin, egg yolks, brown sugar, cinnamon, nutmeg, salt, and cloves. Beat well.
3. Beat egg whites until stiff. Fold into pumpkin mixture.
4. Pour pumpkin mixture over bread cubes and toss gently. Sprinkle wtih remaining pecans.
5. Bake uncovered at 350° for 1 to 1 1/2 hours or until a knife inserted in center comes out clean. Serve warm or chilled with whipped topping.

Banana Pudding

Lisa Schafer
Hampton, VA

Makes 12-14 servings

14-oz. can sweetened condensed milk
1 1/2 cups cold water
1 pkg. instant vanilla pudding
2 cups whipping cream
36 vanilla wafers
3 medium bananas, sliced

1. Combine condensed milk and water. Beat in pudding. Chill 5 minutes.
2. Fold in whipped cream. Spoon 1 cup pudding into 2 1/2-quart glass serving bowl. Top with 1/3 of bananas, 1/3 of wafers, and 1/3 of remaining pudding. Repeat layers twice, ending with pudding. Chill and serve.

Flan

Jeanne Allen
Los Alamos, NM
Baltimore Beauty

Makes 8 servings

2¹/4 cups evaporated milk
1¹/2 cups sugar
³/4 cup water
6 eggs
¹/2 tsp. vanilla
¹/4 cup sugar

1. In double boiler combine milk, 1¹/2 cups sugar, water, eggs, and vanilla. Beat with a hand mixer about 1 minute or until well blended. Heat mixture until warm throughout. Do not boil.
2. In heavy saucepan melt ¹/4 cup sugar over low heat until it is a golden syrup. Stir only if it is browning unevenly.
3. Pour about 1 tsp. sugar syrup into each of 8 custard cups. (The syrup will harden immediately.) Place heavy saucepan in water immediately for easy cleaning.
4. Pour hot, but not boiling, custard into custard cups. Place cups in a large baking pan, making sure the cups are not touching. Add warm water to the pan, enough to cover the bottom ¹/3 of the outside of the custard cups.
5. Bake at 300° for 1³/4 hours, until custard is firm and top is a light brown. Bake up to 15 minutes longer if necessary.

6. Cool for 15-20 minutes. Cover and refrigerate. Chill at least 3 hours before serving.
7. To serve run a knife around the edge of the custard and invert onto serving plates. Shake slightly until the custard lets go. Serve.

Cherry Angel Food Trifle

Anna Oberholtzer
Lititz, PA
Improved Nine Patch

Makes 12-14 servings

¹/2 cup powdered sugar
8-oz. pkg. cream cheese, softened
8-oz. carton whipped topping
5 cups cubed angel food cake
¹/2 cup chopped pecans
21-oz. can cherry pie filling

1. In medium bowl combine sugar and cream cheese. Beat until well blended.
2. Reserve ¹/2 cup whipped topping. Fold remaining whipped topping, cake cubes, and pecans into cream cheese mixture.
3. Spoon mixture into glass bowl. Top with pie filling. Garnish with reserved whipped topping.
4. Cover and refrigerate at least 3 hours before serving.

Chocolate and Cherry Trifle

Sharon Shadburn
Ft. Leavenworth, KS
Northern Stars

Makes 6-8 servings

14-oz. can sweetened condensed milk
¹/2 cup unsweetened cocoa
2 Tbsp. margarine or butter
2 Tbsp. water
1¹/2 tsp. vanilla
8-oz. pkg. cream cheese
8-oz. carton whipped topping
10³/4-oz. pound cake, thawed and cubed
21-oz. can cherry pie filling, chilled
1 cup chopped pecans
6-8 pecan halves

1. In saucepan combine milk, cocoa, margarine, and water. Cook over low heat, stirring until margarine is melted. Remove from heat. Stir in vanilla. Cool.
2. Beat cream cheese until fluffy. Gradually beat in chocolate mixture until well blended. Chill 10 minutes. Fold 1¹/2 cups whipped topping into chocolate mixture.
3. In 3-quart glass serving bowl, layer ¹/2 of cake cubes, then ¹/2 of chocolate mixture. Top with cherry pie filling and 2 cups whipped topping. Sprinkle with pecans. Layer remaining cake cubes and spread remaining chocolate mix-

ture over all. Garnish with additional whipped topping and pecan halves. Chill at least 5 hours before serving.

Pluckets
Esther S. Martin
Ephrata, PA
Dahlia

Makes 6-8 servings

1/2 **cup chopped walnuts**
3-oz. **pkg. non-instant butterscotch pudding**
1 **cup brown sugar**
1/2 **cup margarine**
1 **tsp. cinnamon**
1 **tsp. vanilla**
1/2 **cup milk**
16-oz. **loaf frozen bread dough, partially thawed**

1. Sprinkle walnuts on bottom of greased large bread pan.
2. In medium saucepan combine pudding, sugar, margarine, cinnamon, vanilla, and milk. Bring to a boil and boil for 3-5 minutes, stirring constantly. Let cool, then pour 1 cup pudding over walnuts.
3. Cut bread dough into cubes and place on top. Pour remaining pudding mixture over dough. Cover with waxed paper and refrigerate for at least 8 hours.
4. Bake uncovered at 350° for 30 minutes.
5. Remove from oven and immediately invert onto serving plate.

Graham Cracker Roll
Ruth Liebelt
Rapid City, SD
Woven Heart

Makes 10-12 servings

1 **lb. graham crackers, rolled fine**
1 **lb. marshmallows, cut into pieces**
1 **lb. dates, chopped**
1 **lb. nuts, chopped**
1 **cup thick cream**
1/2 **cup powdered sugar**
1 **tsp. vanilla**

1. Reserve 1/2 cup graham cracker crumbs.
2. Mix together remaining graham cracker crumbs, marshmallows, dates, and nuts.
3. Whip cream until stiff. Slowly add sugar and vanilla. Fold into graham cracker mixture.
4. Divide mixture in half and roll each half into a loaf shape. Roll loaves through reserved cracker crumbs to coat.
5. Refrigerate for 7-8 hours. Slice and serve.

Chocolate Frango
Kareen Armstrong
Rockaway Beach, OR
White on White Heirloom

Makes 8-10 servings

15-20 **vanilla wafers, crushed**
1 **cup butter**
2 **cups powdered sugar**
4 **squares chocolate**
4 **eggs, beaten**
3/4 **tsp. peppermint extract**
2 **tsp. vanilla**

1. Sprinkle half of vanilla wafer crumbs on bottom of 8" x 10" pan.
2. Beat together butter and powdered sugar until fluffy.
3. Melt chocolate in top of double boiler. Stir in eggs and mix well. Remove from heat.
4. Beat chocolate, peppermint extract, and vanilla into powdered sugar mixture. Spoon over crumbs in pan. Sprinkle with remaining crumbs. Freeze. Serve plain or with whipped cream.

Chocolate Sin
Debbie Chisholm
Fallston, MD
Whole Cloth Quilt

Makes 6-8 servings

4 4-oz. bars German
   sweet cooking
   chocolate
1/2 cup butter, softened
4 egg yolks
4 egg whites, room
   temperature
4 tsp. sugar
4 tsp. flour

1. Preheat oven to 425°
2. In double boiler melt
chocolate over hot, not boiling, water, stirring occasionally. Remove from heat and
beat in butter with a spoon.
3. Beat egg yolks until thick
and lemon colored. Slowly
add sugar, beating con-
stantly. Stir in flour until
blended. Stir into chocolate
mixture.
4. Beat egg whites which
have been brought to room
temperature until stiff peaks
form. With rubber scraper
or wire whisk, gently fold
chocolate mixture into egg
whites. Turn into greased
9" x 5" loaf pan.
5. Reduce oven temperature
to 350° and bake for 25
minutes. Let cool com-
pletely in pan on a wire
rack. (Cake will settle like a
cheesecake.) Refrigerate
until well chilled, about 4
hours.
6. To serve loosen cake.
Remove from pan by invert-

ing onto a serving plate.
Decorate with chocolate
curls and cut into slices.

Cheese Cake
Eileen Jarvis
Wexford, PA
Card Trick

Makes 12 servings

Crust:
1 box zwieback cookies,
   crushed
8 Tbsp. margarine or
   butter, softened

Cheesecake:
2 8-oz. pkgs. cream
   cheese, softened
1 lb. ricotta cheese
1 pint sour cream
1 1/4 cups sugar
3 eggs
juice of 1 lemon
1 tsp. vanilla
8 Tbsp. butter or
   margarine, melted
3 Tbsp. flour
3 Tbsp. cornstarch

1. To prepare crust mix
together cookie crumbs and
margarine. Mix thoroughly.
Pat gently into bottom of
springform pan.
2. Mix together cream
cheese, ricotta cheese, and
sour cream. Stir in sugar
and mix well. Gradually
add eggs, one at a time. Stir
in lemon juice, vanilla,
melted butter which has
been brought to room tem-
perature, flour, and cornstarch. Mix thoroughly and

pour over crust in pan.
3. Place in cold oven. Turn
oven to 325° and bake for
70-80 minutes. Turn off the
oven, but do not remove the
cheesecake! Let set in oven
for 2 more hours. Serve
warm or cold.

*Note: This recipe works best
when all ingredients are
brought to room temperature
before mixing.*

Candy Cane
Cheesecake
Rosemarie Fitzgerald
Gibsonia, PA
Nine Patch Baby Quilt

Makes 10 servings

Crust:
1 1/3 cups chocolate
   cookie crumbs
2 Tbsp. sugar
1/4 cup margarine, melted

Filling:
1 1/2 cups sour cream
1/2 cup sugar
3 eggs
1 Tbsp. flour
2 tsp. vanilla
1/4 tsp. peppermint
   extract
3 8-oz. pkgs. cream
   cheese, softened
2 Tbsp. butter, softened
2/3 cup crushed
   peppermint candy
8-oz. carton whipped
   topping

1. To prepare crust combine
cookie crumbs, sugar, and

margarine. Press into bottom of 9" springform pan.
2. To prepare filling cream together sour cream, sugar, eggs, flour, vanilla, and peppermint extract. Add cream cheese and butter, blending until completely smooth. Stir in crushed candy and pour into crust.
3. Bake on lowest rack of oven at 325° for 50-60 minutes or until firm. Allow to cool in oven. Refrigerate for at least 8 hours.
4. Use knife to loosen sides of cake from pan. Remove springform. Spread top of cake with whipped topping and serve.

Pumpkin Swirl Cheesecake
Nancy Jo Marsden
Glen Mills, PA
Plaid Schoolhouse Quilt

Makes 16-20 servings

1 cup graham cracker crumbs
2 Tbsp. margarine, melted
3 8-oz. pkgs. cream cheese, softened
1 cup sugar
1/3 cup brandy
2 tsp. vanilla
4 eggs
1/2 tsp. salt
16-oz. can pumpkin
2 Tbsp. cornstarch
1 tsp. cinnamon
1/2 tsp. allspice
8-oz. carton sour cream

1. In 9" springform pan, stir crumbs and margarine until moistened. Press into bottom of pan.
2. Bake at 325° for 10 minutes. Cool.
3. Beat cream cheese until smooth. Add sugar and mix well. Add brandy, vanilla, eggs, and salt until just blended.
4. Mix together pumpkin, cornstarch, cinnamon, and allspice. Stir 1/2 of cheese mixture into pumpkin mixture until just blended. Stir sour cream into remaining cheese mixture.
5. Reserve 1/2 cup pumpkin mixture. Pour pumpkin mixture over crust. Carefully, pour cheese mixture on top of pumpkin mixture. Spoon dollops of reserved pumpkin onto cheese layer. Cut and swirl with knife.
6. Bake at 325° for 1 hour. Turn oven temperature off, and let cheesecake set in oven for 1 hour longer.
7. Remove from oven and loosen cake from sides of pan with small knife. Cool completely in pan on a wire rack. Cover and refrigerate at least 6 hours before serving.

Barbara's Cheesecake
Barbara Hooley
Shipshewana, IN
Victorian Elegance

Makes 12-16 servings

Pecan Crumb Crust:
1 cup flour
1/2 cup butter, softened
1/4 cup chopped pecans

Filling:
3 8-oz. pkgs. cream cheese, softened
2/3 cup sugar
2 eggs
1/4 cup flour
1 tsp. almond extract

Topping:
1 cup sour cream
2 Tbsp. sugar
1 tsp. almond extract
21-oz. can cherry pie filling

1. To prepare crust mix together flour, butter, and pecans. Press into 10" springform pan.
2. To prepare filling cream together cream cheese and sugar. Beat in eggs. Stir in flour and almond extract. Pour filling mixture into crust.
3. Bake at 350° for 30 minutes.
4. To prepare topping mix together sour cream, sugar, and almond extract. Spread on top of hot cheesecake.
5. Bake at 425° for 5 minutes. Refrigerate. Top with cherry pie filling and serve.

Chocolate Raspberry Cheesecake

Barbara Nolan
Pleasant Valley, NY
*Feed Sack with
Pinwheel Edges*

Makes 6-8 servings

3 squares semi-sweet
chocolate
1/4 cup water
8-oz. pkg. cream cheese
1/2 cup raspberry fruit
spread
8-oz. carton whipped
topping
2 Tbsp. water
2 chocolate wafer
cookies, crushed

1. In saucepan melt chocolate with 1/4 cup water, stirring constantly.
2. Beat together melted chocolate, cream cheese, and 1/4 cup raspberry spread. Immediately stir in 2 1/2 cups whipped topping and beat until smooth. Spread into 9" pie plate or springform pan. Freeze for 3-4 hours.
3. In a small saucepan combine remaining fruit spread and 2 Tbsp. water and heat briefly until just blended. Spread over cheescake. Spread remaining whipped topping to within 1" of edges of cheesecake. Decorate with crushed chocolate wafers.
4. May be served directly from freezer. Or move from freezer to refrigerator for 30 minutes before serving.

Eileen's Good Cheesecake

Eylene Egan
Babylon, NY
Drunkard's Path

Makes 12 servings

3 lbs. cream cheese,
softened
2 cups sugar
4 eggs
2 Tbsp. vanilla

1. Mix together cream cheese and sugar. Beat in eggs and vanilla.
2. Spoon mixture into springform pan.
3. Bake at 350° for 45-60 minutes until lightly browned. Do not open oven while baking. When finished baking, turn oven off and leave cake in oven for 2 more hours.
4. Refrigerate until ready to serve.

Surprise Cheesecake

Barbara Smith
Bedford, PA
Mexican Star

Makes 12 servings

2 pkgs. Pillsbury crescent
rolls
2 8-oz. pkgs. cream
cheese
2 egg yolks
1 tsp. vanilla
3/4 cup sugar
2 egg whites
powdered sugar

1. Knead one package crescent rolls into loose ball of dough and spread to fit the bottom of lightly greased 9" x 13" baking pan.
2. Mix together cream cheese, egg yolks, vanilla, and sugar until fluffy. Spoon over crescent roll crust.
3. Knead remaining package crescent rolls into loose ball of dough and spread over cheesecake filling. Brush lightly with egg whites.
4. Bake at 350° for 25-30 minutes. Sprinkle with powdered sugar and serve.

One year at Christmas my quilt making mother presented each of her seven children with Trip Around the World quilts made from scrap pieces of fabric she had gathered through the years. She had done all the work on all seven of the quilts by herself. The photo of all of us holding our quilts sustains the memory.

—Anna Petersheim, Paradise, PA

Healthy Cheesecake

Kaye Merrill
Olive Branch, MS
Bow Tie

Makes 10 servings

2 8-oz. pkgs. fat-free
  cream cheese
14-oz. can fat-free
  condensed milk
3/4 cup egg beaters
1 tsp. vanilla
1/3 cup lemon juice
1/3 cup flour
1 1/2 cups lowfat graham
  cracker crumbs
2 egg whites

1. Beat cream cheese until fluffy. Beat in milk until smooth. Stir in egg beaters, vanilla, and lemon juice. Mix well. Stir in flour.
2. Mix together graham cracker crumbs and egg whites. Pour into sprayed 10" pie plate. Press down with back of spoon. Pour cream cheese mixture over crust.
3. Bake at 300° for 50-55 minutes. Allow to cool and chill. Serve with your favorite fat-free topping.

Note: The crust does have a small amount of fat, but otherwise this is a very healthy cheesecake.

Pineapple Cheesecake Squares

Katie Zimmerman
Leola, PA

Makes 12 servings

Crust:
2 cups flour
2/3 cup butter, softened
1/2 cup chopped almonds
1/2 cup powdered sugar

Filling:
2 8-oz. pkgs. cream
  cheese, softened
1/2 cup sugar
2 eggs
2/3 cup pineapple juice

Topping:
1/4 cup flour
1/4 cup sugar
1 cup pineapple juice
20-oz. can crushed
  pineapple
1/2 cup whipping cream

1. Drain pineapple listed in topping ingredients and reserve 1 2/3 cups pineapple juice.
2. To prepare crust mix together flour, butter, almonds, and powdered sugar. Press firmly and evenly into bottom of 9" x 13" baking pan.
3. Bake at 350° for 15-20 minutes.
4. To prepare filling beat cream cheese until smooth and fluffy. Stir in sugar, eggs, and pineapple juice. Mix well. Pour over hot crust.

5. Bake until center is set, about 20 minutes. Cool.
6. To prepare topping mix together flour and sugar in a saucepan. Stir in 1 cup pineapple juice and heat to boiling over medium heat, stirring constantly. Boil for 1 minute. Remove from heat and fold in crushed pineapple. Cool.
7. Beat whipping cream until stiff. Fold into pineapple mixture. Spread over dessert. Cover with plastic wrap and refrigerate for 4 hours. Cut into 3" squares and serve.

Pumpkin Pie Dessert Squares
Betty Moore
Plano, IL
Trip Around the World

Makes 15 servings

1 1/2 cups flour
1/2 cup margarine
1/2 cup chopped nuts
2 small pkgs. instant
  vanilla pudding
1 cup milk
2 cups canned pumpkin
1 tsp. cinnamon
1/2 tsp. nutmeg
1/2 tsp. salt
12-oz. carton whipped
  topping

1. Mix together flour, margarine, and nuts. Press into 9" x 13" baking pan.
2. Bake at 350° for 25 minutes. Cool.
3. Combine all remaining ingredients, using half of the whipped topping. Spread over cooled crust. Cover with remaining whipped topping.

Danish Pie Squares
Nettie Miller
Millersburg, OH
Trip Around the World

Makes 24 servings

Filling:
4 1/4 cups flour
1 1/2 tsp. salt
3/4 tsp. baking powder
1 3/4 cups shortening
milk
2 egg yolks, beaten
21-oz. can pie filling
2 egg whites

Glaze:
1 1/2 cups powdered sugar
1/2 tsp. vanilla
2 Tbsp. water

1. Sift together flour, salt, and baking powder. Cut in shortening until mixture becomes crumbly.
2. Add enough milk to egg yolks to make 1 cup. Add to flour mixture and blend well. Divide dough into two parts.
3. Roll half of dough to fit jelly roll pan, sides included. Spread prepared pie filling over bottom crust. Roll out second half of dough and put on top of filling. Cut slits in top crust and pinch edges together.
4. Beat egg whites until stiff. Brush over top of Danish.
5. Bake at 350° for 50-60 minutes or until golden brown. Cool and drizzle with glaze.

6. To prepare glaze mix together powdered sugar, vanilla, and water.

Note: Take a piece of waxed paper the size of jelly roll pan. Under the waxed paper, sprinkle a bit of water onto the table, causing the paper to stick. Roll out dough onto paper. Pick up paper and put it, dough side down, onto the lightly greased pan. Peel paper off.

Coffee Dream Torte
Frani Shaffer
Coatesville, PA
All Hearts Come Home

Makes 10-12 servings

Crust:
1/2 cup butter
1 1/4 cups flour
3/4 cups finely chopped
  pecans

Filling:
1 pkg. instant chocolate
  pudding
1 pkg. instant coffee
  pudding*
2 1/4 cups milk
8-oz. pkg. cream cheese
1 cup powdered sugar
12-oz. pkg. whipped
  topping
1/2 cup chopped pecans
  or walnuts

If you do not find coffee pudding at your grocery, purchase vanilla and add 2 tsp. instant coffee granules to pudding mix.

1. To prepare crust mix together butter, flour, and pecans. Press into greased 9" x 13" baking pan. Bake at 350° for 10-15 minutes. Cool.
2. To prepare filling mix together puddings and milk. Beat well. Pour over crust in pan.
3. Mix together cream cheese, powdered sugar, and half of whipped topping. Spread over pudding.
4. Put remaining whipped topping over top layer and sprinkle with nuts. Serve.

Rugalach
Sherri Lipman McCauley
Austin, TX
Dorothy's Baskets

Makes 4-5 dozen

2 cups flour
1/2 tsp. salt
2 3-oz. pkgs. cream cheese
1/2 cup shortening
2-3 Tbsp. cold water
1/2 cup chopped walnuts
1 tsp. cinnamon
4 Tbsp. sugar
1/2 cup white raisins
1/2 cup powdered sugar

1. Sift together flour and salt. Cut in cream cheese and shortening. Add enough water to hold together. Mix well. Divide into 4 parts. Refrigerate at least 2 hours.
2. Working with one part at a time, roll out into 8" diameter circle on lightly floured

surface. Sprinkle with 1/4 of walnuts, cinnamon, sugar, and raisins. Cut into 12 triangular wedges. Roll up from wide side to narrow. Repeat with each of the other pieces of dough.
3. Bake at 350° for 15-20 minutes. Sprinkle with powdered sugar while still warm and serve.

Frozen Strawberry Cream Squares
Joan Blaes
Chattanooga, TN

Makes 8 servings

1 pint frozen sweetened strawberries
8-oz. can crushed pineapple, drained
1/2 cup pecans, chopped
1/2 lb. miniature marshmallows
1 cup whipping cream
1 cup mayonnaise
3-oz. pkg. cream cheese, softened

1. Mix together strawberries, pineapple, pecans, and marshmallows.
2. Cream together cream, mayonnaise, and cream cheese until smooth. Add to fruit mixture. Mix well.
3. Freeze in mold or flat pan. Cut into squares immediately before serving.

Pumpkin Ice Cream
Marina Salume
Half Moon Bay, CA

Makes 2 servings

1/2 cup cooked mashed pumpkin
1/4 cup packed brown sugar
1/4 cup light cream
1 tsp. pumpkin pie spice
1/2 tsp. vanilla
1 cup whipping cream

1. Mix together pumpkin, brown sugar, light cream, pumpkin pie spice, and vanilla.
2. Whip cream until soft peaks form. Fold into pumpkin mixture. Freeze until firm. Serve.

Fruited Ice Cream Dessert
Donna Wright
Oxford, NY
Tulip Basket Pillow Throw

Makes 6 servings

3-oz. pkg. peach gelatin
1 cup boiling water
1 pint vanilla ice cream
2/3 cup fresh or canned peaches, drained and diced
1 cup sliced peaches for garnish

1. Dissolve gelatin in boiling water. Add vanilla ice cream by spoonfuls, stirring until ice cream is melted. Add fruit. Chill until set, about 30 minutes.
2. Garnish with diced fruit.

Variation: Use strawberry gelatin and strawberries.

Boston Chart House Mud Pie
Barbara G. Winiarski
South Dennis, MA
Sunbonnet Sue Through the Year

Makes 8 servings

Crust:
1 1/2 pkgs. thin chocolate wafers, crushed
1/4 cup butter, melted

Filling:
1 quart coffee ice cream
1 1/2 cups fudge sauce, room temperature
1 cup heavy cream
2 Tbsp. powdered sugar
1 cup slivered almonds, chopped

1. Mix together wafer crumbs and butter. Press into bottom and sides of 9" pie place. Freeze for 30 minutes.
2. Let ice cream stand at room temperature for 10 minutes or until it softens enough to spread. Spread ice cream over crust, smooth the top, and freeze for 1 hour or until it is frozen solid.
3. Spread fudge sauce over the ice cream, smooth the top, and freeze for 1 hour or until the sauce has hardened.
4. In chilled bowl with chilled beaters, beat the cream and sugar until stiff. Refrigerate.
5. Brown almonds on baking sheet at 400° for 8 minutes or until golden. Watch

carefully. Allow to cool completely.
6. Cut pie into 8 individual pieces. Top each piece with whipped cream and browned almonds and serve.

Ice Cream Roll
Lucille Brubacker
Barnett, MO
Double Wedding Ring

Makes 24 servings

5 egg whites
1/2 cup sugar
5 egg yolks
1/4 tsp. salt
1/2 cup sugar
1/4 cup cocoa
3/4 cup flour
1 1/2 pints ice cream
2 cups whipped topping

1. Beat egg whites until light and fluffy. Gradually add 1/2 cup sugar and continue beating.
2. Beat egg yolks and salt until light and fluffy. Gradually add sugar and continue beating.
3. Fold egg whites into egg yolks. Fold in cocoa and flour. Line 11" x 15" shallow pan with greased waxed paper. Pour batter onto waxed paper.
4. Bake at 350° for 25 minutes.
5. Remove from oven and turn onto towel sprinkled heavily with powdered sugar. Remove waxed paper and form into roll. Let stand

about 4 minutes. Unroll and spread with ice cream. Reroll and freeze. Cover with whipped topping. Slice and serve.

Pears Parisienne
Jane S. Lippincott
Wynnewood, PA
*Scrap Trip Around
the World Baby Quilt*

Makes 6 servings

juice and grated rind of 1
  orange
juice and grated rind of 1
  lemon
1 cup sugar
29-oz. can pear halves
1 pint vanilla ice cream
1 square unsweetened
  chocolate, grated

1. In saucepan mix together orange juice, orange rind, lemon juice, lemon rind, and sugar. Cook over low heat for 15 minutes, stirring frequently. Chill.
2. Place 2 pear halves on each individual serving plate. Top with scoop of ice cream, orange sauce, and grated chocolate.

Chocolate Surprise
Shirley A. Carlson
Green Bay, WI
Fourth of July

Makes 24 servings

15-oz. pkg. Oreo cookies,
  crushed
1/3 cup butter, melted
1/2 gallon vanilla ice
  cream, softened
1 pint hot fudge topping
1/2 gallon mint ice cream,
  softened
8-oz. carton whipped
  topping

1. Mix together cookies and butter. Reserve 1 cup. Press remaining mixture into bottom of large pan.
2. Layer vanilla ice cream, hot fudge topping, and mint ice cream. Freeze for half an hour between each layer. Top with whipped topping and sprinkle with reserved crumbs. Serve.

Variation: Use chocolate wafers instead of Oreo cookies for crust.
  Sharron Van Meter
  St. Charles, MO
  Friendship

Butterfinger or Heath Bar Dessert
Sara Ann Miller
Fredericksburg, OH
Mrs. Lester J. Gingerich
Arthur, IL
Janice Yoskovich
Carmichaels, PA
Elizabeth J. Yoder
Millersburg, OH
Marjorie Patterson
North Point, PA
Katie Zimmerman
Leola, PA

Makes 12 servings

60 Ritz crackers, crushed
1/2 cup margarine, melted
2 small pkgs. instant
  vanilla pudding
2 cups milk
1 quart vanilla ice cream,
  softened
8-oz. carton whipped
  topping
4 Butterfinger or Heath
  candy bars, crushed

1. Mix together cracker crumbs and margarine. Press 3/4 of mixture into 9" x 13" pan.
2. Combine pudding and milk. Beat for 1 minute. Stir in ice cream and beat until smooth. Stir in whipped topping and beat until smooth. Pour over cracker crumbs in pan.
3. Mix candy bars with remaining cracker crumbs. Sprinkle on top of ice cream mixture. Freeze.
4. Remove from freezer 20-30 minutes before serving.

Apparently, my parents required us to get dressed on Christmas morning before we could begin opening gifts or have breakfast because I remember sneaking out of bed on Christmas Eve and putting on all my clothes, including shoes. I could then sleep completely dressed and not waste precious time the next morning.
—*Sara Harter Fredette, Williamsburg, MA*

Snowballs
Jan Carroll
Morton, IL
Wedding Autograph Quilt

Makes 8-10 servings

8-10 peppermint sticks
1/2 gallon vanilla ice cream, softened
2 7-oz. pkgs. coconut
8-10 thick birthday candles

1. Place peppermint sticks inside plastic bags. Use a hammer to crush them into small pieces.
2. Mix peppermint into softened ice cream. Refreeze.
3. Form ice cream into orange-sized balls, using large dipper and rolling with hands. Roll the "snow" balls into coconut to cover completely. Place the balls on a cookie sheet. Cover with foil and freeze until needed.
4. To serve place one snowball on each small plate. Place a thick red birthday candle in the top. Turn the lights down low and enjoy.

Note: A small pitcher of hot fudge sauce may be passed to pour over the snowballs after the candles have been blown out and removed.

Cocoa Mint Freeze
Nancy W. Berger
Medina, NY
Irish Chain

Makes 8 servings

Ice Cream:
35 vanilla wafers, finely crushed
4 Tbsp. margarine
1/2 gallon peppermint ice cream, softened

Topping:
2 2-oz. squares unsweetened chocolate
1/2 cup butter
3 egg yolks, beaten
1 1/2 cups powdered sugar
1/2 cup chopped walnuts
1 tsp. vanilla
3 egg whites

1. Mix together vanilla wafer crumbs and margarine. Reserve 1/4 cup. Press remaining crumbs into a 9" square pan.
2. Spread ice cream over crumbs. Freeze.
3. To prepare topping melt chocolate and butter in a saucepan. Stir in egg yolks, sugar, walnuts, and vanilla. Set aside and cool completely.
4. Beat egg whites until stiff. Fold into completely cooled chocolate mixture. Spread on top of ice cream. Sprinkle with 1/4 cup reserved crumbs. Freeze.

Tortoni Squares
Mary Mainwaring
Salem, OR

Makes 8-10 servings

1/3 cup chopped, toasted almonds
3 Tbsp. butter, melted
1 cup finely chopped vanilla wafers
1 tsp. almond extract
3 pints vanilla ice cream, softened
12-oz. jar apricot preserves
whipped topping (optional)

1. Combine almonds, butter, wafer crumbs, and almond extract and mix well. Reserve 1/4 cup crumbs and set aside.
2. Sprinkle 1/2 of remaining crumb mixture over bottom of an 8" square pan. Spoon 1/2 of ice cream over crumb mixture. Drizzle 1/2 of apricot preserves over ice cream. Repeat layers. Sprinkle top with 1/4 cup reserved crumbs.
3. Freeze until ready to serve. Remove from freezer, garnish with whipped topping, and serve.

Fruit Pizza
Rachel Pellman
Lancaster, PA

Makes 6-8 servings

Pizza:
**1 roll refrigerated sugar
  cookie dough**
8-oz. pkg. cream cheese
1/3 cup sugar
1 tsp. lemon juice
**assorted slices of fresh or
  canned fruit**

Orange Glaze:
1/2 cup sugar
2 Tbsp. cornstarch
1 cup orange juice
1/4 cup lemon juice

1. Press sugar cookie dough into a medium-sized greased pizza pan.
2. Bake at 350° for 10-15 minutes or until slightly browned. Cool.
3. Cream together cream cheese, sugar, and lemon juice. Spread over cookie crust.

4. Arrange any variety of fruits over filling. Since fresh fruits are limited at Christmas time, you may use canned peaches, mandarin oranges, fresh red and green grapes, canned pineapple, and kiwi.
5. To prepare glaze mix together sugar, cornstarch, and juices in a saucepan. Cook over medium heat, stirring constantly until thickened. Spoon glaze over fruit while glaze is still hot. Cool pizza several hours. Slice and serve.

Variation: Prepare own crust by combining 1 1/2 cups flour, 3/4 cup margarine, and 1/2 cup powdered sugar. Press into 9" x 13" baking pan. Bake at 350° for 15-20 minutes. Continue as indicated above.
Elizabeth Chupp
Arthur, IL
Nine Patch

Chocolate Sauce
Becky Harder
Monument, CO
Snowball

Makes 3 1/2 cups

**1/2 cup butter or
  margarine**
**2 1-oz. squares
  unsweetened chocolate**
2 cups sugar
**1 cup light cream or
  evaporated milk**
1/2 cup light corn syrup
1 tsp. vanilla extract

1. In saucepan melt together butter and chocolate. Add sugar, cream, corn syrup, and vanilla. Bring to a boil, stirring constantly. Boil for 1 1/2 minutes. Remove from heat.
2. Serve warm or cold over ice cream or pound cake.

Note: This is wonderful over peppermint ice cream. Small jars of this sauce make nice hostess gifts during the holidays.

Hot Fudge Sauce
Marlene Fonken
Upland, CA
Crazy Patch

Makes 2 cups

1 cup sugar
1/3 cup cocoa
2 Tbsp. flour
1/4 tsp. salt
1 cup boiling water
1 Tbsp. butter
1 tsp. vanilla

1. In saucepan mix together sugar, cocoa, flour, and salt. Add water and butter. Cook over medium heat until thickened, stirring constantly. Remove from heat and stir in vanilla.
2. Serve hot over ice cream. May be stored in refrigerator and reheated in microwave.

Candies and Snacks

Pecan Turtles
Lori Berezovsky
Salina, KS
Grandmother's Pride

Makes 4 dozen

2¼ cups packed brown
sugar
1 cup butter or
margarine
1 cup light corn syrup
⅛ tsp. salt
14-oz. can sweetened
condensed milk
1 tsp. vanilla extract
1½ lbs. whole pecans
1 cup semi-sweet
chocolate chips
1 cup milk chocolate
chips
2 Tbsp. shortening

1. In saucepan combine
brown sugar, butter, corn
syrup, and salt. Cook over
medium heat until sugar is
dissolved. Gradually add
milk and mix well.
Continue cooking until

candy thermometer reads
248° (firm-ball stage).
Remove from heat.
2. Stir in vanilla until
blended. Fold in pecans.
3. Drop by tablespoonfuls
onto waxed paper-lined
cookie sheets. Chill until
firm.
4. Melt chocolate chips and
shortening in microwave or
double boiler. Drizzle
melted chocolate over each
pecan cluster. Cool.

Christmas Truffles
Grace Brunelle
Underhill, VT
Amish Square in Square

Makes 2 dozen

⅔ cup heavy cream
⅛ tsp. salt
2 Tbsp. unsalted butter
12-oz. pkg. chocolate
chips

½ cup finely chopped
toasted almonds
1 Tbsp. sugar
½ tsp. almond extract
powdered sugar

1. In saucepan over low
heat, bring cream to a boil.
Remove from heat. Add salt,
butter, chocolate chips,
almonds, sugar, and almond
extract.
2. Pour into a shallow bowl.
Chill for about 3 hours or
until able to roll into 1"
balls. Roll in powdered
sugar. Place in small candy
molds. Keep refrigerated,
but warm slightly immedi-
ately before serving.

*Note: We serve these only
during Christmas week when
visitors stop by.*

Chocolate Dreams
Jean Reistle
Mickleton, NJ
Ohio Star

Makes 1¹/2-2 dozen

3 cups chocolate chips
1 pint marshmallow cream
14-oz. can sweetened condensed milk
1 cup chopped pecans

1. Melt chocolate chips in double boiler. Stir in marshmallow cream and milk. Mix thoroughly. Beat until thick.
2. Drop by teaspoonfuls onto waxed paper-lined cookie sheets. Chill until firm and store in closed container.

Mounds Bar
Sherry Carroll
Delta, PA
Basket

Makes 2-3 dozen

Layer 1:
2 cups graham cracker crumbs
¹/2 cup sugar
¹/2 cup margarine, melted

Layer 2:
7-oz. pkg. coconut
14-oz. can sweetened condensed milk

Layer 3:
12-oz. pkg. chocolate chips
2 tsp. peanut butter

1. Mix together graham cracker crumbs, sugar, and margarine. Press into 9" x 13" pan. Bake at 350° for 10 minutes.
2. Mix together coconut and milk. Spread over 1st layer. Bake at 350° for 15 minutes.
3. Mix together chocolate chips and peanut butter in double boiler or microwave. Spread on top of coconut layer while still warm.
4. Cool before cutting.

Chocolate-Covered Candy
Mary Martins
Fairbank, IA
Log Cabin

Makes 4-5 dozen

¹/2 cup butter, melted
14-oz. can sweetened condensed milk
1¹/2 tsp. maple flavoring
4 cups powdered sugar
1¹/2 cups flaked coconut
1 cup chopped nuts
12-oz. pkg. semi-sweet chocolate chips
¹/2 bar German sweet chocolate
¹/2 bar paraffin

1. Mix together butter, milk, maple flavoring, sugar, coconut, and nuts. Mix well with hands.
2. Roll into small balls and place on trays. Chill overnight.
3. In saucepan melt together chocolate chips, German chocolate, and paraffin.
4. Pick balls up with a toothpick and dip in chocolate. Set aside to cool completely.

Note: These freeze well if you can hide them!

Peanut Butter Squares
Marybeth Romeo
Roanoke, VA
Ugly 70's Quilt

Makes 2-3 dozen

3/4 cup brown sugar
3¹/2 cups sifted powdered sugar
¹/2 cup butter
2 cups peanut butter
12-oz. pkg. chocolate chips
1 Tbsp. butter

1. Cream together sugars and ¹/2 cup butter. Stir in peanut butter. Spread mixture onto 9" x 15" cookie sheet. Press to ¹/4" thickness.
2. In heavy saucepan or double boiler, melt chocolate chips with butter. Spread over peanut butter layer.
3. Refrigerate until firm. Cut into small squares and serve.

Peanut Butter Graham Cracker Squares
Judy Newman
St. Marys, Ontario
School Time

Makes 2-3 dozen

Layer 1:
1 1/3 cups graham cracker crumbs
1 1/2 cups powdered sugar
1/2 cup butter, melted
1 cup peanut butter

Layer 2:
1 1/4 cups chocolate chips
3/4 cups peanut butter

1. Mix together graham cracker crumbs, sugar, butter, and peanut butter. Press into 9" x 13" pan.
2. Mix together chocolate chips and peanut butter. Melt in microwave or double boiler. Spread over graham cracker layer in pan.
3. Refrigerate for 2 hours. Cut into squares.

Peanut Butter Candy
Joan Becker
Dodge City, KS
Licorice Whip

Makes 4-5 dozen

1 Tbsp. corn syrup
2 cups sugar
2/3 cup milk
dash salt
1 cup marshmallow cream
1 cup peanut butter
1 tsp. vanilla

1. Cook together syrup, sugar, and milk until soft-ball stage (see page 279). Stir in remaining ingredients and mix well.
2. Remove from heat and pour into lightly greased 9" square pan.
3. Cut into very small squares and serve.

Rocky Road Candy
Sharon Easter
Yuba City, CA

Makes 5-6 dozen

12-oz. pkg. chocolate chips
12-oz. pkg. butterscotch chips
1 cup peanut butter
10 1/2-oz. pkg. miniature marshmallows
1 cup peanuts

1. Melt together chocolate chips, butterscotch chips, and peanut butter in microwave or double boiler. Stir in marshmallows and peanuts.
2. Press into lightly greased 9" x 13" pan and refrigerate.
3. Cut into bite-sized pieces and serve.

About twenty years ago, my extended family began a holiday tradition of meeting at a motel centrally located among all our homes. We were twenty-four that first time with lots of small children and had decided that a swimming pool was important. The person taking the reservation assured my sister that, yes, the motel had a pool. We met on a weekend in early December with swimsuits in tow. Evidently, having a pool and using a pool were not closely linked in the motel management mind because to our surprise we discovered an outdoor pool covered with ice. After the initial disappointment, we found other ways to entertain ourselves and had a great time. Our family has grown to include about sixty people, and we still get together at a central location sometime between mid October and early December each year.
—Pat Unternahrer, Wayland, IA

Microwave Rocky Road Fudge

Kim McEuen
Bear, DE
Feathered Star
Rosemarie Fitzgerald
Gibsonia, PA
Baby Nine Patch

Makes 2-3 dozen

1¹/2 cups sugar
2 cups miniature
  marshmallows
5-oz. can evaporated milk
¹/4 cup margarine or
  butter
12-oz. pkg. semi-sweet
  chocolate chips
1 tsp. vanilla
10-12-oz. can mixed nuts,
  chopped

1. In 2-quart glass measuring cup, microwave sugar, 1 cup marshmallows, milk, and margarine on high for 4¹/2-5¹/2 minutes until melted, stirring once after 2¹/2 minutes.
2. Stir in chocolate chips and vanilla and mix until smooth. Fold in nuts and remaining marshmallows.
3. Spread into foil-lined 8" square pan. Refrigerate until firm. Cut into pieces and serve.

Million Dollar Fudge

Darla Sathre
Baxter, MN
Off Center Log Cabin

Makes 10-12 dozen

4¹/2 cups sugar
12-oz. can evaporated
  milk
2 8-oz. Hershey chocolate
  bars
1 cup butter
12-oz. pkg. milk
  chocolate chips
12-oz. pkg. semi-sweet
  chocolate chips
3 tsp. vanilla

1. In saucepan combine sugar and milk. Bring to a boil and cook for 6 minutes.
2. Combine all other ingredients in a large bowl. Pour milk mixture over ingredients and mix until smooth.
3. Pour into lightly greased 11" x 16" jelly roll pan with sides.
4. Chill overnight. Cut into squares and serve.

Nana's Million Dollar Fudge

Debra Botelho Zeida
Mashpee, MA
Sunbonnet Sue
Kathie Weatherford
Stockton, CA
In Memory of Samantha

Makes 10-12 dozen

4¹/2 cups sugar
pinch salt
2 Tbsp. butter
12-oz. can evaporated
  milk
12-oz. can semi-sweet
  chocolate chips
12-ozs. German sweet
  chocolate squares
1 pint marshmallow
  cream
2 cups chopped nuts

1. In a saucepan combine sugar, salt, butter, and milk. Bring to a boil and boil for 6 minutes.
2. In a large bowl combine chocolate chips, chocolate squares, marshmallow cream, and nuts. Pour boiling syrup over chocolate mixture and beat until mixture has completely melted.
3. Pour onto lightly greased large jelly roll pan. Chill overnight.
4. Cut and store in covered tins until ready to serve.

Easy Holiday Fudge
Maricarol Magill
Freehold, NJ
Round Robin

Makes 4-5 dozen

1/2 lb. butter
4 cups sugar
1 tsp. vanilla
1 cup milk
25 large marshmallows
2 1/2-lb. Hershey chocolate bars
12-oz. pkg. semi-sweet chocolate chips
2 ozs. unsweetened chocolate

1. In saucepan mix together butter, sugar, vanilla, and milk. Bring to boil, stirring constantly, and simmer for 2 minutes. Remove from heat.
2. Immediately stir in all remaining ingredients and mix until smooth.
3. Pour into lightly greased 9" x 13" pan. Chill for 6-8 hours. Cut into small squares.

Perfect Chocolate Fudge
Alice Kennedy
Dallas, TX
Ye Olde Bow Tie

Makes 3-4 dozen

3 cups sugar
1/4 tsp. salt
1/2 cup corn syrup
4 squares bitter chocolate
1 cup milk
3 Tbsp. butter
1 tsp. vanilla
1 cup chopped nuts

1. In saucepan mix together sugar, salt, corn syrup, chocolate, and milk. Heat over low heat, stirring constantly, until mixture boils.
2. While fudge cooks, remove crystals that form on sides of pan with damp brush or fork wrapped in damp cheesecloth. Do not stir during this step.
3. Continue cooking fudge until it forms a soft ball or reaches 238° on candy thermometer. Remove from heat. Stir in butter. Cool to warm. Add vanilla and beat until creamy. Stir in nuts.
4. Pour into greased 9" x 13" dish. Cool completely before cutting into squares.

Toffee Fudge
Tracey B. Stenger
Gretna, LA
Baby Quilt

Makes 2-3 dozen

2 cups butterscotch chips
1/2 cup smooth peanut butter
1 Tbsp. instant coffee granules
1/2 tsp. water
2/3 cup sweetened condensed milk

1. In top of double boiler, combine morsels and peanut butter. Place over simmering water. Stir until morsels are melted and mixture is well blended. Remove from heat.
2. Combine coffee with water. Stir into condensed milk. Stir into butterscotch mixture and blend well.
3. Spread in greased 8" square pan. Chill until firm. Cut into squares.

Velveeta Fudge
Anna Petersheim
Kinzers, PA
Noah's Ark

Makes 4-5 dozen

1/2 lb. Velveeta cheese, cut
   into 1" cubes
1 cup butter or
   margarine
1/2 cup unsweetened
   cocoa
2 lbs. powdered sugar
1/3 cup cornstarch
2 tsp. vanilla

1. In top of double boiler,
combine cheese, butter, and
cocoa. Simmer, stirring frequently, until cheese melts
and mixture is smooth.
2. Combine powdered sugar
and cornstarch. With electric mixer on medium
speed, add powdered sugar
mixture to cheese mixture,
beating until smooth. Beat
in vanilla.
3. Spread evenly into
greased 9" x 13" pan. Cover
with plastic wrap and chill
for 24 hours.
4. Cut into squares and
serve.

*Variation: Delete cornstarch.
Fold in 1 1/2 cups chopped
pecans or walnuts at the end
of Step 2.*
   Joyce B. Suiter
   Garysburg, NC
   Pieced Tulip

Sugar-Free Peanut Butter Fudge
Kaye Merrill
Olive Branch, MS
Bow Tie

Makes 1 1/2-2 dozen

2 8-oz. pkgs. cream
   cheese
1 cup sugar-free peanut
   butter
24 pkgs. sweetener (sugar
   substitute)
1 tsp. vanilla extract
1/2 cup chopped pecans

1. Beat cream cheese until
soft and fluffy. Stir in
peanut butter, sweetener,
and vanilla. Mix well. Add
pecans.
2. Spread into 8" square pan
which has been prepared
with non-stick cooking
spray. Cover and refrigerate.

*Note: This is a special treat I
make for my dad who is dia-
betic. His face always lights
up when I walk in the door
with a pan of "his" peanut
butter fudge.*

Peanut Butter Fudge
Karen Ferebee
Hastings, NE

Makes 1 1/2-2 dozen

2 cups sugar
2/3 cups milk
1 cup chunky peanut
   butter
1 pint marshmallow
   cream

1. In saucepan cook
together sugar and milk
until it reaches the soft ball
stage, stirring constantly.
2. Pour over peanut butter
and marshmallow cream
and beat until smooth.
3. Pour into greased 8"
square pan. Cool. Cut into
pieces.

*Note: To test for soft ball
stage, remove pan with boiling
candy from heat to prevent
overcooking. Pour about 1/2
tsp. candy into 1/2 cup cold
water. Pick candy up with fingers. If it is at softball stage,
the candy will form a soft ball
which quickly loses its shape
when removed from water
(can be picked up but flattens
immediately).*
   Audrey L. Couvillon
   Dallas, TX

Shortcut Fudge
Roberta Poscharscky
Goshen, IN

Makes 5-6 dozen

1 1/3 cups sweetened
   condensed milk
2 1/4 cups semi-sweet
   chocolate chips
1/8 tsp. salt
1 1/2 cups chopped nuts
1 tsp. vanilla

1. In double boiler mix
together milk, chocolate,
and salt. Stirring frequently,
cook over rapidly boiling
water for 10 minutes.
Remove from heat.
2. Stir in nuts and vanilla.
Pour into greased 9" square
pan. Chill until firm (about
3 hours). Cut into very
small squares.

Divinity Candy
Ruth Ann Collins
Waseca, MN
Roberta Poscharscky
Goshen, IN
Inez E. Dillon
Tucson, AZ

Makes 2-3 dozen

2 cups sugar
1/2 cup light corn syrup
1/2 cup water
2 egg whites
pinch salt
1 tsp. vanilla
1 cup chopped walnuts

1. In saucepan mix together
sugar, corn syrup, and
water. Boil to a hard ball
stage or 265° on candy thermometer.
2. Whip eggs whites with
salt until stiff peaks form.
Pour syrup over whites and
continue beating on high
until candy starts to lose its
shine. When beaters are
lifted out of candy, mixture
should fall in a ribbon that
mounds on itself.
3. Fold in vanilla and nuts.
Drop by teaspoonfuls onto
a sheet of waxed paper.
Cool.

Angel Cookie
Candy
Alyce C. Kauffman
Gridley, CA
Sailing Away

Makes 4 1/2 dozen

3-oz. pkg. cream cheese,
   softened
2 Tbsp. milk
1/2 tsp. vanilla
3 cups powdered sugar,
   sifted
2 squares unsweetened
   chocolate, melted and
   cooled
1 cup quick oats
1 cup miniature
   marshmallows
1/2 cup chopped nuts or
   raisins
3/4 cup flaked coconut

1. Blend together cream
cheese, milk, and vanilla
until creamy and smooth.

Gradually add powdered
sugar, beating until well
blended.
2. Beat in chocolate. Stir in
oats, marshmallows, and
nuts or raisins. Stir until all
ingredients are evenly
blended.
3. Shape dough to make two
7" logs. Roll each log in
coconut. Wrap in waxed
paper and refrigerate
overnight. Slice each log
into 1/4" pieces. Serve immediately.

Cathedral
Windows
Chris Peterson
Green Bay, WI
Star Medallion

Makes 1 dozen

6-oz. pkg. chocolate chips
2 Tbsp. butter or
   margarine
1 egg, beaten
3 cups miniature
   marshmallows
1 cup chopped nuts
powdered sugar

1. Melt chocolate chips and
butter over low heat.
Remove from heat. Stir in
egg. Mix well. Cool about 5
minutes.
2. Mix together marshmal-
lows and nuts. Pour chocolate mixture over marshmallows and nuts. Mix well.
Divide mixture in half.
3. On waxed paper which
has been sprinkled with
powdered sugar, shape each

half into a log, approximately 8" long. Wrap the log in waxed paper. Chill several hours. Slice to serve.

Variation: I roll the logs in coconut and wrap in plastic wrap. Keep in refrigerator until ready to serve. Our teenagers love this sweet treat so much I have to hide it in the back of the fruit and vegetable drawer to make it last at all!
Rebecca Meyerkorth
Wamego, KS
Challenge Quilt

Christmas Wreath
Anna Stoltzfus
Honey Brook, PA
Deer on White

Makes 1 wreath

1/2 cup butter
35 large marshmallows
2 tsp. green food coloring
4 1/2 cups cornflakes
red cinnamon candies

1. Melt together butter and marshmallows. Stir in food coloring and mix well. Stir in cornflakes.
2. Shape into a large wreath and trim with red cinnamon candies for berries.

Note: This makes a nice centerpiece for a Christmas party. It tastes good, too.

Kris Kringle Kandy
Sharon Timpe
Mequon, WI
ABC Quilts

Makes 1 1/2-2 dozen

1 1/2 lbs. white chocolate
14-oz. can sweetened condensed milk
1/8 tsp. salt
1 cup chopped pecans
1 cup candied red and green cherries, cut in half
1 tsp. vanilla

1. In top of double boiler, melt white chocolate, condensed milk, and salt together. Stir in pecans, cherries, and vanilla. Mix well.
2. Spoon into a waxed paper-lined 9" square pan. Chill 4 hours or until firm. Cut into small serving-sized pieces.

Buckeyes
Kathy Hale
Eaton, IN
Bargello

Makes approximately 8 dozen

1 cup margarine
10 ozs. peanut butter
1 lb. powdered sugar
1/4 bar paraffin
16-oz. pkg. chocolate chips

1. Mix together margarine, peanut butter, and powdered sugar. Roll into 3/4" balls. Put toothpick in center of each ball, arrange on cookie sheets, and freeze.
2. In double boiler melt together paraffin and chocolate chips. Dip each ball in chocolate, leaving a small part of top showing. Set on waxed paper until hard. Store in refrigerator until ready to serve.

In November of 1971, a friend who was a newlywed and I decided the time had come to do some of our own Christmas baking and candy making. I was single at the time, but by the third year of this new tradition, I had also married and from that point on, we each supplied half of the ingredients and divided the resulting goodies. Christmas 1996 will mark our 25th anniversary of baking Christmas cookies and making Christmas candy.
—Carolyn Shank, Dayton, VA

Peanut Butter Cups

Emma Z. Martin
Lititz, PA
Diamond Star Log Cabin

Makes approximately 8 dozen

1¹/2 cups creamy peanut butter
1¹/2 cups powdered sugar
2 tsp. vanilla
¹/4 cup margarine or butter
2 lbs. coating chocolate
2 cups creamy peanut butter

1. Mix together 1¹/2 cups peanut butter, powdered sugar, vanilla, and margarine until creamy.
2. Shape into balls the size of small walnuts, then flatten slightly. Place on waxed paper.
3. In double boiler melt together coating chocolate and 2 cups peanut butter. Mix well.
4. Place 1 tsp. melted chocolate into candy paper cup. Place peanut butter candy in center, then fill with melted chocolate. Chill to harden. Serve.

Sponge Candy

Charlotte Fry
St. Charles, MO
Basket

Makes 6-8 dozen

1 cup sugar
1 cup dark corn syrup
1 Tbsp. white vinegar
1 Tbsp. baking soda
2 12-oz. pkgs. chocolate chips

1. In saucepan mix together sugar, corn syrup, and vinegar. Cook, stirring constantly, until sugar dissolves. Cover for 1 minute so steam can wash down sides.
2. Uncover and insert candy thermometer. Cook to 300°. Remove from heat and stir in baking soda. Stir fast and pour immediately onto greased jelly roll pan. Cool. Break into pieces.
3. Melt chocolate chips in double boiler. Dip sponge candy pieces in melted chocolate.
4. Cool completely. Store in airtight container.

Note: Be sure not to use old baking soda, and it is better not to make this on a damp day.

Stained Glass Christmas Candy

Jan Steffy Mast
Lancaster, PA
Bow Tie

Makes 3 dozen

12-oz. pkg. semi-sweet chocolate chips
¹/2 cup butter or margarine
10¹/2-oz. pkg. red/green holiday miniature marshmallows
2 cups finely chopped nuts

1. Melt together chocolate chips and butter in microwave on high for 1 minute. Stir. Heat on high for 1 more minute. Stir. Heat more if needed to melt. Let stand for 5 minutes.
2. Stir in marshmallows and 1 cup nuts. Do not melt marshmallows.
3. On waxed paper shape mixture into 2 rolls, each 2" in diameter. Wrap in aluminum foil and chill for 15 minutes. Roll candy rolls in remaining 1 cup nuts to cover. Re-wrap and chill overnight.
4. Cut rolls into ¹/4" slices and serve.

Holiday Peppermint Bark
Sandra Fulton Day
Oxford, PA
Road to Oklahoma

Makes 1 lb. candy

12-oz. pkg. white chocolate chips
24 hard peppermint candies

1. Melt white chocolate chips in medium-sized bowl for 1-2 minutes on high in microwave, stirring every 30 seconds until smooth.
2. Crush peppermint candies in heavy plastic bag, using a rolling pin.
3. Holding a strainer or colander over melted white chocolate, pour crushed candy into strainer. Shake to release all small candy pieces into chocolate. Set aside larger candy pieces.
4. Stir chocolate and candy to mix. Spread onto waxed paper-lined baking sheet. Sprinkle with remaining candy pieces. Chill for 1 hour until firm. Break into pieces and store at room temperature.

Coconut Candy
Carolyn Shank
Dayton, VA
Double Wedding Ring

Makes 5-6 dozen

Layer 1:
1 Tbsp. unflavored gelatin
2 Tbsp. water
2 cups sugar
1 cup light cream
1 Tbsp. butter
1 tsp. vanilla
1 cup coconut

Layer 2:
1 Tbsp. unflavored gelatin
2 Tbsp. water
2 cups sugar
1 cup light cream
1 Tbsp. butter
1 cup coconut
3 drops red food coloring

Layer 3:
1 Tbsp. unflavored gelatin
2 Tbsp. water
2 cups sugar
1 cup light cream
1 Tbsp. butter
1 cup coconut
2-oz. square unsweetened chocolate

1. To prepare layer 1, soak gelatin in cold water for 5 minutes.
2. In heavy saucepan combine sugar and cream until mixture reaches soft ball stage or 240° (see page 279). Stir often at first until sugar is dissolved. Stir only once after sugar is dissolved.
3. Remove from heat. Stir in gelatin, butter, and vanilla. Beat about 5 minutes with electric mixer until mixture is creamy.
4. Stir in coconut. Spread into greased 7" x 11" baking dish.
5. To prepare layer 2, follow Steps 1-4 as stated, except be sure to omit vanilla. Stir in red food coloring immediately before beating. Pour red layer on top of white layer in baking dish.
6. To prepare layer 3, add chocolate, which has been broken into small pieces, to heavy saucepan. Follow Steps 1-4 as stated, except be sure to omit vanilla. Pour chocolate layer on top of red layer in baking dish.
7. Chill until firm. Cut into small squares.

Note: Be sure to wash pans and utensils after each layer to prevent scorching.

Mint Meringues
Becky Harder
Monument, CO
Churn Dash

Makes 2 dozen

2 egg whites, room
temperature
1/4 tsp. cream of tartar
3/4 cup white sugar
1/2 tsp. peppermint
flavoring

1. In a glass or stoneware
bowl, beat egg whites and
cream of tartar until frothy.
Very slowly beat in sugar.
Add flavoring. Continue
beating until stiffened and
peaks form.
2. Put rounded teaspoonfuls
onto ungreased cookie
sheets. Bake at 375° for
only 1 minute. Then turn
off oven. Leave in oven
without opening door for 4
hours or more.

*Note: I like to make these in
the evening, leaving them in
the oven overnight. At
Christmas time I often add
red or green food coloring to
make them more festive.*

Cream Cheese Mints
Sara Wilson
Blairstown, MO
A Calendar Kite

Makes 5-6 dozen

Mints:
3 cups powdered sugar
3-oz. pkg. cream cheese,
softened
1 Tbsp. butter
flavoring of choice (see
note below)

Chocolate Dip:
12 ozs. almond bark
6-oz. pkg. semi-sweet
chocolate chips
1 tsp. cooking oil
1/2 of 5" bar paraffin

1. Cream together sugar,
cream cheese, and butter.
By hand work into a smooth
ball. Divide into 3 portions.
Flavor and color each portion as desired. (See note
below.) By hand work fla-
voring and coloring into
candy until desired color.
3. Roll each portion into
small balls.
4. To prepare chocolate dip,
melt together almond bark,
chocolate chips, oil, and
paraffin in top of double
boiler.
5. Dip mints into chocolate.
Let excess drip off. Cool on
waxed paper and wrap in colored candy papers, if desired.

*Note: I buy the small .25-oz.
bottles of flavoring. For each
1/3 of candy, I flavor with my*

choice of the following combi-
nations: 1) 1 bottle cherry flavoring and red food coloring;
2) 1 bottle wintergreen flavoring and green food coloring; 3)
1 bottle spearmint flavoring
and blue food coloring; 4) 1
bottle orange flavoring and
orange food coloring; or 5) 1
bottle maple-pecan flavoring
and no food coloring. (Add as
much food coloring as you
need to reach desired color for
options 1-4.)

Pomanders
Marge Reeder
State College, PA
Sara's Log Cabin

Makes 3-4 dozen

6-oz. pkg. chocolate chips
1/2 cup sugar
1/4 cup light corn syrup
1/4 cup water
2 1/2 cups vanilla wafer
crumbs
1 cup chopped nuts
1 tsp. orange extract
sugar for dipping

1. Melt chocolate chips in
double boiler or microwave.
Stir in 1/2 cup sugar and
corn syrup. Blend in water.
2. Combine crumbs and
nuts. Add chocolate mixture
and orange extract. Mix
well.
3. Form into 1" balls and
roll in sugar for dipping. Let
ripen in covered container
for several days. These candies improve in flavor when
stored.

Caramels
Ilene Bontrager
Arlington, KS
Country Bride

Makes 2-3 dozen

1 cup sugar
3/4 cup light corn syrup
11/2 cups cream
1 tsp. vanilla
1 cup chopped walnuts

1. Cook together sugar, syrup, and 1/2 cup cream until it reaches the soft ball stage. (Drip a small dab in cold water and push together with your fingers. Cook until you can push into a lump in cold water, but it looses its shape when you pick it up.)
2. When candy has reached soft ball, slowly add another 1/2 cup cream. Cook again until soft ball stage. Slowly add another 1/2 cup cream. Cook until hard ball stage. (Drip small dab in cold water and cook until it holds its shape when picked out of water.)
3. Fold in vanilla and walnuts and pour into well greased pan. Cool and cut into squares. Wrap individually in waxed paper and store.

Toffee Butter Crunch
Laura Ashby
Boulder Creek, CA
Elaine Ribas
Miami, FL
Charlotte Shaffer
Ephrata, PA

Makes 2 dozen

1/2 lb. almonds, blanched and peeled
1 cup butter
11/2 cups sugar
3 Tbsp. water
1 Tbsp. light corn syrup
1 lb. milk chocolate, broken into pieces

1. Chop almonds coarsely and spread onto baking sheet. Toast the almonds at 350° for 5-10 minutes or until lightly browned.
2. In saucepan melt butter. Add sugar, water, and corn syrup. Stirring occasionally, cook the mixture over medium heat until it reaches the hard crack stage, 300° on candy thermometer. (Watch carefully to avoid burning.)
3. While still hot, spread mixture onto a well greased 9" x 13" baking sheet. Cool thoroughly and turn sheet of candy onto waxed paper.
4. Melt chocolate in double boiler or microwave. Spread 1/2 of melted chocolate over candy. Sprinkle with 1/2 of almonds. Cover the top with waxed paper and flip sheet of candy over. Spread the bottom side with remaining 1/2 of melted chocholate and sprinkle with remaining 1/2 of almonds. Chill until firm.
5. Break the toffee into about 24 pieces.

❖

Old-Fashioned Taffy
Sara Wilson
Blairstown, MO
Calico Puppy

Makes approximately 2 lbs.

3 cups white sugar
1 cup light corn syrup
1 cup hot water
1 Tbsp. vinegar
1/2 tsp. cream of tartar
1/2 cup butter
1/4 tsp. baking soda
1/2 tsp. vanilla

1. In saucepan mix together sugar, syrup, water, and vinegar. Bring to boil.
2. Stir in cream of tartar, butter, and baking soda. Cook to hard ball stage (260° on candy thermometer).
3. Stir in vanilla. Pour onto greased cookie sheet.
4. Chill to touch. Butter hands and with a friend pull until the taffy is white in color.
5. With a scissors or knife, cut into pieces and wrap individually in waxed paper. Store in airtight container.

Microwave Praline Candy

Trudy Kutter
Corfu, NY
Cathedral Window

Makes 1½ lbs.

2 cups chopped pecans
½ cup unsalted butter
⅔ cup packed brown
  sugar
14-oz. can sweetened
  condensed milk
1 tsp. vanilla

1. Place pecans in glass pie plate and microwave on high for 8 minutes, stirring every 2 minutes. Set aside.
2. In 8-cup glass measuring cup, microwave butter on high for 1 minute. Stir in brown sugar and milk and microwave on high for 8 minutes, stirring every 2 minutes.
3. Beat with wooden spoon until stiff, about 5 minutes. Stir in nuts and vanilla and quickly spread on greased 8" square pan.
4. Chill. Cut in 1" squares and serve.

Microwave Peanut Brittle

Kathie Weatherford
Stockton, CA
Kelly Bailey
Mechanicsburg, PA
Beverly Simmons &
Kimberly Davison
Boulder, CO

Makes approximately 1 lb.

1 cup raw peanuts
1 cup sugar
½ cup light corn syrup
⅛ tsp. salt
1 tsp. butter
1 tsp. vanilla
1 tsp. baking soda

1. In 1½-quart glass casserole dish, stir together peanuts, sugar, syrup, and salt. Cook on high for 8 minutes, stirring after 4 minutes.
2. Mix in butter and vanilla. Cook 1 minute longer.
3. Add baking soda and quickly stir until mixture is light and foamy. Immediately pour onto lightly greased large baking sheet and spread out into thin layer. Cool.
4. Break into pieces and store in an airtight container.

Note: This mixture becomes very hot so use caution. For stirring in Step 1 and for spreading onto baking sheet in Step 3, use two table knives.

Skillet Peanut Brittle

Sylvia Netterville
Metairie, LA
Maple Leaf

Makes 2-3 dozen pieces

1 cup sugar
½ cup light corn syrup
1 cup raw peanuts
1 tsp. baking soda

1. In a fairly large iron skillet, mix together sugar and corn syrup. Cook on high for 4 mintues.
2. Stir in peanuts and continue cooking on high for 3½ minutes or until candy thermometer reaches 290°.
3. Remove from heat and quickly stir in baking soda to mix completely. (Mixture will become foamy.) Quickly pour onto greased cookie sheet. Cool.
4. Break into small pieces, using a knife handle.

Peanut Brittle

Esther Lantz
Leola, PA
Broken Star

Makes 3-4 dozen pieces

1 cup sugar
1 cup light corn syrup
1 Tbsp. water
2 cups raw peanuts
¾ tsp. baking soda
½ tsp. salt
½ tsp. cinnamon

1. Combine sugar, corn syrup, and water in medium saucepan. Bring to a boil and let boil for 2 minutes. Stir in peanuts and cook until 290° on candy thermometer.

2. Remove from heat and quickly stir in baking soda, salt, and cinnamon. (Mixture will become foamy.) Quickly spread into thin layer on large, well greased cookie sheet. Cool.

3. Break into small pieces and serve.

Jerry's Cashew Brittle

Sharron Van Meter
St. Charles, MO
Friendship

Makes 5 lbs. of brittle

4 cups sugar
1¹/8 cups white corn syrup
1¹/3 cups water
1 lb. cashews
¹/4 tsp. salt
4 Tbsp. margarine
1 tsp. baking soda
1 tsp. vanilla

1. In large saucepan combine sugar, corn syrup, and water. Cover and bring to a boil. Uncover, put in candy thermometer, and boil until mixture reaches 275°.

2. Stir in cashews, salt, and margarine. Stir with wooden spoon until temperature reaches 300°.

3. Remove thermometer and

remove from heat. Quickly stir in baking soda and vanilla. Quickly pour this very hot mixture onto 2 large well greased cookie sheets.

4. Let cool and break into pieces.

Nibbler's Delight

Karen Kay Tucker
Manteca, CA
Baltimore Bride

Makes 3 cups

1¹/2 cups sugar
¹/4 tsp. salt
¹/2 cup sherry
1 tsp. grated orange rind
¹/2 tsp. cinnamon
3 cups walnut halves or pecans

1. In saucepan combine sugar, salt, and sherry and bring to soft ball stage (see page 279) or 240° on candy thermometer. Remove from heat.

2. Add orange rind, cinnamon, and walnuts. Stir until syrup is cloudy and walnuts are coated.

3. Turn out onto waxed paper and quickly separate nuts with table knives.

4. Cool and store in airtight container.

Chocolate Peanut Balls

Tanya Potenta
Bridgewater, NJ
Biscuit Crib Quilt

Makes 100 1" balls

¹/2 cup butter
2 cups chunky peanut butter
1 tsp. vanilla
1 lb. powdered sugar
3 cups Rice Krispies
3 6-oz. pkgs. milk chocolate chips
3 tsp. vegetable oil

1. Melt butter in saucepan. Stir in peanut butter. Mix well. Add vanilla, powdered sugar, and cereal. Mix with hands and form 1-inch balls. Freeze balls for ¹/2 hour.

2. In top of double boiler combine chocolate chips and oil and melt.

3. Dip cereal balls in chocolate and place in mini cupcake liners. Refrigerate. Serve at room temperature. Store in refrigerator or freezer.

Best-Ever Peanut Butter Balls
Robin Schrock
Millersburg, OH
Irish Chain

Makes 2 dozen

1 cup powdered sugar
1/2 cup peanut butter
3 Tbsp. butter
1 lb. coating chocolate

1. In a mixing bowl, cream together sugar, peanut butter, and butter. Shape into 1" balls and place on waxed paper-lined cookie sheet. Chill for 30 minutes or until firm.
2. Meanwhile, melt coating chocolate in top of double boiler.
3. Using a toothpick, dip balls in chocolate and place on waxed paper to harden. Store in candy tins.

Peanut Butter Balls
Janice Deel
Paducah, KY
Mariner's Compass

Makes 3-4 dozen

1 cup crunchy peanut butter
1 cup shredded coconut
1/2 cup instant oats
1 lb. powdered sugar
1 cup margarine, softened
1 tsp. vanilla
4 ozs. paraffin
1 cup chocolate chips

1. Mix together peanut butter, coconut, oats, sugar, margarine, and vanilla. Shape into balls. Chill for 2 hours.
2. In top of double boiler, melt together paraffin and chocolate chips. Turn to very low heat while dipping.
3. Dip peanut butter balls into melted chocolate. Place on waxed paper to cool.
4. Store in cool place.

Peanut Butter Crunch Balls
Wanda S. Curtin
Bradenton, FL
Lancaster Rose

Makes 3 dozen

4 cups miniature marshmallows
1/2 cup butter
1/2 cup peanut butter
1 cup unsalted peanuts
3 cups toasted oat cereal
1 cup red and green M&Ms

1. In a medium saucepan or double boiler, melt together marshmallows, butter, and peanut butter over low heat, stirring until smooth. Remove from heat. Cool for 15 minutes.
2. In a large bowl combine all remaining ingredients. Pour marshmallow syrup over cereal. Mix until evenly coated.
3. By hand roll mixture into 2" balls. Cool on waxed paper. Store in airtight container.

When I was growing up in Chicago, my grandmother always made a traditional Swedish meal for Christmas Eve. We would make faces at the lutefisk and herring, but we all loved the Swedish meatballs, limpa bread, and rice pudding for dessert. I only wish I had learned how to cook that meal for my daughter!

—*Nancy Vance, Carterville, IL*

Date Balls
Sharleen White
Arnold, MD
Dawn J. Ranck
Strasburg, PA
Naomi Stoltzfus
Leola, PA

Makes 3 dozen

8 Tbsp. butter
1 cup sugar
1 egg, beaten
1 cup chopped dates
1/2 cup chopped nuts
2 cups Rice Krispies
1/2 tsp. vanilla
powdered sugar or
   coconut

1. In saucepan mix together butter, sugar, egg, and dates and bring to a boil. Cook for 10 minutes.
2. Cool to lukewarm, and add nuts, cereal, and vanilla.
3. Shape into 1" balls and roll in powdered sugar or coconut. Store in airtight container.

Apricot Balls
M. Jeanne Osborne
Wells, ME

Makes 3-4 dozen

8-oz. pkg. dried apricots,
   ground
2 1/2 cups flaked coconut
3/4 cup sweetened
   condensed milk
1 cup finely chopped
   nuts

1. Mix together apricots, coconut, and milk.
2. Shape into small balls. Roll in finely chopped nuts.
3. Chill for about 2 hours until firm. Serve.

Note: For tangy apricot balls, add 2 Tbsp. lemon juice.

Orange Balls
Ashlene Drake
Salem, OR

Makes 5-6 dozen

6-oz. can frozen orange
   juice, thawed
12-oz. pkg. vanilla wafers,
   crushed
1/2 cup butter, softened
1 lb. powdered sugar
1 1/4 cups chopped pecans
   or walnuts
3 cups coconut
1 Tbsp. water

1. Mix together orange juice and wafer crumbs. Stir in softened butter and mix well.

2. Sift powdered sugar over wafer mixture and stir well. Stir in nuts, 2 cups coconut, and water.
3. Form into small balls and roll balls in remaining 1 cup coconut. Air dry in cool, out of the way place for at least 2 days.

Note: The flavor of these orange balls is enhanced after several days.

Health Candy
Lucille Metzler
Conestoga, PA
Country Love

Makes 2-3 dozen

1 cup peanut butter
1 cup honey
1 1/2 cups powdered milk
1 1/2 cups wheat germ
1 tsp. nutmeg
1 cup crushed cornflakes

1. Mix together peanut butter, honey, powdered milk, wheat germ, and nutmeg.
2. Shape into 1" balls.
3. Roll in cornflake crumbs. Chill.

Note: These make a nice, healthy addition to the Christmas cookie plates I fix as gifts.

Date Nut Balls
Irma H. Schoen
Windsor, CT
Log Cabin

Makes 30 1" balls

7-oz. pkg. slivered
  almonds
1 cup walnuts
8 ozs. dates
1 cup raisins
1/2 cup craisins*

*Craisins are dried cranber-
ries.

1. Combine all ingredients
in a food processor and
chop until fine. Knead
together by hand, adding a
few Tbsp. water, if needed.
2. Wrap in plastic wrap, and
refrigerate for at least two
days. Break off pieces and
roll into balls.

*Note: Any other dried fruit
may be substituted for
craisins, a relatively new
product which may be much
easier to find here in New
England than in other parts of
the country.*

Yummy
Chocolate Squares
Anna Musser
Manheim, PA
PA Dutch Sampler

Makes 1 8" square pan

1 lb. marshmallows
2 cups chocolate chips
3 Tbsp. butter
1/2 tsp. salt
2 cups Rice Krispies
1 tsp. vanilla

1. Melt marshmallows,
chocolate chips, and butter
in microwave.
2. Using heavy metal or
wooden spoon, stir in salt,
cereal, and vanilla, working
quickly. Spoon into greased
8" square pan. When set,
cut into squares and serve.

Cornflake Squares
Anna Musser
Manheim, PA
PA Dutch Sampler

Makes 1 9" x 13" pan

1/4 cup butter
2 cups molasses
1 cup sugar
2 cups peanut butter
3 1/2 quarts cornflakes

1. In saucepan over medium
heat, melt together butter,
molasses, sugar, and peanut
butter. Do not bring to boil.
Remove from heat.
2. Stir in cornflakes. Press

into greased 9" x 13" pan.
3. Cool completely and cut
into squares.

Peanut Rice
Krispie Squares
Alvina Werning
Emery, SD
Flower Garden

Makes 3 dozen

Crust:
1 1/2 cups flour
2/3 cup brown sugar
1/2 tsp. baking powder
1/2 tsp. salt
1/4 tsp. baking soda
1/2 cup butter, softened
1 tsp. vanilla
2 egg yolks
3 cups miniature
  marshmallows

Topping:
2/3 cup light corn syrup
1/4 cup butter
2 tsp. vanilla
12-oz. pkg. peanut butter
  chips
2 cups Rice Krispies
2 cups salted peanuts

1. Combine flour, brown
sugar, baking powder, salt,
baking soda, butter, vanilla,
and egg yolks until crumb
mixture forms. Press into
bottom of ungreased 9" x
13" pan. Bake at 350° for
12- 15 minutes or until
golden brown. Immediately
sprinkle with marshmallows
and bake 1-2 minutes longer
or until marshmallows just
begin to puff. Cool.

2. In saucepan heat corn syrup, butter, vanilla, and peanut butter chips until chips are melted and mixture is smooth, stirring constantly. Remove from heat. Stir in cereal and nuts.
3. Immediately spoon warm cereal topping over marshmallow layer and spread to cover.
4. Chill and cut into squares.

Holiday Party Mix
Emilie Kimpel
Arcadia, MI
Joanne Kennedy
Plattsburgh, NY
Cindi Dafoe
Marquette, MI
Emma S. Byler
Paradise, PA
Ilene Bontrager
Arlington, KS

Makes 40-45 cups

12-oz. box Rice Chex
12-oz. box Cheerios
12-oz. box Kix
16-oz. box Wheat Chex
15-oz. bag pretzels
2 lbs. peanuts
1 lb. butter
1/2 cup bacon fat or vegetable oil
1/4 cup peanut butter
2 Tbsp. onion salt
3 Tbsp. Worcestershire sauce
1/4 tsp. Tabasco sauce
1 Tbsp. garlic salt
2 Tbsp. celery salt
1/2 tsp. Accent (optional)

1. Mix together all cereals, pretzels, and peanuts in large baking pan or roaster.
2. In saucepan melt together butter, bacon fat, and peanut butter. Add salt, Worcestershire sauce, Tabasco sauce, garlic salt, celery salt, and Accent and mix well. Pour over dry ingredients.
3. Bake covered at 200° for 1 hour. Stir and bake uncovered for 1 more hour.

Holiday Crunch Mix
Marlene Fonken
Upland, CA
Crazy Patch

Makes 5-6 cups

1 cup whole almonds
2 cups small knot pretzels
1 cup dried cranberries
1/2 cup dried blueberries
1 egg white
1/2 cup sugar
1/2 tsp. cinnamon
1/2 tsp. salt

1. Spread almonds on cookie sheet. Bake at 350° for 8 minutes or until almonds are slightly darker. Remove from oven. Reduce oven temperature to 225°.
2. Combine almonds, pretzels, cranberries, and blueberries in a large bowl.
3. Beat egg white until foamy. Pour over nut and berry mixture and toss to coat.

4. Combine sugar, cinnamon, and salt. Sprinkle over mixture and toss to coat.
5. Spread onto greased baking sheet.
6. Bake at 225° for 1 hour, stirring every 15 minutes.
7. Cool and store in airtight container.

Reindeer Feed
Lorene P. Meyer
Wayland, IA
Sampler

Makes 8-9 cups

6 cups assorted cereals*
1 cup pecan halves
1 cup walnuts
1/2 cup slivered almonds
1/2 cup brown sugar
1/2 cup dark corn syrup
1/4 cup margarine
1/2 tsp. salt

Cheerios, Rice Krispies, Corn Chex, or Wheat Chex

1. Mix together cereals, pecans, walnuts, and almonds in large bowl.
2. In saucepan heat together sugar, syrup, margarine, and salt until sugar is dissolved. Remove from heat. Pour over cereal and stir until coated. Spread onto 2 greased cookie sheets.
3. Bake at 325° for 10 minutes. Stir and return to oven to bake another 10 minutes.
4. Cool and break mixture apart. Store in airtight container.

Wicked Bad Munchy Mix
Sara Harter Fredette
Williamsburg, MA
Springtine at Bear Hollow

Makes 24-26 cups

1 lb. bacon
3 10-oz. boxes cheese crackers
16-oz. bag thin pretzel sticks
2 cups coarsely chopped pecans
8 Tbsp. margarine, melted
4 Tbsp. Worcestershire sauce
6-oz. can French-fried onion rings

1. Fry, drain, and crumble bacon. Set aside. Reserve 8 Tbsp. drippings.
2. Combine drippings with cheese crackers, pretzels, pecans, margarine, and Worcestershire sauce. Pour onto 2 10" x 15" baking sheets.
3. Bake at 300° for 15 minutes, stirring occasionally.
4. Stir in onion rings and bake another 5 minutes.
5. Remove from oven, stir in crumbled bacon, and set aside to cool.
6. Store in airtight container.

Note: This is a salty snack. To decrease salt, use some no-salt ingredients.

Honey Crunch
Doris H. Blue
Mechanicsburg, PA

Makes 5-6 cups

3 cups corn bran
1 cup quick oats
1 cup coarsely chopped nuts
1 tsp. cinnamon
1/4 tsp. salt
1/2 cup butter or margarine
1/3 cup honey
1/4 cup firmly packed brown sugar
1/2 cup raisins

1. In large bowl combine corn bran, oats, nuts, cinnamon, and salt.
2. In small saucepan combine butter, honey, and brown sugar. Cook over low heat, stirring constantly until butter is melted and ingredients are well blended. Pour over cereal mixture. Mix thoroughly. Spread evenly onto 10" x 15" baking pan.
3. Bake at 325° for 20-25 minutes or until golden brown, stirring occasionally. Remove from oven and stir in raisins. Immediately spread on waxed paper. Cool completely and store in airtight container.

Nuts and Bolts
Pauline J. Morrison
St. Marys, Ontario
Cinderella

Makes 12 cups

1/2 cup melted butter
1 tsp. celery salt
1 tsp. onion salt
1/2 tsp. garlic salt
4 tsp. Worcestershire sauce
3 cups peanuts
3 cups tiny shredded wheats
3 cups thin pretzels
3 cups Cheerios

1. Blend together melted butter, celery salt, onion salt, garlic salt, and Worcestershire sauce.
2. Measure peanuts, tiny shredded wheats, pretzels, and Cheerios into large roasting pan. Stir in butter mixture.
3. Bake at 250° for 1 hour, stirring frequently.
4. Cool and store in airtight container.

Nutty O's
Joyce Shackelford
Green Bay, WI
Double Irish Chain

Makes 15 cups

1/2 cup butter or
  margarine
1 cup brown sugar
1 cup dark corn syrup
12 cups Cheerios
2 cups pecan halves
1 cup whole almonds

1. In saucepan heat butter, brown sugar, and corn syrup until sugar is dissolved.
2. In large bowl combine Cheerios, pecans, and almonds. Mix well. Pour syrup over mixture and stir until well mixed. Spread onto 2 greased 10" x 15" baking pans.
3. Bake at 325° for 15 minutes. Cool for 10 minutes, then stir to loosen from pan. Cool completely.
4. Store in airtight container.

Confetti Party Mix
Juanita Marner
Shipshewana, IN
Grandmother's Flower Garden

Makes 7 1/2 cups

4 cups corn bran
1 cup raisins
1 cup M&Ms
1 cup salted peanuts
1/2 cup dried banana
  chips

1. Combine all ingredients.
2. Store in tightly covered container at room temperature.

Crunchy Caramel Snack Mix
Juanita Marner
Shipshewana, IN
Grandmother's Flower Garden

Makes 10 cups

3 cups chocolate-flavored
  puffed corn cereal
3 cups bite-sized rice
  square cereal
2 cups small twisted
  pretzels
1 cup peanuts
1 cup packed brown
  sugar
1/2 cup margarine or
  butter
1/2 cup light corn syrup
1/4 tsp. baking soda
1/4 tsp. cream of tartar
1/2 tsp. vanilla

1. In a large bowl, combine the chocolate-flavored corn cereal, rice cereal, pretzels, and peanuts. Set aside.
2. To prepare syrup combine the brown sugar, margarine, and corn syrup in a medium saucepan. Cook and stir over medium heat until margarine melts and mixture begins to boil. Boil for 4 minutes.
3. Remove saucepan from heat and stir in baking soda and cream of tartar. Then stir in vanilla. Pour syrup over cereal mixture, stirring until cereal is coated with syrup.
4. Bake at 170° for 1 hour, stirring every 15 mintues. Let cool completely before storing.

Christmas Cereal Mix
Katie Esh
Ronks, PA

Makes 14-16 cups

2 cups white coating
  chocolate
5-7 cups Cheerios
5-7 cups Rice Chex
2 cups peanuts

1. Melt chocolate in double boiler. Pour over cereal and nuts and mix well.
2. Pour onto waxed paper to cool. When cool, break into pieces.

Frosted Christmas Nuts

Marjorie Patterson
North Point, PA
Betty Gray
Ellicott City, MD
Kimberly Davison
Coral Gables, FL

Makes 5 cups

2 egg whites
1 cup sugar
1/2 tsp. cinnamon
1/4 tsp. salt
4-5 cups walnuts and
    pecans
1/2 cup margarine

1. Beat egg whites until fluffy. Stir in sugar, cinnamon, and salt. Stir in nuts until coated.
2. In shallow baking pan or dish, melt margarine. Add nut mixture to baking pan.
3. Bake at 325° for 45-60 minutes, stirring every 10-15 minutes. Remove from oven when lightly browned and all margarine has been absorbed. Cool completely.

Spicy Pecans

Shirley Taylor
Yuba City, CA

Makes 2 1/2 cups

1 egg white
1 tsp. vanilla
2 Tbsp. water
2 1/2 cups pecan halves
1/2 cup sugar
1/4 cup cornstarch
2 tsp. cinnamon
1/2 tsp. salt
1/2 tsp. ginger

1. Beat slightly egg white, vanilla, and water. Stir in pecans until well moistened.
2. Combine sugar, cornstarch, cinnamon, salt, and ginger. Sift this mixture onto the pecans. Toss pecans in mixture until well coated. Place on non-stick 10" x 15" baking sheet.
3. Bake at 250° for 1/2 hour, stirring often.
4. This recipe keeps well in the freezer.

Glazed Nuts

Carol Jensen
Watchung, NJ
Morning Star
Mary Lou Kirtland
Berkeley Heights, NJ
Storm at Sea

Makes 3 lbs.

1 lb. blanched almonds
1 lb. pecans
1 lb. cashews
4 egg whites
2 cups sugar
1 cup butter

1. Arrange almonds, pecans, and cashews on baking sheet. Toast lightly at 325° for 8-10 minutes or until lightly browned. Remove from oven and salt lightly.
2. Beat egg whites until stiff. Fold in sugar. Gently fold in nuts and mix until well coated.
3. Melt butter in shallow roasting pan. Spread nuts into the butter.
4. Bake at 325° for 35-40 minutes, stirring every 10 minutes.
5. Cool completely and store in airtight container.

Several years ago my son's girlfriend gave me a Christmas present without realizing it. She asked me to teach her how to quilt so she could make Patrick a quilt for Christmas. I pieced a queen-sized Bear Paw top, and within three months, she had quilted it. Her handwork was beautiful, and Patrick was delighted. Since then she has won ribbons for her quilting. I am proud of her and glad that my love of quilting has been passed on to the next generation.
—*Theresa Leppert, Schellsburg, PA*

Sour Cream Candied Walnuts
Sharon Easter
Yuba City, CA

Makes 4 cups

1 cup brown sugar
1/2 cup white sugar
1/2 cup sour cream
1 tsp. vanilla
4 cups walnut pieces

1. In saucepan mix together sugars and sour cream. Bring to a boil and cook to soft ball stage, 236° on candy thermometer (about 10-15 minutes). Remove from heat.
2. Stir in vanilla and beat until it become thick and has lost its gloss.
3. Stir in nuts to coat. Spread out onto waxed paper to cool.

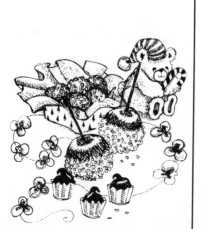

Spiced Nuts
Helen Plauschinn
Pickering, Ontario
Autumn Breeze

Makes 6 cups

2 cups salted mixed nuts
2 cups salted peanuts
2 egg whites, slightly beaten
10 Tbsp. white sugar
8 tsp. cinnamon
2 cups raisins
1 tsp. salt

1. Combine nuts, peanuts, and egg whites. Toss until well coated.
2. Combine sugar and cinnamon. Sprinkle over nuts, stirring until well coated. Spread onto baking sheet.
3. Bake at 325° for 20 minutes, stirring several times.
4. Stir in raisins and sprinkle with salt. Cool and store in covered tins in a cool place.

Glazed Walnuts
Janet Derstine
Telford, PA
Double Wedding Ring
Laura Ashby
Boulder Creek, CA
Leap Frog

Makes 4 cups

1 cup sugar
1/4 tsp. cinnamon
6 Tbsp. milk
1 tsp. vanilla
1 lb. shelled walnuts

1. In saucepan cook together sugar, cinnamon, and milk until mixture comes to soft ball stage (see page 279). Remove from heat. Stir in vanilla and walnuts.
2. Spread onto greased baking pan. Cool, then separate.

Crystallized Orange Nuts
Susan Ketcherside
St. Charles, MO
Lone Star

Makes 2 cups

1/4 cup orange juice
1 cup sugar
2 cups pecan halves

1. Combine orange juice and sugar in 2-quart glass baking dish. Mix well. Stir in pecans.
2. Microwave on roast for 6 minutes. Stir and continue cooking on roast for 8-10 minutes until syrup has crystallized. Spread immediately on greased cookie sheet or waxed paper and separate as they cool.

Spiced Orange Pecans

Janice Muller
Derwood, MD
Canadian Geese

Makes 5 1/2 cups

1/4 cup orange juice
1 Tbsp. grated orange
  rind
1/2 tsp. cinnamon
1/4 tsp. allspice
1/4 tsp. ginger
1 cup sugar
4 cups pecan halves

1. In a large skillet, combine orange juice, orange rind, cinnamon, allspice, ginger, and sugar. Cook on medium heat until mixture comes to a full boil. Stir in pecan. Cook until well coated and syrup is absorbed, stirring occasionally.
2. Remove from heat, and stir until pecans separate. Spread onto waxed paper to cool.

Walnut Crackers

Anona M. Teel
Bangor, PA
Irish Chain

Makes 100 crackers

1/2 lb. ground walnuts
1 cup coconut
1/2 cup brown sugar
1 cup butter, softened
1 box club crackers

1. Mix together walnuts, coconut, brown sugar, and butter.
2. Spread on unsalted side of each cracker and place on cookie sheet.
3. Bake at 350° for 7 minutes. Serve at a party.

Praline Crackers

Martha Ann Auker
East Waterford, PA
Trip Around the World

Makes 40-50 crackers

40-50 club crackers
1/4 cup butter
1/4 cup margarine
1/3 cup sugar

1. Arrange club crackers on 10" x 15" jelly roll pan.
2. In a saucepan cook together butter, margarine, and sugar for 1 minute or until butter and margarine have melted. Pour over crackers.
3. Place in cold oven. Turn to 350° and bake for 10 minutes. Remove from oven and cool on wire rack. Cool completely and store in airtight container.

Grandma's Popcorn Balls

Judy Sharer
Port Matilda, PA
Sew Charming

Makes 1-2 dozen

1-1 1/4 cups unpopped
  popcorn
3/4 cup molasses
1/4 cup light corn syrup
2 Tbsp. water
1 Tbsp. vinegar
1 cup sugar
1 tsp. vanilla
2 tsp. butter
1 tsp. baking soda

1. Pop popcorn. Set aside in large bowl.
2. In a skillet combine molasses, corn syrup, water, vinegar, and sugar. Stir over medium high heat. Boil mixture until it turns brittle when dropped in cold water (hard ball stage).
3. Add vanilla, butter, and baking soda, stirring constantly until completely mixed.
4. Immediately pour over prepared popcorn and mix until all popcorn is covered. Coat hands with a little butter and form popcorn into balls.
5. Place on tray and air dry. Wrap in plastic wrap or cellophane and tie with a ribbon to give as gifts.

Caramel Corn
Robin Schrock
Millersburg, OH
Thelma A. Stein
Tavares, FL
Grace Brunelle
Underhill, VT
Charlene Bement
Rancho Cucamonga, CA

Makes 30-34 1-cup servings

1/2 cup light corn syrup
2 cups brown sugar
1 cup margarine or
  butter
1 tsp. salt
1/4 tsp cream of tartar
1/2 tsp. baking soda
1/2 tsp. vanilla
8 quarts popped popcorn
1 cup peanuts (optional)

1. In saucepan combine corn syrup, sugar, margarine, salt, and cream of tartar. Bring to a boil and boil for 5 minutes or until mixture reaches 260° on candy thermometer.
2. Remove from heat and stir in baking soda and vanilla. (Mixture will foam.)
3. Carefully pour this very hot syrup over popcorn in very large roasting pan or several large cookie sheets.
4. Bake at 250° for 75 minutes, stirring every 15 minutes.
5. Let cool and break apart before serving or storing.

Caramel Nut Popcorn
Carole M. Mackie
Williamsfield, IL
Sunbonnet Sue

Makes 4 quarts

3 quarts freshly popped
  corn
1 cup roasted, unsalted
  cashews
1 cup roasted, salted
  macadamia nuts
1 cup pecan halves
1 cup firmly packed
  brown sugar
1/2 cup light corn syrup
1/2 cup butter
1/2 tsp. salt
1 tsp. vanilla
1/2 tsp. baking soda

1. Mix popcorn and nuts in large roasting pan. Turn oven to 250°, and place popcorn and nuts in the oven while it heats and while preparing glaze.
2. In large, heavy saucepan, combine brown sugar, corn syrup, butter, and salt. Bring to a boil over medium heat, stirring constantly until sugar dissolves. Boil for 4 minutes without stirring.
3. Remove from heat. Stir in vanilla and baking soda. Gradually pour glaze over popcorn and nuts, stirring to coat well.
4. Bake at 250° for 1 hour, stirring every 15 minutes. Remove from oven. Using a metal spatula, free popcorn from bottom of pan. Let

cool completely in pan. Break into clumps.
5. Will keep in tightly closed container at room temperature for about 1 week.

Maple Popcorn
Judy Newman
St. Marys, Ontario
Schooltime

Makes 4-5 quarts

1 cup unpopped popcorn
1 cup butter
1/2 cup maple syrup
2 cups brown sugar
dash salt
1/2 tsp. baking soda
1 tsp. vanilla

1. Pop popcorn and pour into large roasting pan. Set aside.
2. Combine butter, maple syrup, brown sugar, and salt in large saucepan. Bring to a boil and boil for 5 minutes without stirring.
3. Stir in baking soda and vanilla and immediately pour over popcorn, stirring quickly. (Be careful as this mixture is very hot.)
4. Bake at 250° for 1 hour, stirring every 15 minutes. Cool and serve.

Praline Coffee Popcorn
Millie Hohimer
Independence, MO
Heart of Roses

Makes 12 cups

10 cups popped popcorn
1 cup pecan halves
3/4 cup brown sugar
2 tsp. instant coffee granules
1/3 cup butter
2 Tbsp. light corn syrup
1 tsp. vanilla

1. Combine popcorn and pecan halves in large bowl.
2. In a 4-cup glass measure, mix together brown sugar, coffee, butter, and light corn syrup. Microwave on high for 1 1/2 to 2 minutes. Stir and microwave for 2 more minutes.
3. Stir in vanilla and quickly pour over popcorn mixture, tossing until evenly coated.
4. Transfer 1/2 of mixture to an ungreased microwave-safe dish and microwave on high for 2-3 minutes, stirring after each minute. Spread out on aluminum foil to cool. Repeat with remaining mixture.
5. Popcorn will become crisp as it cools. Serve.

Italian Popcorn
Rose Hankins
Stevensville, MD
Bow Tie

Makes 6 cups

6 cups freshly popped popcorn
1/2 tsp. Italian seasoning
1/2 tsp. garlic powder
3 Tbsp. Parmesan cheese

1. Mix together seasonings and cheese. Stir.
2. Sprinkle over hot popcorn, let stand several minutes, and serve.

Seasoned Oyster Crackers
Lucille Reagan
Salem, OR

Makes 3-4 cups

1/3 cup corn oil
10-oz. box small oyster crackers
1/2 pkg. Hidden Valley Herb dressing mix
1 pkg. Hidden Valley Ranch dressing mix
1/2 tsp. garlic powder
1/2 tsp. dill weed

1. Heat corn oil slightly in small skillet. Pour over oyster crackers and mix well.
2. Combine all remaining ingredients in large plastic bag. Pour in crackers and shake well to cover crackers with seasonings. Serve.

Oyster Cracker Snack
Katie Esh
Ronks, PA

Makes 5-6 cups

1 cup cooking oil
1/4 tsp. garlic salt
1/4 tsp. lemon pepper
1 pkg. Hidden Valley Ranch dressing mix
2 12-oz. pkgs. oyster crackers

1. Mix together first four ingredients and pour over oyster crackers.
2. Allow to sit at least 1 hour, stirring occasionally.
3. Store in a tight container.

Breakfast Foods

Holiday Quiche
Sara Harter Fredette
Williamsburg, MA
Cabin in the Woods

Makes 8 servings

2 cups lightly cooked
  broccoli, cut into bite-
  sized pieces
1/2 cup chopped onion
1/2 sweet red pepper, cut
  into bite-sized pieces
1 1/3 cups shredded cheese
1 1/3 cups skim milk
2/3 cup biscuit mix
4 eggs
salt and pepper to taste

1. Place broccoli, onion, red
pepper, and cheese in large
greased pie plate.
2. In blender mix together
milk, biscuit mix, eggs, salt,
and pepper. Mix well. Pour
over vegetables in pie plate.
3. Bake at 375° for 30 minutes. Allow to set for 5 minutes before serving.

Quiche New Mexico Style
Colleen Konetzni
Rio Rancho, NM
Double Wedding Ring

Makes 4-6 servings

1/2 lb. ground beef
1 cup shredded cheddar
  cheese
1 cup milk
2 eggs, beaten
2 tsp. minced onion
2 ozs. chopped green
  chilies
1 9" unbaked pie shell

1. In skillet brown ground
beef. Drain well.
2. Mix together beef,
cheese, milk, eggs, onion,
and chilies.
3. Pour mixture into
unbaked pie shell.
3. Bake at 400° for 10 minutes. Reduce oven temperature to 350° and bake
another 35 minutes or until
center is set. Serve.

Quiche
Sherri Lipman McCauley
Austin, TX
Dorothy's Baskets

Makes 6 servings

1/4 lb. cubed ham chunks
2 cups grated cheese*
4 Tbsp. flour
3 eggs
1/2 cup milk
1/2 cup half-and-half
1/4 tsp. salt
1/4 tsp. dry mustard
1 9" unbaked pie shell

*Swiss, provolone, mozzarella,
or cheddar*

1. Sprinkle ham chunks in
bottom of unbaked pie shell.
2. Mix together cheese and
flour. Sprinkle over ham.
3. Mix together eggs, milk,
half-and-half, salt, and mustard. Beat until smooth.
Pour over cheese.
4. Bake at 375° for 35 minutes.

Pepperoni Mushroom Quiche

Marsha Sabus
Fallbrook, CA
Diamond in the Rough

Makes 6-8 servings

1 cup finely diced pepperoni
1/2 lb. mushrooms, sliced
1/2 cup chopped green onions
2/3 cup grated Parmesan cheese
1 1/2 cups half-and-half
3 eggs, beaten
1/2 tsp. crushed basil
1/2 tsp. salt
3 Tbsp. Parmesan cheese
1 9" unbaked pie shell

1. In a skillet cook pepperoni over low to medium heat for 3-4 minutes.
2. Stir in mushrooms and green onions and sauté until tender and moisture has evaporated.
3. Sprinkle 2/3 cup Parmesan cheese in bottom of unbaked pie shell. Spoon pepperoni mixture over cheese.
4. Mix together half-and-half, eggs, basil, and salt. Pour over pepperoni mixture in pie shell. Sprinkle with remaining 3 Tbsp. Parmesan cheese.
5. Bake at 350° for 45-50 minutes or until knife inserted in center comes out clean. Let stand 5-10 minutes before cutting.

Racey Ricey Quiche

Anne Townsend
Albuquerque, NM
Christmas Appliqué

Makes 6-8 servings

1/2-3/4 lb. hot spicy sausage
1 cup cooked rice
1/4 lb. Monterey Jack cheese, grated
4 eggs
1 Tbsp. flour
1/2 tsp. dry mustard
12-oz. can evaporated milk

1. In a skillet brown sausage. Drain well and crumble.
2. Spread rice over bottom and slightly up the sides of greased pie pan.
3. Sprinkle cheese and sausage on top of rice.
4. Beat together eggs, flour, mustard, and milk. Pour over ingredients in pie pan.
5. Bake at 375° for 40 minutes or until set. Let stand 10 minutes before slicing.

Salmon Quiche

Amy Picard
Leesburg, FL
Sampler

Makes 6 servings

1 cup whole wheat flour
2/3 cup shredded sharp cheddar cheese
1/4 cup chopped nuts
1/2 tsp. salt
1/4 tsp. paprika
6 Tbsp. cooking oil
15-oz. can salmon
3 eggs, beaten
1 cup sour cream
1/4 cup mayonnaise
1/2 cup shredded sharp cheddar cheese
1 Tbsp. grated onion
1/4 tsp. dried dill weed
3 drops hot pepper sauce

1. Mix together flour, 2/3 cup cheese, nuts, salt, and paprika. Stir in oil. Reserve 1/2 cup of crust mixture. Press remaining mixture into the bottom and up the sides of a 9-inch pie plate. Bake crust at 400° for 10 minutes. Remove from oven. Reduce oven temperature to 325°.
2. Drain salmon, reserving liquid. Add water to reserved liquid, if necessary, to make 1/2 cup liquid. Flake salmon, removing bones and skin. Set aside.
3. Blend together eggs, sour cream, mayonnaise, and salmon liquid. Stir in salmon, 1/2 cup cheese, onion, dill weed, and hot pepper sauce. Spoon filling

into crust. Sprinkle with reserved crust mixture.
4. Bake at 325° for 45 minutes or until firm in center.

Ham and Crab Quiche

Rosaria Strachan
Old Greenwich, CT
Friendship

Makes 6-8 servings

1/2 lb. Swiss cheese, grated
1/2 cup milk
1/2 cup mayonnaise
2 Tbsp. flour
1/4 cup onion, minced
2 eggs
1 cup chopped ham
4-oz. can crab meat, drained
1 9" unbaked pie shell

1. Combine all ingredients except pie shell and mix well. Pour into pie shell.
2. Bake at 350° for 35-40 minutes or until knife inserted in center comes out clean. Let set 5 minutes and slice to serve.

Belgian Waffles

Audrey Romonosky
Austin, TX
Pineapple Quilt

Makes 5-6 waffles

2 cups flour, sifted
3 tsp. baking powder
1 tsp. salt
2 Tbsp. sugar
2 egg yolks, beaten
1 1/2 cups milk
6 Tbsp. cooking oil
2 egg whites, stiffly beaten
1 pint strawberries, sliced
2 Tbsp. sugar
whipped topping

1. Sift together flour, baking powder, salt, and sugar.
2. Mix together egg yolks, milk, and cooking oil.
3. Pour wet ingredients onto dry ingredients and stir just enough to moisten dry ingredients.
4. Fold in egg whites.
5. Pour batter onto preheated, greased waffle iron. Each time pour batter within about 1" of edge of iron. Close iron and cook until browned. Watch carefully. Add dab of butter each time to grease iron and repeat to use all remaining batter.
6. Mix together strawberries and sugar. Serve over waffles. Top with whipped topping.

Walnut Waffles

Alyce C. Kauffman
Gridley, CA
Sailing Away

Makes 6-8 servings

2 eggs
2 cups buttermilk
1 tsp. baking soda
2 cups flour
1/2 tsp. salt
2 tsp. baking powder
6 Tbsp. softened shortening
3/4 cup chopped nuts
1 tsp. cinnamon
2 Tbsp. sugar

1. Beat together eggs, buttermilk, baking soda, flour, salt, baking powder, and shortening. Batter will be thin.
2. Stir in nuts, cinnamon, and sugar.
3. Bake in preheated and greased waffle iron. Spread batter to within about 1" of edge of iron. Close iron and cook until browned, watching carefully. Add dab of butter each time to grease iron and repeat to use all remaining batter.
4. Serve with butter, sour cream, and maple syrup.

Mama's Christmas Waffles

Joyce R. Swinney
Mooresville, IN
Dresden Heart

Makes 8 large waffles

Waffles:
2 1/2 cups flour
4 1/2 tsp. baking powder
3/4 tsp. salt
3 Tbsp. sugar
3 egg yolks, beaten
3 cups milk
1/2 cup cooking oil
3 egg whites
1 1/2 cups shredded
    coconut

Honey Butter Topping:
1 cup butter, softened
4 Tbsp. milk
1/3 cup honey

1. Sift together flour, baking powder, salt, and sugar.
2. Mix together egg yolks, milk, and oil. Slowly stir egg mixture into flour. Never beat.
3. In medium bowl beat egg whites until stiff.
4. Fold egg whites and coconut into batter. This will be lumpy.
5. Pour some of batter into preheated and greased waffle iron. Spread within 1" of edge. Close iron and cook until browned, watching carefully. Add dab of butter each time to grease iron and repeat to use all remaining batter.
6. To prepare honey butter topping, beat together butter and milk until fluffy. Continuing to beat, drizzle in 1/3 cup honey. Serve over waffles.

The Christmas when I was seventeen years old, my mother was baking her usual homemade yeast rolls which had to rise three times. My cousin and I were fooling around and knocked two trays behind the steam radiator. We picked out the lint, reformed the rolls, and set them back on the radiator to continue rising. After we confessed, my mother said she didn't think they looked right, but she had gone ahead and baked them. The family raved about how good they were, but after our confession, it was declared that we should never be permitted to do the yeast rolls. I'm forty-one and the rule has held.
—*Grace Brunelle, Underhill, VT*

Evelyn's Overnight French Toast

Sara Harter Fredette
Williamsburg, MA
Storm at Sea

Makes 4-6 servings

1 long oval loaf French
    bread
5 eggs
3/4 cup milk
1/4 tsp. baking powder
1 Tbsp. vanilla
20 oz. pkg. frozen
    strawberries
4 bananas, sliced
1/2 cup sugar
1 Tbsp. apple pie spice
1 tsp. cinnamon

1. Cut bread into 8 thick slices and place in greased 9" x 13" baking pan.
2. Mix together eggs, milk, baking powder, and vanilla. Pour over bread and refrigerate overnight.
3. Place frozen strawberries in bottom of another greased 9" x 13" baking pan. Lay banana slices on top of frozen fruit.
4. Mix together sugar and pie spice and sprinkle over strawberries.
5. Arrange bread over top of strawberries. Sprinkle with cinnamon.
6. Bake at 450° for 20-25 minutes or until crusty and brown.

Note: Substitute raspberries, blueberries, or a combination of berries for the strawberries.

Oven French Toast with Orange Sauce
Jennet C. Parker
Stroudsburg, PA
Around the Garden Twist

Makes 8-10 servings

French Toast:
1/2 cup butter, melted
1/2 cup orange juice
1 Tbsp. honey
4 eggs
1 loaf French bread cut into 1" slices

Orange Sauce:
1/2 cup butter, melted
1/2 cup dark brown sugar
2 Tbsp. honey
1/4 tsp. lemon juice
1/4 cup orange juice

1. Pour 1/2 cup melted butter into 10" x 15" jelly roll pan. Cover bottom evenly. Place in refrigerator to chill.
2. Mix together orange juice, honey, and eggs and mix well. Dip bread into mixture, and place on pan. Cover and refrigerate up to 24 hours.
3. Bake at 400° for 8-10 minutes or until bottom of bread browns. Turn and bake 7-8 minutes longer until golden brown.
4. To prepare orange sauce, melt butter in medium saucepan. Remove from heat and stir in brown sugar, honey, lemon juice, and orange juice. Return to low heat, and stir to blend for about 1 minute. Serve warm over toast.

Stuffed French Toast
Elaine Headley
Salina, KS
Strippy Grandmother's Fan

Makes 6-8 servings

French Toast:
8-oz. pkg. cream cheese, softened
1 tsp. vanilla
1/2 cup chopped walnuts
1 loaf French bread
4 eggs
1 cup whipping cream
1/2 tsp. nutmeg
1/2 tsp. vanilla

Topping:
12-oz. jar apricot preserves
1/2 cup orange juice

1. Cream together cream cheese and vanilla until fluffy. Stir in walnuts and set aside.
2. Cut bread into 10-12 slices, 1 1/2" wide. Cut a pocket in the top of each slice.
3. Fill each pocket with 1 1/2 Tbsp. cream cheese filling.
4. Beat together eggs, whipping cream, nutmeg, and vanilla. Dip stuffed slices in the egg and cream mixture. Be careful not to squeeze out the filling.
5. In a skillet with melted butter, fry bread on both sides until golden brown. Keep warm in 225° oven, if necessary.
6. To prepare topping combine apricot preserves and orange juice in a saucepan. Heat over low temperature until bubbly hot, stirring frequently. Serve over French toast.

Note: Serve with maple syrup instead of apricot topping, if desired.

Overnight French Toast
Nancy J. Robinson
Kealakekua, HI
Nine Patch

Makes 10-12 servings

9 eggs, beaten
3 cups light cream
1/3 cup sugar
1 1/2 tsp. rum extract
2 tsp. vanilla
1 tsp. ground nutmeg
24-30 slices French bread (3/4"-1" thick)

1. Mix together eggs, cream, sugar, rum extract, vanilla, and nutmeg.
2. Arrange bread slices in a single layer on two 10" x 15" baking pans. Pour egg mixture over bread slices. Turn over once. Cover with foil and refrigerate overnight.
3. Bake uncovered at 400° for 20-25 minutes or until golden brown. Serve with butter and warm syrup.

Sallie's Orange Toast
Marge Reeder
State College, PA
Sara's Log Cabin

Makes 12 servings

1 loaf very thin, sliced
   white bread
1 cup margarine,
   softened
1 cup sugar
2 Tbsp. grated orange
   peel

1. Mix together margarine, sugar, and orange peel. Spread mixture on one side of each slice of bread.
2. Cut slices into halves. Bake on cookie sheet at 250° for 1 hour. Cool on wire rack to prevent sogginess.

Apple-Puffed Pancake
Margaret F. Moehl
Pinckney, MI
Christmas Treasures

Makes 8 servings

Pancakes:
6 eggs, beaten
1 1/2 cups milk
1 1/2 cups flour
3 Tbsp. sugar
1 tsp. vanilla
1/2 tsp. salt
1/2 tsp. cinnamon
8 Tbsp. butter
2 apples, peeled and sliced

Raspberry Sauce:
16-oz. pkg. frozen
   raspberries, thawed
1/8 cup Grand Marnier or
   orange juice

1. In blender or mixing bowl, mix eggs, milk, flour, sugar, vanilla, salt, and cinnamon until well blended.
2. In a preheated 425° oven, melt butter in 12" quiche dish or 9" x 13" casserole dish. Add apples. Place in hot oven for several minutes. Do not brown. Remove from oven. Pour pancake batter over apples.
3. Bake for 20 minutes or until puffed and brown.
4. To prepare raspberry sauce, combine raspberries and Grand Marnier in a small saucepan. Heat, stirring occaionally, for 5-10 minutes.
5. Serve hot apple puffed pancakes with raspberry sauce.

Apple Pancakes
Jan Steffy Mast
Lancaster, PA
Bow Tie

Makes 10-12 servings

Pancakes:
4 cups biscuit mix
1 tsp. cinnamon
2 eggs, beaten
2 2/3 cups milk
1 1/2 cups chopped apples

Apple Sauce:
1 cup sugar or less
2 Tbsp. cornstarch
1/4 tsp. cinnamon
1/4 tsp. nutmeg
2 cups apple cider
2 Tbsp. lemon juice
1/4 cup butter

1. Mix together all pancake ingredients. Fry on hot griddle.
2. To prepare sauce mix together sugar, cornstarch, cinnamon, and nutmeg in a saucepan over medium heat. Gradually stir in cider and lemon juice and bring to a boil. Boil and stir for 1 minute. Add butter and remove from heat. Stir until butter melts. Serve apple sauce over pancakes for a delicious holiday breakfast.

Mama's Best Blueberry Pancakes

Joyce R. Swinney
Mooresville, IN
Dresden Heart

Makes 6-8 servings

1 1/4 cups flour
2 1/2 tsp. baking powder
2 Tbsp. sugar
3/4 tsp. salt
2 eggs, beaten
1 cup milk
4 Tbsp. cooking oil
3/4-1 cup fresh or frozen blueberries

1. Sift together flour, baking powder, sugar, and salt.
2. Mix together eggs, milk, and oil. Slowly stir into dry ingredients. Mix only until dry ingredients are wet. (Mixture will be lumpy.)
3. Carefully spoon batter onto well greased griddle. Sprinkle 8-12 blueberries on each pancake. Flip pancakes when surface is about 3/4 covered with bubbles. Flip over carefully.
4. Serve with peanut butter and syrup.

Note: If pancakes are doughy inside, griddle is too hot. If pancakes are leathery and heavy, griddle is not hot enough.

Hot Stuffed Eggs

Ann Gouinlock
Alexander, NY
Dresden Plate

Mapes 4 servings

1/2 cup chopped mushrooms
1/4 cup chopped onions
1 Tbsp. flour
2 Tbsp. butter
1/2 cup milk
1/2 tsp. salt
1/8 tsp. pepper
1/4 tsp. mustard
4 hard-cooked eggs
buttered bread crumbs

1. Brown mushrooms and onion in butter.
2. Add flour and blend.
3. Add milk gradually and stir until thick. Mix in salt, pepper, and mustard.
4. Remove shell from eggs and slice in half lengthwise. Remove yolks and crush.
5. Add yolks to cream sauce and seasonings.
6. Stuff egg whites with mixture.
7. Sprinkle eggs with buttered bread crumbs.
8. Broil 5 minutes or until browned.

Savory Eggs

Jennet C. Parker
Stroudsburg, PA
Around the Garden Twist

Makes 8 servings

2 cups grated American cheese
1/4 cup butter or margarine
1 cup light cream or milk
1/2 tsp. salt
1/4 tsp. pepper
2 tsp. prepared mustard
12 eggs, slightly beaten

1. Spread cheese in greased 8" square baking dish. Dot with butter.
2. Mix together cream, salt, pepper, and mustard. Pour half over cheese in baking dish. Pour eggs on top. Add remaining cream mixture.
3. Bake at 325° for 40 minutes or until set. Stir once or twice while cooking.

Note: This can easily be mixed the day before and kept in refrigerator until ready to serve.

Eggs in a Hurry
Mary Bartlet
Schenectady, NY
I Believe

Makes 6 servings

8 slices bacon
6 eggs
1/3 cup milk
1/2 cup mayonnaise
1/4 cup chopped green
    pepper
salt and pepper to taste
4 thin tomato slices

1. Fry, drain, and crumble bacon.
2. Beat together eggs, milk, and mayonnaise. Stir in bacon, green pepper, salt, and pepper.
3. Pour into 8" square glass baking dish. Top with tomato. Cover with plastic wrap.
4. Microwave on medium for 10-12 minutes or until set. Let stand covered for 5 minutes before serving.

Eggs in a Nest
Brenda Joy Sonnie
Newtown, PA
Nine Patch

Makes 4 servings

1 lb. bacon
10-oz. pkg. frozen leaf
    spinach
10 3/4-oz. can cream of
    celery soup
4 eggs
2 slices American cheese
4 bagels, toasted

1. Fry bacon and set aside to drain.
2. Cook leaf spinach according to package directions. Drain in colander, pressing with spoon to remove as much liquid as possible.
3. Pour celery soup into glass casserole dish with a lid. Stir spinach into soup. Make 4 depressions in spinach, deep enough for egg. Crack and place 1 raw egg into each depression. Place a triangle of cheese over each egg. Cover with glass lid.
4. Bake at 350° 10-15 minutes or until eggs set.
5. Serve with bacon and toasted bagels.

Baked English Omelette
Eileen B. Jarvis
Wexford, PA
Card Trick

Makes 4 servings

3 slices bacon
6 eggs, beaten
2/3 cup milk
1/8 tsp. pepper
1 1/2 cups shredded
    cheddar cheese
1 green onion, thinly sliced
1 Tbsp. margarine or
    butter
1 Tbsp. grated Parmesan
    cheese

1. Fry, drain, and crumble bacon. Set aside.
2. Mix together eggs and milk.
3. Stir in pepper, cheddar cheese, onion, and bacon.
4. Melt butter in a 9" frying pan or omelette pan. Pour egg mixture into pan. Sprinkle with Parmesan cheese.
4. Bake at 400° for 20 minutes or until set and golden. Serve immediately.
5. Garnish with additional bacon if desired. Serve immediately.

Brunch Baked Eggs

Susan Orleman
Pittsburgh, PA
Hilton Head Memories

Makes 10-12 servings

12 ozs. Monterey Jack
cheese, shredded
12 ozs. fresh mushrooms,
sliced
1/2 medium onion,
chopped
1/4 cup sweet red pepper,
thinly sliced
1/4 cup margarine, melted
8 ozs. cooked ham, cut
into strips
12 ozs. Monterey Jack
cheese, shredded
8 eggs, beaten
1 3/4 cups milk
1/2 cup flour
2 Tbsp. snipped fresh
chives or basil
1 Tbsp. snipped fresh
parsley

1. Sprinkle 12 ozs. Jack
cheese in bottom of 9" x 13"
baking dish.
2. In saucepan cook the
mushrooms, onion, and red
pepper in margarine until
vegetables are tender but
not brown. Drain well.
Place vegetables on top of
cheese.
3. Arrange ham strips over
vegetables. Sprinkle with
remaining 12 ozs. Jack
cheese.
4. Cover and chill in refrigerator overnight.
5. In the morning combine
eggs, milk, flour, herb of
choice, and parsley.
6. Bake at 350° for 45 minutes. Let stand 10 minutes
before serving.

*Variation: Substitute 12 ozs.
shredded cheddar cheese and
12 ozs. shredded mozzarella
for the 24 ozs. Monterey Jack
cheese.*

Joanne Spatz
Lebanon, PA
Lovers Knot
Donna Wright
Oxford, NY
Tulip Basket

Spanish Tortilla

Alice Turner Werner
St. Charles, MO

Makes 4 servings

2 medium potatoes,
peeled and cubed
1 medium onion, diced
1/2 green pepper, diced
1/2 red pepper, diced
1/2 cup olive oil
8 large eggs, lightly
beaten
1/2 cup cubed ham
salt and pepper to taste

1. Sauté potatoes, onion,
and peppers in 2-3 Tbsp. oil
until soft.
2. Mix together sautéed vegetables, eggs, and ham. Pour
into a large, hot skillet with
remaining olive oil.
3. As the tortilla cooks, pull
gently from sides and let
uncooked egg flow under-
neath. When tortilla is fairly
firm, slide onto a large
plate, and turn back into
skillet with uncooked side
down. Let cook about 1
minute more and turn back
onto plate.

*Note: Substitute ham with
shrimp, crab, or leftover beef.
We learned to eat this dish
when we lived in Spain. It is
usually cooked early in the
day and served cold for lunch.
We always have this for
breakfast on Christmas morning with a fruit salad and
rolls.*

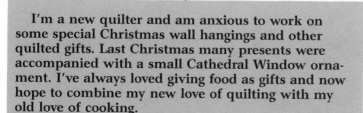

I'm a new quilter and am anxious to work on
some special Christmas wall hangings and other
quilted gifts. Last Christmas many presents were
accompanied with a small Cathedral Window ornament. I've always loved giving food as gifts and now
hope to combine my new love of quilting with my
old love of cooking.
—*Claire Amick, Pine Grove Mills, PA*

Overnight Potato Breakfast Casserole

Susan Ketcherside
St. Charles, MO
Lone Star

Makes 6-8 servings

6-8 slices bacon
6-oz. pkg. hash brown
  potato mix
1 quart hot water
5 eggs
1/2 cup cottage cheese
1 cup shredded Swiss
  cheese
1 green onion, chopped
1 tsp. salt
1 tsp. paprika
1/8 tsp. pepper
4 drops hot sauce

1. Fry, drain, and crumble bacon. Set aside.
2. Cover hash browns with hot water. Let stand 10 minutes. Drain well.
3. Beat eggs and add to potatoes. Stir in cottage cheese, Swiss cheese, onion, salt, paprika, pepper, and hot sauce.
4. Pour mixture into lightly greased 10" pie pan. Sprinkle with bacon and paprika. Cover and refrigerate overnight.
5. Place cold pie pan in cold oven. Bake uncovered at 350° for 35 minutes or until done.

Breakfast Egg Delight

Emilie Kimpel
Arcadia, MI
Dancing Daffodils

Makes 12-15 servings

2 lbs. pork sausage
1/2 loaf fresh Italian
  bread, cubed
1/2 lb. Monterey Jack
  cheese, shredded
10-12 eggs, beaten
2 cups milk
paprika

1. Brown sausage. Drain well and set aside.
2. Layer bread into greased 9" x 13" baking pan. Arrange sausage over top and sprinkle with cheese.
3. Mix together eggs and milk and pour over bread. Refrigerate overnight.
4. Bake at 350° for 30 minutes or until set.
5. Sprinkle with paprika and serve.

Christmas Breakfast Casserole

Jan Carroll
Morton, IL
Dede Peterson
Rapid City, SD
Vicky Jo Bogart
Fargo, ND

Makes 8 servings

1 lb. bulk sausage
2 1/2 cups plain croutons
1 cup shredded cheddar
  cheese
6 eggs, beaten
2 1/4 cups milk
10 3/4-oz. can cream of
  mushroom soup
1/2 soup can of milk

1. Cook sausage until browned. Drain well.
2. In a large mixing bowl, mix croutons, sausage, and cheese.
3. Pour eggs and 1 cup milk into blender. Beat. Add remaining 1 1/4 cups milk and pour over crouton-sausage mixture. Stir.
4. Pour into greased 9" x 13" pan. Refrigerate overnight.
5. In the morning mix together cream of mushroom soup and 1/2 soup can of milk. Pour over casserole.
6. Bake at 325° for 1 1/2 hours or until knife comes out clean when inserted in center.

Breakfast Sausage Special
Katie Esh
Ronks, PA
Maricarol Magill
Freehold, NJ
Pat Unternahrer
Wayland, IA
Grace Ketcham
Wilmington, DE

Makes 6-8 servings

1 lb. mild sausage
6 slices bread, cubed
6 eggs, beaten
2 cups milk
1 tsp. salt
1 tsp. dry mustard
1 cup cheddar cheese, grated

1. Brown sausage. Drain well.
2. Arrange bread cubes in lightly greased 9" x 13" baking dish. Spread sausage over bread cubes. Combine eggs, milk, salt, and mustard and pour over sausage layer. Sprinkle with cheese. Cover and refrigerate overnight.
4. Bake at 350° for 30 minutes.

Variations: 1. Add 10³/4-oz. can cream of mushroom soup and 4-oz. jar mushrooms, drained, to egg and milk mixture in Step 2.
Rhonda Yoder
Goshen, IN
Joan Becker
Dodge City, KS

2. Add 1/4 cup chopped green pepper and 4-oz. jar pimientos, drained, to egg and milk mixture in Step 2.
Dorothy B. Williams
Keezletown, VA

Breakfast Casserole
Andrea O'Neil
Fairfield, CT
Irish Chain
Rayann Rohrer
Allentown, PA
The Twist

Makes 8-10 servings

12 slices white bread
1 cup grated cheddar cheese
1¹/2 cups chopped ham
7 eggs, beaten
4 cups milk
salt and pepper to taste
3 spring onions, diced

1. Remove crusts from bread. Butter bread on both sides and arrange six slices in 9" x 13" baking pan. Cover with 1/2 cup grated cheese and 3/4 cup ham. Repeat layers.
2. Beat together eggs and milk. Add salt, pepper, and onions and mix well. Pour over layers in casserole dish. Cover and refrigerate overnight.
3. Bake at 350° for 45-60 minutes or until knife inserted in center comes out clean.

Variations: 1. Add 1 tsp. prepared mustard to egg and milk mixture in Step 2.
Mary Jane Wackford
Oxford, NJ
Log Cabin

2. Omit ham. Add 1/4 tsp. dry mustard and a dash of red pepper to egg and milk mixture in Step 2.
Nancy Jo Marsden
Glen Mills, PA
Country Plaid

3. Substitute 1/2 lb. bacon, fried, drained, and crumbled, for ham.
Linda Sluiter
Schererville, IN
Birds and Blooms

Our grandson Michael amuses us often with his imagination and his great ability to express himself. At age two-and-a-half, he attended a party at church. Michael played the games and won several prizes, one of which was a goldfish. On the way home, his parents asked what he wanted to name the fish. He responded, "Santa Claus!" A few days later the hapless goldfish died and was flushed down the toilet. The next Sunday morning Michael announced to his Sunday school class, "Santa Claus is dead, and Mama and Daddy flushed him away!"
—*Violette Harris Denney, Carrollton, GA*

Breakfast Casserole

Cora J. Peterson
Frederic, WI
Wagon Tracks

Makes 8 servings

1 lb. mild sausage
6 eggs, beaten
2 cups milk
1 tsp. dry mustard
1 tsp. salt
3 English muffins, cubed
8-oz. pkg. shredded
  cheddar cheese

1. Brown sausage. Drain and set aside to cool.
2. Mix together eggs, milk, mustard, and salt. Add English muffin cubes and stir.
3. Stir in cheese and sausage.
4. Pour into greased 8" square baking dish. Refrigerate overnight.
5. Bake at 350° for 35-45 minutes until light brown around the edges.

Note: We serve this every year at our Christmas brunch at church, along with fresh fruit, sweet breads and rolls, orange juice, and coffee.

Sausage Broccoli Breakfast Casserole

Arlene Wengerd
Millersburg, OH
Double Wedding Ring
Thelma A. Stein
Tavares, FL
Hollywood

Makes 8-10 servings

12 slices bread, torn in small pieces
1 lb. cheddar cheese, grated
1 lb. bulk sausage or 2 cups diced, cooked ham
1/2 cup sliced mushrooms
10-oz. pkg. chopped frozen broccoli
6 eggs, slightly beaten
2 Tbsp. minced onion
1/4 tsp. dry mustard
3 1/2 cups milk
1/2 tsp. salt

1. Line bottom of greased 9" x 13" baking dish with 3/4 of bread. Spread 3/4 of cheese on top.
2. Sauté sausage and mushrooms together.
3. Layer broccoli and sausage mixture over cheese. Sprinkle remaining bread over the top.
4. Mix together eggs, onion, mustard, milk, and salt. Pour over casserole. Refrigerate for a few hours or overnight.
5. Bake at 325° for about 50-60 minutes. Sprinkle with remaining 1/4 cup cheese. Return to oven for 5 minutes. Cut into squares and serve.

Grits New Mexico Style

Karen Bryant
Corrales, NM
Morning Star

Makes 16 servings

6 cups boiling water
1 1/2 cups grits
1/2 cup margarine
4-oz. can green chilies, chopped
3 eggs, separated
1 lb. cheddar cheese, grated
1 tsp. salt
1 tsp. savory salt
dash Tabasco sauce

1. Cook grits in boiling water until thickened.
2. Fold in margarine, green chilies, egg yolks, cheese, salt, and Tabasco sauce.
3. Beat egg whites until slightly stiffened. Fold into grits mixture.
4. Pour into 4-quart baking dish.
5. Bake at 325° for 60 minutes. (Or at high altitude, bake at 350° for 80 minutes.)

Christmas Coffee Cake

Beverly Roberts Kessler
Marietta, SC
Mint Green Gingham

Makes 8-10 servings

Coffee Cake:
1 cup milk
1/2 cup sugar
1 tsp. salt
1/2 cup shortening
1/4 cup warm water
2 pkgs. yeast
41/2 cups flour
11/2 tsp. cardamom
1/2 cup raisins
1/4 cup citron
1/2 cup diced cherries
1/4 cup slivered almonds

Glaze:
1/2 cup powdered sugar
1 tsp. vanilla
few drops water

1. Scald milk. Stir in sugar, salt, and shortening. Cool to lukewarm.
2. Add yeast which has been dissolved in warm water. Stir in 2 cups flour. Beat thoroughly. Cover. Let rise until double (approx. 30 minutes).
3. Stir down and blend in cardamom raisins, citron, cherries, and almonds.
4. Add remaining 21/2 cups flour. Turn out onto board. Knead. Place in greased bowl. Cover. Let rise in warm place until double (55 minutes). Punch down. Form into a round ball. Place on a greased cookie sheet. Let rise 1 hour.
5. Bake on cookie sheet at 400° for 10 minute. Reduce oven temperature to 350° and bake for 40 more minutes. Remove from oven and cool on wire rack.
6. To prepare glaze combine powdered sugar, vanilla, and a few drops of water until it has glaze consistency. Spread on cooled cake and serve with coffee.

Streusel-Filled Coffee Cake

Jeannine Dougherty
Tyler, TX
Joe's Cows

Makes 8-10 servings

Coffee Cake:
11/2 cups flour
3 tsp. baking powder
3/4 cup sugar
1/4 cup shortening
1 egg, beaten
1/2 cup milk

Filling:
1/2 cup brown sugar
2 tsp. butter, melted
1/2 cup chopped nuts
2 tsp. cinnamon
2 Tbsp. flour

1. Sift together flour, baking powder, and sugar. Cut in shortening. Blend in egg and milk.
2. Spread 1/2 of batter in greased and floured 8" square baking pan.
3. Mix together all filling ingredients. Sprinkle 1/2 of filling over batter in pan.
Layer with remaining batter and remaining filling.
4. Bake at 375° for 25-30 minutes. Serve warm.

Cinnamon Pecan Coffee Cake

Marianne Miller
Millersburg, OH
Trip Around the World
Pam Wilkins
Belchertown, MA
Thousand Pyramids

Makes 12 servings

Coffee Cake:
1/2 cup margarine
1 cup sugar
2 eggs
1 tsp. vanilla
1 cup sour cream
11/2 cups flour
1 tsp. baking soda

Topping:
1/2 cup white sugar
1/2 cup chopped pecans
2 tsp. cinnamon

1. To prepare cake cream together margarine and sugar. Beat in eggs and mix well.
2. Add vanilla, sour cream, flour, and baking soda. Pour 1/2 of batter into greased and floured 8" square baking pan.
3. Mix together all topping ingredients. Pour 1/2 of topping over batter in pan. Spoon on remaining batter and sprinkle with remaining topping.
4. Bake at 350° for 30-35 minute.

Hungarian Coffee Cake

Patricia Fielding
Stone Mountain, GA
Georgia on My Mind

Makes 12-15 servings

1 cup margarine
1 cup white sugar
1 cup brown sugar
3 cups sifted flour
1/2 cup chopped pecans
1 tsp. baking powder
1 tsp. baking soda
2 eggs
1 cup sour milk or
    buttermilk

1. Cream together margarine and sugars. Add flour and nuts and mix until crumbly. Reserve 1 cup crumbs for topping.
2. Add baking powder, baking soda, eggs, and milk to remaining crumbs. Mix well. Spoon into 2 greased and floured 8" square baking pans.
3. Sprinkle reserved topping evenly over cake batter.
4. Bake at 350 for 30-35 minutes.

Maple-Nut Coffee Twist

Marian Brubacker
Barnett, MO
Country Bride

Makes 12-15 servings

Coffee Twist:
3/4 cup milk
1/4 cup margarine
2 3/4-3 cups flour
3 Tbsp. sugar
1/2 tsp. salt
1 Tbsp. dry yeast
1 tsp. maple flavoring
1 egg, beaten
1/4 cup margarine, melted

Filling:
3/4 cup brown sugar
1/3 cup chopped nuts
1 tsp. cinnamon
1 tsp. maple flavoring

Glaze:
1 cup powdered sugar
2 Tbsp. margarine,
    melted
1-2 Tbsp. water
1/2 tsp. maple flavoring

1. In small saucepan heat milk and 1/4 cup margarine to scalding.
2. In large bowl combine warm milk, 1 cup flour, sugar, salt, yeast, maple flavoring, and egg. Beat 2 minutes.
3. Stir in remaining flour by hand to make a soft dough.
4. On floured surface knead dough until smooth and elastic, about 2 minutes. Place in greased bowl, cover, and let rise in warm place until light and doubled in size (about 45-60 minutes).
5. Meanwhile, combine all filling ingredients. Set aside.
6. Punch down dough. Divide and shape into 3 balls. On lightly floured surface, roll out 1 ball of dough to cover bottom of greased 12" pizza pan. Brush dough with 1/3 of melted margarine. Sprinkle with 1/3 of filling. Repeat procedure twice to have three layers.
7. Place a drinking glass, about 2" in diameter, in center of dough. Using a scissors, cut 16 pie shaped wedges to glass. Carefully, twist each wedge 5 times. Remove glass. Let rise for 30-40 minutes.
8. Bake at 375° for 18-20 minutes. Cool for 5 minutes. Remove from pan.
9. Mix together all glaze ingredients and drizzle over warm coffee twist. Serve with coffee.

Crumb Cake
Barbara Nolan
Pleasant Valley, NY
Feed Sack
Irene Klaeger
Inverness, FL
Bear Paw

Makes 10-12 servings

Cake:
1/2 cup margarine
1/2 cup sugar
1 egg, beaten
1/2 cup milk
1 tsp. vanilla
1 cup flour
1 tsp. baking powder
1/2 tsp. salt

Crumbs:
1/2 cup butter or margarine
1/2 cup sugar
1 cup flour
1-2 Tbsp. cinnamon

1. Cream together margarine and sugar. Beat in egg and mix well.
2. Mix together milk and vanilla.
3. In separate bowl sift together flour, baking powder, and salt.
4. Alternating with milk, add dry ingredients to creamed ingredients. Mix well. Spoon into greased 8" cake pan with removable sides and bottom.
5. To prepare crumbs combine all ingredients and mix by hand until crumbly. Spread evenly over top of cake batter.
6. Bake at 375° for 30 minutes or until toothpick inserted in center comes out clean.

Cherry Cheese Coffee Cake
Susan Miller
Millersburg, OH
Susan J. Miller
Millersburg, OH
Laura Troyer
Sugarcreek, OH

Makes 12 servings

Coffee Cake:
2 8-oz. pkgs. cream cheese, softened
2/3 cup powdered sugar
1 egg yolk
1/2 tsp. vanilla
2 8-oz. pkgs. crescent rolls
21-oz. can cherry pie filling
1 egg white, beaten

Glaze:
1 cup powdered sugar
1/4 cup water

1. Beat together cream cheese, powdered sugar, egg yolk, and vanilla until smooth.
2. Arrange 12 crescent rolls on a round pizza pan, pinching together to completely cover pan. Spread cream cheese mixture over dough. Top with pie filling.
3. Cut 4 crescent rolls into a total of 8 strips. Twist each strip and lay over filling, securing edges to crescent rolls crust.
4. Brush dough with beaten egg whites.
5. Bake at 350° for 20 minutes.
6. To prepare glaze slowly add water to powdered sugar until it becomes a glaze. Drizzle over coffee cake and serve.

Overnight Coffee Ring
Ann Sunday McDowell
Newtown, PA
Jessica's Froggy Patchwork
Rosemarie Fitzgerald
Gibsonia, PA
Nine Patch

Makes 8-10 servings

18 frozen yeast rolls
3-oz. pkg. non-instant butterscotch pudding mix
1/4 cup butter or margarine
1/2 cup brown sugar
1 tsp. cinnamon
1/2 cup chopped pecans

1. Arrange rolls in greased bundt pan. Sprinkle dry pudding over rolls.
2. In a saucepan melt butter with brown sugar. Pour over yeast rolls. Sprinkle with cinnamon and pecans.
3. Cover pan with tea towel and place in cold oven overnight.
4. In the morning remove tea towel. Bake at 350° for 25-30 minutes.
5. Invert onto plate and serve.

Apple Breakfast Treat

Doris L. Orthmann
Wantage, NJ
Kissing Cousins

Makes 8-10 servings

1/2 cup margarine
2-3 apples, peeled and
  thinly sliced
6 eggs, beaten
1 1/2 cups milk
1 cup flour
3 Tbsp. sugar
1 tsp. vanilla
1/2 tsp. salt
1/2 tsp. cinnamon
4 Tbsp. brown sugar

1. Melt margarine at 425° in 9" x 13" baking pan.
2. Add apple slices to pan (should sizzle). Remove dish from oven immediately to keep apples from burning.
3. Mix together eggs and milk. Beat in flour, sugar, vanilla, salt, and 1/4 tsp. cinnamon.
4. Pour batter over apples and sprinkle with brown sugar and remaining 1/4 tsp. cinnamon.
5. Bake at 425° in middle of oven for 20 minutes or until puffed and brown.
6. Serve immediately.

Porridge

Joyce Bowman
Lady Lake, FL
Single Wedding Ring

Makes 4 servings

1 cup old-fashioned
  oatmeal*
3 cups milk
1 cup water
2" cinnamon stick
2 Tbsp. sugar
1/2 tsp. vanilla
1/2 tsp. salt
freshly grated nutmeg

* Do not use quick oats.

1. Soak oatmeal in 1 cup milk for 15 minutes.
2. In saucepan bring 1 cup water with the cinnamon stick to a boil. Boil for 15 minutes. Add remaining 2 cups milk and scald the mixture.
3. Stir in oatmeal, sugar, vanilla, and salt and simmer for five minutes, stirring constantly.
4. Remove and discard cinnamon stick. Serve porridge sprinkled with freshly grated nutmeg.

Groovy Granola

Carol Homewood
Stevensville, MD
Good Things Come in Threes

Makes 10-12 cups

8 cups rolled oats
1/4 cup sesame seeds
1 cup nuts
1/4 cup sunflower seeds
1/2 cup wheat germ
1/2-1 cup brown sugar
1 Tbsp. salt or less
3/4 cup water
3/4 cup vegetable oil
1 Tbsp. vanilla
2 cups raisins

1. In large bowl combine oats, sesame seeds, nuts, sunflower seeds, wheat germ, brown sugar, and salt and mix thoroughly.
2. In medium bowl combine water, oil, and vanilla. Pour over dry ingredients and mix to moisten.
3. Divide mixture in 2 9" x 13" baking pans.
4. Roast at 325° for 45-60 minutes, stirring every 15 minutes. Remove from oven and stir in raisins. Cool thoroughly and store in air-tight container. Serve with milk.

Beverages

Spicy Cranberry Warmers
Martha Bender
New Paris, IN
Boston Commons

Makes 8-10 servings

3 whole cloves
2 cinnamon sticks
2 whole allspice
4 cups apple cider
1/3 cup packed brown
   sugar
4 cups cranberry juice
8-10 cinnamon sticks

1. Place whole cloves, 2 cinnamon sticks, and whole allspice in a double thickness of cheesecloth. Bring up corners of cloth and tie with a string. Place with cider in a large saucepan. (Or, if desired, place loose spices in saucepan and strain before serving.) Simmer covered for 5 minutes.
2. Stir in sugar and simmer for 5 more minutes.

3. Add cranberry juice and heat to just below boiling.
4. Serve hot in mugs. Garnish each mug with a cinnamon stick for stirring.

Variation: Garnish each mug with a cinnamon stick and a slice of apple.
Susanne Troise
West Hills, CA
Amish Love

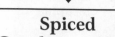

Spiced Cranberry Cider
LaVerne H. Olson
Willow Street, PA
Crooked Log Cabin

Makes 20-25 servings

4 3" cinnamon sticks
1 1/2 tsp. whole colves
2 quarts apple cider
1 1/2 quarts cranberry
   cocktail
1/4 cup brown sugar,
   packed
1 lemon, thinly sliced

1. Put cinnamon sticks and cloves into piece of cloth and tie into bag.
2. Combine remaining ingredients in a large kettle. Add spice bag. Heat to boiling. Reduce heat and simmer for 15-20 minutes.
3. Remove spice bag and serve.

Hot Buttered Cranberry Punch
Jeanne Allen
Los Alamos, NM
Scrap-a-holic

Makes 8-10 large servings

1/3 cup firmly packed
  brown sugar
1/2 cup water
1/2 tsp. cloves
1/4 tsp. allspice
1/4 tsp. cinnamon
1/8 tsp. nutmeg
1/4 tsp. salt
1 quart cranberry juice
1 quart pineapple juice
butter

1. In saucepan combine sugar, water, cloves, allspice, cinnamon, nutmeg, and salt. Bring to a boil.
2. Stir in cranberry juice and pineapple juice. Heat to boiling.
3. Serve hot and dot each mug with butter.

Spiced Grape Punch
Joyce Parker
North Plainfield, NJ
Friendship Quilt

Makes 2 1/2 quarts

6 cups water
1 quart red grape juice
1 cup sugar
6-oz. can frozen
  lemonade concentrate
6-oz. can frozen orange
  juice concentrate
4" stick cinnamon,
  broken
6 whole cloves

1. In a large saucepan, combine water, grape juice, sugar, lemonade, and orange juice. Tie cinnamon and cloves in cheesecloth bag or place in tea ball and add to punch.
2. Simmer about 15 minutes. Remove spices before serving. Serve hot.

Hot Spiced Apple Cider
Elaine Ribas
Miami, FL

Makes 1 gallon

1 gallon apple cider
1/2 cup brown sugar
16 whole cloves
16 whole allspice
dash salt
2 sticks cinnamon

1. In saucepan mix together all ingredients. Use cheesecloth bags to place spices in cider or strain mixture after it has been heated.
2. Simmer over low heat for 15-20 minutes. Serve in mugs.

Variations: 1. Delete brown sugar and use 4 sticks cinnamon. Serve with thick slice of apple floating on top.
Mary Puskar
Forest Hill, MD
Snowbound

2. Prepare in a 30-cup coffee maker. Pour cider into coffee maker. Put spices in coffee filter in coffee maker basket. Add dash of nutmeg and 1 orange, seeded, and cut into wedges.
Marsha Sabus
Fallbrook, CA
Diamond in the Rough

3. Serve in mugs with a slice of orange floating on top and a cinnamon stick to use as a stirrer.
Jeanne Sanson
Chatham, IL

I live in the small agricultural town of Manteca, California, and belong to a quilting club of one hundred seventy-five members. From this large group have come numerous smaller groups that meet every other week to quilt, laugh, and enjoy each other's company.

My group has only six members and is kept small so we can all get into one car for shopping trips and for an annual trip to the Sisters, Oregon, quilt show. We call ourselves the Wednesday Wasters because our goal is to have a good time even though we may waste away the day.

—*Shirley Odell, Manteca, CA*

Holiday Cider
Carol A. Findling
Princeton, IL
Sampler

Makes 1 1/4 gallons

1 gallon apple cider
1 quart cranberry juice
3/4 cup brown sugar
2 sticks cinnamon
1 tsp. whole allspice
1 tsp. whole cloves

1. In a 30-cup coffee maker, combine apple cider and cranberry juice.
2. Put all remaining ingredients in a coffee filter in the coffee maker basket. Serve hot when it has finished percolating.

Quilters' Punch
Elinor L. Briggs
Eaton, IN
Devil's Puzzle

Makes 1 1/4 gallons

1 gallon apple cider
6-oz. can frozen orange juice concentrate
6-oz. can frozen lemonade concentrate
1 Tbsp. cloves
1 Tbsp. allspice
1/2-1 tsp. nutmeg
cinnamon sticks

1. In a large saucepan mix together apple cider, orange juice, lemonade, cloves, allspice, and nutmeg.

2. Simmer over low heat for 30 minutes. Serve hot.

Hot Cider Punch
Darla Sathre
Baxter, MN
Off Center Log Cabin

Makes 1 1/2 gallons

1 gallon apple cider
3-oz. pkg. raspberry gelatin
3 12-oz. cans diet 7-up, room temperature

1. Stir together apple cider and dry gelatin in a 30-cup coffee pot. Percolate.
2. Immediately before serving, stir in 7-up.

Wassail
Claire H. Perkins
Inverness, FL

Makes 1 1/2 quarts

1 1/2 cups sugar
4 cups boiling water
3 allspice berries
6 whole cloves
1 Tbsp. ground ginger
1" stick cinnamon
1 1/2 cups orange juice
2/3 cup lemon juice

1. In saucepan combine sugar and 2 cups boiling water. Boil for 5 minutes. Stir in spices. Cover and allow to stand for 1 hour.
2. Add remaining water, orange juice, and lemon juice and mix well. Strain to separate spices. Heat to boiling point. Serve immediately in small cups.

Note: In the British tradition, wassail is a liquid with or without liquor which one drinks when wishing health to another person.

Mother's Wassail
Emma B. Ebersole
Lancaster, PA
Drunkard's Path

Makes 3 quarts

2 quarts apple cider
2 cups orange juice
1 cup lemon juice
1 stick cinnamon
1 Tbsp. honey
1 tsp. ground ginger
6 whole cloves
1 1/2 cups pineapple juice
1 orange

1. In a saucepan combine all ingredients except orange and simmer for 15-20 minutes. Strain to separate spices and pour into a punch bowl.
2. Garnish with orange slices. Serve hot.

Note: I served this as the family arrived for our Christmas get-together.

Spiced Tea
Diana Ziffer
Batavia, IL

Makes 1 quart

4 cups water
3" cinnamon stick
1" piece fresh ginger, cut
  into 4 slices
10 cardamom pods or
  1/2 tsp. ground
  cardamom
1/2 tsp. black pepper
1/2 tsp. whole cloves
1 tsp. whole coriander
  seeds
3 tea bags of black tea
1 cup milk
honey

1. In saucepan mix together
water and spices. Bring to
boil. Reduce heat, cover,
and simmer for 20 minutes.
2. Add tea bags and milk
and simmer for 3-4 minutes.
Remove tea bags. Sweeten
to taste with honey.
3. Strain to separate spices.
Serve.

Laura's Holiday
Tea
Laura Barrus Bishop
Boerne, TX
Log Cabin

Makes 1½ quarts

1 quart boiling water
2 family-sized tea bags
1/2 cup sugar
1 cup orange juice

1 cup pineapple juice
1 cup cranberry juice
dash cinnamon or 1
  cinnamon stick
lemon or lime slices

1. In a saucepan pour boiling water over tea bags.
Brew 4 minutes. Remove
tea bags. Stir in sugar and
juices. Heat through.
2. Add cinnamon and simmer
another 15 minutes. Serve
with lemon or lime slices.

*Variation: Omit cinnamon
and serve with ice for a summer drink.*
Betty Dennison
Grove City, PA

Christmas Brunch
Almond Tea
Cheryl Bartel
Hillsboro, KS
Angels Gather Here

Makes 2 quarts

9 cups water
1 cup sugar
1 tsp. vanilla
1 tsp. almond flavoring
1 heaping Tbsp. instant
  tea
1/2 cup lemon juice

1. In a saucepan mix
together water and sugar.
Bring to a boil and cook for
5 minutes. Stir in remaining
ingredients. Turn off heat
and stir.
2. Serve hot.

Johnny Appleseed
Tea
Sheila Plock
Boalsburg, PA
Christmas Sampler

Makes 2 quarts

2 quarts water
6 tea bags
6-oz. can frozen apple
  juice, thawed
1/4 cup plus 2 Tbsp. firmly
  packed brown sugar

1. Bring 1 quart water to
boil. Add tea bags. Remove
from heat. Cover and let
steep for 5 minutes. Remove
tea bags.
2. Stir in remaining 1 quart
water, apple juice, and
sugar. Cook over low heat
until thoroughly heated.
Serve hot.

*Note: This may also be pre-
pared in a crockpot.*

Friendship Tea
Violette Harris Denney
Carrollton, GA
Mary Lou Rowe
Batavia, IL
Donna Barnitz
Rio Rancho, NM

Makes many servings

18-oz. jar Tang
3-oz. pkg. unsweetened
  lemonade mix
2 cups sugar
1¼ cups instant tea

1 tsp. ground cloves
2 tsp. cinnamon

1. Mix together all ingredients. Store in an airtight container.
2. To serve stir in 2 tsp. tea mix per cup of hot water.

Variation: Omit the lemonade mix. This mixture makes a nice gift when put into pint jars and presented with a cloth lid skirt.
Karen Weber
Alexandria, SD
Appliqué in a Day

Apple-Honey Tea
Jeanne Allen
Los Alamos, NM
Trip Around the World

Makes 1¹/₂ quarts

12-oz. can frozen apple cider concentrate
2 Tbsp. instant tea powder
1 Tbsp. honey
¹/₂ tsp. ground cinnamon

1. In a saucepan prepare apple cider concentrate according to package directions.
2. Add tea powder, honey, and cinnamon and stir to blend. Heat through and serve.

Chocolate Marshmallow Punch
Jeanne Allen
Los Alamos, NM
Scrap-a-holic

Makes 12 servings

3 12-oz. cans evaporated milk
2 cups chocolate syrup
2 cups water
12 large marshmallows
1 Tbsp. vanilla marshmallows
grated chocolate

1. In large saucepan mix together milk, chocolate

syrup, water, and 12 large marshmallows. Heat over medium heat, stirring until marshmallows are melted. Stir in vanilla.
2. Pour into cups. Garnish with marshmallows and grated chocolate. Serve.

Hot Cocoa Mix
Mary Lou Rowe
Batavia, IL
Garden Twist

Makes many servings

6 cups nonfat dry milk
2 cups nonfat, non-dairy creamer
2 cups cocoa mix
2 cups powdered sugar

1. Mix together all ingredients. Store in an airtight container.
2. To serve stir 5 heaping tsp. into each 1 cup boiling water.

Variation: Add 1 pkg. miniature marshmallows to the mixture before storing. I put this mixture into glass jars, decorate the lids with quilted covers, and add labels which say "Serve 2 ozs. mix with 8 ozs. hot water." I recycle my applesauce, mayonnaise, and peanut butter jars for these gifts. To make the gift really special, add a festive mug.
Dianna Milhizer
Springfield, VA
Windows Friendship

Our family often reminisces about a Christmas breakfast twenty-some years ago. My husband and I were exhausted with the usual holiday preparations so our four children decided to let us sleep in while they prepared breakfast. One child was scrambling a dozen eggs in the blender when the lid flew off.

Egg landed on the ceiling, the floor, and the kitchen table, including the dishes and silverware which had been set for breakfast. The mishap startled our son and when he jumped, he knocked over a bowl of Christmas balls, which disintegrated into a million pieces! We were soon awakened, and everyone pitched in to clean up the mess. Breakfast on that Christmas morning consisted of cold cereal.
—*Gertrude Hedrick, Willow Grove, PA*

Cappuccino Mix

Gloria R. Yoder
Dundee, Ohio
Annabelle Unternahrer
Shipshewana, IN
Susan Miller
Millersburg, OH

Makes 3 cups dry mix

1 cup dry coffee creamer
1 cup instant chocolate
  drink mix
2/3 cup instant coffee
  granules
1/2 cup white sugar
1/2 tsp. ground cinnamon
1/4 tsp. ground nutmeg

1. Combine all ingredients.
Mix well. Store in an airtight container.
2. To prepare one serving,
add 3 Tbsp. mix to 6 ozs.
hot water. Stir well.

*Note: This would make an
excellent gift in fancy jars with
a ribbon tie and directions
attached in a small folder. This
is what I plan to do.*
  Barbara Sparks
  Glen Burnie, MD

New Mexican
Hot Chocolate

Jane Talso
Albuquerque, NM
Snapshot

Makes 6 servings

1/2 cup sugar
1/4 cup cocoa mix

1 1/2 cups cold water
1 tsp. cinnamon
1/2 tsp. nutmeg
6 cups milk
1 Tbsp. vanilla
whipped topping
nutmeg
cinnamon or cinnamon
  sticks

1. In a saucepan combine
sugar, cocoa, water, cinnamon, and nutmeg. Simmer
over medium heat. Add
milk and scald, stirring until
smooth. Stir in vanilla.
2. Pour into mugs. Top with
whipped topping. Add dash
of nutmeg and cinnamon.
Or insert cinnamon stick to
use as a stirrer. Serve.

Sparkling
Cranberry Punch

Dottie Geraci
Burtonsville, MD
The Homestead

Makes 2 1/2 quarts

1 quart cranberry juice
  cocktail
6-oz. can frozen orange
  juice, thawed
6-oz. can frozen
  lemonade, thawed
2 cups water
2 cups ginger ale
orange slices

1. Combine cranberry cocktail, orange juice, lemonade,
and water. Chill well.
2. Immediately before serving, pour juice mixture over
ice. Gently stir in ginger ale.

Garnish with orange slices
and serve.

Banana Cow

Chris Peterson
Green Bay, WI
Star Medallion

Makes 1 glass

3-4 ozs. crushed ice
1/2 ripe banana
2 ozs. plain or vanilla
  yogurt
1 tsp. maple syrup

1. Put ingredients in blender
and stir to blend.
2. Serve in fancy glasses and
enjoy.

Raspberry
Surprise

Chris Peterson
Green Bay, WI
Star Medallion

Makes 1 glass

3-4 ozs. crushed ice
3-4 Tbsp. raspberries
1 tsp. maple syrup
2 ozs. plain or vanilla
  yogurt

1. Put ingredients in blender
and stir to blend.
2. Serve in fancy wine glass
and enjoy.

Coconut Cooler
Linda Gruhlkey Pond
Los Alamos, NM
Fields of Purple

Makes 5-6 cups

3 cups orange juice
10-oz. can cream of
  coconut
1 cup club soda
1/2 cup lime juice

1. Combine all ingredients in blender.
2. Serve over ice.

Holiday Punch
Marianne Miller
Millersburg, OH

Makes 50 small servings

3 6-oz. pkgs. cherry
  gelatin
13 cups boiling water
4 cups sugar or less
2 cups lemon juice
46-oz. can pineapple juice
2 2-liter bottles ginger ale

1. Dissolve gelatin in 9 cups boiling water.
2. Dissolve sugar in 4 cups boiling water. Add to gelatin mixture and mix well.
3. Stir in lemon and pineapple juice. Put in containers and freeze. Remove from freezer 1 1/2 hours before serving. Add ginger ale and serve in a large punch bowl.

Holiday
Cranberry Punch
Alyce C. Kauffman
Gridley, CA
Sailing Away

Makes 5 1/2 quarts

1 quart cranberry juice
12-oz. can frozen orange
  juice concentrate
12-oz. can frozen
  lemonade concentrate
12-oz. can frozen
  pineapple concentrate
1 quart ginger ale
2 1/2 quarts water

1. Combine juices and ginger ale. Add enough water and mix well.
2. Pour punch over ice to serve.

Citrus Slush
Lucille Metzler
Conestoga, PA
Country Love

Makes 2 gallons

2 1/2 cups sugar
3 cups water
12-oz. can frozen orange
  juice concentrate
12-oz. can frozen
  lemonade concentrate
46-oz. can pineapple juice
3 cups cold water
4 quarts lemon-lime soda
  or ginger ale, chilled

1. In a saucepan boil 3 cups water and sugar over high

heat until dissolved, stirring constantly. Remove from heat.
2. Stir in frozen orange juice and lemonade concentrate until melted. Stir in pineapple juice and water until well blended. Pour into two 9" x 13" pans. Cover and freeze until firm.
3. Cut each pan into 24 squares. Place squares in punch bowl. Slowly pour chilled soda over squares. Stir until punch is slushy.

Banana Slush
Jeanne Allen
Los Alamos, NM
Baltimore Beauty

Makes 5 quarts

4 cups sugar
6 cups water
4 6-oz. cans frozen orange
  juice concentrate
juice of 2 lemons
5-6 bananas, mashed
3 quarts lemon-lime soda

1. In a saucepan mix together sugar and water. Cook until syrupy. Cool.
2. Stir in fruit juices and bananas. Pour mixture into freezer containers. Freeze.
3. Let stand at room temperature until mushy. Break up with a potato masher. Add soda immediately before serving. Serve in a punch bowl.

Holiday Banana Beer

Annabelle Unternahrer
Shipshewana, IN
Round Robin

Makes 10-15 servings

2 cups boiling water
2 cups sugar
12-oz. can frozen orange
   juice concentrate
1¹/2 cups cold water
16-oz. can crushed
   pineapple, undrained
4 large bananas, mashed
¹/4 cup maraschino
   cherries, diced
1 liter lemon-lime soda

1. Stir sugar and boiling water together until sugar dissolves. Stir in orange juice, cold water, pineapple, and mashed bananas. Freeze, stirring 3 or 4 times during freezing time. When mixture becomes slushy, spoon into ice cube trays and freeze solid.
2. When ready to serve, fill glass with cubes and pour soda over. Serve as appetizer.

Lime-Pineapple Punch

Mary Jane Musser
Manheim, PA
Friendship
Ruth Ann Hoover
New Holland, PA
Spinning Star

Makes 1 gallon

2 pkgs. lemon-lime drink
   mix
1¹/2 cups sugar
2 quarts water
1 quart pineapple juice
1 quart ginger ale
1 quart lime sherbet

1. Mix together drink mix, sugar, water, and pineapple juice.
2. Immediately before serving, mix in ginger ale and lime sherbet in a large punch bowl.

Orange Sherbet Party Punch

Elva J. Miller
Sugarcreek, OH
*Green Embroidered
Flower Pattern*

Makes 6-7 quarts

6-oz. pkg. strawberry
   gelatin
2 cups boiling water
1¹/2 cups sugar
3 cups cold water
46-oz. can pineapple juice
46-oz. can orange juice
1 cup lemon juice
¹/2 gallon orange sherbet
2-liter bottle ginger ale

1. Dissolve gelatin in boiling water. Stir in sugar until dissolved. Add cold water and juices.
2. Immediately before serving in a large punch bowl, add sherbet and pour in ginger ale.

Condiments

Fresh Cranberry Chutney

Marybeth Romeo
Roanoke, VA
Ugly 70's Quilt

Makes 2 pints

2 cups fresh cranberries
3/4 cup packed brown sugar
1/2 cup light raisins
1/2 cup chopped celery
1/2 cup chopped apple
1/4 cup chopped walnuts
1 tsp. ground ginger (or to taste)
2 Tbsp. lemon juice
1 tsp. onion salt
1/4 tsp. ground cloves
1/2 cup water

1. In large saucepan combine all ingredients.
2. Bring to boil, stirring constantly.
3. Simmer uncovered for 15 minutes, stirring occasionally.
4. Store covered in refrigerator. Serve chilled.

Cranberry Chutney

Sharon Timpe
Mequon, WI

Makes 2 pints

1 cup raisins
1/4 cup warm brandy
12-oz. pkg. cranberries
11/2 cups sugar
1 cup water
1 cup orange juice
1 cup chopped walnuts
1 cup chopped celery
1 apple, chopped
1/4 tsp. ground ginger

1. Soak raisins in warm brandy. Set aside.
2. In saucepan mix together cranberries, sugar, and water. Simmer for 15 minutes.
3. Stir in all remaining ingredients, including raisins, and heat through, simmering at least another 15 minutes. Remove from heat and cool.

4. Store in refrigerator. Freezes well.

Pesto

Dawn J. Ranck
Strasburg, PA
Patchwork

Makes 2 cups

2 cups freshly washed, firmly packed basil leaves
2-4 cloves garlic, peeled and crushed
1/2 cup olive or vegetable oil
3 Tbsp. pine nuts
1 cup freshly grated Parmesan cheese

1. Put basil and garlic in blender or food processor. Pour in oil and process until smooth. Add pine nuts and process for a few seconds. Stir in Parmesan cheese.
2. If pesto seems too thick, add a bit more olive oil. Do

not heat pesto because it will turn dark.

3. If you are not using pesto immediately, store in sterilized jar in refrigerator with a skim of oil on top. Cover with plastic wrap. Pesto will keep for several weeks.

4. To freeze pesto for the winter, process basil, garlic, and oil and freeze in plastic containers. When ready to use, thaw slowly at room temperature. Add pine nuts and Parmesan cheese and serve.

Orange Honey Glaze for Turkey
Linda Gruhlkey Pond
Los Alamos, NM
Fields of Purple

Makes 1¹/2 cups

12-oz. can frozen orange juice concentrate, thawed
1 cup honey
1 Tbsp. Worcestershire sauce

1. In a blender or food processor, mix together all ingredients.

2. Apply glaze to turkey during the last 40 minutes of baking turkey. Baste every 10 minutes, watching carefully as this glaze burns easily.

Note: It is best if oven temperature is turned to 375° during this basting. Gives a beautiful color to turkey.

Jezebel Sauce for Ham
Eldeen Carter
Charleston, SC
A Charleston Basket

Makes 3 cups

10-oz. jar apple jelly
12-oz. jar pineapple preserves
5-oz. jar horseradish
1 tsp. dry mustard

1. In a saucepan mix together all ingredients and heat until melted, stirring constantly.

2. Cool and refrigerate. Serve warm with ham or pork chops.

Horseradish Sauce
Irma Harder
Mountain Lake, MN
Angel Wallhanging

Makes about 1 cup

¹/2 cup whipping cream
2²/3 Tbsp. horseradish, well-drained
1¹/3 Tbsp. salad dressing

1. Whip cream until stiffened. Blend in horseradish and salad dressing.

2. Serve with Christmas ham.

Grandma's Chili Sauce
Gail Skiff
Clifton Park, NY
Tree Everlasting II

Makes 4 pints

2 28-oz. cans peeled tomatoes
4 medium onions
2 cups sugar
2 cups vinegar
2 tsp. salt
1 tsp. pepper
1 tsp. cinnamon
1 tsp. allspice
1 tsp. cloves

1. Chop together tomatoes and onions in food processor (or through an old-style food grinder as Gram did). Stir in remaining ingredients and blend.

2. Pour into saucepan and bring to a boil, stirring often. Simmer for 45 minutes.

3. Pour into pint jars. Refrigerate when cool.

Note: If you wish to give this as gifts, purchase small pint canning jars and seals. Proceed with canning according to manufacturer directions. Makes a wonderful gift for the men in the family.

Ernie's Barbecue Sauce
Glenna Keefer Smith
Punxsutawney, PA
North Star

Makes 2 cups

1/4 cup olive oil
1/8 cup wine vinegar
2/3 cup ketchup
1/3 cup water
1 small onion, diced
1/3 cup brown sugar
juice from 1 lemon
few dashes Tabasco

1. In saucepan combine all ingredients and bring to a boil. Simmer for 20 minutes.
2. Baste chicken, pork, or beef during the last 20 minutes of grilling or roasting.

Sauerkraut Relish
Inez E. Dillon
Tucson, AZ
Crazy Quilt

Makes 2 quarts

1 quart sauerkraut, well drained
1/3 cup diced green pepper
1/3 cup diced red pepper
1/3 cup diced yellow pepper
1 cup diced onion
4-oz. jar pimiento
1 cup chopped celery
1/2 cup shredded carrot
3/4 cup sugar

1/2 cup vegetable oil
1/2 cup vinegar
1 tsp. celery seed

1. Mix together sauerkraut, peppers, onion, pimiento, celery, and carrot.
2. Mix together sugar, oil, vinegar, and celery seed.
3. Pour liquid mixture over other ingredients and stir well. Let stand overnight or for a minimum of 12 hours.

Mother's Pepper Relish
Mary Puskar
Forest Hill, MD

Makes 6 pints

12 green peppers
12 red peppers
15 onions
4 Tbsp. salt
3 cups sugar
4 cups vinegar
2-3 Tbsp. celery seed

1. Grind together peppers and onions. Sprinkle with salt and stir well. Let stand for 20-30 minutes.
2. Squeeze out excess liquid by hand. Stir in sugar, vinegar, and celery seed. Bring to a boil and boil for 40 minutes.
3. Sterilize 6 pint jars. Carefully, pour hot relish into hot jars, leaving about 1" of headspace. Wipe rims of jars and cover with seals which have also been sterilized in hot water. Tighten firmly by hand.

4. Place jars on a rack in canner. Add enough hot water to cover jars 1"-2" over top. Bring to a full rolling boil. Process in boiling water bath for 15 minutes. Remove jars from water and set aside to seal. Store in cool place.

Note: This relish makes a great holiday gift because of the colors. I prepare it during the summer when the peppers are plentiful.

Cranberry Red Pepper Relish
Eunice B. Heyman
Baltimore, MD
William's Clown Parade

Makes 1 1/2 pints

2 red peppers, seeded and finely diced
2 cups cranberries, coarsely chopped
1 medium onion, finely chopped
3/4 cup sugar
1 small jalapeno pepper, minced
1/4 tsp. salt
1/4 tsp. red pepper flakes

1. In a saucepan combine all ingredients. Bring to a boil and simmer for 30-40 minutes, stirring occasionally.
2. Cool and store in refrigerator. Serve with poultry or baked ham.

Fresh Tomato Salsa

Carol Ambrose
Napa, CA
Kittens in the Attic

Makes 5 cups

15-25 firm tomatoes
1 medium to large onion, chopped
1-2 jalapeno peppers, chopped
2 tsp. garlic powder, chopped
2 tsp. salt
1 tsp. pepper
1 Tbsp. fresh, chopped parsley
1 Tbsp. fresh, chopped cilantro (optional)

1. Chop tomatoes into pieces about the size of a pencil eraser.
2. Mix together all ingredients. Stir and refrigerate overnight to blend flavors.
3. Serve with corn chips or chips of choice.

Hot Tomato Salsa

Janie Canupp
Millersville, MD
Double Wedding Ring

Makes 3 pints

12 ripe tomatoes, peeled and chopped
3 sweet peppers, chopped
3 hot peppers
3 large onions, chopped
1 cup sugar
1 tsp. salt
1 1/2 tsp. pepper
1 cup vinegar
2 heaping Tbsp. cornstarch
1/2 cup water

1. In large saucepan mix together tomatoes, peppers, hot peppers, and onions.
2. Stir in sugar, salt, pepper, and vinegar and bring to a boil. Simmer for 1 hour, stirring occasionally.
3. Mix cornstarch with water. Stir into salsa and cook 10 more minutes.
4. Sterilize 3 pint jars. Carefully, pour hot salsa into hot jars, leaving about 1" of headspace. Wipe rims of jars with wet cloth and cover with seals which have also been sterilized in hot water. Tighten firmly by hand.
5. Place jars on rack in canner. Add enough water to cover jars 1" to 2" over top. Bring to a full rolling boil. Process in boiling water bath for 25 minutes. Remove jars from water and set aside to seal. Store in cool place.

Mary's Salad Dressing

Mary Mainwaring
Salem, OR

Makes 2 cups

1 cup vegetable oil
1/2 cup sugar
1 tsp. Worcestershire sauce
2 Tbsp. white vinegar
1 tsp. salt
1 tsp. dry mustard
juice from 1 lemon
1/2 cup ketchup
dash paprika
4 garlic cloves, minced

1. Blend together all ingredients except garlic. Stir in garlic.
2. Refrigerate until ready to serve.

I am a fourth generation quilter and enjoy remembering my mother and grandmother and the love they passed on to me through their quilts. I treasure the stories of my great-grandmother sitting at her spinning wheel as she created the cloth for her quilts. Our home has always been filled with quilts, family, food, and love. Today my daughter, Tracey Stenger, is the fifth generation to quilt in my family line.

—*Barbara R. Zitzmann, Metairie, LA*

Raspberry Poppy Seed Salad Dressing
Carmen Kleager
Scottsbluff, NE
Carrie Nation

Makes 1³/4 cups

3/4 cup sugar
1 tsp. dry mustard
1 tsp. salt
1/3 cup raspberry vinegar
1 Tbsp. grated onion
1 cup vegetable oil
2 tsp. poppy seeds

1. Mix together all ingredients.
2. Serve over tossed spinach garnished with red onions and mandarin oranges.

Blue Cheese Dressing
Ruth Bruffey
Nipomo, CA
Duck in a Flower Garden

Makes 3 cups

1 pint mayonnaise
1/2 pint sour cream
4¹/2-ozs. blue cheese, crumbled
1 tsp. salt
1 tsp. freshly ground pepper
1/2 Tbsp. garlic powder
1 tsp. Worcestershire sauce
5-6 Tbsp. buttermilk

1. Mix together mayonnaise and sour cream.
2. Stir in blue cheese, salt, pepper, garlic powder, and Worcestershire sauce. Mix well. (This will be very thick.) Store in the refrigerator.
3. Immediately before serving, thin with buttermilk.

Light French Dressing
Ann Driscoll
Albuquerque, NM
Christmas Wallhanging

Makes 3/4 cup

1/2 cup corn oil
1 Tbsp. sugar
1 tsp. garlic salt
3 Tbsp. vinegar
paprika to taste and for color

1. Mix together all ingredients. Shake well and let stand overnight to blend flavors.
2. Serve with favorite green salad.

French Dressing
Jennie Walsh
Port Hawkesbury, Nova Scotia
Casey's Stars

Makes 3¹/2 cups

10³/4-oz. can tomato soup
1 cup vegetable oil
1 cup sugar
3/4 cup vinegar
1¹/2 Tbsp. prepared mustard
1 Tbsp. paprika
1¹/2 Tbsp. garlic salt
1 Tbsp. parsley flakes
1 Tbsp. Worcestershire sauce
1 tsp. salt
1/2 tsp. pepper
1 tsp. onion salt

1. Mix together all ingredients and shake well.
2. Serve with choice of greens.

Easy Salad Dressing
Nan Mitchell
Peru, NY
Kansas Album

Makes 1/2 cup

1 clove garlic, halved
1/2 tsp dry mustard
1/4 tsp. black pepper
1/4 tsp. salt
3 Tbsp. vinegar
1/3 cup vegetable oil

1. Place garlic in glass jar.

Add mustard, pepper, salt, and vinegar. Cover container and shake well. Let stand 30 minutes.
2. Strain out garlic. Add oil and shake well again.
3. Each time before serving, shake well.

Raspberry Rhubarb Jam

Beverly Simmons
Boulder, CO
Spirit of the Carousel

Makes 5 cups

5 cups diced rhubarb
1 cup crushed pineapple, drained
2 1/2 cups sugar
2 3-oz. pkgs. raspberry gelatin

1. Combine rhubarb, pineapple, and sugar and cook for 20-25 minutes, stirring occasionally until sugar has dissolved and mixture is clear.
2. Remove from heat and stir in gelatin until dissolved.
3. Cool and pour into jars. Keep refrigerated.

Christmas Apple Butter

Claire H. Perkins
Inverness, FL

Makes 24 half pints

14 cups fine applesauce
7 cups sugar
6-oz. pkg. cherry gelatin
1/2 lb. red cinnamon candies

1. Mix together all ingredients. Pour into large baking pan.
2. Bake at 350° for 1 hour, stirring occasionally.
3. Sterilize 24 half pint jars. Carefully pour hot apple butter into hot jars, leaving about 1" of headspace. Wipe rims of jars and cover with seals which have also been sterilized in hot water. Tighten firmly by hand.
4. Place jars on rack in canner. Add enough water to cover jars 1" to 2" over top. Bring to a full rolling boil. Process in boiling water bath for 20 minutes. Remove jars from water and set aside to seal. Store in cool place.

Note: I tie a bow onto these jars and give as Christmas gifts.

Hot Pepper Jelly

Wanda Curtin
Bradenton, FL
Lancaster Rose
Alyce C. Kauffman
Gridley, CA
Sailing Away

Makes 6 6-oz. jars

3 jalapeno peppers
1 medium green pepper, cut into strips
1 1/4 cups vinegar
6 cups sugar
3 drops red or green food coloring
8-oz. bottle Certo (liquid pectin)

1. Put peppers and 1/4 cup vinegar into blender and blend until liquid.
2. In large saucepan mix together pepper mixture, remaining 1 cup vinegar, and sugar. Bring to a boil. Skim off the layer of scum.
3. Stir in food coloring and Certo. Bring to a hard rolling boil, stirring constantly for 2 minutes. Remove from heat, stirring occasionally to cool.
4. Pour into small jars. Refrigerate or give as gifts.

Note: To serve spoon jelly over an 8-oz. block of cream cheese. Serve with crackers.

Green Pepper Jelly
Carmen Kleager
Scottsbluff, NE
Carrie Nation

Makes 6-8 small jars

3 large green bell peppers
1 1/2 cups cider vinegar
1/2 tsp. salt
6 1/2 cups sugar
1 Tbsp. cayenne pepper
1 packet Certo (2 per box)
2 drops green food coloring

1. Cut peppers and remove seeds. Blend in blender with 1/2 cup vinegar.
2. In saucepan combine pepper mixture, remaining 1 cup vinegar, salt, sugar, and cayenne pepper. Bring to a boil and boil for 5 minutes, stirring constantly.
3. Remove from heat and cool for 2 minutes. Stir in Certo and food coloring. Pour into sterilized jars and seal.

Freezer Blackberry Jelly
Marilyn Chandler
Louisburg, KS
Double Wedding Ring

Makes 8 cups

3 cups blackberry juice*
6 cups sugar
1 box pectin
3/4 cup water
* Process 1 1/2 quarts fresh

blackberries or 3 12-oz. pkgs. frozen blackberries in a Foley food mill to obtain 3 cups juice.

1. Stir sugar into blackberry juice. Set aside for 10 minutes.
2. In small saucepan mix together pectin and water. Bring to a boil, stirring constantly. Boil for 1 minute.
3. Stir hot pectin mixture into blackberry juice mixture, stirring constantly for 3 minutes.
4. Fill small jelly jars to within 1/2" of top. Cover tightly with lids. Let stand for 24 hours. Freeze jelly until ready to use.

Lemon Jam
Claire H. Perkins
Inverness, FL

Makes 3 8-oz. jelly jars

6 eggs
2 1/4 cups sugar
1/4 lb. butter or margarine
juice of 3 lemons
grated rind of 2 lemons

1. In medium saucepan beat eggs until thick and frothy. Stir in sugar, butter, lemon juice, and lemon rind. Mix well.
2. Heat over low to medium heat, stirring constantly with a wooden spoon. Do not allow mixture to come to a boil. Stir until mixture thickens, about 15-20 minutes. Pour into jelly jars and cover tightly.

3. Store in refrigerator for 4-6 weeks.

Note: If mixture does not thicken in Step 2, remove from heat and stir in 1/2 pkg. unflavored gelatin.

Garlic and Herb Spread
Rose Hankins
Stevensville, MD
Bow Tie

Makes 1 cup

2 cloves garlic, minced
1 Tbsp. dried oregano
1/2 cup margarine, softened
1/4 cup olive oil

1. Mix together all ingredients and stir to mix well.
2. Cover and refrigerate up to 30 days.
3. Serve with crackers or spread on Italian bread slices and broil for 1-2 minutes.

Dill Pickles
Anita Coker
Bellville, TX
12 Days of Christmas

Makes 4 pints

2 cups water
1 cup vinegar
1/2 cup sugar
1/4 tsp. salt
1 head dill
2 cloves garlic
2 dried red peppers
3-4 green grapes and
    grape leaves
small cucumbers

1. In a saucepan combine water, vinegar, sugar, and salt and bring to a boil, stirring occasionally. Set aside.
2. Put piece of dill, bit of garlic, bit of red pepper, 1 grape, and 1 grape leaf in each of 4 pint jars. Fill with small cucumbers. Pour vinegar solution over cucumbers to within 1/2" of top of jar. Cover tightly with sterilized seal.
3. Place jars on rack in canner. Add enough water to cover jars 1" to 2" over top. Bring to a full rolling boil.

Process in boiling water bath for 15 minutes. Remove jars from water and set aside to seal. Let stand at least 2 weeks in cool place before serving.

Refrigerator Pickles
Lorene P. Meyer
Wayland, IA
Sampler

Makes 3-4 quarts

8 large cucumbers, thinly
    sliced
4 medium onions, thinly
    sliced
4 cups sugar
4 cups vinegar
1/4 cup salt
1 1/3 tsp. turmeric
1 1/3 tsp. celery seed
1 1/3 tsp. mustard seed

1. Layer cucumbers and onions in 3-4 quart jars.
2. Mix together sugar, vinegar, salt, turmeric, celery, and mustard seed. Stir until sugar has dissolved.
3. Cover cucumbers and

onions with cold syrup and fasten lids.
4. Refrigerate for 5 days before using. Will keep in refrigerator for 6-8 weeks.

In my Polish heritage, Christmas is a time for making peace. My grandmother would set an extra plate at the dinner table and light a lone candle for the window facing the street. The candle flickering through the darkness signified our hope that Christ in the form of a stranger would see our light and join the family for dinner. It also served as a beacon to help guide the spirit of any family member who could not travel the distance in person to be with us.
—*Charmaine Caesar, Lancaster, PA*

Index

Index

About the Authors

Louise Stoltzfus learned the arts of quilting and cooking from her mother, Miriam Stoltzfus. While she puts occasional stitches in one of the many quilts her mother always has in frame, Stoltzfus regrettably seldom finds time for quilting.

Stoltzfus authored the first quilters' cookbook, *Favorite Recipes from Quilters.* She also co-authored *The Central Market Cookbook, The Best of Mennonite Fellowship Meals,* and *Lancaster County Cookbook.*

Stoltzfus is an editor for Good Books and director of The People's Place Gallery in Intercourse, Pennsylvania.

Dawn Ranck helped to make her first quilt—a doll quilt—at age seven, with the help of her Grandma Engel. She is currently handpiecing a Grandmother's Flower Garden quilt.

Ranck also enjoys cooking and gardening and combines the two by growing herbs and using them in her cooking.

Ranck is Designer and Production Manager for Good Books.